THE ARAB MIDDLE EAST AND THE UNITED STATES

Inter-Arab Rivalry and Superpower Diplomacy

Twayne's International History Series

Akira Iriye, Editor
Harvard University

THE ARAB MIDDLE EAST AND THE UNITED STATES

Inter-Arab Rivalry and Superpower Diplomacy

Burton I. Kaufman

Virginia Polytechnic Institute and State University

TWAYNE PUBLISHERS • NEW YORK
AN IMPRINT OF SIMON & SCHUSTER MACMILLAN

PRENTICE HALL INTERNATIONAL • LONDON • MEXICO CITY • NEW DELHI
SINGAPORE • SYDNEY • TORONTO

Twayne Publishers
An Imprint of Simon & Schuster Macmillan
866 Third Avenue
New York, New York 10022

Library of Congress Cataloging-in-Publication Data

Kaufman, Burton Ira.
    The Arab Middle East and the United States : inter-Arab rivalry and superpower diplomacy / Burton I. Kaufman.
        p.   cm.—(Twayne's international history series ;)
    Includes bibliographical references and index.
    ISBN 0-8057-7911-6 (alk. paper).—ISBN 0-8057-9211-2 (pbk.)
    1. Arab countries—Foreign relations—United States.   2. United States—Foreign relations—Arab countries.   3. United States—Foreign relations—1945–   I. Title.   II. Series.
    DS63.2.U5K38   1995
    327.730174927—dc20   95-19575
                                                                                CIP

The paper used in this publication meets the minimum requirements of American National Standard for Information Sciences—Permanence of Paper for Printed Library Materials. ANSI Z39.48-1984. ⊚ ™

10 9 8 7 6 5 4 3 2 1 (hc)
10 9 8 7 6 5 4 3 2 1 (pb)

Printed in the United States of America

For Lois, Sid, Eleanor, Tom, Shirley,
Jennifer, Jack, Jan, and Steve

CONTENTS

MAPS

FOREWORD

Twayne's International History Series seeks to publish reliable accounts of post–World War II international affairs. Today, more than fifty years after the end of the war, the time seems opportune for a critical assessment of world affairs in the second half of the twentieth century. What themes and trends have characterized international relations since 1945? How have conceptions of warfare and visions of peace changed? These questions must be addressed if one is to arrive at an understanding of the contemporary world that is international—with an awareness of the linkages among different parts of the world—and historical—with a keen sense of what the immediate past has brought to human civilization. Hence Twayne's International History Series. It is hoped that the volumes in this series will help the reader to explore important events and decisions since 1945 and to develop the global awareness and historical sensitivity required for confronting today's problems.

The first volumes in the series examine the United States' relations with other countries, groups of countries, or regions. The focus on the United States is justified in part because of the nation's predominant position in postwar international relations, and also because far more extensive documentation is available on American foreign affairs than is the case with other countries. The series addresses not only those interested in international relations, but also those studying America's and other countries' histories, who will find here useful guides and fresh insights into the recent past. Now more than ever, it is imperative to understand the linkages between national and international history.

This volume offers a balanced, thorough, and timely account of the United States' dealings with the Arab states in the Middle East since 1945.

This has been one of the most complex phenomena in postwar international history, not least because the United States was a relative newcomer to the scene. The Middle East was traditionally an arena for the interplay of European power politics, on one hand, and for the intermingling of diverse ethnic and religious identities, on the other. How the United States became steadily drawn into the region to replace the European powers, and how its foreign policy sought to cope with Arab nationalism, the Arab-Israeli antagonism, and the problem of regional security, are important issues whose relevance has increased in the wake of the ending of the cold war.

To examine these and many other questions, we have been fortunate to obtain the services of Professor Burton Kaufman, a well-known authority on postwar U.S. foreign affairs. He has written an excellent survey, based on extensive reading in primary and secondary sources. As in his other published work, in this book Kaufman brings to the subject judiciousness and balance, qualities that are particularly needed in the discussion of Middle Eastern affairs. At a time when Israeli-Arab relations are moving fast, one hopes in a positive direction, this book should serve as an invaluable guide, carefully charting the course of postwar U.S.-Arab relations and pointing to future possibilities.

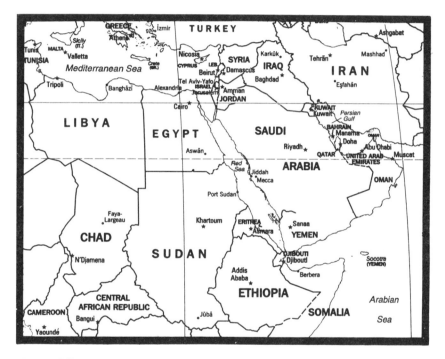

The Middle East

INTRODUCTION

As the title indicates, this book is intended as a general introduction to the history of the United States' relations with the Arab Middle East since the end of World War II. It is mainly a synthesis of the extant primary and secondary literature, which is voluminous. But I have also incorporated research that I conducted at the libraries of each of the postwar presidents.

Although there are a number of fine books that cover much the same ground, I have tried to differentiate this book from the others by the coverage I give to the Arab side of U.S.-Arab relations. Indeed, one of the recurring themes of this book is the internal divisions of the Arab world. One simply cannot understand relations between the United States and the Arab countries without some comprehension of the historical differences, rivalries, competing ambitions, and confrontations that characterize inter-Arab relations. The very concept of an "Arab world" has to be approached with care since it suggests a degree of Arab unity that is not always present.

Another theme of this book is the impact of the cold war on U.S.-Arab relations. Like so much of American foreign relations in the postwar period, Washington's abiding concern with communist expansion after 1945 acted like a malignancy on the nation's relations with the Arab states, pervading and perverting the United States' approach to the Arab world.

Yet concern about growing communist influence in the Middle East diminished considerably following the Yom Kippur War of 1973. Because of the Arab states' initial success on the battlefield and the harmful impact of their oil embargo on the American economy, Washington no longer looked upon them primarily in the context of the cold war. Nor were more radical Arab leaders viewed largely as agents (or dupes) of Moscow. The United States became more attentive to Arab concerns and more responsive to the

Arab position in the Arab-Israeli dispute. At the same time, the Soviet presence in the Middle East diminished considerably as a result of Soviet attempts at detente with the United States, growing Arab disenchantment with Moscow's policy in the region, and Secretary of State Henry Kissinger's concerted efforts at limiting Soviet influence within the Arab world. Although the United States continued to express concern about the Soviet role in the Middle East, the Soviet threat there no longer seemed as great as it had prior to the Yom Kippur War.

Increasingly important for American policymakers was the West's growing dependence on Arab-controlled oil. Yet the role of oil in U.S.-Arab relations can be easily overstated. There can be no question that the need for Mideast oil was always a major concern for those who made American foreign—and domestic—policy. An antitrust case brought after World War II against the multinational corporations that controlled the flow of oil from the Middle East was largely abandoned because of the need for Middle Eastern oil and the important role these companies played in that region of the world. A major reason—but not the only, or even primary, reason—for Washington's concern about a Soviet presence in the Middle East was the specter of Soviet domination of the region's vast oil resources. Those who maintain that President George Bush would never have attempted to free Kuwait from Iraq during the 1991 Persian Gulf War if Kuwait and Saudi Arabia were not major oil producers are probably correct (although that type of counterfactual argument is somewhat beside the point). But what I find significant is how greatly factors other than the prize of oil (specifically the cold war and the United States' special relationship with Israel) influenced the United States' relations with the Arab world throughout most of the period covered in this book.

As I have already indicated, writing about "the Arab world" can be misleading since it suggests a degree of Arab unity that has not always been present. But writing about the "Arab Middle East" can be even more misleading since, as so many historians have pointed out, not all Arabs live in the Middle East, and not all of the Middle East is Arab. Even defining the geographical extent of the Mideast is fraught with danger. For the purposes of this book, I have defined the region as extending from Libya in the west to Iraq in the east and from Syria in the north to the Arabian Peninsula and the Sudan in the south. Except for Libya and the Sudan, this is the definition that William L. Cleveland uses in his excellent A History of the Modern Middle East.[1] It is also similar to that used by the eminent scholar L. Carl Brown, who defines the region as "the Afro-Asian lands of the former Ottoman Empire." Brown's definition includes the entire Arab world except Morocco and Mauritania.[2] I have also excluded Algeria and Tunisia because they were marginal players in the issues and developments covered in this book.

Israel was, of course, not a marginal player. As a result, it receives considerable attention in the pages that follow. So does Iran after the Iranian Revolution of 1979. But the focus of this book remains the United States' relations with the Arab states of the Middle East.

I wish to thank Professor Akira Iriye for his patience with a long overdue manuscript. I also wish to acknowledge my deep gratitude to my colleague, William Ochsenwald, co-author of one of the leading texts on the history of the Middle East, who read the entire manuscript, helped me with Arabic names, corrected factual errors, and made numerous other helpful recommendations for improving the text.

I dedicate this book to my sisters and brothers by birth and by marriage: Lois and Sid Kaufman, Eleanor and Tom Sprowl, Shirley Novack, Jennifer and Jack Kallison, and Jan and Steve Rosenberg.

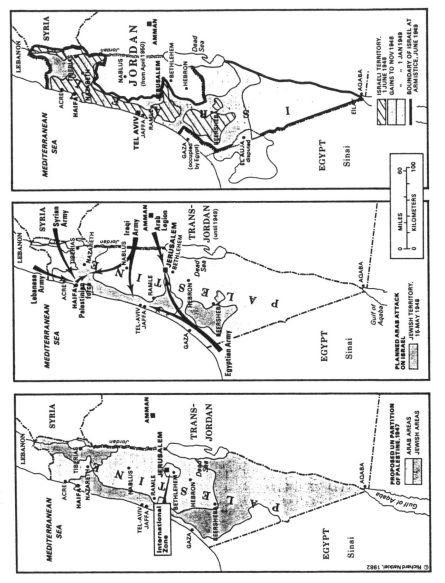

Formation of Israel, 1947–49
Courtesy Richard Natkiel

chapter 1

FORGING POLICY IN THE POSTWAR ERA: 1945–1953

Until the end of World War II in 1945, the United States' interest in the Middle East had largely been limited to the quest for oil. Americans did engage in some commerce and trade in the region. Missionary societies had been active in the area since the nineteenth century, and an organized movement was already underway among American Jews to establish a Jewish homeland in Palestine. But to most Americans, the Middle East was a strange and alien place with which the United States had far less contact than with Europe, Latin America, and most of Asia. Not until 1939 did Washington even accredit the first American minister to Saudi Arabia.

Oil drove the United States' interest in the Middle East. Although the full extent of Mideast oil wealth was not known when World War II ended, government and industry officials had long been aware of the region's immense oil reserves and understood oil's importance in bringing about Europe's postwar economic recovery and growth. The State Department had promoted or endorsed the expansion of American oil interests in the Middle East since the 1920s. On the eve of World War II, five American and two European multinational oil companies (the majors)—Standard Oil of New Jersey (now EXXON), Standard Oil of New York (now Mobil), Standard Oil of California (SOCAL, now Chevron), the Texas Oil Company (Texaco), Gulf Oil, Royal Dutch Shell, and Anglo-Iranian (now British Petroleum or BP)—controlled the oil industry in the Middle East. Two of the American companies, SOCAL and Texaco, jointly owned the California Arabian Standard Oil Company (CASOC), which had the concession to develop the oil fields of Saudi Arabia. Nevertheless, at San Remo in 1920, the League of Nations had awarded the Levant (modern day Syria and Lebanon) as a mandate to France, and Iraq and Palestine (including what is now Jordan) as a mandate to Britain, so the United States' role in the Middle East was limited mainly to oil. In fact, Washington regarded the region as largely a British sphere of interest in which the U.S. served as a junior partner. In Saudi Arabia, the British maintained a strong political presence and provided an annual subsidy to King Ibn Saud.

The situation began to change during World War II. The decline of domestic reserves as a result of the war effort underscored the importance of securing independent control of oil sources abroad, particularly to conserve the strategically more important Western Hemispheric reserves. The war also left the United States as the world's unrivaled economic and military power. No longer prepared to play junior partner to the British in the Middle East, the United States was now committed to a postwar world predicated on the Wilsonian principles of self-determination, anti-imperialism, and an open-door economic policy.

These developments were played out in Saudi Arabia, which became the focal point of British-American rivalry.[1] American oil interests and Arab hands at the State Department's Division of Near Eastern Affairs were afraid that London might use its economic assistance to the financially strapped Saudis to increase its political influence at the expense of the CASOC oil concession. The State Department also recognized the country's strategic location linking the Persian Gulf with the rest of the Middle East. As a result, it persuaded President Franklin D. Roosevelt in 1943 to extend lend-lease aid to the Saudis.

Without conferring with London, administration officials began planning for a government-owned, trans-Arabian pipeline linking the Persian Gulf to the eastern Mediterranean. About the same time, Secretary of State Cordell Hull proposed opening negotiations with the British about "problems concerning Middle East oil," which the British interpreted as a challenge to their preferred position in the region. In a sharply worded exchange of letters with President Roosevelt, British prime minister Winston Churchill virtually accused the United States of seeking to overturn Britain's concession rights in Iraq and Iran (where it maintained an oil monopoly). Roosevelt responded with his own concern "about the rumor that the British wish[ed] to horn in on Saudi Arabian oil reserves." In a more conciliatory vein, the president assured Churchill that the United States did not harbor designs on British oil interests. To resolve wartime differences and plan for the postwar world, an Anglo-American oil agreement was negotiated later that year. Nevertheless, there remained widespread distrust in Washington about Britain's postwar imperial ambitions.[2]

Washington's interest in Mideast oil remained strong after the war, but in terms of shaping American policy, it merged with such considerations as the cold war, recognition of Britain's decline as a world power, the quest for a Jewish homeland in Palestine, and growing Arab nationalism. Most historians attribute the beginning of the cold war to the failure of the Soviet Union to allow free elections in eastern and central Europe. But the crises of the cold war took place in the Near and Middle East. In the United States and Britain had to apply intense diplomati before the Soviet Union agreed to withdraw its troops from the northern Iranian province of Azerbaijan. Later that year, Moscow applied pressure on Turkey to accept joint control of the Dardanelles Straits linking the Black Sea with the Mediterranean. In 1947, President Harry Truman responded to the Soviet pressure on Turkey and to a civil war in Greece between communist-led forces and forces loyal to the Greek monarchy by addressing Congress and asking it for $400 million in economic and military assistance to Greece and Turkey. In what became known as the Truman Doctrine, he also vowed that the United States would resist communist expansion throughout the world.

Iran, Turkey, and Greece are not Arab countries, but events involving the three nations (the so-called northern tier) focused Washington's attention on the Middle East, serving as reminders of its importance both geopolitically and in terms of its oil resources. American policymakers became increasingly concerned that the region's economic destitution would make it a breeding ground for communist influence. At the same time, the Pentagon's strategic plans factored in America's Dharan airfield in Saudi Arabia and, more importantly, British air bases in Egypt, which were closer to the Soviet Union's oil fields and refineries than any airfield in western Europe.[3]

At the end of the war, Britain was still the predominant power in the Middle East. Indeed, it was the only big power in the region, because the war had resulted in the end of French colonial rule in Syria and Lebanon. Near the conclusion of the conflict, France had tried to impose preferential treaties on the two countries and had even bombed Damascus. But the French were widely condemned for their actions. Together with the British—who had moved forces into the Levant in 1941 because France's Vichy government failed to stop Axis activity there—they withdrew the last of their occupation forces in 1946. With the Italians, who had occupied Libya since 1911, also gone, the British had no European rival in the Middle East.

World War II, however, had sapped much of Britain's economic strength and, in the process, dealt a further blow to the British imperium, which had been in decline since the end of the nineteenth century. The corollary was an expanded American political presence in the Middle East. In fact, the president announced the Truman Doctrine in response to London's notification that it could no longer supply economic and military assistance to Greece and Turkey and to his concern that the British might also withdraw from Egypt.

Except for events in the northern tier, though, the region was not of paramount concern to the United States. Despite the global thrust of the Truman Doctrine, the cold war was largely fought over western Europe. Notwithstanding the increased strategic importance of the Middle East,

Britain's decline as a world power, and serious economic and political differences with London over Middle East policy, Washington preferred a British military presence in the region to its own. It held to this position even when it resulted in conflict with Arab aspirations and nationalist sentiments, as in the case of the Anglo-Egyptian dispute over Britain's bases in the Suez Canal Zone and control over the Sudan. By a 1936 agreement with the Egyptians, which was supposed to run for 20 years, Britain was given the right to station 10,000 soldiers, 500 pilots, and an unspecified number of support personnel in Egypt and to use naval and air bases in the canal zone.

But during the war the zone had become a huge military enclave which extended three-quarters of the way between the Suez Canal and Cairo and held as many as 38 camps and 10 airfields. Even after the war ended, there were more than 80,000 British troops stationed in Egypt. Britain was willing to withdraw its combat troops but not to give up its bases where it wanted to maintain air defense forces and maintenance personnel. Britain and Egypt were also at odds over the Sudan, which, according to an 1899 agreement, they were supposed to govern jointly but which was effectively under British authority. London refused to relinquish its control over the Sudan, which Cairo claimed was part of Egypt, without first providing for Sudanese self-determination. Although sensitive to Egyptian nationalism, the United States backed the British in their negotiations with Cairo.[4]

Of more immediate and lasting importance than the cold war in Washington's relations with the Arab Middle East was the growing pressure in the United States to establish a Jewish homeland in Palestine. The complex story behind the creation of the state of Israel in May 1948 and its almost immediate recognition by the United States is beyond the scope of this book.[5] Nevertheless, the Palestinian question—by whom and under whose control Palestine should be inhabited—was central to America's relations with the Arab world even before Britain decided in 1947 to relinquish its mandate over Palestine. Arabs had opposed, sometimes violently, the establishment of a separate Jewish state in Palestine since the Balfour Declaration of 1917 had promised a Jewish homeland there. Largely in response, Britain altered its policy on Palestine in the years between World Wars I and II. In 1939, London announced that it would restrict Jewish immigration to Palestine to 15,000 a year for five years, after which it would be stopped completely, and that in certain areas Jews would not be allowed to purchase Arab-owned lands. But its new policy encountered strong opposition even from Arab leaders, who demanded an immediate end to Jewish immigration and the establishment of a separate Arab state.

Palestine's fate remained undecided during the war. Fighting against the Axis powers for its very survival, Britain adopted a policy in Palestine of maintaining the status quo, limiting Jewish immigration to 1,500 a month. But an estimated 20,000 Jews came in illegally, and both Jews and Arabs armed themselves for conflict. In March 1945, Arab leaders formed the Arab

League to promote Arab unity and to lobby against a Jewish state in Palestine. In the United States, Zionist support grew within the small but politically influential Jewish community, as American Jews learned about the Holocaust taking place in Europe. On Capitol Hill strong backing also developed for a Jewish state. President Roosevelt sent out conflicting signals. During the 1944 presidential campaign he stated that he supported the Zionist program. But he assured Saudi King Ibn Saud, whom he met on his way back from the Yalta Conference in 1945, that he would consult with Arab leaders before taking any action that affected Arab interests in Palestine.[6]

With the end of the war and the full extent of the Holocaust revealed, pressure mounted for a Jewish homeland. Stunned by the enormity of the Jewish tragedy in Europe, the new American president, Harry Truman, urged that 100,000 displaced European Jews be settled in Palestine. His proposal was received coolly by most officials in the State Department and Pentagon. Although not unsympathetic to the plight of European Jews, they were more concerned about maintaining good relations with the Arab nations than about establishing a homeland in Palestine for Holocaust victims. Defense planners were also concerned that as many as 150,000 American troops might be needed just to keep Arabs and Jews from killing each other, when the armed forces were being demobilized and the remaining troops were needed for the German and Japanese occupations.[7]

The British also opposed the massive immigration Truman was proposing. Although a declining power, Britain had no intention of withdrawing from the Middle East. Its oil resources in Iran and Iraq, its military installations in Iraq, the Sudan, Bahrein, Aden, and Jordan (at the time known as Transjordan), and its control of the Suez Canal dictated a strong British presence in the region. British foreign minister Ernest Bevin sought to retain his country's preeminent position in the Middle East by supporting moderate Arab leaders and developing bilateral arrangements with each Arab nation. At the same time, he maintained a jaundiced view of the establishment of a Jewish state in Palestine and feared increased conflict between Arabs and Jews if Jewish immigration continued.[8]

In an attempt to delay, and possibly sidetrack, Truman's suggestion to open Palestine to 100,000 Jewish immigrants, London proposed, and the United States agreed to, the establishment of an Anglo-American Committee of Inquiry to consider the question of the permanent settlement of Europe's displaced Jews. In May 1946, the committee recommended that 100,000 Jews "who had been the victims of Nazi and Fascist persecution" be permitted into Palestine, that the 1939 restrictions on land sales to Jews be lifted, and that the region be brought under United Nations (UN) trusteeship in preparation for its eventual independence as a binational state.[9] President Truman welcomed the recommendation on immigration while holding off comment on the other proposals. But Arab leaders condemned the entire report. The Arab League warned that it would not sit idly by while the committee's proposals were instituted. Even most Zionists opposed the concept of a binational state in Palestine. In the United States, American Jews called instead for the establishment of a Jewish state through the partition of Palestine. In October, Truman seemed to endorse this proposal in a message he sent to American Jewish leaders on the eve of Yom Kippur, the holiest day in the Jewish religion.

The president's Yom Kippur statement angered the British, who were already upset that he had endorsed the committee's recommendation on immigration without consulting them and that the United States had offered no financial assistance in the settlement of Jews in Palestine. "My annoyance is with the Americans who forever lay heavy burdens on us without lifting a little finger to help," Prime Minister Clement Attlee told Richard Crossman, a British member of the committee. Attlee insisted that both Arabs and Jews in Palestine would have to disarm before his government would proceed further with the committee's recommendations.[10]

Meanwhile, Britain sat on a powder keg as Palestinian Jews undertook a concerted effort to get the British to give up their mandate and get out of Palestine. Jewish extremist groups like the Irgun and Stern Gang, which had already been engaged in terrorism against the British, stepped up their activities. In 1946, they shocked the world by bombing the King David Hotel in Jerusalem, which housed the British military command, killing 92 persons and injuring many more. A more moderate group, the Haganah, smuggled arms and, less successfully, immigrants into Palestine and committed its own acts of violence and sabotage against British rule.

Totally frustrated and finding themselves in an increasingly intolerable position, the British were no longer willing to incur the odium of occupation. In April 1947, they requested that the UN establish a committee to review the Palestinian situation and make recommendations to the UN General Assembly at its next regular session in September. Over the succeeding three months, the United Nations Special Committee on Palestine (UNSCOP) met with Jewish and Arab leaders in New York, Jerusalem, Beirut, and Geneva. In September, UNSCOP recommended that the Palestinian mandate be terminated as soon as possible and that Palestine be partitioned into an Arab state, a Jewish state, and an independent Jerusalem under UN trusteeship. Despite warnings against partition from Defense and State Department officials, who considered the establishment of the state of Israel the height of folly, Truman decided to support UNSCOP's recommendations. On 29 November 1947, the General Assembly approved the committee's report by a vote of 33 to 13.[11]

Approval of the partition resolution came at a time of growing Arab nationalism and despite nearly unanimous Arab rejection of a Jewish state in Palestine. Indeed, the Palestinian question probably did more than anything else to foster Arab nationalism. Although the concept of an Arab people with a common heritage and language, shared values, and a sense of community can be traced back at least to the Arab revolt against the Ottoman Empire during World War I, division more than unity characterized relations within the Arab world. The most obvious fissure was between the pro-British Hashimite rulers of Iraq and Transjordan (which Britain had detached from its Palestinian mandate in 1921) and their anti-Hashimite foes closely identified with King Ibn Saud, the Wahhabi ruler of Saudi Arabia. The enmity between these Arab leaders can be traced back to at least 1924, when Ibn Saud drove the Hashimite family, which had led the Arab revolt against Ottoman rule during World War I, from the Arabian Peninsula and then consolidated his rule and established the kingdom of Saudi Arabia.

Along similar lines, bitter rivalry also existed between Iraq, which sought in 1943 to establish a Hashimite Confederation that would include Iraq, Syria, Lebanon, Palestine, and Transjordan, and Egypt, which sought to lead the Arab unification movement and had assumed a leadership role in establishing the Arab League. Likewise, Transjordan's King Abdullah's ambition for a "Greater Syria" that would unite Syria, Lebanon, Palestine, and Transjordan was strongly opposed by Egypt and by the anti-Hashimite leader of the Palestinian Arabs, Hajj Amin al-Husayni. Meanwhile, the system of mandates accentuated regional differences, created separate political entities, and promoted psychological barriers to coordinated activity.[12]

King Abdullah and Prime Minister Sidqi Pasha of Egypt had earlier maintained indirect contact with Zionist leaders. But even moderate Arab leaders were constrained by Arab public opinion, which remained resolutely opposed to the establishment of a Jewish state in Palestine. Aware of the intensity of Arab feeling, officials at the State Department and Pentagon tried to get Truman to change his position on Palestine. Reminding the president of the importance of Middle East oil for European reconstruction, they maintained that American support for partition might lead Saudi Arabia to impose sanctions against the Arabian-American Oil Company (ARAMCO), successor to CASOC. They also pointed to the armed conflict between Arabs and Jews that had broken out immediately following the partition announcement as proof that partition was not politically viable and could even result in American military intervention. Alternatively, they expressed fear that the instability created by partition would invite a Soviet presence in the region. According to Walter Bedell Smith, the American ambassador to Moscow, the Soviets believed that partition would "soften up" the area for Soviet infiltration.[13]

This argument weighed heavily on Truman, who had grown increasingly concerned about Soviet expansionism as a result of a communist coup in Czechoslovakia in February. In March the president indicated that "in principle" he supported turning Palestine into a United Nations trusteeship. But changing his mind after meeting with the British scientist and Zionist leader Chaim Weizmann, whom he greatly admired, Truman announced on 14 May, just 10 minutes after Israel proclaimed its independence, that he was

_ it de facto recognition (that is, acknowledgment of the fact of Israel's existence as opposed to de jure recognition, or the right of Israel to exist, which involved the establishment of formal diplomatic ties with the new state).[14]

Truman's vacillation on the future of Palestine over the 20 months between his Yom Kippur statement of October 1946 and his recognition of Israel in May 1948 has become the subject of considerable historical speculation. Historians argue over the degree to which he acted for domestic political reasons (to maintain the support of the American Jewish community), for humanitarian reasons (in sympathetic response to the tragedy of European Jews), and even for national security reasons (to preempt Soviet influence in Israel).[15] But several points are clear. First, he was never prepared to use American forces to keep Arabs and Jews apart. He agreed with the Pentagon that the United States could not station troops in Palestine when the size of the military was being cut. Second, he became increasingly annoyed at the pressure being put on him by Jewish leaders and pro-Zionist forces on Capitol Hill, particularly after the American ambassador to the UN, Warren Austin, announced in March that the United States supported a proposal to bring Palestine under UN trusteeship. Third, his administration was badly divided over the issue of a Jewish state in Palestine. While most State Department and Pentagon officials, including Secretary of State George Marshall, Undersecretary of State Dean Acheson, and George Kennan, the head of the recently established Policy and Planning Staff, opposed statehood, at the White House presidential advisers Clark Clifford and David Niles worked effectively in its support. Finally, and perhaps most importantly, Truman concluded by May that he had no alternative other than to recognize Israel. By this time, the tide of battle had turned in favor of the Jews. In April, Jewish forces had taken control of the port of Haifa. The next month, they captured the town of Jaffa. Not to have recognized the new Jewish state under these circumstances would have been to deny the realities of the battlefield.

Only hours after declaring its independence, Israel was invaded by forces from Egypt, Iraq, Syria, Transjordan, and Lebanon. At first the war went poorly for the Israelis, who lacked arms and still had not adequately organized their forces. Had Arab military leaders coordinated their battle plans better and pursued the Israelis with more determination, they might have won the war. Instead, they lacked a unified command, quarreled among themselves, and held back their forces, thereby allowing the Israeli forces to switch fronts to meet emergency situations.

Both sides were exhausted after a month of intense fighting. In what proved to be a turning point of the war, they agreed on 11 June to a four week truce worked out by UN mediator Count Folke Bernadotte. During this time, Israel received large shipments of arms from Czechoslovakia and managed to build a small but effective air force by smuggling planes from the United States and Britain. As a result, when the truce expired in July, the Israelis went on the offensive. Although intermittent periods of fighting were followed by longer periods of inaction and cease-fires, by the beginning of 1949 Israel had seized the western Galilee and the entire Negev Desert and had mauled the Egyptian army.

Throughout this period, the Truman administration continued to struggle over its policy toward the Arab-Israeli conflict. In September, Bernadotte was assassinated by Jewish terrorists in Jerusalem shortly after sending a plan to the UN that would have given the Negev to the Arabs in return for giving the Galilee to Israel. The rationale for the plan was that it would provide for geographical consolidation of Israel, afford a natural land bridge between the Arab states east and west of the Negev, and assure that a region largely inhabited by Arab Bedouins remained Arab. Bernadotte's plan was similar to one which the State Department had developed in November 1947 shortly before the UN vote on partition and to a plan Secretary of State George Marshall had sent on 1 September to America's ambassador in Israel, James McDonald. Before forwarding his plan to McDonald, the secretary had cleared it with Truman. Therefore, Marshall believed that he spoke for the president when he announced shortly after Bernadotte's murder that the United States supported the slain diplomat's proposals "in their entirety."[16]

To the embarrassment of the secretary and the White House, his statement created a brouhaha similar to the one in the spring over Truman's reversal on partition. The Bernadotte Plan was strongly opposed by Israel and by Israeli supporters in the United States both because it would deny the new Jewish state an area it hoped to populate with newly arrived immigrants and because it would prevent Israeli access to the Gulf of Aqaba and the Red Sea. It was an election year, and the secretary's statement also conflicted with the Democratic Party platform, which provided that any modifications to Israel's boundaries at the time of partition "should be made only if fully acceptable to the State of Israel."[17] Faced with losing Jewish votes in key industrial states, Truman declared in October that he stood behind the Democratic platform. He also promised to grant Israel de jure recognition as soon as it held elections, and he expressed the hope that he would soon be able to extend financial assistance to the new nation.

On 7 January, the fighting between Arabs and Jews stopped. The next month an armistice was worked out between Egypt and Israel by Dr. Ralph Bunche, the UN mediator who had replaced Bernadotte. Over the next five months, similar agreements were reached between Israel and the other Arab belligerents. Transjordan, whose British-trained Arab Legion had fought well against the Israelis, annexed the West Bank of the Jordan River to form the Hashimite Kingdom of Jordan. Egypt held onto the Gaza Strip, a small part of southwest Palestine inhabited entirely by Arabs. Israel acquired an additional 2,400 square miles of territory, which increased its size by about 40 percent (from 5,600 to 8,000 square miles). Arab Palestine no longer existed as a political entity.

The Arab-Israeli war underscored the lack of unity within the Arab world that would continue to characterize its relations with the United States and other Western powers. King Abdullah's ambition to create a Syrian federation under his leadership conflicted with Egypt's desire to nullify partition and even create a client state in Palestine. As a result, Transjordan was more willing to end the war than Egypt, which regarded Jordan as little more than a British puppet; while Egyptian forces were suffering a humiliating defeat, Transjordan's forces, and those of its Hashimite ally Iraq, did nothing to relieve the pressure on the Egyptians. After the conflict, Egypt responded to Transjordan's annexation of the West Bank by establishing a Palestinian Arab government in the Gaza Strip, which laid claim to the whole of Palestine.

One tragic result of the war was the permanent displacement of more than 750,000 Palestinian refugees who had fled or been forced from their homes. A UN resolution in December called for Israel to allow the Palestinians to return. But Israel refused, claiming the Palestinians would be a threat to its security. Consequently, the UN established the United Nations Relief and Work Agency (UNRWA) to ensure a measure of subsistence for the Palestinians, most of whom lived in squalid refugee camps.

Although armistices were arranged between Israel and its Arab enemies, neither side had much incentive to conclude a permanent peace agreement. Before Arab leaders would agree to peace with Israel, they insisted that the Israelis settle the Palestinian refugee problem and return to the boundaries provided for in the 1947 UN partition resolution. But with their superior military force, Israeli leaders had no reason to abide by the Arab terms. Not even considerable American pressure, including a thinly veiled threat to withdraw a $49 million loan to Israel, could get the Israelis to change their position on the repatriation of Palestinian refugees. As for the Arab states, their leaders had been embarrassed by their defeat at the hands of a nation that they had confidently told their people they would easily overpower. To agree now to a peace on Israeli terms would result in a public humiliation that could threaten their very political survival. The United States understood the problem Arab leaders faced. According to a joint memorandum prepared by the National Security Council (NSC) and the Central Intelligence Agency (CIA) in August 1948, while hostilities were still underway, "fear of popular reaction will still prevent any Arab government from recognizing or negotiating with a Jewish state."[18] Nothing occurred between August and the end of the war in January to alter that assessment. Indeed, the end of hostilities was followed by three military coups in Syria, the assassination in 1951 of Jordan's King Abdullah, and a successful military coup the next year in Egypt, all of which were related directly or indirectly to Israel's victory in the conflict.

Several features of Mideast politics reflected in the Arab-Israeli conflict would remain fairly constant over the next 45 years. Two of these—disunity in the Arab world and the intrusion of the cold war into the Middle East—have been commented upon already. But the influence of the cold war cannot be stressed too much, for it led Washington to view regional problems in a largely global context, ignoring the internal dynamics of the Middle East and creating a lack of balance between regional and global approaches. Compounding this problem was a third feature of Mideast politics synonymous with, but apart from, the cold war: this was what the historian Carl Brown has referred to as "the politics of Arab nationalism," which took the form of increasingly strident appeals to Arab nationalism by leaders seeking to bring about fundamental change in the region and to position themselves at the head of a pan-Arab movement.[19] The coincidence of radical Arab nationalism and a hardening of the cold war resulted in an American myopia toward the Middle East that a more regional perspective might have avoided.

An illustration of the harm that such a distorted focus could cause was the ill-fated proposal by the United States and Britain in October 1951 to establish a Middle East Command (MEC) that would include forces from the United States, Britain, France, Egypt and Turkey. Profound political changes had taken place both globally and regionally between the end of the first Arab-Israeli war and the time of the proposal. The formation of the North Atlantic Treaty Organization (NATO) in 1949 and the outbreak of the Korean War in June 1950 meant that the cold war had become militarized and internationalized. America's cold war policy of containment, which had been confined largely to Europe, took on worldwide dimensions. A crisis atmosphere developed in the United States in response to a sense that the West was losing its struggle against the communist threat. Collective security became the imperative for containing communist expansion.

In the Middle East, major developments included the crystallization of Arab nationalism and Egypt's ongoing struggle with the British over Britain's refusal to withdraw its forces guarding the Suez Canal or to turn over the Sudan to Egypt. Although Britain remained the paramount power in the region, the Labour government's policy of working with moderate Arab regimes in anticipation of developing relationships that would preserve British interests in the Middle East was being challenged by the growth of revolutionary nationalism and anti-imperialism. In non-Arab Iran, the Tehran government had to contend with ever growing economic and political turmoil, which would culminate in 1951 with the assassination of Prime Minister Ali Razmara and the nationalization of the Anglo-Iranian Oil Company. Even Iraq's staunchly pro-British government faced increasing opposition from groups demanding social and economic reforms and denouncing Britain's military presence in the country. Although Iraq's strongman, Nuri al-Said, was able to contain the nationalist opposition, it was powerful enough in 1948 to defeat a treaty by which Britain would have shared control of its two air bases in Iraq with the Baghdad government and established an Iraq-British Joint Defense Board. London intended the treaty to be a model for agreements with other Arab governments. But nationalists forced Baghdad to withdraw the agreement on the basis that it did not fulfill "the national aspirations" of the Iraqi people.[20]

blesome to London, though, was the Egyptian demand in 1950,
s of unsuccessful negotiations, that they withdraw their forces
the Suez air base and cede control of the Sudan to Egypt. Britain was
prepared to relinquish dominion over its Suez operation. But it was not willing to give up its bases or to recognize Egyptian sovereignty over the Sudan.
The partition of Palestine meant that it could not be used as an alternative
military base for British forces, as London had once contemplated. According
to the British chiefs of staff, in fact, there was no suitable alternative to the
Suez base. The British high command also concluded that the Egyptians
lacked both the technical prowess to administer such a complex operation as
the Suez Canal and the ability to defend themselves.[21]

Increasingly concerned about a worldwide communist threat and worried
about instability in the Middle East, the United States sought to coordinate
its diplomatic and political efforts more closely with Britain. In May, the
United States, Britain, and France issued the Tripartite Declaration limiting
arms sales to the Middle East to those weapons needed for internal stability
and self-defense. The decision to issue the statement followed the lifting in
1949 of an arms embargo imposed by the UN after the outbreak of the Arab-
Israeli conflict and the subsequent sales of arms to the Arab states by Britain.
Under domestic pressure to sell arms to Israel but fearful of a destabilizing
arms race that could result in another conflict in the Middle East, the
United States decided to supply arms to Israel. At the same time, however, it
joined Britain and France in an agreement to reduce overall arms sales in the
region. The three Western powers also pledged to "immediately take action,
both within and outside the United Nations, to prevent . . . violation[s of
existing territorial borders]."[22]

Although the Arab League and other Arab leaders attacked the declaration as an infringement on national sovereignty and an unacceptable
endorsement of the territorial status quo, it received a generally favorable
reception in the Middle East. Nowhere was this truer than in Egypt, where it
was viewed by Egyptian King Farouk as a way of reducing tensions in the
region. But the statement had no effect on Egypt's ongoing quarrel with the
British over military bases and the Sudan. Elections in Egypt in 1950 brought
to power the Wafd Party, which was committed to Egyptian sovereignty over
the canal zone and the Sudan and the immediate withdrawal of all British
forces from Egypt.

Britain remained determined, however, not to be driven out of Egypt
willy-nilly. It insisted instead on a phased withdrawal of its troops from Egypt
during which time Egyptians could be trained to run the Suez operation. It
also maintained that it had a trustee responsibility to the Sudanese people.
The United States pressured the British to compromise on the Sudan but
otherwise supported London. The outbreak of the Korean War in 1950
underscored the strategic importance of the Suez Canal and British air bases
in Egypt for transporting personnel and equipment to the Far East, protect-

ing the Middle East oil fields, and striking at Soviet oil facilities in the event of an expanded war.[23]

The establishment of a Middle East Command was intended by Britain and the United States as a means of satisfying Egypt's nationalist sensibilities while maintaining a Western military presence in Egypt. The proposal for MEC came from the British, who had long been interested in having the United States assume greater responsibility for defense in the Middle East. Secretary of State Dean Acheson liked the concept of a regional security system, which he viewed as a complement to NATO. The British would still have most of the responsibility for the defense of the region, but the United States would provide some small weapons and training and military schooling for Arab officers.

In October 1951 the British presented the proposal for MEC to Egypt. But Cairo rejected it almost immediately, announcing that it was ending further discussions with the British and abrogating the treaty of 1936. Washington strove for an accommodation between London and Cairo. Secretary Acheson proposed an agreement by which Britain would accept Farouk's title as "King of Egypt and the Sudan." In return, Egypt would agree to join MEC and to permit a referendum on Sudanese self-determination. But London rejected the American plan. What Britain wanted was strong backing from Washington in dealing with Egypt, not proposals for compromise on the Sudan.[24]

The collision of Egyptian nationalism and British intransigence left American policymakers successively bemused, bewildered, and totally frustrated. On the one hand, Egypt's unilateral abrogation of the 1936 treaty resulted in a wave of increasingly violent demonstrations against the British. On the other, the British responded with a growing show of force and repression, including fatally shooting Egyptian demonstrators, airlifting paratroopers into the canal zone, establishing roadblocks, and seizing power plants and telephone exchanges. This spiraling escalation of violence and coercion undermined the already slim chances of getting Egypt and other Arab states to join MEC (renamed the Middle East Defense Organization, or MEDO, in order to avoid the appearance of being dominated by the West) and placed the United States in the awkward position of berating Britain for its inflexibility and use of force, yet publicly supporting the British and reluctantly sanctioning the use of force to keep the Suez Canal open. All the elements that would soon result in a decidedly anti-Western, pan-Arab revolution in Egypt were thus already in play by the fall of 1951.[25]

The revolution did not begin, though, until the end of July 1952, when a group of military officers seized control of the government and forced King Farouk to abdicate. Although the reasons for the uprising were complex, Egypt's miserable military performance in the 1948 Arab-Israeli war and Farouk's debauched lifestyle were important causes. The nominal leader of the military coup was a popular general, Muhammad Naguib. But its real leader was Colonel Gamal Abdel Nasser, who would replace Naguib as prime minister within a year and declare himself president of Egypt in 1954.

National security considerations had dictated America's response to the Anglo-Egyptian quarrel over military bases and troop withdrawals. A similar concern about national security also determined American policy with respect to Mideast oil. By the early 1950s, Mideast oil production was already expanding significantly, as oil producers began realizing the full extent of the region's oil resources. Oil production in Iraq, for example, increased from 3.5 million metric tons in 1948 to 34 million metric tons by 1954. Even more dramatic were increases in Saudi Arabian production, which grew from 1 million metric tons in 1944 to 47 million metric tons by 1954, and in Kuwaiti production, which rose from 830,000 metric tons in 1946 to over 55 million metric tons by 1956.[26] Most oil from the Middle East, moreover, was controlled by American companies. In addition to ARAMCO's exclusive control of Saudi oil, these corporations had a partial interest in the exploration rights of all the other territories on the western side of the Persian Gulf. Indeed, the only major producing area still closed to Americans was the Iranian oil fields, which remained the exclusive property of the British-owned Anglo-Iranian Oil Company.

Even as the production of Mideast oil increased dramatically, the Federal Trade Commission (FTC) undertook an investigation into the extent of concentration within the oil industry. The FTC's report on the oil industry, which was published at the beginning of 1952, found that concentration in the form of jointly owned subsidiaries, affiliated companies, and other contractual tie-ins was "probably more widespread in the international petroleum industry than in any other field of enterprise."[27] On the basis of the FTC's report and a follow-up recommendation by the Justice Department, President Truman ordered a grand jury investigation of the oil industry on 2 June 1952, for the purpose of bringing criminal indictments against the majors.

The Truman administration actually considered giving the multinational corporations immunity from the antitrust laws in the production and distribution of oil from Iran. Throughout the crisis that followed Iran's nationalization of Anglo-Iranian Oil in 1951, the United States used the oil companies to accomplish specific foreign policy objectives, such as avoiding oil shortages in Europe and Japan, which were by now heavily dependent on Middle Eastern oil, bolstering Iran's economy by agreeing to give it a larger share of oil profits, preventing Iran from slipping within the Soviet orbit, and achieving an American oil presence in Iran. The administration regarded these objectives as vital to the nation's security in light of the expanding cold war.[28]

In similar fashion, the Treasury and State Departments encouraged in 1950 a highly controversial scheme worked out between Saudi Arabia and ARAMCO, which resulted in the transfer to Saudi Arabia of income taxes previously paid by ARAMCO to the United States. The transfer was accomplished by having Saudi Arabia issue new income tax laws that gave it 50 percent of ARAMCO's Arabian profits. Under a 1918 provision, ARAMCO could deduct these revenues from its United States income taxes. ARAMCO developed the scheme in response to demands by King Ibn Saud for a larger share of its profits. The United States supported the plan as a means of bolstering the pro-Western Saudi government. The alternative of direct foreign aid to the Saudis would have encountered strong opposition from the American Jewish community and from pro-Israeli forces on Capitol Hill. The administration also wanted to avoid damaging the profit structure of ARAMCO, which claimed it could not meet Ibn Saud's money demands and still pay high American taxes. By satisfying Ibn Saud's demands, the United States also intended to protect its exclusive oil concessions in Saudi Arabia against a nationalist takeover or a possible British challenge. In all these respects, the government regarded the oil companies as a means of accomplishing interrelated foreign policy and national security objectives.[29]

By the time Truman had left office in January 1953, in fact, oil had taken on such importance within the administration that the president decided to scale down the antitrust action that the Justice Department was pursuing against the major oil corporations even though lawyers at the department maintained that the industry was one of the worst violators of the nation's antitrust laws. In a prepared paper, the Departments of State, Defense, and Interior recommended that the investigation be dropped. They based their position on the important role played by the multinational oil companies in carrying out national policy in the Middle East, on the harm that a criminal antitrust prosecution would do to the nation's image abroad, and on the cooperation that had developed between the oil industry and the State Department. Over the strong objections of the Justice Department, which questioned the wisdom of using private corporations to carry out foreign policy, Truman accepted these arguments. "I am of the opinion," he wrote Attorney General James P. McGranery on 12 January 1953, just eight days before leaving office, "that the interest of national security might best be served at this time . . . in the context of civil litigation rather than in the context of a criminal proceeding."[30]

Clearly, by the time Truman left office on 20 January the Middle East was assuming increasing importance in American foreign policy. But at the same time, the major foreign policy concern of the Truman administration remained containing communist expansion. Although the Korean War had turned containment from a largely economic policy limited to Europe to a global economic and military policy, the communist threat did not appear to imperil the Arab Middle East in the same way it did Europe, the Far East, or even the northern tier. As a result, the Middle East did not have the same priority for Truman as these other regions. The same was true of his successor, Dwight D. Eisenhower. Yet the spread of Arab nationalism, an increased Soviet presence in the Middle East, and the growing dependence of western Europe, Japan, and to a lesser extent, the United States, on Mideast oil forced the new administration to pay ever more attention to the region.

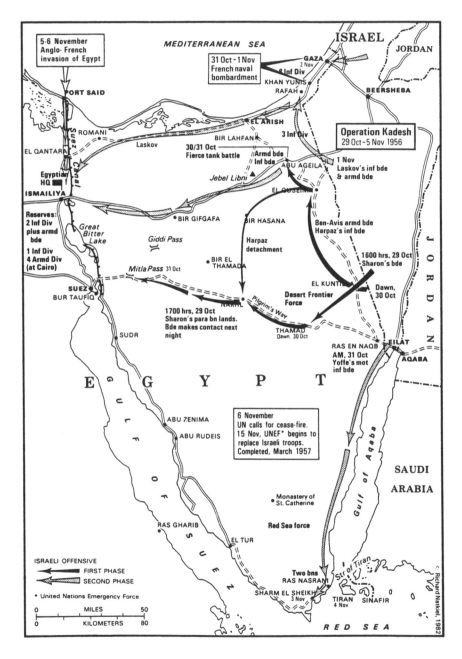

5-6 November
Anglo-French
invasion of Egypt

MEDITERRANEAN SEA

ISRAEL

JORDAN

31 Oct-1 Nov
French naval
bombardment

GAZA
2 Nov

8 Inf Div

KHAN YUNIS

RAFAH

BEERSHEBA

PORT SAID

ROMANI

EL QANTARA

Laskov

EL ARISH

BIR LAHFANE

3 Inf Div

30/31 Oct
Fierce tank battle

Armd bde
Inf bde

ABU AGEILA

Operation Kadesh
29 Oct-5 Nov 1956

Jebel Libni

EL QUSEIMA

1 Nov
Laskov's inf bde
& armd bde

Egyptian
HQ

ISMAILIYA

BIR GIFGAFA

BIR HASANA

Ben-Avis armd bde
Harpaz's inf bde

Reserves:
2 Inf Div
plus armd
bde

1 Inf Div
4 Armd Div
(at Cairo)

*Great
Bitter
Lake*

Giddi Pass

Harpaz
detachment

1600 hrs, 29 Oct
Sharon's bde

*BIR EL
THAMADA*

J
O
R
D
A
N

Mitla Pass 31 Oct

SUEZ

BUR TAUFIQ

NAKHL

EL KUNTIL

Dawn,
30 Oct

Desert Frontier
Force

Pilgrim's Way

1700 hrs, 29 Oct
Sharon's para bn lands.
Bde makes contact next
night

THAMAD
Dawn, 30 Oct

RAS EN NAQB
AM, 31 Oct
Yoffe's mot
inf bde

EILAT

AQABA

SUDR

E   G   Y   P   T

G
U
L
F

O
F

S
U
E
Z

ABU ZENIMA

ABU RUDEIS

6 November
UN calls for cease-fire.
15 Nov, UNEF* begins to
replace Israeli troops.
Completed, March 1957

Gulf of Aqaba

SAUDI

ARABIA

RAS GHARIB

EL TUR

*Monastery of
St. Catherine*

Red Sea force

© Richard Natkiel, 1982

ISRAELI OFFENSIVE

FIRST PHASE

SECOND PHASE

* United Nations Emergency Force

Two bns
RAS NASRANI

SHARM EL SHEIKH
3 Nov

Str of Tiran

TIRAN
4 Nov

SINAFIR

0   MILES   50

0   KILOMETERS   80

RED SEA

1956 Suez War
Courtesy Richard Natkiel

chapter 2

EISENHOWER, CONTAINMENT, AND ARAB NATIONALISM: 1953–1961

Although Eisenhower was the first Republican president of the cold war era (and the first Republican in the Oval Office since 1933), the contours of his foreign policy were fundamentally the same as those of his Democratic predecessor. Like Truman's, Eisenhower's objective was a Wilsonian world order characterized by openness, interdependence, and commitment to democratic principles. Similarly, his strategy for achieving this world order was containment, and his tactics were collective security. Finally, like Truman, he was far more concerned with European matters, particularly maintaining the Atlantic alliance, than with developments in the Middle East.

Yet there were significant differences between Eisenhower and Truman in the construction and implementation of foreign policy, which greatly affected Eisenhower's Mideast policy. Eisenhower and his secretary of state, John Foster Dulles, expanded upon the concept of collective security by establishing around the Soviet Union a chain of collective security agreements, which besides NATO included the Southeast Asia Treaty Organization in the Far East (1954) and the Baghdad Pact in the Middle East (1955). Also, Eisenhower resorted to new tactics for carrying out containment, such as greater reliance on covert operations and foreign economic policy. In addition, he was more sensitive than Truman to the rising tide of nationalism sweeping much of the third world, including the Middle East. But he perceived the communist threat in even more apocalyptic terms than Truman, regarding it as a cancer that menaced the third world by latching onto and undermining nationalist political movements. As a result, his foreign policy in the Middle East was strewn with contradictions and inconsistencies.

Concerns about stability, security, and the Soviet threat guided Eisenhower's Mideast policy. As stated in a report on the Middle East approved by the National Security Council (NSC) on 15 July 1953, security meant having access to the region's resources and strategic positions while denying them to the Soviet Union. Stability inferred the existence of friendly governments strong enough to withstand communist subversion and aggression. In the NSC's view, the greatest threat was internal and had to do with anti-Western nationalism and Arab-Israeli antagonism. Therefore, the United States should strive to resolve the outstanding differences that contributed to anti-Western sentiment.[1]

Beginning at the end of 1954, the administration even engaged in a top secret diplomatic initiative with England, given the code name "Project Alpha," which was meant to resolve the Arab-Israeli dispute by having the West guarantee Israel's borders. In return Israel would be expected to make territorial compromises with its Arab neighbors and provide for the repatriation of Palestinian refugees. But escalating tensions in 1955 killed whatever chance Project Alpha might have had for resolving the Arab-Israeli dispute, and by early 1956 it had been abandoned in favor of other initiatives.[2]

In 1954, however, the United States' most immediate problems in the Middle East were resolving the dispute between London and Cairo over the British base in the canal zone and implementing an Anglo-Egyptian agreement on the Sudan. The agreement was made possible by the decision of the Naguib government following the overthrow of King Farouk to recognize the right of Sudanese self-determination. In return Britain agreed to surrender its claims over the Sudan. An Anglo-Egyptian accord was signed on 12 February 1953 abolishing the 1899 condominium and allowing the Sudanese to choose between complete independence or union with Egypt.

The issue of the British base in the canal zone was more complicated, however, and promised to delay implementation of the Sudan agreement. The Middle East nations were determined to end the last vestiges of colonialism in the region, and they remained particularly distrustful of Britain because of its former colonial practices. That was one reason why the NSC wanted London to be more flexible in negotiating with Cairo. At the same time, the NSC remained persuaded that it was in America's security interests to have the British continue to "assume as much responsibility [in the Middle East] as feasible under present conditions." Also, Washington did not want to do anything—such as trying to pressure Britain into negotiating with Egypt—that might cause a rift within the Western alliance.[3]

Actually, both the United States and Britain had already begun to devalue British military operations in Egypt. On the basis of a three day visit to Egypt in May, Secretary of State John Foster Dulles determined that while it was still important to maintain a Western military presence in the canal zone, the United States should concentrate its efforts on building a military defense pact around the northern tier. Similarly, the NSC concluded that "special consideration" should be given to Turkey, Iraq, Syria, Iran, and Pakistan because they were "most keenly aware of the threat of Soviet

Russia" and were "located geographically to stand in the way of possible Soviet aggression." The British were worried that their 81,000 troops stationed in Egypt were in harm's way because of the Soviet Union's possession of the atomic bomb and the proximity of its airfields to Egypt. Almost daily acts of violence against the British in Egypt also sapped troop morale and raised questions about the security of British military operations. Budgetary constraints provided an additional reason for the British to leave Egypt.[4]

Nevertheless, there was strong opposition in Britain to withdrawing from Egypt and mounting annoyance with the United States' pressure to compromise on all outstanding issues in the Middle East, including the ongoing imbroglio in Iran over the nationalization of Anglo-Iranian Oil. Foreign Secretary Anthony Eden suspected the United States of trying to supplant Britain in the region. He also did not care for Secretary of State Dulles, with whom he had disagreed on a number of issues; indeed, he had lobbied unsuccessfully against Dulles's appointment as secretary of state. He insisted that before Britain would relinquish its bases in the canal zone, Cairo would have to participate in a Middle East Defense Organization (MEDO), which London was trying to establish for the region.[5]

As a result, the United States found itself torn between the need to maintain Anglo-American unity and the desire to respond positively to Egyptian nationalism by not seeming to gang up with Britain against Egypt. It tried to finesse this problem by approving $11.7 million in economic and technical assistance and $11 million in military equipment for the country. The White House also expressed interest in financing the proposed High Dam at Aswan, which would open millions of acres to farming and provide an abundant source of hydroelectric power. But opposition to the arms agreement was so great from Britain and lawmakers on Capitol Hill that the administration backed down and refused to approve any new military purchases.[6]

After considerable negotiations with Egypt and much pressure from Washington, in July 1954 London finally agreed to an accord with Egypt providing for the withdrawal of British troops from the canal zone. But the agreement also allowed British civilian technicians to remain in Egypt and British troops to return in case of an attack on any member of the Arab League or on Turkey. The headquarters for British forces in the Middle East was transferred to Cyprus. The United States received considerable credit in Egypt for helping arrange the withdrawal of British troops. But the good feeling between the two countries was short-lived. The administration's priorities in the Middle East conflicted sharply with those of Egyptian leader Gamal Abdel Nasser. Eisenhower's priorities were dictated by the exigencies of the cold war. Nasser was motivated by his sense of Egyptian and Arab nationalism.[7]

The inherent conflict between these two sets of interests was clearly revealed in the events surrounding the formation in February 1955 of the Baghdad Pact, a military agreement among Britain and the northern tier of states bordering on the Soviet Union. Questions still exist as to whether the United States or Britain was primarily responsible for putting together this defense organization. Britain had the most to gain from its formation, since the pact would enhance Britain's weakened position and offer protection to its still considerable interests in the Middle East.

But the NSC also concluded that it was in the United States' security interest to organize such an alliance. Essential to the Eisenhower administration's foreign policy, in fact, was the establishment of a series of security agreements and organizations that would surround the Soviet Union and communist China. Although Dulles had, at one point, thought of building a defense pact in the Middle East around Egypt, he determined by June 1953 that the Arab states in the southern tier (Egypt, Saudi Arabia, Jordan, and Lebanon) were "too lacking in the realization of the international situation to offer any prospect of becoming dependable allies."[8]

In contrast to the British, who hoped Arab states in the southern tier, especially Jordan, would become members of the pact, the United States sought to confine the agreement to the northern tier. Sensitive to Arab nationalism and the strong opposition of Nasser and other Arab leaders to a MEDO, the administration did not want to pressure the Arab states into becoming members of the organization. Unlike Britain, which wanted Western participation in the pact, Washington also preferred that it remain distinctly regional, without Western membership. In addition, the administration had reservations about the military capability of the new defense organization and feared the domestic political backlash that membership in the pact would create because of Israel's opposition to the agreement. These different perceptions of a Middle East defense organization led to considerable friction and antagonism between London and Washington. The United States' "tendency to ignore the feeling of its allies," Eden wrote the British ambassador to the United States, Roger Makins, "is creating mounting difficulties for anyone in this country who wants to maintain close Anglo-American relations."[9]

What mattered to Nasser, however, was not so much who was responsible for the pact as its implications in terms of both a continuing Western presence in the Middle East and his own ambitions and plans for the region. Depending on one's perspective, Nasser was either crafty or ingenuous, devious or shrewd, principled or unprincipled. But several things about this fiery and charismatic leader seem clear. He was ambitious, he distrusted the West, and he was determined to make Egypt the recognized leader of the Middle East. Although committed more to Egyptian nationalism than to Arab nationalism when he led the coup that overthrew King Farouk in 1952, he became the leader of the pan-Arab movement after replacing Naguib as head of state in 1954.[10]

The formation of the Baghdad Pact came as a stunning blow to Nasser's plans to build a defense organization around his own leadership. At the same time, it gave Egypt's arch foe in the Arab world, Iraq, new status among Arab nations. As an NSC report commented, "a struggle for Arab leadership developed [following the Baghdad Pact] with Iraq on one side and Saudi Arabia, Egypt, and Syria on the other."[11] Nasser regarded the pact as a tool of Western imperialism and a move by which Britain could still maintain a strong military presence in the region. He was determined, therefore, that other Arab nations would not join the Baghdad Pact. When it appeared that Jordan might become a member, Nasserites in the Hashimite kingdom were able to pressure its leader, King Hussein, into backing down by threatening to overthrow the monarchy.[12]

Because the United States did not want to antagonize Israel or those countries such as Egypt and Saudi Arabia whose traditional foes were members of the Baghdad Pact, Washington decided against joining the organization. But America's involvement in the pact's formation and its support for the organization were well known to Nasser. Despite the administration's determination to pursue a more evenhanded policy in its dealings with Israel and the Arab nations, the Egyptian leader also resented American efforts to convince Egypt to allow ships carrying cargo bound for Israel through the Suez Canal and to open the canal to Israeli shipping.[13]

Meanwhile, Israel adopted a more militant policy toward its Arab enemies. Increasingly fearful for its own security following Britain's decision to withdraw its troops from Egypt and worried about the formation of a regional defense organization from which it was excluded, Israel engaged in a campaign of sabotage against Western embassies and other facilities in Egypt. The Israelis hoped this would compel the British to reconsider withdrawing, either because they would blame the attacks on a fanatical but politically powerful group in Egypt known as the Muslim Brotherhood or because the attacks would underscore Egypt's inability to carry out the agreements it had signed. The scheme was uncovered and twelve Israelis were arrested and tried in Cairo. Two were acquitted, two executed, and eight given long prison terms.

On 28 February 1955, following raids from Egyptian-controlled Gaza into Israel, Israeli forces attacked the Gaza Strip. This action undermined Eisenhower's efforts to establish a defense organization directed against Moscow. It emphasized for Nasser and other Arab leaders that their enemy was Israel, not the Soviet Union. It also convinced Nasser that his most urgent need was for more weaponry, including jet fighters, tanks, and naval vessels. Apparently Dulles gave serious consideration to selling weapons to Egypt, but Nasser would not agree to the establishment of a military assistance advisory group as required by the Mutual Security Act of 1954. Instead, he turned to the Soviet Union for help.[14]

America's perspective was global, the Arab perspective was regional, and the two were not always compatible. But this was not readily apparent to the White House, which still counted on Egypt to play a major role in preventing the spread of communism into the Middle East. In April 1955, Nasser attended a conference of 28 Afro-Asian nations at Bandung, Indonesia. He emerged from the conference as a leading spokesman for cold war neutrality and the recognized leader of the Arab world. About the same time, the Soviet Union launched an "economic offensive" designed to gain favor among third world nations by providing them with economic assistance, mainly in the form of barter agreements and soft loans (loans with concessionary repayment terms by the lender). The United States was greatly concerned that the Soviets' economic efforts might tie the world's underdeveloped areas closely to the Communist bloc. The continued growth of Arab nationalism and the "economic offensive" led the Eisenhower administration to stress the urgency of increasing the United States' own programs of economic aid in the Middle East.[15]

Remarking that "Soviet expansionism has merely taken on a somewhat different guise and that its fundamental objective is still to disrupt and in the end to dominate the free nations," President Eisenhower called for a $100 million fund for the Middle East and Africa. About the same time, the administration restated its earlier interest in helping to finance the Aswan High Dam.[16] But in September, Egypt shocked the West by concluding a major arms deal with Czechoslovakia. Although the United States and Britain responded by agreeing, along with the World Bank, to back the dam financially, Nasser refused to modify his behavior. Instead, he continued to lash out against the Baghdad Pact, to attack the stringent terms which the World Bank attached to its offer of a loan for the dam, and to be uncompromising in his position against Israel.

Nasser's actions caused the White House to reconsider its plan to help finance the Aswan Dam project. When the president had agreed to back the project, he anticipated that it would encourage Nasser to seek a settlement of the Arab-Israeli dispute. He also expected that the Egyptian leader would no longer turn to the Soviet bloc for economic and military assistance. But by March, he realized that he had been wrong on both counts. In November 1955, the administration had undertaken another diplomatic effort (code-named "Project Gamma") at resolving the Arab-Israeli dispute by sending a special emissary, Robert Anderson, to the Middle East. But the Egyptian leader showed little interest in settling with the Israelis, and intelligence reports indicated that he was about to conclude a second arms deal with Czechoslovakia. Furthermore, the administration was under strong pressure from several quarters to back away from the High Dam project. British prime minister Anthony Eden blamed Nasser for Jordan's dismissal of the British commander of the Arab Legion, Sir John Glubb. The other members of the Baghdad Pact pointed to Nasser's efforts to subvert the pact. On Capitol Hill, the opposition to the High Dam came from the Israeli lobby and southern cotton interests concerned about Egyptian competition.[17]

In March, Eisenhower decided to adopt a tougher policy toward Nasser, which included canceling America's participation in the Aswan project; the president even raised the possibility of joining the Baghdad Pact with the Joint Chiefs of Staff. "A fundamental factor [in the Middle East]," he noted in his diary toward the end of the month, "is the growing ambition of Nasser, the sense of power he has gained out of his association with the Soviets, [and] his belief that he can emerge as a true leader of the entire Arab world."[18] Although Secretary of State Dulles did not formally announce that the United States was withdrawing from the project until 19 July, the current of events—mounting opposition in Congress, sustained British pressure, and Nasser's decision on 16 May to recognize Communist China (the first nation to do so since the end of the Korean War in 1953)—left little doubt as to the action Eisenhower would take.[19]

Even though Nasser had anticipated the administration's action, he was outraged by what he considered the insulting tone of Dulles's announcement. The United States, the secretary of state said, would not give the High Dam its financial backing because Washington did not believe the Egyptian economy was strong enough to meet the projected repayment costs of the project. On 27 July, the Egyptian leader responded to the American decision and to Britain's subsequent announcement that it, too, was withdrawing from the dam project, by nationalizing the Suez Canal Company and stating that he would use the proceeds from its operations to finance construction of the High Dam.[20]

Nasser's seizure of the Suez Canal was a direct and unacceptable challenge to Britain's and France's vital interests. Three-quarters of Europe's oil supply passed through the canal. The French were also angry at Nasser's support of an independence movement in Algeria, which they considered an integral part of France. A decade after World War II, the specter of the 1938 Munich agreement in which Czechoslovakia was sold out in the hope of avoiding war remained very real for both Paris and London. Curiously, they regarded Nasser both as an Arab version of Adolf Hitler with similar territorial ambitions and as a Soviet dupe, and they believed he had to be stopped before he threatened the entire Middle East.[21]

Over the summer and into the fall, the French, later joined by the British, conducted secret talks with the Israelis about a joint military venture against Egypt. The rearming of Egypt, the increasing militancy of Nasser's rhetoric, raids by Egyptian-sponsored commandos (fedayeen) from the Gaza Strip, and the blockade of Israel's southern port of Eilat convinced the Israelis that it was only a matter of time before Egypt would launch a full-scale attack against Israel in a renewed effort to destroy the Jewish state. The Israelis, therefore, shared a common interest with the British and French in taking military action to depose Nasser and discipline Egypt. Nasser's seizure of the Suez Canal provided them with pretext as well as provocation.

On 24 October, the three nations reached final agreement on a plan whereby Israel would attack Egypt across the Sinai, striking toward the Suez Canal. Britain and France would warn the Egyptians and Israelis to stay away from the canal, and if the warning was ignored, they would send troops into Egypt, justifying their action on the need to keep that vital waterway open. Five days later, Israel dropped paratroopers and sent its forces into the Sinai, quickly destroying part of Nasser's army. Britain and France then delivered their ultimatum, and when the Egyptian leader rejected it as they had anticipated he would, they began bombing Egyptian air fields. A few days later, they carried out their invasion of the canal zone. Meanwhile Nasser took the waterway out of service by sinking ships filled with rocks and cement.

President Eisenhower, who had been kept in the dark about the secretly arranged scheme but knew something was afoot, was outraged by the duplicity of his two erstwhile European allies. Although not ruling out military action, the president had made it clear over the summer and fall that the United States would not tolerate the use of force to resolve the Suez crisis until other options had been tried, such as establishing an international authority to operate the canal in cooperation with Egypt. He was certain that otherwise the West would be playing into the hands of the Soviet Union, Nasser, and other militant nationalists in the region. He was also angry that the attack against Egypt deflected world attention from the simultaneous Soviet suppression of an anti-Soviet revolution in Hungary. He was determined, therefore, to make Britain and France stop fighting and withdraw their forces from Egypt. According to Undersecretary of State Robert Murphy, he did not intend to have the United States "used as a cat's paw to protect British oil interests" in the Middle East.[22] At the United Nations, the United States sponsored a resolution calling for an immediate cease-fire. Then to compel the British and French to stop their attack, the administration prevented London from drawing on the International Monetary Fund (IMF) in response to a run on British reserves triggered by the crisis.[23] Under this pressure the British and French halted hostilities on 7 November. But they were reluctant to pull their forces out of Egypt. To persuade them to change their minds, Eisenhower applied additional pressure based upon their need for oil.

As much as any world leader, the president was fully aware of the growing dependence of western Europe and Japan on oil from the Middle East. In 1957, he even raised the possibility of war against the oil-producing countries in the event of an oil embargo. Responding to his friend and sometime adviser Dillon Anderson, who noted the growing danger of relying too heavily on foreign oil, Eisenhower replied, "I think you have . . . proved that should a crisis arise threatening to cut the Western world off from Mid East oil, we would *have* [Eisenhower's italics] to use force. . . . [T]he West must, for self-preservation, retain access to Mid East Oil."[24]

Recognizing Europe's dependence on oil, the administration had established the Middle East Emergency Committee (MEEC) after Nasser's seizure of the canal in July 1956. Composed of the major American petroleum concerns having foreign operations, MEEC's purpose was to prepare a plan for meeting Europe's emergency needs in case of a substantial petroleum stoppage. The plan it drafted provided for replacing Persian Gulf oil with increased Western Hemispheric production. Although most of Britain's and France's oil supply was suspended when the Suez Canal was closed and the Iraqi pipeline to the eastern Mediterranean was cut by the Syrian army, Eisenhower refused to put the plan into operation until Britain and France agreed to withdraw their forces from Egypt. As a result, British prime minister Anthony Eden and French premier Guy Mollet, who had hoped for American support for the military action they had taken against Egypt, had little choice but to come to terms. But Israel refused to pull its forces out of the Sinai until March, and it only did so then under the threat of American support for UN sanctions and after an agreement was reached on maintaining a UN peacekeeping force in the Gaza Strip and at Sharm al-Sheikh at the entrance of the Strait of Tiran.[25]

The Suez crisis severely strained the Western alliance. Eden and Secretary of State John Foster Dulles, whom the British prime minister blamed for what he regarded as America's betrayal at a moment of crisis, would barely speak to each other.[26] In contrast, the Soviets, by supporting Egypt during the crisis and even threatening to send rockets against London and Paris, gained considerable favor in the Middle East. At the same time, the crisis turned Nasser into an even greater hero in Arab and nonaligned nations than he already was. Nasser had defied the Western powers and won. At the end of the crisis, Cairo was in control of the Suez Canal, and the British and French had been forced to withdraw their forces from Egypt.

The Suez crisis stripped Britain and France of their last pretense of great power status. Hitherto, the United States had been satisfied to follow Britain's lead in the Middle East. But in Eisenhower's view that policy was no longer possible. A political vacuum had been created in the region, which the United States could not allow the Soviet Union to fill. Accordingly, Eisenhower went before Congress in January 1957 and asked for what became known as the Eisenhower Doctrine, a package of economic and military assistance and authorization to use armed force in defense of any country in the Middle East "requesting such aid against overt armed aggression from any nation controlled by International Communism." Despite considerable misgivings on Capitol Hill from lawmakers reluctant to hand over to the president such a blank check, in March Congress gave the president the authority he requested. Approval of the Eisenhower Doctrine meant that the United States would now assume primary responsibility for protecting Western interests in the region.[27]

This responsibility placed a heavy burden on the United States, for the Middle East had entered a period of considerable internal upheaval encouraged by Nasser and characterized by the spread of radical Arab nationalism and considerable inter-Arab rivalry and divisiveness, which the eminent scholar Malcolm H. Kerr has referred to as the "Arab Cold War."[28] In Jordan, King Hussein, who was generally regarded in Washington as a moderate Arab leader, held parliamentary elections in 1956, which unlike previous and subsequent elections were relatively free of rigging. Following the elections, a new government was formed headed by Sulayman al-Nabulsi. Al-Nabulsi and his cabinet were pro-Nasser, pan-Arab nationalists; indeed, al-Nabulsi would have been happy to integrate Jordan into an Arab federation under Nasser's leadership. In the wake of the Suez crisis, Hussein was also forced to sever relations with Britain, replacing the considerable subsidy he still received from the British with a subvention from Egypt, Syria, and Saudi Arabia. In 1957, the Jordanian leader established diplomatic relations with the Soviet Union.[29]

In February 1958, Egypt and Syria announced that they were joining to form the United Arab Republic (UAR). In 1949, Syria had considered union with Iraq, only to be persuaded against it by Egypt and Saudi Arabia. Both countries had feared Hashimite rule in Syria and provided the Damascus government with financial support in order to prevent it. In the 1950s, however, Egypt and Saudi Arabia competed for political influence in Syria, with Egypt emerging the clear winner.

Along with Egypt, Syria was among the most radical of the Arab states in its promotion of Arab nationalism and its opposition to alleged Western imperialism, which it closely associated with support for Israel. Syria's Communist Party was small but politically strong. The country's major party, the Ba'th, advocated a combination of revolutionary activism, pan-Arab nationalism, and social reform that attracted thousands of adherents even outside Syria. The signing of the Baghdad Pact in 1955, which Syrians regarded as a way of entrenching Western interests in the Middle East at the expense of Arab nationalism (and nonalignment), drove Damascus into closer affiliation with Egypt. In October 1957, Nasser tightened the bonds between Egypt and Syria by sending forces to the Syrian coastal city of Latakia during a border dispute between Turkey and Syria that threatened to result in hostilities.[30]

Like Egypt, Syria also turned to the Soviet Union for economic and military assistance, receiving by 1957 an estimated $60 million in tanks and other military hardware. Although the White House had followed a generally passive policy toward political developments in Syria, Eisenhower became increasingly concerned about growing Soviet influence in the country and the leftist drift of its politics. The chief of staff of its armed forces was widely believed to be a Communist, and according to Eisenhower, by 1957 "the suspicion was strong [within the administration] that the Communists had taken control of the government."[31]

Fearful that the contagion of communism might spread to Syria's neighbors, the president participated in a scheme to overthrow the Syrian government. The plot involved the massing of military forces along Syria's borders by its neighbor states and the deployment of Iraqi forces into Syria. The United States would provide arms and stand guard against Soviet (or even Israeli) interference. Although the plan collapsed after Jordan and Iraq backed away from it, the president ordered American aircraft from Europe to the United States base at Adaba, Turkey, "to be available in case of need." He also dispatched the Sixth Fleet into the eastern Mediterranean.[32]

In July 1958, Arab nationalists overthrew the Hashimite monarchy in Iraq. The Iraqi political situation was complicated by the fact that the Communists were also a powerful political force in the country, perhaps the most powerful. Even so, they were not primarily responsible for the revolution. Pressure had been building for years against the royal family and Iraq's pro-Western leader, Nuri al-Said. Between January 1948 and July 1958, when the monarchy was overthrown by a military coup and the royal family and al-Said were executed, 20 different cabinets had held office. Nasser's nationalization of the Suez Canal, which was hailed by massive demonstrations throughout Iraq, only hastened the process of political disintegration already underway. Furthermore, while the new government of Abd al-Karim Qasim relied heavily on the Iraqi Communist Party (IPC) to hold on to power against Nasserites favoring a union with Egypt and Syria, Qasim was a reformer rather than a revolutionary. He displayed little enthusiasm for communism, something even Secretary of State Dulles later acknowledged. He excluded Communists from important positions within government, the civil service, and the military.[33]

Nevertheless, the Eisenhower administration saw little distinction between Arab nationalism and communism. In its view, one reinforced the other, and the anti-Western character of Nasser's actions and rhetoric opened new avenues of opportunity for the Soviet Union. In Jordan, King Hussein was able to play on America's fear of communism as part of his successful effort to oust al-Nabulsi and gain American economic and military support. Responding to Hussein's claims that he was under attack from "international communism" and its followers, Eisenhower ordered the Sixth Fleet to return to the eastern Mediterranean nearer Jordan and provided $10 million in assistance. Shortly thereafter, Hussein dissolved parliament and all political parties and declared martial law.[34]

What most concerned the president, however, was the formation of the UAR and the Iraqi revolution. Hitherto, Eisenhower had regarded Iraq "as a bulwark of stability and progress in the region." But now he believed that the entire Middle East, with its rich oil resources, was in danger of becoming a

Soviet sphere of influence, something he could not allow. When on the heels of the coup in Iraq the pro-Western president of Lebanon, Camille Chamoun, urgently asked for help against so-called rebels seeking to oust him from power, the president immediately sent 14,000 American troops into Lebanon. He acted even though he and Dulles had earlier concluded that armed intervention would play into Nasser's hands by creating additional Arab resentment against the West. Recalling earlier communist coups in Czechoslovakia and China, Eisenhower argued that the troops were needed to forestall another communist coup in the Middle East.[35]

In justifying his actions in this manner, Eisenhower was being disingenuous. As he well understood, the problem in Lebanon involved an armed revolt by Muslims angered that Chamoun, a Maronite Christian, was seeking to change the country's constitution, which limited him to one term, in order to run for reelection. The White House was concerned not so much with a communist coup as with the fact that the rebels appeared to be receiving considerable support from the UAR. According to the director of the CIA, Allen Dulles (the brother of John Foster Dulles), the level of support was "massive." Furthermore, Chamoun's likely successor was General Fuad Chehab, commander of Lebanon's small army, who Dulles reported was being backed by Nasser.[36]

When the coup failed to materialize, the administration came under heavy criticism at home and abroad. The invasion and the simultaneous British dispatch of 2,200 paratroopers to prop up King Hussein's shaky regime after Syria closed its frontier to Jordan stirred Arab anger. Iraqis feared that the buildup of American forces in Lebanon was directed against them, a view encouraged by the UAR. Although Iraq was still a member of the Baghdad Pact, no one expected it to be for long.

Ironically, America's intervention in Lebanon was followed by improved relations between the United States and Egypt over the next two years. Nasser let up on his campaign to reduce Western influence in the Middle East, and in 1959 the United States resumed economic assistance to Egypt for the first time since the Suez crisis.[37] One reason for Nasser's restraint was his concern about the Qasim regime in Iraq, which posed a challenge to Nasser's previously unquestioned leadership of the pan-Arab movement. In early 1959, the UAR even promised—but apparently never delivered—military assistance to a group of Iraqi military officers who led an unsuccessful revolt against Qasim.[38]

Furthermore, the Egyptian leader became increasingly distrustful of Moscow. Nasser's visit to the Soviet Union in May 1958 was a keen disappointment for him. According to CIA Director Dulles, there appeared "to have been a great deal of talk but very little in the way of concrete accomplishment" while the Egyptian leader was in Moscow. The Soviets bargained hard on Nasser's request for a reduction in the price of military equipment. Moreover, the Soviet press failed to echo very strongly the violently anti-

Israeli speeches that the Egyptian leader made while in the Soviet Union. As a result, Nasser no longer saw an identity of interests between Arab nationalism and the Soviet desire to establish a sphere of influence in the Middle East, especially given the strength of the Communist Party in Iraq and its opposition to union with the UAR. The Arab leader was also forced to deflect much of his attention from pan-Arabism to internal problems relating to the administration and development of the UAR.[39]

For its part, the White House came to regard the Qasim government as a greater threat to American interests in the Middle East than Nasser. By the beginning of 1959, the White House was convinced that Iraq was becoming a communist satellite. In response, the NSC discussed the possibility of military intervention in Iraq to oust Qasim. An interdepartmental committee formed in April 1959 to determine what could be done to prevent communists from seizing power in Iraq concluded in October that "dramatic action" by the United States was not desirable and that "restraint by Arab countries [was] the best means of restraining Iraq." Still, the administration's concern about the Qasim government made it look more kindly on Nasser, whom it now viewed as a countervailing force in the Middle East. Eisenhower hoped that if Qasim were forced out of office, Nasser would agree to the establishment of a nationalist, noncommunist government in Baghdad independent of Cairo.[40]

Despite this shimmer of hope, the White House remained pessimistic about the Middle East. "The Near East is still in the throes of a major nationalist and social-economic revolution," concluded a report by the NSC Planning Board in June 1960. "The predominant force in the area is nationalism with strong anti-Western overtones."[41] The administration was especially concerned about access to Mideast oil, particularly following the formation of the UAR. As a historian of the oil industry, Daniel Yergin, has pointed out, the union of Egypt and Syria "ominously brought together the two countries which—with the Suez Canal in Egypt and the Saudi and Iraqi pipelines passing through Syria—dominated the transit routes for Middle East oil." At any time, Nasser had the ability to choke off most of the supply of Arab oil to the West.[42]

The need to maintain the flow of oil from the Middle East also helped determine the administration's position on the oil cartel case that had been initiated during the Truman administration. For national security reasons having largely to do with Iran's nationalization of the Anglo-Iranian Oil Company in 1951, President Truman had decided just before leaving office in 1953 to replace criminal with civil proceedings against members of the alleged oil cartel. On 21 April 1953, the new administration filed a civil suit against the litigants. By filing a civil suit rather than a criminal action and then approving a National Security Council memorandum stating "that the enforcement of the antitrust laws of the United States against the western oil companies operating in the Near East [were to be] deemed secondary to the national interest," Eisenhower made clear that he was in full accord with Truman's handling of the case.

Accepting Truman's plan to gain an American presence in Iran, in 1954 the White House helped put together a consortium for the production and marketing of Iranian oil that included America's largest oil corporations. It took this action even though it undercut much of the Justice Department's case against the multinational giants. Similarly, the administration displayed little concern about the antitrust implications of allowing—indeed encouraging—the establishment of the MEEC by the major United States petroleum concerns engaged in foreign operations during the 1956 Suez Canal crisis.[43]

The Eisenhower administration, in other words, considered Western access to Mideast oil far more important than prosecution of alleged violators of the nation's antitrust laws. As a result, the Justice Department was forced to circumscribe its case against the nation's major oil companies and then to reach an out-of-court settlement with three of them (Exxon, Gulf, and Texaco), which prohibited such practices as price-fixing and joint-marketing ventures but left the multinational oil giants virtually in control of Mideast oil.[44] In asking for dismissal of the cases against Exxon and Gulf, Wilbur Fugate of the Justice Department chose to mask the true purpose behind the settlements by claiming that they represented a victory for free trade at the expense of multinational cartels. But privately he made clear that foreign policy considerations—and not free trade—were the principal cause of the settlements. "I do not intend to bring into my statement anything about national defense security factors," he explained to his superior, W. Wallace Kirkpatrick, in outlining how he proposed to justify the settlements. "The national defense argument which I would not go into," he added, "is, in a nutshell, that separating these joint interests at this time might jeopardize the position of United States oil companies abroad vis-a-vis the Russians."[45]

In formulating his policy toward the Middle East, President Eisenhower had shown an awareness of Arab nationalism and had fully understood western Europe's (and Japan's) growing dependence on Middle East oil. But the containment of communism was his overarching concern. In the view of Eisenhower's successor, John F. Kennedy, who was more sensitive to Arab nationalism, such a concern assured a deterioration of relations between the United States and the Arab world. Yet Kennedy was only marginally more successful than Eisenhower in carrying out American foreign policy in the Middle East.

chapter 3

_____

KENNEDY AND ARAB NATIONALISM: 1961–1963

John F. Kennedy was the first American president to recognize Arab nationalism as a force independent of the cold war. But traditional American support for Israel, the strength of the American Jewish community, ongoing concern about Soviet influence in the Middle East, and divisions within the Arab world itself, particularly following a coup in Yemen believed to have been instigated by Nasser, undermined Kennedy's efforts at an even-handed policy and actually pushed Nasser closer to the Soviet Union than he was at the time Kennedy assumed office.

Like Eisenhower, Kennedy was sensitive to the rising tide of nationalism in the third world, but in contrast to his predecessor, he did not equate radical nationalism with communism. As a senator, he had spoken out in 1953 and 1954 against French colonial rule in Indochina, and in 1957 he attracted considerable international attention for his attack on the Senate floor against French rule in Algeria. The next year he tried to explain the attraction of communism to third world nations. Countries "with relatively primitive, top-heavy economies and low industrial capacity," he said, were attracted by the speed of "the Russian and even the Chinese passage to modernity."[1]

Kennedy understood the wave of Arab nationalism sweeping the Middle East. He was also aware of Arab sensitivities on such questions as the Palestinian refugee problem and American support for Israel. During the 1960 presidential campaign, he attacked previous administrations for dealing with the Arab world "almost exclusively in the context of the East-West struggle."[2] He took office, therefore, committed to following a more balanced Middle East policy.

As president, Kennedy gave Cuba, Berlin, and Vietnam far more attention than the Middle East, which was relatively quiet during his three years in office.[3] But this did not lessen his desire to improve America's relations with the Arab world. Soon after taking office the new president sent identical letters to five Arab leaders promising that he would support the efforts of the United Nations Palestine Conciliation Commission to resolve the refugee problem "on the basis of the principle of repatriation and compensation for property." Meeting with Israeli prime minister David Ben Gurion in May 1961, he pressed the case for a mediated settlement of the refugee problem. The next year the administration instructed the U.S. delegation at the United Nations to vote in favor of a resolution condemning Israel for a retaliatory raid it had conducted against Syria.[4]

The president was especially anxious to mend ties with Nasser. According to Arthur Schlesinger Jr., who served as a White House aide to Kennedy, the president's National Security Adviser, McGeorge Bundy, and the State Department's policy planning chief, Walt Rostow, "placed very high" on their list of priorities "the question of whether better relations were possible with the most powerful leader of the Arab world."[5]

Kennedy admired Nasser, whom he considered one of the great leaders of the nonaligned nations along with Nkrumah of Ghana, Sukarno of Indonesia, and Ben Bella of Algeria. Believing that the Eisenhower administration had needlessly alienated Nasser because of its preoccupation with the Soviet-American conflict, the new president was determined to reverse course. As a first step in that direction, he appointed John S. Badeau, an Arabist and former president of the American University of Cairo, as the United States' new ambassador to Egypt.[6]

The president also approved increased shipments of American grains to Egypt under the so-called PL 480 program, which made food aid available to friendly foreign governments. In October, the administration announced an agreement to provide Egypt with $432 million of PL 480 assistance over the next three years. During Kennedy's term in office, American grain shipments accounted for more than 30 percent of Egypt's entire supply of wheat and wheat flour.[7]

Nasser welcomed the aid he received from the United States. Despite Kennedy's pro-Israeli speeches during his campaign, the Egyptian leader liked the new American president, and he hoped that relations between Egypt and the United States might improve while Kennedy was in office. His response to the president's circular letter on Palestinian refugees—the start of a frank but generally friendly correspondence between the two leaders that would last until Kennedy was assassinated in 1963—suggested that a new direction in Egyptian-American relations was possible.[8] Nasser even indicated an interest in reaching a mutually acceptable settlement of the Arab-Israeli dispute. He made clear that he would resist efforts by the American president to carry out his campaign promises "to Zionism." But Egypt's ambassador to the United States, Mohamed Ibrahim Kamel, went so far as to suggest putting the Arab-Israeli issue "in the refrigerator."[9]

Undoubtedly motivating Nasser was the continued breach in Egypt's relations with Moscow. The Egyptian leader was willing to take economic and military aid from the Soviets. But he was scathing in his critique of Marxist ideology, and he ordered the arrest of a number of Egyptian Communists. Despite this, the Soviet Union continued to provide Egypt with assistance, so that by the end of 1960 relations between the two countries had begun to improve. Nevertheless, Moscow accused Egypt of conducting "a reign of terror" against suspected Communists, and when an Egyptian delegation visited Moscow the following April, Nikita Khrushchev warned the Egyptians "not to cut down the tree that gives you shade."[10]

The breakup of the UAR in September 1961 also influenced Nasser's policy toward the United States. The Egyptian leader had never been that eager for a union with Syria. Syria's Ba'th Party, with its strong pan-Arab orientation, advocated union with Egypt as a way of preventing Syria from drifting toward the Communists, the other powerful party in the country. As the leading spokesman for Arab unity, Nasser could hardly turn Syria down. But he saw the potential for conflict. The two countries were very different politically and socially. Egypt was far more centralized and less doctrinaire than Syria. Compared to Nasser, who, notwithstanding his sometimes bombastic rhetoric, was fundamentally a pragmatist, Syria's leaders were ideologues. Syrian society was also more fractious, individualistic, and disdainful of authority than that of Egypt. Similarly, landowners and the developing middle class in Syria had a greater voice in government, and political alignments were more complex and in greater flux than in Egypt.[11]

In short, there was an inherent conflict between the internal dynamics of Syrian and Egyptian politics and society that became evident following the merger of the two countries. From the very start, Egypt, larger and more populated than Syria, became the dominant partner. Syrian leaders were forced to live in Cairo; Syrian political parties were abolished; Syrian military officers were dismissed and replaced by Egyptians; and Syrian government bureaucrats lost their jobs to their Egyptian counterparts. In 1961, Nasser also nationalized major sectors of the Egyptian and Syrian economies and imposed a program of land reform, which alienated just about every politically influential group in Syrian society. Finally, in September 1961, a group of Syrian military officers in Damascus rebelled against their Egyptian commanders, effectively bringing an end to Syria's union with Egypt.[12]

The breakup of the UAR was a major blow to Nasser's prestige and pan-Arab ambitions. Afterward, he became more concerned with cementing his leadership in Egypt and limiting the political influence in Egypt of "bourgeois elements," which he held responsible for Syria's decision to withdraw from the UAR,[13] than with continuing his verbal assaults on the West. In addition, he appreciated that the United States did not exploit the breakup of the UAR and that it did not object when Egypt sent troops to newly independent Kuwait as part of British and Arab forces to protect Kuwait from a possible Iraqi invasion.[14] According to Ambassador Badeau, the Egyptian leader "realized that we were trying to act in good faith and not try some trick to catch him off balance."[15] The following February, Ambassador Chester Bowles, whom Kennedy had sent to Egypt to assess its economic development program and to reassure Nasser of America's friendly intentions toward the Arab states, also told the president that it was "clear that [Egypt] had made a decision to improve relations with the United States."[16]

By the end of 1962, however, the administration's policy of evenhandedness was in trouble. One problem was the opposition of the American Jewish community. In contrast to Eisenhower who had not needed the support of Jewish voters to get elected, Kennedy could not have won the presidency in 1960 without strong Jewish backing in key states like New York and Illinois. Furthermore, he did not see any contradictions between his support for Israel and his efforts to build bridges to the Arab world. On the contrary, he spoke about a new partnership between Jerusalem and Washington, and he went beyond either Truman or Eisenhower in the reassurances he gave Israel about defending its national security.[17]

In Kennedy's view, the United States would best serve Israel's interests as well as its own by channeling Arab nationalism along constructive lines. "To be effective in our own interests and to help Israel," he told Israeli foreign minister Golda Meir in December 1962, "we have to maintain our position in the Middle East generally. . . . We are in a position then to make clear to the Arabs that we will maintain our friendship with Israel and our security guarantees."[18] But his conciliatory gestures toward Nasser and his apparent opposition to Israel on such matters as the refugee problem and the use of military force against neighboring states upset American Jews and pro-Israeli lawmakers on Capitol Hill. Many of these same lawmakers also opposed the shipment of food to Nasser because they still regarded him as a foe of the West.

A more serious problem, however, was the civil war raging in Yemen following a revolution there by pro-Nasser army officers. It is hard to imagine how a domestic conflict in such an economically underdeveloped place as Yemen, a remote and isolated country in the southwest corner of the Arabian peninsula best known for the Yemeni custom of chewing qat, a local leaf and mild narcotic, could have such far-reaching consequences. But it did. Led by Colonel Abdullah al-Sallal, the new military regime seized power on 26 September 1962 following the death of the Imam (ruler) of Yemen, Ahmad Hamid al-Din. The regime then established the Yemen Arab Republic, issued a promise to modernize the country, and demanded that Britain withdraw from its neighboring protectorate of Aden. But although al-Sallal took control of the government, Ahmad's son, Muhammad al-Badr, fled into the mountains in northern Yemen where he and his royalist followers waged war against the republican forces. In a manner not unlike that of the Spanish Civil War in the 1930s, the opposing sides in Yemen's civil war became proxies in a much larger struggle involving Egypt, Saudi Arabia, and Jordan.[19]

The new regime naturally looked to Nasser for help in sustaining the revolution, and it did not have long to wait. The Egyptian leader had not been involved in the plot to overthrow the monarchy. According to Ambassador Badeau, Nasser's decision to intervene in Yemen was "a pragmatic one made at the time of the revolt."[20] Nevertheless, it was almost predictable that he would intervene, for he was at the nadir of his power following the breakup of the UAR and was anxious to reassert his leadership in the Arab world. He also hoped that Arab radicalism might spread to Saudi Arabia and Jordan. In order to assure the victory of the republican forces in Yemen, he concluded a military agreement with the country's controlling junta and then sent 6,000 Egyptian troops to fight against the royalists. Eventually 70,000 Egyptian troops were sent to Yemen. Without Egypt's support, the republican regime would probably have collapsed.

For the very reasons that Nasser backed the radical regime in Yemen, Saudi Arabia and Jordan supplied the royalists with arms and money. The Saudis and Jordanians were frightened by Nasser's radicalism. Nasser had broken off relations with Jordan in 1961 after it recognized the new regime in Syria and before the Egyptian leader was prepared to concede the dismemberment of the UAR. Jordan's King Hussein was also convinced that Nasser was involved in plots to assassinate him and his followers. Because he and Saudi Arabia's King Ibn Saud believed that Washington's support of Nasser increased his proclivity to intervene in their countries, they were greatly upset by Kennedy's efforts to court him. Kennedy tried to reassure Hussein, arguing that if he improved ties with Cairo, Jordan would likely be among the countries to benefit the most. But neither Hussein nor King Ibn Saud were persuaded by Kennedy's arguments.[21]

Their concerns about Nasser deepened when, following the breakup of the UAR, he stated that henceforth Egypt would maintain close relations only with those countries that agreed with its revolutionary goals. This looked like a direct challenge to Saudi Arabia and Jordan. Moreover, if the revolution succeeded in Yemen, it could spread to these two countries, thereby threatening the very existence of the monarchies. For that reason, Hussein turned Jordan, in the words of historian Uriel Dann, "into a center of support for royalist resistance."[22]

This intrusion of other Arab powers into the Yemeni civil war placed the Kennedy administration in an extremely difficult position. At the State Department, the head of the Near Eastern Bureau, Phillip Talbot, and other Middle East experts favored recognition of the new regime in the hope that this would limit Nasser's involvement in Yemen. In response to a warning from Washington that the United States had a "vital interest" in maintaining security in the Persian Gulf, the Egyptian leader assured Ambassador Badeau that Yemen would not be used as a base from which to attack Saudi

Arabia. Badeau and other State Department officials took him at his word. Secretary of State Dean Rusk even made the point that pressing Nasser too hard on withdrawing his forces from Yemen would only increase the likelihood of such an attack.[23]

Spokesmen for the oil industry and officials at the Pentagon, however, disagreed. In their view, the establishment of a radical regime in Yemen would threaten the stability of Saudi Arabia and its immense and strategically important oil reserves.[24] In support of their position, they could point to American intelligence sources that reported evidence of disaffection among pro-Nasser forces within the Saudi military. In fact, seven Saudi pilots defected to Egypt with their planes, and several of King Ibn Saud's half brothers sought asylum in Cairo. The establishment of the new regime in Yemen would also endanger Jordan, where pro-Nasser sentiment was much stronger and more open than in Saudi Arabia. Should King Hussein be overthrown, Jordan could fall under Nasser's control, thereby destroying the tenuous equilibrium existing in the Middle East and almost assuring an Israeli military response. Pentagon officials were also troubled by the threat a radical regime in Yemen posed to its neighbor to the east, the British protectorate of Aden. Strategically located on the oil routes from the Persian Gulf, Aden was one of the world's busiest ports and the site of the most important military base east of Suez.[25]

Saudi Arabia and Jordan protested vigorously against any proposal to recognize the Yemen Arab Republic. In a meeting with Kennedy in October, Crown Prince Faisal warned the United States that establishing ties with al-Sallal would be inviting Nasser to try to topple the Saudi monarchy. The next month he received a letter from the American president affirming his "deep and abiding" commitment to the Saudi government but also offering a plan for recognizing the new regime in Yemen. As part of the plan, Saudi Arabia would stop its aid to al-Badr in return for a promise by Nasser to withdraw his troops from Yemen. According to Ambassador Parker T. Hart, when the Saudi prince was presented with the plan, he became "absolutely furious," saying he would not be a party to it. King Hussein of Jordan expressed similar sentiments, telling the president in November that an emboldened Nasser would be a constant threat to Amman and Riyadh.[26]

Scarcely less vigorous in its opposition to Kennedy's proposal was Great Britain, which was seeking to establish a federation in southern Arabia before its imminent departure from Aden. At a meeting with Kennedy in Bermuda in November, Prime Minister Harold Macmillan made clear the threat he believed a pro-Nasser regime in Yemen posed for Aden and British plans for a southern Arabian federation. If Nasserites in Yemen were victorious, Macmillan said, then moderate elements in Aden and southern Arabia would be too intimidated to cooperate with British plans. A few weeks later, he urged the president to delay recognition of the republican regime in

Yemen "as long as possible." But privately, he felt certain Kennedy would soon recognize the new government.[27]

Macmillan was correct. Divided over what course to pursue regarding the civil war in Yemen, the administration waited three months before finally deciding on 19 December 1962 to recognize the Yemen Arab Republic. The decision was made only after Nasser agreed to a phased withdrawal of his troops from Yemen and the Yemeni republic agreed to live at peace with its neighbors. In granting de facto recognition to the new Yemeni regime, the administration could argue that it was merely acknowledging the fact that the regime was in control of most of the country, the sina qua non for recognition. But more was involved than that. As Arthur Schlesinger Jr. later explained, by recognizing the Yemen Arab Republic, President Kennedy hoped to "stabilize the situation in Yemen and begin the job of modernizing that fifteenth century country." He also hoped to preclude the reentry of the Soviet Union as a major player in the Middle East.[28]

Despite Kennedy's decision to recognize the Yemen Arab Republic, the Saudis and Jordanians refused to stop their assistance to al-Badr. For the rulers of Saudi Arabia, King Ibn Saud and his younger and more able brother Faisal—who, because of Ibn Saud's financial irresponsibility and general incompetence, replaced him in February as effective head of government— support of the royalist forces was a matter of both honor and self-interest. On the one hand, they felt honor-bound to support a fellow monarch. On the other, the fall of another royal family would weaken their own hold on power. As Nasser stepped up his threats to overthrow the Saudi monarchy, they also considered it increasingly important to have a buffer zone in the mountains of northern Yemen to protect against an Egyptian attack. But as the Saudis continued to assist the Yemeni royalists, Nasser began bombing royalist camps inside Saudi Arabia.[29]

Pressure mounted on Kennedy to reconsider his policy on Yemen. Faisal responded to the bombing raids by accusing the United States of giving the Egyptian leader "a hunting license to go after Saudi Arabia."[30] During a visit to the United States at the end of December, Israeli foreign minister Golda Meir warned the president that his recognition of the Yemeni republic would only fuel Nasser's ambitions in the Middle East. Britain made clear that it would not follow the United States' lead in recognizing the new Yemeni regime. Lobbyists for ARAMCO expressed concern that the Saudi government might retaliate against the United States by changing the terms of the contract under which ARAMCO was allowed to operate.[31]

Faced with this opposition, Kennedy began to backpedal. He still sought to identify himself with what he regarded as the progressive currents of Arab nationalism and to remain on good terms with Nasser. But as tokens of America's commitment to the Saudi government, he dispatched two American destroyers to the Saudi port of Jedda and agreed to send the Saudis a squadron of American airplanes. But he made clear that the squadron was not to engage in combat without his authorization and that sending the squadron (in a mission known as Operation Hard Surface) was contingent on Saudi agreement not to aid the royalist forces in Yemen. Furthermore, he recommended that the ruling family broaden its base of support among the Saudi people to avoid possible domestic turmoil.[32]

Egyptian involvement in the Yemeni civil war helped persuade Kennedy that Nasser was untrustworthy. On 19 January 1963, he wrote the Egyptian leader to complain about an attack by Egyptian planes against the Saudi town of Najran. "Each time we have felt we were making some progress toward disengagement [in Yemen]," he commented, "such actions as the Najran bombings have set us back."[33]

In an effort to end the war in Yemen before it totally undermined his policy in the Middle East, the president dispatched Ellsworth Bunker, a seasoned diplomat, to the Middle East to confer with Faisal and Nasser. After considerable negotiation, Faisal agreed to stop aiding the royalists, and Nasser promised to withdraw his forces from Yemen. Both agreements were contingent on compliance by the other side. The two adversaries also agreed to underwrite the cost of a UN monitoring team in Yemen.[34]

Unfortunately, the UN team did not arrive in Yemen until July, and by that time the fragile cease-fire had been broken. Notwithstanding his agreement with Bunker, Nasser actually increased his troop strength in the war-torn country and authorized air strikes using bombs containing poisonous gas against royalist strongholds in northern Yemen. Thoroughly frustrated, in October, just one month before he was killed, Kennedy wrote Nasser to complain about Egypt's noncompliance with the disengagement agreement worked out by Bunker. The president told Nasser that, unlike the Saudis, the Egyptians were not making "phased withdrawals to a scale consistent with our understanding of the spirit of the agreement."[35]

Other developments in the Middle East had also led Kennedy to reconsider his policy with respect to Nasser. In February and March 1963, the Iraqi and Syrian governments were overthrown by more radical, pan-Arab regimes composed of Ba'th Party members and other Arab nationalists who looked to Nasser for leadership. In April, the leaders of the two new governments met with Nasser in Cairo where they announced that a new federation (a new UAR) would be formed within four months. A week after the meeting, there were riots on the West Bank of Jordan organized by followers of the Egyptian leader, who demanded that Jordan join the UAR.[36]

This latest wave of radical Arab nationalism posed new dangers for Saudi Arabia and Israel. Should Hussein fall, Israel would most likely try to protect itself by seizing the West Bank, thereby setting off a general war in the Middle East. As a show of force in support of Hussein, Kennedy ordered the Sixth Fleet to the eastern Mediterranean and raised the possibility of military intervention with reporters on 21 April. Although preferring a peaceful resolution of the developing crisis in the Middle East, he told the journalists that he was prepared to resort to "other courses of action on our own to prevent or to put a stop to such aggression."[37]

The crisis was short-lived. Hussein took quick and forceful action, declaring martial law after receiving news of a planned coup against his government, arresting the leaders of the disturbances, and forming a new government that was unquestionably loyal to him. Also, the new UAR quickly unraveled. The old jealousies and resentments that had led to the demise of the first attempt at federation between Syria and Egypt undid this latest effort at union. Nasser and the Ba'th leaders of Syria and Iraq simply did not trust each other. As a result, the Cairo agreement was abandoned two months after it had been signed. The rift between Syria and Egypt further widened toward the end of the year when a group of pro-Nasser army officers ousted the Ba'th regime in Iraq. Although Iraq and Egypt grew closer following the coup, they were never able to form a true federation. Still, this latest threat to American interests in the Middle East provided additional reasons for Kennedy to question his efforts at rapprochement with the Egyptian leader.

The president was also concerned about the rapid growth in Egypt's defense spending, which increased from about 7 percent of the country's estimated gross national product (GNP) in 1960–1961 to approximately 11 percent in 1963–1964. Part of the increase was attributable to the Egyptian intervention in Yemen, which was costing about $1 million a day by 1962, but a substantial portion went to the development of an expensive guided-missile system.

Moreover, the Soviets had been rebuilding Egypt's military stockpile since the Suez War of 1956.[38] In 1963, Moscow concluded the largest package of military equipment with Cairo thus far. Included in the package, whose value was estimated at anywhere between $220 million and $500 million, were late model T-54B medium tanks, TU-16 medium bombers, and MiG-21 supersonic interceptors. This was the first time that Moscow sold Egypt its most modern equipment.[39]

In response to this military buildup in Egypt, Kennedy lifted an embargo on the sale of arms to the combatants in the Arab-Israeli dispute that had been in place since the Tripartite Declaration of 1950. In August 1962, he agreed to sell Israel HAWK surface-to-air missiles. Israeli prime minister David Ben Gurion had requested permission to purchase the missile system during a meeting with Kennedy in New York in May 1961. But the president had delayed approving the sale for more than a year, waiting until a comprehensive review of Israel's defense needs had been completed, and America's relations with the Arab states had improved to the point that he thought they would not be adversely affected by the sale. He also waited until he was certain that neither Cairo nor Moscow was interested in an arms limitation agreement. He informed Nasser beforehand about the sale, and he made clear

> willing to sell HAWK missiles to the Arabs. He also justified
> rounds that it was intended for defense purposes only.[40]

......dy's decision to provide Israel with a HAWK missile system represented a major departure from previous policy and indicated the White House's concern about the military buildup taking place in Egypt under Soviet auspices. Not only did Kennedy believe that it threatened the precarious balance of power in the Middle East, but he also worried that it might damage Egypt's efforts at economic development. For an administration that tended to equate economic growth with political democracy and social progress, this was not an inconsequential matter.[41]

By the fall of 1963, relations between the United States and Egypt had deteriorated to the point that Congress was moving to cut off economic assistance to Cairo. Reports in the press and on Capitol Hill that Egypt's missile program was being directed by former Nazi scientists did not help matters. On 7 November, the Senate voted 65 to 13 in favor of an amendment that would deny economic assistance to any country engaged in, or preparing for, military aggression against the United States or any country receiving U.S. aid.[42]

President Kennedy was not yet willing to relinquish entirely his efforts at improving relations with Nasser. On 14 November, just one week before his assassination, he spoke out against the Senate amendment, saying it would cause difficulty in his dealings with the Egyptian leader and the heads of other nonaligned nations. Clearly, though, at the time of Kennedy's death his efforts at rapprochement with Nasser were being openly challenged in Washington, and the president himself was having second thoughts about the policy he had been pursuing toward Nasser.

The Egyptian leader was having his own second thoughts about his relationship with the United States. According to West Berlin's mayor, Willy Brandt, who met with Nasser in Cairo on 8 November, the Egyptian leader "spoke bitterly and at length about the tactic of using aid to pressure him."[43] Nasser's sense of Arab nationalism and America's interest in the Middle East were simply incompatible, as were Kennedy's commitment to reform and Nasser's espousal of radical change.

Yet as historian Douglas Little has remarked, Kennedy's policy toward the Middle East was far from a failure. "By fostering Egyptian development and accepting Nasser's neutralism, JFK [had] managed to keep the Palestinian question on ice and to prevent fresh Kremlin inroads in the Middle East for nearly three years."[44] His successor, Lyndon Johnson, would not be so fortunate.

chapter 4

JOHNSON AND THE SIX-DAY WAR: 1963–1969

In terms of foreign relations, the administration of Lyndon Johnson will be remembered for the war in Vietnam, which eventually overwhelmed the president, undermined his Great Society programs, tore the nation apart, and forced him out of office. Although events in the Middle East did not consume the president in the same way as the Vietnam War did, they were nevertheless of considerable concern to the White House, and their legacy has been at least as profound as that of the Vietnam conflict.

In particular, the president became increasingly worried during the spring of 1967 that the Arab-Israeli dispute might result in yet another round of hostilities that this time would draw the United States and the Soviet Union into a dangerous superpower confrontation. This concern was shared by Soviet premier Alexsei Kosygin. When war broke out on 5 June 1967 between Israel and its Arab enemies, the two leaders responded almost immediately by using the so-called hotline between the Kremlin and the White House to avoid an escalation of the conflict.

Although the two leaders were successful in containing hostilities and in helping to end the war on 10 June, just six days after it had begun, Israel refused to return the territories it had seized during the war. Together with the problem of the Palestinian refugees, Israel's occupation of the lands taken during the Six-Day War—specifically, the Gaza Strip, the West Bank of the Jordan River, the Golan Heights, and East Jerusalem[1]—has remained at the core of the Arab-Israeli dispute to the present. Interestingly, President Johnson, whose foreign policy had been roundly criticized as a result of America's growing involvement in Vietnam, displayed considerable prescience in predicting the long-term consequences of the Six-Day War. But he also welcomed Israel's victory over the Arabs and, at the cost of consider-

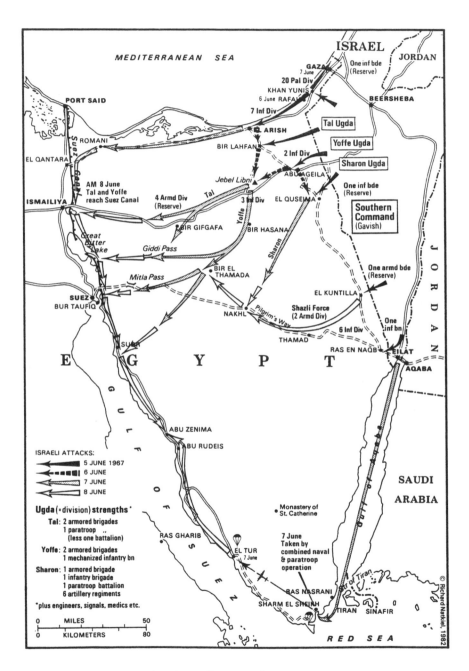

1967 Six-Day War—Southern Command
Courtesy Richard Natkiel

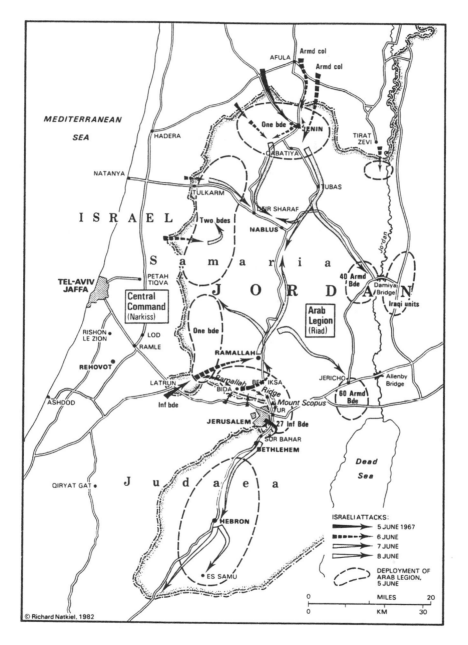

MEDITERRANEAN
SEA

AFULA Armd col
Armd col

HADERA

One bde JENIN
QABATIYA
TIRAT
ZEVI

NATANYA
TULKARM

I S R A E L DEIR SHARAF TUBAS

Two bdes NABLUS

S a m a r i a

JORDAN 40 Armd
Bde Damiya
Bridge

TEL-AVIV PETAH
JAFFA TIQVA Iraqi units

Central
Command
(Narkiss)

Arab
Legion
(Riad)

RISHON
LE ZION LOD
RAMLE

One bde RAMALLAH

REHOVOT JERICHO Allenby
Bridge

LATRUN Ramallah BEIT IKSA
BIDA Ridge

ASHDOD Inf bde Mount Scopus 60 Armd
Bde

TUR

JERUSALEM 27 Inf Bde

SUR BAHAR

QIRYAT GAT J u d a e a BETHLEHEM

Dead
Sea

HEBRON ISRAELI ATTACKS:
5 JUNE 1967
6 JUNE
7 JUNE
8 JUNE

ES SAMU DEPLOYMENT OF
ARAB LEGION,
5 JUNE

© Richard Natkiel, 1982

0   MILES   20
0   KM   30

1967 Six-Day War—Central Command
Courtesy Richard Natkiel

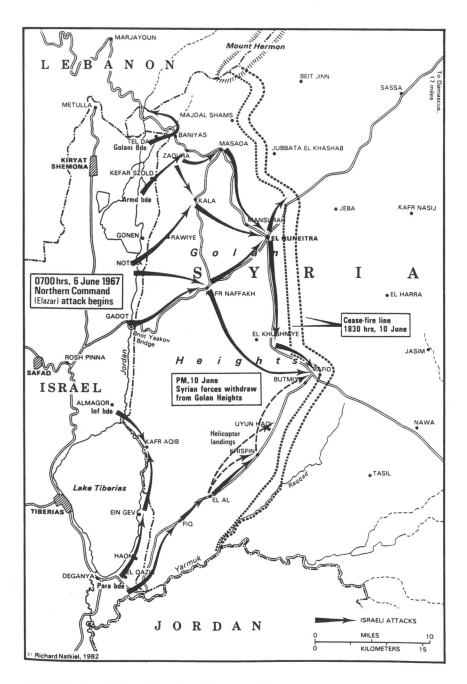

MARJAYOUN

L E B A N O N

Mount Hermon

BEIT JINN

SASSA

METULLA

MAJDAL SHAMS

To Damascus, 17 miles

TEL DAN
Golani Bde
BANIYAS

MASADA

JUBBATA EL KHASHAB

KIRYAT SHEMONA

ZAOURA

KEFAR SZOLD

KALA

JEBA

KAFR NASIJ

Armd bde

MANSURAH

EL QUNEITRA

GONEN

RAWIYE

G o l a n

NOTERA

S Y R I A

0700 hrs, 6 June 1967
Northern Command
(Elazar) attack begins

KAFR NAFFAKH

EL HARRA

GADOT

Bnot Yaakov
Bridge

H e i g h t s

EL KHUSHNEYE

Cease-fire line
1830 hrs, 10 June

JASIM

ROSH PINNA

Jordan

SAFAD

RAFID

BUTMIYE

ISRAEL

PM, 10 June
Syrian forces withdraw
from Golan Heights

ALMAGOR
Inf bde

KAFR AQIB

UYUN HADI

NAWA

Helicopter
landings

KHISFIN

Lake Tiberias

TASIL

TIBERIAS

EIN GEV

EL AL

FIQ

Raqqad

HAON

EL QAZIR

Yarmuk

DEGANYA
Para bde

J O R D A N

ISRAELI ATTACKS

0   MILES   10
0   KILOMETERS   15

© Richard Natkiel, 1982

1967 Six-Day War—Northern Command
Courtesy Richard Natkiel

able Arab resentment, came to regard Israel as one of three "pillars" (the others being Saudi Arabia and non-Arab Iran) on which the United States would rely to protect and promote Western interests in the Middle East.

There was very little difference between Johnson's approach to foreign and domestic policy. The key to understanding both was that Johnson was the consummate "horse trader." He believed in extending favors, but he expected something in return. Although he had been a strong supporter of John F. Kennedy's Alliance for Progress and had a real commitment to combating world hunger, he believed that, at the very least, recipients of American economic assistance should display some public gratitude.[2] That Nasser not only failed to show his appreciation for the food Egypt had received under the PL 480 program but also increasingly challenged America's interests in the Middle East and Africa was one reason Johnson abandoned Kennedy's more evenhanded approach to the Arab-Israeli dispute.[3]

While one can easily overstate the importance of the Kennedy-Nasser relationship in Washington's relations with Cairo, one can just as easily understate the significance of the personal animus between Johnson and Nasser. Simply put, neither man liked the other very much. If the American president found Nasser a stubborn and uncompromising radical with whom negotiation was impossible, the Egyptian leader had an equally unfavorable impression of Johnson. As Nasser's close ally Mohamed Heikal later wrote, Nasser "did not like what he had heard about this Texas politician, the party man, the wheeler-dealer." He found him rude, crude, and unsophisticated.[4]

Johnson's strong support of Israel did not help matters. Shocked by the horror of the Holocaust, the president had enthusiastically backed the establishment of the Jewish state after World War II and had actually helped facilitate the secret—and illegal—sale of arms to Israel following its independence in 1948. As majority leader in the Senate in the 1950s and a potential presidential candidate, he had courted American Jewish voters in the key industrial states of the North, and in turn he had been successfully courted by the pro-Israeli lobby on Capitol Hill. Thus he spoke out in early 1957 against imposing U.N. sanctions on Israel after the Jewish state refused to withdraw from the Gaza Strip or Sharm al-Sheikh following the end of the Suez War. At the same time, he developed a warm relationship with Israeli ambassador Abba Eban, whose eloquence greatly impressed him.[5]

Never a student of foreign affairs, Johnson failed to make the types of distinctions between communism, nationalism, and neutralism that Kennedy had made; in this sense his administration was a throwback to the Eisenhower presidency. But since he was from an oil-rich state and had close ties to the domestic oil industry, he understood the threat that political instability in the Middle East posed to oil prices in the United States and western Europe; from this perspective alone, radical Arab nationalism represented a real danger to the national interest.[6]

Johnson reaffirmed his strong support for Israel following Kennedy's funeral on 25 November 1963 when he told Israeli president Zalman Shazar and foreign minister Golda Meir, who had come to the United States to attend the funeral, that they could continue to rely on the United States as a close friend. But preoccupied with his Great Society programs and increasingly with events in Southeast Asia, during his first two years in office Johnson paid relatively little attention to problems in the Middle East, which for the most part did not seem to require much. In contrast to the two years of inter-Arab turmoil after the breakup of the UAR in 1961, the two years beginning in 1964 were characterized by Arab unity and solidarity.

At the end of 1963, Nasser called for a summit meeting in Cairo of Arab leaders ostensibly to deal with Israel's plan to divert the Jordan River, which flowed through Syria, Israel, and Jordan. But he also wanted to find a way to end the costly war in Yemen and, more importantly, to deal with a challenge from Syria, which was taunting Nasser for not taking military action against Israel. At the Cairo summit in January 1964, the Arab leaders responded to Israel's plans for the Jordan by promising to develop schemes to divert the Jordan upstream from Israel. They also agreed to ignore their differences in order to unite against the common Israeli threat. King Hussein reestablished relations with Egypt, and Nasser emerged from the summit with his prestige and leadership within the Arab world intact or even enhanced.[7]

The Cairo summit was followed by a second summit in Alexandria in September and a third at Casablanca the subsequent September. At the meeting in Alexandria, the Arab leaders established a Unified Arab Command under an Egyptian general and created the Palestine Liberation Organization (PLO) as the official representative of the Palestinian people. At the Casablanca conference, they raised the possibility of eventually establishing a Palestinian Liberation Army as the military unit of the PLO. At both Alexandria and Casablanca, they emphasized the need for maintaining unity and harmony within the Arab world.[8]

By 1966, the political landscape of the Arab nations had become clouded again. The summits of Arab leaders had papered over, rather than resolved, existing differences among the Arab governments. Nasser's pragmatic concerns as Egypt's head of state and as leader of both the Arab world and non-aligned nations prevailed over any doctrinaire commitment to Arabist beliefs and made him far more cautious than the more ideological adherents of pan-Arabism. In this regard, he helped establish the PLO not so much as a vanguard of Palestinian liberation but as a means of controlling the Palestinian movement, thereby angering such militants as Yasir Arafat, the head of the radical Palestinian group known as al-Fatah. While Nasser argued that achieving Arab unity was a prerequisite for success in the struggle against Israel, Arafat and other Palestinians maintained that war against Israel was needed to bring about Arab unity.[9]

Syria's Ba'th regime scarcely concealed its contempt for Nasser. The enmity between the president of Syria's National Revolutionary Council, General Amin al-Hafiz, and the Egyptian leader was evident even at the Cairo summit. Al-Hafiz was the only head of state whom Nasser did not personally receive. For his part, the Syrian leader lashed out at Nasser for not doing more to help the Palestinians reclaim their lands from Israel, remarking that if Egypt was not prepared to take military action against the Jewish state, Syria was. Indeed, the Syrians felt uncomfortable even mixing with what they considered "reactionary regimes" at the Arab summits and had attended them largely to show Arab unity and to avoid the opprobrium within the Arab world that their absence might engender.[10]

Relations between Egypt and Saudi Arabia also remained strained. Diplomatic ties between Riyadh and Cairo had resumed in 1965, and efforts were made by both countries to end the civil war in Yemen. But a conference planned for November 1964 that was supposed to bring the warring factions together never materialized, and the conflict continued. Meanwhile, the British concluded a £100 million arms deal with the Saudis which convinced Nasser that Saudi Arabia was involved in an unholy alliance with London. More specifically, he was persuaded that Britain intended to use Saudi Arabia to suppress Nasserist forces in the southern Arabian federation of Aden and the surrounding protectorates that the British had hastily put together after deciding to give up their protectorate of Aden. Furthermore, Nasser was infuriated when, in obvious response to his efforts at summitry and his attempt to control and manipulate the force of Arab nationalism, King Faisal joined the Shah of Iran in December 1965 in calling for a competing conference of Islamic states. Probably more than any other consideration, Faisal's attempt to form an alignment of Muslim states persuaded the Egyptian leader to remain in Yemen.[11]

Despite efforts at coexistence, the Palestinians living in Jordan often found themselves at odds with Jordan's leader, King Hussein, and their differences became even more pronounced as the newly formed PLO began to organize the Palestinians and groups like Fatah competed for their allegiance. These groups promised self-government for the Palestinians either through the establishment of a Palestinian entity within Jordan and/or a "war of liberation" against Israel, both of which could result in the destruction of the Hashimite kingdom.[12]

With few exceptions, none of the major Arab leaders actually wanted war with Israel. In fact, at the Casablanca summit, they had stressed the importance of avoiding a conflict with the Jewish state. Nasser's rhetorical outbursts and threats against Israel were designed primarily to maintain his leadership within the Arab world. Taunted by the Syrians, the Egyptian leader was backed into a corner from which he had to lash out against Israel to maintain his credibility among the Arab people. Even Syria's leaders did not plan to soon start a war with the Jewish state. They limited guerrilla operations across their border, and although they allowed some Palestinians to cross into Israel, it was intended as a substitute for a more general war.[13]

Nevertheless, Egypt, Syria, and Iraq had developed formidable military machines. Since the end of the Suez War, the Soviet Union had supplied these countries with some of its most advanced weaponry, including T-54 and T-55 tanks, TU-16 medium bombers, IL-28 light bombers, MiG-19 all-weather fighters, and MiG-21 interceptors. Egypt alone boasted 1,200 tanks and assault guns, of which at least 450 were T-54 tanks, as well as 70 TU-16 and IL-28 bombers, 80 MiG-19s, and 130 MiG-21s.[14]

The administration worried about the Soviet Union's arms sales and growing influence in the Middle East. In a March 1965 memorandum to the American embassies in all the Arab capitals, Under Secretary of State Phillip Talbot pointed to the "irresponsible way in which [the] Soviets have sought to buy Arab friendship by weapons sales."[15] Talbot and other American diplomats were especially concerned about a possible sale of Soviet weaponry to Jordan. During a visit to Washington in April 1964, King Hussein had asked for American tanks and planes and had hinted that he would buy them from the Soviet Union if he could not purchase them from the United States. In keeping with America's policy of not becoming an arms dealer in the Middle East, Johnson refused the Jordanian leader's request. But faced with Hussein's repeated warning that he was prepared to do business with Moscow if he could not do business with Washington and wanting to bolster his moderate regime against Palestinian militants, the White House agreed in 1965 to sell Jordan 250 M-48 tanks and to help it obtain sophisticated jet aircraft in Europe.[16]

The United States could hardly sell arms to Jordan without selling weapons to Israel. Israel had wanted to purchase the sophisticated and very powerful M-48 Patton tank to counterbalance the Soviet T-54 and T-55 tanks. But the State Department opposed the sale, which would have been in violation of the Tripartite Declaration of 1950. Although President Johnson agreed to a plan whereby Germany would have supplied Israel with 200 of its older Patton tanks in return for 200 newer M-48s from the United States, the plan fell apart when Egypt threatened an economic boycott against Germany if it went through with the deal.[17]

Unable to buy the American-built tanks, the Israelis were almost certain to object to a Jordanian arms deal, especially if they did not have a corresponding agreement with Washington. The pro-Israeli lobby in the United States was bound to do the same. Military aid to Israel would both moderate some of the criticism the administration expected to receive over the Jordanian arms agreement and help offset the arms imbalance in the region. Accordingly, the White House agreed in March 1965 to provide Israel with 210 M-48 tanks. As the price for Jerusalem's tacit acquiescence in the Jordanian arms sale, the administration also stated that it would consider selling the Israelis 24 jet fighters if they could not obtain similar planes from western Europe.[18]

In terms of military hardware and personnel, Israel remained at a distinct disadvantage to the Arab states in 1966. As a result of its arms agreement with the United States, it had about 1,000 tanks of which about 200 were M-48 Pattons. In addition, it had about 300 aircraft of various types purchased mainly from France. This fleet was far outnumbered by Egypt's tanks and planes alone, and some military experts thought the Soviet T-54 and T-55 tanks were superior to the American Pattons. Israel's regular military forces numbered only about 50,000, approximately the same as just Syria's forces.[19]

As Arab leaders understood, however, such figures were misleading. Syria's army, for example, was poorly trained, and its officer corps was short-handed and ill-equipped to lead the nation into war. Only about half its tanks were operational, and its air defense missile system was limited and primitive. Moreover, Israel's regular military force was augmented by about 200,000 well-trained reservists who could be mobilized at a moment's notice. Its forces were highly mechanized and mobile and, therefore, able to cover long distances quickly.[20]

Israel also had one of the best and most admired air forces in the world with an elite group of pilots flying highly sophisticated French Mirage and Super Mystère interceptors and Mystère fighter bombers. Unlike its Arab enemies, Israel had developed a coherent military doctrine predicated on fighting on enemy rather than Israeli territory and providing for preemptive strikes by the air force, armored vehicles, and paratroopers.[21] In contrast, Moscow structured its arms sales to the Arab states in a way that allowed them to respond to Israeli attacks rather than launch preemptive strikes of their own. Tanks and interceptor fighters would neutralize an Israeli attack, but as Jon Glassman, an authority on Soviet arms sales to the Arabs, has pointed out, the Soviets had intentionally "denied [Egypt and Syria] significant numbers of contemporary ground-attack aircraft and tactical rockets, which would have improved their fire-support and, hence, their offensive capabilities."[22]

Thus, while the Arab-Israeli dispute was always dangerous, the United States had relatively little cause for concern about the Middle East prior to 1966. There were serious problems, to be sure, such as the continuing civil war in Yemen, the Jordan River dispute, the arming of the region, and above all, the Soviet Union's growing influence, which increasingly troubled the president and Middle East experts at the State Department and White House. Nevertheless, war in the Middle East did not appear imminent, and problems in the region were relatively minor compared to the escalating war in Vietnam.

Beginning in the late winter of 1966, however, matters deteriorated rapidly. After London announced on 22 February that it was preparing to withdraw its troops from Aden in 1968 and a coup occurred in Syria the next day,[23] the Soviet Union intensified its diplomatic efforts in the Middle East as it sought to extend its influence into the southernmost regions of the Arabian Peninsula. A study of Soviet influence in the region undertaken at the request of the president found "a pattern of serious Soviet advances . . . including the active expansion of Soviet power and missile capability." On the basis of the study, Johnson concluded that the Middle East represented another arena in the global confrontation between Washington and Moscow.[24]

Relations between the United States and Egypt grew increasingly strained. In 1965, President Johnson, already under considerable pressure from a Congress hostile toward Nasser, had suspended PL 480 food shipments to Egypt. His action followed a number of incidents between Cairo and Washington that included: Egypt sending arms to leftist guerrillas battling the American-backed government in the Congolese civil war; an angry and uncontrolled mob of African students burning the United States Information Service Library in Cairo in November; an American cargo plane owned by Johnson's Texas friend John Mecom being downed; and a particularly vituperative speech Nasser delivered against the United States in December.[25]

At the end of 1965, the president resumed food shipments and consented to a new six-month PL 480 agreement after the Egyptian leader moderated—but never entirely stopped—his anti-American rhetoric, apologized for the burning of the American library, stopped arms shipments to the Congo, and reached agreement with Saudi Arabia to end outside involvement in the Yemeni civil war. Despite his request in April 1966 for additional food aid for Egypt, President Johnson showed little interest in continuing the PL 480 program with a government whose leader attacked the United States and whom he personally disliked.[26]

Nasser remained persuaded that the United States was plotting to overthrow his government. During the last two years, three well-known leftist leaders of nonaligned nations—Ben Bella of Algeria, Nkrumah of Ghana, and Sukarno of Indonesia—had been toppled from power. The Egyptian leader concluded that they had been victims of a CIA plot and that he was its next target. He also determined that the CIA had sponsored the proposal by Saudi Arabia and Iran to establish an Islamic alliance directed against his leadership of the Arab world and that both the United States and Britain were using the Saudi monarchy to organize the Middle East into a pro-Western alliance similar to that envisioned by Eisenhower at the time of the Eisenhower Doctrine.[27]

Although Nasser may have been off the mark about the conspiratorial nature of Washington's relations with Saudi Arabia, the United States certainly sought to bolster the conservative Saudi regime against the threat posed by the Egyptian leader and his followers. At stake was not only the balance of power in the Middle East but also the West's need to protect the vital oil flow from the Arabian Peninsula. This was a point that had been brought home to the administration as early as January 1965 when Thomas Barber, president of ARAMCO, warned other oil executives and a group of State Department officials against allowing the "unthinking use of oil as a political weapon by radical Arabs."[28] Despite strong objections from the Israelis and opposition on Capitol Hill, President Johnson agreed in December 1965 to provide Saudi Arabia with a $300 million military aid package that included HAWK missiles and combat aircraft.[29]

But Arab politics was not merely a response to Western interests or cold war politics. A far more important development in Arab politics in 1966 was that the period of Arab summitry and efforts at Arab unity gave way to the pressures of traditional rivalries and the emergence of new political forces, which added to the area's inherent instability. In February 1966, a bloody coup in Syria resulted in the establishment of a particularly radical and repressive military regime. Paranoid about foreign influence in the Middle East, the new regime was convinced that Israel was part of a larger plot by enemies of the Ba'th revolution to destroy the movement. Determined to right the wrongs they believed had been inflicted on the Arabs in general and Syria in particular, they permitted Palestinians to use Syria as a base of operations from which to attack Israel.[30]

Also in 1966, PLO leaders angrily criticized King Hussein for not allowing the PLO to recruit and train Palestinians in Jordan for the Palestinian Liberation Army. More ominously, Egypt parted ways with Jordan and in October concluded a mutual defense agreement with Syria, which provided for a unified military command under Egyptian leadership. Although the immediate cause for Egypt's break with Jordan was Hussein's conflict with the PLO, a more fundamental reason was the ideological polarization of Arab politics. Nasser was alienated by the Jordanian king's support of Faisal's proposed Islamic alignment. At the same time, he was forced to distance himself from Amman by Syrian attacks on Jordan's "reactionary" regime.[31]

With Syria's encouragement and Egypt's acquiescence—but not its consent or approval—Fatah began attacking Israel from Jordan in the first concerted effort at guerrilla violence since before the Suez War in 1956. (As early as 1964, Fatah had attacked Israel from Jordan, but not as part of a systematic campaign of guerrilla activity.) Meanwhile, Hussein arrested more than 200 "subversives," including Ba'thists and most of the staff of the PLO office in Amman. In a speech on 14 June, he stated that cooperation with the PLO was no longer possible. Syria and the PLO responded by declaring that Palestine could not be liberated until Jordan was freed from Hussein's rule.[32]

If the purpose of Fatah's raids into Israel was to provoke a military response that might lead to an all-out conflict between Israel and the Arab states, they succeeded. Although the attacks across the border did relatively little damage and caused few casualties, they raised the level of fear among Israelis and prompted the Israeli government to take countermeasures. Prime

Minister Levi Eshkol and other Israeli leaders concluded that unless Israel responded with military force, the raids would become more frequent and the damage more severe.[33]

On 13 November 1966 Israeli army units crossed into Jordan and attacked the village of Samu on Jordan's West Bank, blowing up 125 homes in retaliation for the deaths of three Israeli soldiers who had been killed by a mine. What was intended to be a limited punitive action against a local guerrilla base turned into a major battle lasting four hours, involving units of Jordan's Arab Legion, and leaving 15 Jordanian soldiers and three civilians dead and many others wounded. The Samu raid provoked worldwide condemnation of Israel and resulted in a censure by the UN Security Council. Even friends of the Jewish state were disturbed because the guerrilla activity against Israel had been supported by the Damascus government, not by Amman, which had sought to prevent the guerrillas from using Jordan as a base.[34]

In the Arab world, the Samu raid weakened moderate leaders like Hussein, who wanted to avoid war with Israel. Outraged by the apparent helplessness of the government to protect its citizens, angry mobs took to the streets in Jordan, demonstrating and rioting against Hussein and nearly toppling him from power. Egyptian radio also attacked the Jordanian leader, claiming he was too weak to stand up to Israel. Similarly, Syrian leaders made clear their view that so long as Hussein stayed in power, Palestinians living in Jordan would be at the mercy of Israel.[35]

In Israel, too, the Samu raid undermined moderate leaders while strengthening the hand of hardliners. The UN resolution of censure, which the United States chose not to veto, left Israel feeling isolated and vulnerable. Israeli leaders, including Prime Minister Eshkol, who just six months earlier had been actively pursuing a negotiated settlement of the Arab-Israeli dispute, found it difficult to understand why Israel should be censured for its attack on Samu when no action had been taken against the Arab states allowing or supporting terrorism against Israel. Believing also that the condemnation of Israel would encourage more terrorist attacks, Israel concluded that to protect itself, it would have to engage in stepped-up military retaliation against suspected guerrilla bases irrespective of world opinion.[36]

Guerrilla raids and Israeli reprisals multiplied throughout the remainder of 1966 and into 1967. Both Arabs and Israelis seemed headed down an ineluctable path toward war, even though most Arab and Israeli leaders wanted to avoid a third Arab-Israeli conflict. Even Egypt's defense pact with Syria was intended by Nasser as a way of avoiding conflict rather than as a step toward war. By requiring Damascus to confer with Cairo before undertaking any major military operation and placing both the Syrian and Egyptian armies under Egyptian command, Nasser sought to prevent any precipitate action on Syria's part. But by obligating Egypt to come to Syria's assistance if it appeared threatened by Israel, the agreement increased the chance that local skirmishes between Israel and Syria would escalate into a major war.[37]

The very lack of unity among the Arab states and the Middle East's inherent instability had a similar impact. As the political scientist Malcolm Kerr has observed, the Palestinian issue has generally served to divide, rather than to unite, Arab states. When they are in a cooperative mood, they tend to put the issue aside. But "when they choose to quarrel, Palestine policy readily becomes a subject of dispute."[38] During the two years of detente beginning in 1964, Arab leaders had successfully contained the Palestinian issue to avoid provoking hostilities with Israel. But with the Arab world divided, the issue became a political weapon that Syria, the most militant of the Arab states, used in an effort to enhance its own position within the Arab world and to undermine traditional foes like Jordan and Saudi Arabia. Driving Syria's leaders was also the humiliation they suffered when, on 7 April, Israeli planes shot down six Syrian MiGs and then flew unchallenged over Damascus following an exchange on the ground between Israeli and Syrian tanks and artillery.[39]

The Palestinian raids and Israeli reprisals set in motion a process that led directly to the Six-Day War beginning on 5 June 1967.[40] Between 9 April and 8 May, 14 military clashes took place along the Syrian-Israeli border. UN secretary general U Thant termed the incidents "very deplorable," especially since they seemed to involve persons who "had more specialized training than has usually been evidenced in El Fatah incidents in the past."[41] Although Syria denied responsibility for the attacks, it made clear it would do nothing to stop them, claiming that Israel was massing troops and moving them toward the Syrian border. The Soviets told the Egyptians much the same thing. These reports were erroneous, but rumors in Damascus and Cairo of an imminent Israeli invasion raised war fevers.[42]

Nasser concluded that he had to demonstrate his solidarity with Syria. On 14 May, Egyptian and Syrian military leaders held joint meetings as provided for under the Egyptian-Syrian defense pact, and a large Egyptian force was moved into the Sinai. The next day Iraq promised to assist Syria if it was attacked, and Israel put its forces on a state of alert. On 16 May, Nasser suddenly and unexpectedly requested the withdrawal of United Nations Emergency Forces (UNEF) from observation posts along the Egyptian-Israeli border. When Secretary General U Thant responded that a partial withdrawal was impossible, Egypt demanded that the entire force be withdrawn as soon as possible, including the UN personnel deployed along the coast of the Gulf of Aqaba in the Sinai Peninsula. U Thant acceded to the Egyptian request almost immediately. Israel moved a tank unit and three infantry battalions toward the Egyptian frontier around the Gaza Strip. On 21 May, Israeli General Yitzhak Rabin told the Israeli cabinet that in the past few days Egypt had increased the number of its troops in the Sinai from 35,000 to 80,000.

On 22 May, Nasser announced that he had seized the outpost of Sharm al-Sheikh on the Egyptian side of the Strait of Tiran and declared a blockade of the strait, through which shipping passed from the Red Sea to the Gulf of Aqaba and the Israeli port of Eilat. The gulf would be closed to all Israeli shipping and to the ships of any other country carrying strategic goods to Israel. The Egyptian leader justified his action on the grounds that the strait was within Egypt's territorial waters and that Egypt was still technically at war with Israel.

In closing the strait to Israeli shipping, Nasser turned an increasingly dangerous situation in the Middle East into a full-blown diplomatic crisis and probably made a third Arab-Israeli war inevitable. The issue for Israel was not so much the economic damage that the blockade would do; Eilat was important mainly for the oil that it received from Iran, and no Israeli ships had gone through the strait in two years. But closing the strait constituted a direct challenge to Israel's national sovereignty. To cave in to Nasser's blockade, the Israeli government believed, would encourage the Egyptian leader to apply additional pressure and make new demands on Israel. At stake also was the sanctity of international obligations, since Israel's freedom to navigate the strait had been guaranteed both by a UN resolution and by the United States, Britain, and France following the Suez War.

The United States had watched the developments in the Middle East with increasing alarm. For President Johnson the mounting crisis could not have come at a worse time, faced as he was with both growing opposition on Capitol Hill to the Vietnam War and public accusations that he was conducting his office in an imperious manner. Harassed and isolated because of the Vietnam War, the president was determined not to become embroiled in another quagmire possibly involving the use of military force. At the very least, he wanted full congressional and public support for whatever course he pursued.[43]

As the situation had darkened in the Middle East, the president had urged Israeli and Arab leaders to practice restraint. In a letter to Israeli prime minister Eshkol on 17 May, he commented sympathetically on the stress placed on Israel by the actions of Egypt and Syria. But he warned that the United States would not support or condone precipitate or unilateral action by Israel.[44] Two days later, he sent a personal message to Soviet premier Kosygin asking the Soviets to use their influence on behalf of restraint. Johnson even made conciliatory gestures toward Nasser. In a letter to the Egyptian leader on 22 May, he held out the promise of a carrot rather than the threat of a stick. Far from manifesting unfriendliness toward Egypt, he wrote, the United States was interested in efforts being made to modernize the country. He hoped the Arab leader would keep foremost in mind his responsibility to his people and to the world to avoid hostilities with Israel.[45]

On the very day the president sent his letter to Nasser, he learned that Egypt was imposing a blockade on the Gulf of Aqaba by closing the Strait of

Tiran. The Egyptian action elicited an immediate White House response. In the administration's view, more was involved in the closing of the strait than a violation of international law or even Israel's national sovereignty. As NSC Adviser Walt Rostow put it to the president on 23 May, "the issue in the Middle East today is whether Nasser, the radical states and their Soviet backers are going to dominate the area. A related issue is whether the US is going to stand up for its friends, the moderates, or back down as a major power in the Near East."[46] As soon as the blockade was imposed, the State Department informed Egypt that the United States considered its action illegal and a threat to peace in the Middle East. The White House also responded favorably to a British proposal for a declaration by the principal maritime powers of their intention to assure free passage through the Gulf of Aqaba and for the organization of a naval force in the Red Sea. President Johnson later noted that he wanted to work through the United Nations, but he was not optimistic. "I want to play every card in the UN," he told his advisers, "but I've never relied on it to save me when I'm going down for the third time."[47]

On 25 May, Israeli foreign minister Abba Eban came to Washington, where he held two days of talks with Secretary of State Dean Rusk and President Johnson. They reassured Eban that the United States was committed to defending the right of free passage through the strait and stated that they were considering the British proposal for an international naval force to keep it open. But they were not prepared to go further than that. Claiming that an Egyptian and Syrian attack on Israel was imminent, Eban in effect asked for a public promise from the administration that it would regard an attack on Israel as an attack on the United States. With Congress in mind, the president refused to make such an open-ended commitment, especially since reports from the CIA and other U.S. intelligence agencies contradicted the Israeli claims. Instead, the president warned Israel again against any preemptive strike. "Israel will not be alone unless it decides to go alone," Johnson told Eban rather cryptically.[48]

The Soviets applied similar pressure on the Arab states. Although Moscow regarded the Middle East as a realm of opportunity and had armed the most militant of the Arab countries as part of its effort to strengthen its influence in the region, the Soviets were determined to avoid involvement in renewed hostilities in the Middle East, which could pit them against the United States. Because Moscow sought improved relations with Washington but faced the roadblock of the Vietnam War, it was anxious to avoid a second roadblock. Accordingly, Soviet premier Kosygin informed the president on 27 May that Moscow would join the United States in urging restraint in the Middle East.[49]

The combined pressure of the two superpowers staved off war momentarily. On 30 May, Prime Minister Eshkol told the president that Israel, which almost launched a preemptive strike on 27 May, would for the moment refrain from attacking. Under pressure from the Soviet Union and the United States, Nasser also changed his mind about a renewed Arab-Israeli war. Throughout the months prior to the closing of the strait, the Egyptian leader had tried to avoid a conflict with Israel. Notwithstanding his swagger, he was not certain Arab forces could win such a war, and his rhetoric and actions, including the closing of the Strait of Tiran, were intended largely to maintain his leadership of the Arab world.[50]

The Arab response to his blockade, however, was so overwhelmingly favorable that he got caught up in his own inflammatory words. Even Jordan's King Hussein swallowed his pride and went to Cairo, where he negotiated a defense pact with Nasser that placed Jordan's armed forces under the command of an Egyptian general. Nasser's military commanders also began to talk confidently of defeating the Israelis. According to Heikal, "some of us . . . were dazzled by the spectacle of the force we moved into Sinai between May 11th and May 20th."[51] But at a meeting on 2 June with former treasury secretary Robert Anderson, whom Johnson had sent to Cairo as his personal representative, the Egyptian leader was surprisingly conciliatory, promising free passage of shipping in Arab territorial waters (presumably for all nations except Israel), denying any complicity in the terrorist activities of Palestinian Arabs, and suggesting a visit to the United States on the part of Egyptian vice president Zakariya Mohiedden.[52]

By this time, however, the momentum toward war was too strong to be stopped. Johnson thought he had until at least the second week in June to reach a settlement of the crisis before Israel would attack; Israeli officials had indicated that much to him. But sentiment was growing in Israel for a preemptive strike, even among those like Abba Eban who had played a decisive role in keeping Israel from attacking on 27 May.[53]

The United States and the Soviet Union continued to urge restraint on the part of both Israel and the Arab states, and Washington pursued Britain's proposal for an international naval force to assure free navigation to Eilat. But few countries wanted to become involved in a dispute that affected them marginally, if at all. Only Britain, the Netherlands, Canada, and, later, Australia indicated that they might join a naval task force, and lawmakers on Capitol Hill were opposed to the United States unilaterally using force to reopen the strait. The Joint Chiefs of Staff told Defense Secretary Robert McNamara that such an action would be "operationally unsound." They also expressed "reservations concerning the ability of the United States to meet worldwide military commitments and contingencies beyond the current Southeast Asia conflict."[54] The United States had nothing else to offer Israel. As far as Israel was concerned, American policy was bankrupt.

Furthermore, steps taken by each side in the developing crisis only boosted the fears of the other side. For example, Jordan's treaty with Egypt raised the specter for Israelis of being encircled by Arab forces preparing to attack. Conversely, the establishment by Israel of a government of national unity, which included the militant hero of the 1956 Suez War Moshe Dayan as defense minister and the even more hawkish Menachem Begin as minister without portfolio, convinced Arabs that Israel was preparing for war.[55]

The Arabs were essentially correct. Although Israel would probably have attacked even without Dayan's presence in the cabinet, the defense minister was convinced that only a war would reopen the Strait of Tiran, and his voice in the cabinet carried great weight. On 4 June, the cabinet decided in favor of war, and the next day Israeli bombers and fighters launched a pre-emptive strike, destroying the Egyptian air force in the morning and doing the same to the much smaller Jordanian and Syrian air forces in the after-noon.[56] Although he later claimed that the establishment of the coalition government in Israel had persuaded him that an attack was imminent, Nasser was taken completely by surprise. According to his biographer, Robert Stephens, the Egyptian leader actually thought the United States would be able to keep Israel from attacking: he simply "misunderstood the relationship between Israel and Washington, and under-estimated the readiness and ability of the Israelis, especially the Dayan generation, to go it alone."[57]

Over the next six days, Israel inflicted a smashing and humiliating defeat on its Arab neighbors.[58] Israeli strategy was first to concentrate its forces against Egypt. Having destroyed the Egyptian air force, Israel then proceeded to systematically destroy Egyptian ground forces. Israeli forces nearly wiped out Egypt's Seventh Division and seized the Gaza Strip in the northern Sinai. They also forced a general withdrawal of Egyptian forces across the middle and southern regions of the peninsula toward the mountain passes at Mitla, Giddi, and Bir Gifgaga where they were decimated by Israeli air and ground attacks. Meanwhile, Israeli forces carried to shore by patrol boats from Eilat captured Sharm al-Sheikh and reopened the Strait of Tiran. By 9 June, Israeli advance forces had reached the eastern bank of the Suez Canal and could have marched into Cairo with little resistance had they been given the order, so completely had Egypt been defeated.

By this time, Israel had also defeated Jordan and was engaged in battle with Syrian forces defending the Golan Heights overlooking the Galilee region of northeastern Israel. Privately, Israel had let King Hussein know that it would not attack Jordan unless it was attacked first. But as both an Arab and a ruler of a country whose population was overwhelmingly Palestinian, Hussein felt he had to abide by his defense agreement with Egypt; his honor and very survival were at stake.[59] Although Jordan's Arab Legion fought well, by 8 June Israel had overrun the West Bank of the Jordan River and captured the Old City of Jerusalem. Fighting along Syria's border with Israel was light during the first four days of the war. But on 9 June after Israeli planes had softened up Syrian fortifications on the Golan Heights, Israeli armor and infantry attacked, and by late afternoon, they had routed Syrian forces along the entire front.

Throughout the fighting, American—and Soviet—policy was to end to the war as quickly as possible. Immediately following news of the conflict, Kosygin contacted Johnson over the hotline. Over the next six days, the two leaders used the hotline 20 times.[60] In his very first message to the president, Kosygin urged an immediate end to the fighting and an Israeli withdrawal to the 1949 armistice line. At the United Nations, the Soviets sought similar cease-fire terms along with condemnation of Israel by the Security Council. Such terms would have left the Strait of Tiran in Egyptian hands and required the Israelis to withdraw their forces from all the territories they had taken during the war.[61]

In marked contrast, Washington favored a simple cease-fire. But the White House wanted more than just another truce. Once a cease-fire had been arranged, it hoped to negotiate a permanent settlement of the Arab-Israeli dispute. According to the National Security Council's Middle East expert, Harold H. Saunders, "the men around the President just started talking this way—apparently at first with little discussion of what was possible."[62] Apparently concerned by Egypt's massive losses, the Soviets agreed to the American position on a cease-fire, and on 6 June, the Security Council passed a resolution calling for an immediate end to the fighting with no mention of withdrawal or condemnation of Israel.[63]

The Israelis, though, were in no hurry to agree to a cease-fire. Israel had earlier assured the United States that it did not intend to use the war to enlarge its territory and that it would seek to localize the conflict.[64] Even if these were true—and the evidence suggests otherwise—Israel had a number of war aims, the most important of which were the downfall of Nasser and the destruction of Soviet weaponry in Arab hands. Until these objectives were achieved, Israel was not particularly interested in ending the war.[65]

In contrast, Jordan was desperate for a cease-fire, and King Hussein accepted the UN resolution as soon as it was approved. The United States urged Israel to implement a cease-fire immediately lest Hussein be overthrown. But angered that he had initiated hostilities and placed his forces under an Egyptian commander, the Israelis were not interested in saving the Jordanian leader or his regime.[66] They were not even certain Hussein still had charge of the country. As a result, Israel did not agree to a cease-fire with Jordan until the evening of 7 June, by which time it was in control of all of Jerusalem and the West Bank.

Egypt and Syria proved more reluctant than Jordan to end hostilities. Not completely aware of how massive a defeat Egypt was sustaining, Nasser rejected the UN cease-fire resolution outright. Even after he gained some sense of the enormity of his losses, he held out, not knowing how to explain Egypt's defeat to the Egyptian people and perhaps hoping that Moscow would rescue him. Not until Israeli armies reached the Suez Canal and encircled Egyptian forces in the Sinai did he agree to a cease-fire, which went into effect on 8 June.[67]

Syria accepted the principles of a cease-fire on 9 June. Israel did the same, but claiming that Syria was still shelling Israeli villages in the Galilee, it continued to fight. Moscow broke off diplomatic relations with Israel, and Kosygin hinted to Johnson that the Soviets would intervene with their own military forces if Israel did not cease its military operations. As a signal to the Soviet leader that he would not countenance such action, the president ordered the Sixth Fleet in the Mediterranean to move from 100 miles off the Syrian coast to just 50 miles. The warning had its desired effect, and after an exchange of messages with Johnson, Kosygin backed away from his earlier threat. Meanwhile, Secretary of State Dean Rusk told the Israelis that if they did not stop their attack, the UN would pass a resolution condemning Israel. Chastened by the Soviet threat, not wanting to antagonize the United States, and having achieved its objective of capturing the Golan Heights, Israel finally agreed to a cease-fire with Syria on 10 June, thereby ending the Six-Day War.[68]

Israel's overwhelming victory caused deep resentment in the Arab world toward the United States. Egypt's ambassador to Washington, Mohamed Ibrahim Kamel, upbraided the American news media and Congress for encouraging or endorsing Israel's attack. Unable to understand how the Israelis could have destroyed his air force so swiftly and so totally, Nasser attributed its destruction to the participation of American and British planes operating from aircraft carriers in the Mediterranean and air bases in Cyprus. Reports from Jordan on the first day of fighting that planes from the U.S. Sixth Fleet had landed in Israel lent credence to this view. In an angry statement in which he accused Washington of being the prime instigator of the Arab-Israeli conflict and called for an all-out war against "imperialism," the Egyptian leader broke off diplomatic relations with the United States. Syria, Iraq, Yemen, Algeria, and the Sudan followed suit. Lebanese foreign minister Georges Hakim warned Secretary of State Dean Rusk that the results of the conflict would be undying Arab enmity for the United States and long-term Soviet-Arab cooperation.[69]

Militancy rather than submission characterized the Arab reaction to defeat. There had been widespread expectation within the administration that Nasser would be forced out of power as a result of the war; a CIA estimate of likely scenarios even concluded that the Soviets would try "to get rid" of him.[70] But in Egypt and other Arab countries, people took to the streets in an apparently spontaneous outburst of emotion when, in the wake of military defeat, Nasser announced he was stepping down. In response to their pleas, the Egyptian leader decided to remain in power. Sporadic hostilities between Arabs and Israelis continued after the cease-fire. In July, fighting between Egyptian and Israeli forces along the Suez Canal became so intense that the UN sent peace observers to get both sides to stop the shooting. Although peace was restored, it was fragile.[71]

Even during the conflict, President Johnson had expressed concern about the long-term consequences of an Israeli victory, particularly an overwhelming one. Not only did he appreciate the resentment the Arab states would have for the United States, but he also predicted that Israel would be reluctant to give up the lands it had just captured, and he realized that this would indefinitely delay a final settlement of the Arab-Israeli dispute. "[B]y the time we get through with all the festering problems," he remarked at a meeting of the NSC on 7 June, "we are going to wish the war had not happened."[72]

Nevertheless, Americans welcomed Israel's victory enthusiastically, and the White House, gladdened that Nasser, his surrogates, and his patron (the Soviet Union) had suffered a major political and military defeat, joined in the celebration. Although intelligence experts at the Pentagon and CIA had anticipated that Israel would prevail in another Arab-Israeli dispute, most Americans had been far less confident and viewed Israel's victory as another instance of David slaying Goliath. Scant attention was paid in the press to the plight of the inhabitants of the occupied territories, thousands of whom were forced out of their homes or left fearing for their lives. Instances of brutality and pillaging by Israeli forces, even an attack on the American surveillance ship USS Liberty by Israeli aircraft, which may or may not have been committed intentionally,[73] were also largely ignored or downplayed by the media and the American public. For the vast majority of Americans, the image of Israelis was nothing less than heroic.[74]

Once the cease-fire was in place, the question became whether the Israelis would withdraw from the territories they had seized. All signs indicated that Israel intended to keep the lands, at least until an agreement had been reached with the Arab states that recognized Israel's legitimacy as a nation and provided it real security. Even with such an agreement, it was far from certain that Israel would return the Old City of Jerusalem, where the biblical Western Wall so important in the Jewish faith was located, or the Gaza Strip and the West Bank from which Palestinian attacks against Israel had been launched in the past. On CBS's "Face the Nation," Moshe Dayan declared that none of these territories should be given back to the Arabs. Prime Minister Eshkol also commented that it would be a mistake to think that Israel was prepared to return to the antebellum status quo.[75]

America's position on the territorial issue was equivocal. Toward the end of June, Premier Kosygin came to the United States to speak before the UN General Assembly. At the UN, he again called for the condemnation of Israel and for the Israelis to withdraw from the occupied territories. In a nationally televised speech just before Kosygin's UN address that was meant to upstage the Soviet leader, Johnson also called for the withdrawal of Israeli troops from the territories. Privately, the White House also tried to get Jerusalem to assume a moderate position on the lands.[76]

In his televised speech, the president linked Israeli withdrawal to five principles of peace, one of which was "respect for [the] political independence and territorial integrity of all the states of the area," including, of course, Israel; in other words, the occupied territories would form part of a quid pro quo in which a lasting peace would be exchanged for the territories. The president maintained the same position when he met with Kosygin at Glassboro State College in New Jersey where the two leaders discussed, among other things, the Mideast situation but made no progress in reconciling their differences.[77]

Unfortunately, the White House's strategy of a quid pro quo largely ignored the overwhelming sentiment in Israel in favor of keeping at least some of the lands and wrongly assumed that, at some point, the Arab states would be willing to bargain with the Israelis. In contrast to what the administration hoped for, the Knesset passed legislation at the end of June effectively annexing Jerusalem and almost doubling its size by extending the city limits 9 miles in the north and 10 miles in the south. Even Foreign Minister Abba Eban made clear that Israel was not likely to return the occupied territories anytime soon.[78]

Typically, the Arab states were divided over the course to pursue after the war. The two nations that had suffered the most from the conflict, Egypt and Jordan, were prepared to reach some kind of political settlement with Israel. Even Nasser was willing to try diplomacy, if only to gain time for Egypt to recover from the war and to be perceived in world opinion as a conciliator rather than as an aggressor. But Syria and Algeria, the two most militant Arab states, rejected diplomacy in favor of a continued campaign of terrorist activity against Israel, even though Damascus refused to let Syria be used as a base for guerrilla operations and Algeria was too far away to worry very much about Israeli reprisals.[79]

At the end of August, 13 Arab states met at Khartoum in the Sudan, where they declared a policy toward Israel of "no peace, no negotiations, no recognition" and promised not to abandon the struggle for Palestinian rights. This strongly worded decree may have hid more than it revealed, for after the meeting Nasser and Hussein indicated that the Arab states were willing to end the war with Israel; that by "no peace," they meant only no peace treaty; that by "no negotiations," they meant no direct negotiations (negotiations through third parties could still take place); and that by "recognition," they meant de jure rather than de facto recognition (which was still possible).[80]

But perceptions are sometimes more important than intent, and the Israelis interpreted the Khartoum statement to mean that the Arab leaders were not prepared to negotiate a withdrawal of Israeli troops from the occupied territories in return for a lasting and secure peace with Israel. Conversely, Israel's move to annex Jerusalem (and perhaps keep other territories) indicated to even moderate Arab leaders Israel's unwillingness to withdraw from the occupied territories. Furthermore, Arabs and Israelis were divided over whether negotiations should precede withdrawal (the Israeli position) or follow it (the Arab position).

At Khartoum, the Arab states did agree to lift an embargo on oil that during the war they had imposed on countries friendly to Israel (i.e., the United States, Britain, and Germany). In contrast to later embargoes, the embargo of 1967 proved worthless as a political or diplomatic weapon. With the administration's approval, the major American oil companies worked closely with each other and with foreign companies to redirect non-Arab oil to the embargoed countries while sending Arab oil destined for these countries elsewhere. At first, there was a shortage of tankers and problems in rerouting so much oil. The problems were exacerbated at the beginning of the Six-Day War by the Arab states closing the Suez Canal and oil pipelines to the Mediterranean, which necessitated long hauls from the Persian Gulf around the Cape of Good Hope. But the logistical difficulties were worked out, and supertankers that had gone into service over the last decade more than compensated for the long journey around the tip of Africa. Splits also developed between the conservative oil-producing countries such as Saudi Arabia and Kuwait, which were losing revenues because of the selective embargo, and radical nonproducing countries like Egypt and Syria, which favored a total embargo. Instead of cutting back oil production, some oil producers increased their normal production, so that by the Khartoum meeting, Arab oil production was actually 8 percent higher than before the embargo.[81]

Rather than precipitating significant movement toward a settlement of the Arab-Israeli dispute, the Khartoum conference was followed by continued bloodshed. Military skirmishes along the Suez Canal and terrorist attacks and counterattacks, sometimes on a significant scale, became almost routine. In October 1967, Egyptian missiles sank one of Israel's largest warships, the destroyer *Elath*, while it was off Egypt's Mediterranean coast. Israel responded by destroying much of Egypt's refinery capacity in the southern canal city of Suez.[82]

The sinking of the *Elath* and Israel's response emphasized the need to resolve the Arab-Israeli dispute, and the administration sought to achieve this within the framework of the United Nations. Over the summer and early fall, the White House had grown increasingly annoyed at Israel as it became apparent that the Israelis intended to hold on to at least some of the occupied territories. The administration's position remained that a Middle East settlement required both the withdrawal of Israeli forces from the occupied territories (with some minor boundary adjustments for security purposes) and Arab acceptance of Israel's right to exist in peace and security.[83]

On 22 November 1967 the Security Council unanimously approved UN Resolution 242, which largely embodied these views. The resolution called for the "withdrawal of Israeli armed forces from territories occupied in the recent conflict" in return for Arab acknowledgment of "the sovereignty, territorial integrity and political independence of every state in the area and their right to live in peace within secure and recognized boundaries." It also called for freedom of navigation through international waterways in the region and a just settlement of the Palestinian refugee problem.[84]

Although UN Resolution 242 became the basis for subsequent efforts at bringing peace to the Middle East, it may have done more harm than good. The British diplomat who drafted the resolution, Lord Caradon, left it purposely ambiguous on the issue of the occupied territories, omitting the article "the" before "territories." This was an artful piece of diplomatic finesse intended to gain the support of both Arabs and Israelis. The resolution's ambiguity allowed Arab leaders to argue that the resolution required Israel to give up all the occupied territories, while the Israelis maintained with equal vigor that it meant for Israel to give up only some of the territories. Seemingly endless debate would be devoted in subsequent years to discerning the Security Council's real intent.[85] At best, UN Resolution 242 allowed Arab and Israeli leaders to agree to disagree without the resumption of full-scale hostilities in the hope that, at some point, a common ground for peace predicated on the principles set forth in the resolution might be found.

Following approval of UN Resolution 242, the White House lost much of its interest in trying to bring about a lasting peace in the Middle East. At a meeting with Prime Minister Eshkol in January, the president urged the Israelis to make concessions on the occupied territories and the question of Palestinian refugees. Apparently dissatisfied by Israel's lack of movement on these issues, Johnson held up the sale of 50 highly sophisticated F-14 Phantom fighters to Israel. But preoccupied with the war in Vietnam, he had neither the will nor the commitment needed to settle the Arab-Israeli dispute—even if it was possible. The Tet offensive of January 1968 and the president's decision two months later not to seek reelection virtually assured that his administration would undertake no new major initiatives regarding the Middle East.[86]

Nevertheless, the Six-Day War had had a profound impact on America's Mideast policy. Prior to the war, Johnson had to confront the problem of how to contain radical Arab nationalism and Soviet expansionism in the Middle East without some form of American military intervention. Part of the answer was to provide military assistance to Saudi Arabia—and Iran—which had impeccable antiradical and anticommunist credentials. But by its overwhelming victory in the third Arab-Israeli conflict, Israel had shown that it, too, was a major regional power. Oriented toward the West, it also deserved American support, which, not incidentally, would resonate well domestically.

The administration was also deeply concerned about Soviet shipments of weapons to Egypt and Syria. Almost as soon as the Six-Day War had ended, the Soviet Union had begun to resupply Egypt and Syria with weapons. By the end of 1968, most of their losses from the war had been replaced. Thousands of Soviet advisers also helped reform and strengthen Egypt's military forces. While Soviet weapons and advisers may not have tipped the military balance in favor of the Arab states, they nevertheless posed a growing threat to Israel (and even to moderate Arab regimes like Jordan). As a result, the United States became Israel's main arms supplier, replacing France. In December 1968, it concluded a deal with the Jewish state for the 50 Phantom jets that Johnson had refused to sell Israel 11 months earlier. Henceforth, Israel would serve—along with Saudi Arabia and Iran—as a pillar of American (and Western) interests in the Middle East.[87]

The corollary of that development, however, was further polarization of the Arab world, further Arab militancy, further Soviet influence in the Middle East, and further erosion in American relations with most Arab nations.

chapter 5

NIXON, KISSINGER, AND THE YOM KIPPUR WAR: 1969–1974

No recent president has been regarded with such disdain by Americans as Richard Nixon. Long before he was driven out of office in August 1974 by the revelations of the Watergate affair, a legion of Nixon's detractors had concluded that he was insecure and mean spirited at best, sinister and criminal at worst. Yet even Nixon's harshest critics have found much to praise in his conduct of foreign policy. He and his national security adviser (later secretary of state), Henry Kissinger, have been widely viewed as master geopoliticians who ended the Vietnam War, opened ties with the People's Republic of China, and established a policy of detente with the Soviet Union. In the Middle East, they helped end the fourth Arab-Israeli war (the Yom Kippur War of October 1973) in a way that promoted America's interests in the region and raised the possibility of a major diplomatic breakthrough in the Arab-Israeli dispute while, in the process, curtailing the Soviet diplomatic presence in the region.

Yet both Nixon and Kissinger viewed the Middle East through the prism of the cold war struggle between Washington and Moscow. They were not particularly sensitive to the stirrings of Arab nationalism or especially aware of the internal dynamics of Arab politics that affected the region's relations with the rest of the world. Although Nixon was proud that he was not as beholden to the American Jewish lobby as some of his predecessors, his view of the "special relationship" between the United States and Israel differed little from theirs. Like Lyndon Johnson before him, he came to view Israel as one of the pillars of American foreign policy in the Middle East.

As a private citizen in 1963, Nixon had visited Egypt and met with its leader, Gamal Abdel Nasser. Although he was impressed by Nasser's intelligence, charisma, and dignified demeanor, he thought the Egyptian was too

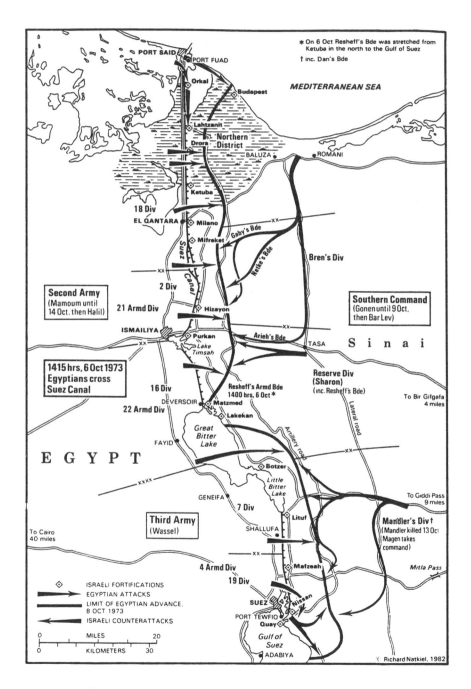

1973 October War—Egyptian Front, Phase One
Courtesy Richard Natkiel

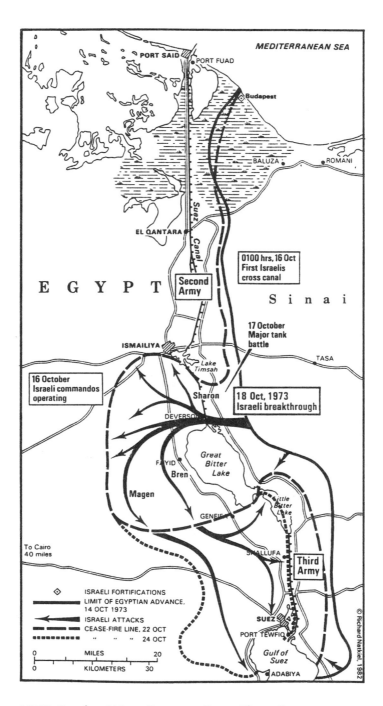

1973 October War—Egyptian Front, Phase Two
Courtesy Richard Natkiel

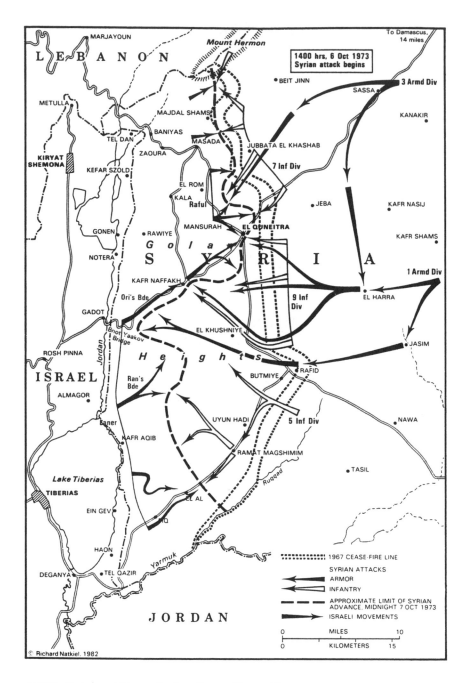

1973 October War—Syrian Front, Phase One
Courtesy Richard Natkiel

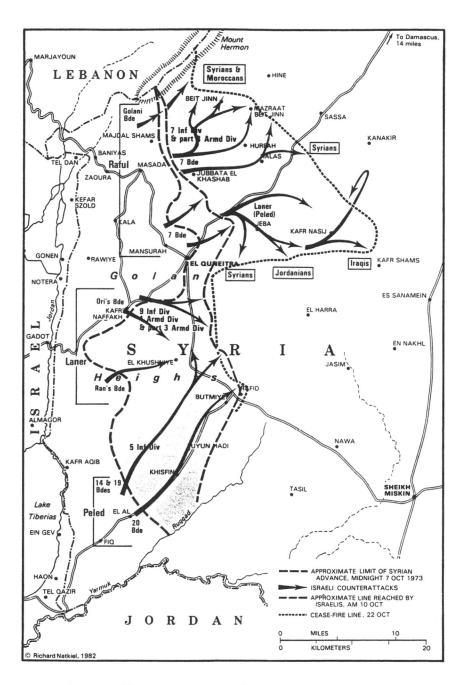

1973 October War—Syrian Front, Phase Two
Courtesy Richard Natkiel

concerned with grandiose schemes of Arab unity and not concerned enough with Egypt's internal problems. Yet he left Egypt convinced that the Arab nations under Nasser's leadership "would in the end submerge the Israelis and defeat them by sheer weight of numbers unless some accommodations were reached [between the warring parties]." Disturbed also by Soviet influence within the Arab world, he felt that it was essential that the United States broaden and improve its relations with the Arab countries.[1]

As president, Nixon continued to worry about the Soviet Union's growing influence in the Middle East; indeed, reducing the Soviet threat in the region was the paramount aim of his Mideast policy. To accomplish this, he believed that the United States needed to improve its relations with the Arab states, especially Syria and Egypt, which were the largest beneficiaries of Soviet weaponry and posed the greatest military threat to Israel. But he felt no progress could be made in resolving the Arab-Israeli dispute without Soviet willingness to allow the peace process to go forward. "The key to peace in the Middle East lay as much in Moscow as it did in Cairo and Damascus," he later wrote. Accordingly, he sent a personal letter to Soviet premier Alexsei Kosygin soon after taking office urging the Soviets to practice restraint in the region.[2]

Unlike Nixon, Kissinger had never visited an Arab country nor displayed much interest in the Middle East. "When I took office," he later acknowledged, "I knew little of the Middle East. . . . My personal acquaintance with the area before 1969 was limited to three brief visits to Israel during the 1960's."[3] For the first two years of the Nixon administration, Kissinger was not in charge of Mideast policy. That was left to Secretary of State William Rogers, who had served as attorney general in the Eisenhower administration and was Nixon's long-time friend. Nixon thoroughly distrusted the State Department, and he intended that Rogers, as secretary of state, would largely be an administrator and watchdog over its bureaucracy. The president and his national security adviser would be responsible for conceptualizing and formulating foreign policy.[4] In the case of the Middle East, however, Nixon made an exception. He was concerned that Kissinger's Jewish faith might create difficulties for him in dealing with the Arab states, and he wanted Kissinger to concentrate on other matters, most notably the war in Vietnam, Soviet-American relations, and America's relations with its European allies and Japan. "You and I will have more than enough on our plate [without the Middle East]," he told Kissinger. He also gave Rogers responsibility for the Middle East because he felt the region "required full time and expert attention," and he wanted to distance the White House from the domestic whiplash that Mideast issues often produced on Capitol Hill.[5]

The president's decision to delegate responsibility for the Middle East to the State Department while empowering Kissinger with most other foreign policy responsibilities contributed to a rift between the secretary of state and the national security adviser that hampered the development of a clearly defined and consistent American policy for the region. Kissinger favored a low profile for the Middle East; Rogers wanted an activist policy. Kissinger believed in what became known as step-by-step diplomacy; Rogers advocated a comprehensive approach. Kissinger believed that a prerequisite to negotiations had to be a willingness by all parties to make concessions; Rogers was convinced that this would happen as talks proceeded. Kissinger preferred limits to the Soviet Union's involvement in the peace process; Rogers thought Moscow's presence was essential to it. The differences between the two administration officials were, therefore, fundamental as well as bureaucratic, and they proved unbridgeable.[6]

Kissinger did not easily accept Nixon's decision to delegate responsibility for the Middle East to the State Department. He sought to undermine Rogers's efforts to launch an initiative between Israel and the Arab states based on UN Resolution 242 (Israeli withdrawal from Arab territories in return for secure and recognized frontiers). He was against rushing into negotiations when neither side appeared ready to make concessions. If there were to be negotiations, he wanted them to be between Israel and Jordan (two "friendly" states) rather than to include Soviet "clients," like Egypt or Syria. Otherwise, the negotiations would enhance Soviet influence in the region, antagonize the Israelis, who would be under intense pressure to make concessions they were not prepared to make, and benefit the radical Arab states, who had little to offer and the most to gain from negotiations.[7]

But Kissinger's views did not prevail. In March 1969, Egypt launched a "war of attrition" along the Suez Canal. Nasser hoped to inflict such high casualties on Israeli forces and to make Israel maintain such a prolonged— and expensive—military mobilization that it would be forced to withdraw its troops from the canal. But the Egyptian leader underestimated Israel's retaliatory capability. Israeli planes destroyed most of Egypt's anti-aircraft system along the canal, and Israeli commandos raided Egyptian installations in the Nile Valley. An Israeli armored unit even penetrated 50 miles behind Egyptian lines.[8]

As the fighting between Egyptian and Israeli forces escalated, the situation threatened to develop into another full-scale war. Nasser warned that, with the United States supporting Israel, there was "no longer any way out except to use force to open our own road toward what we want—over a sea of blood and under a horizon of fire."[9] Nixon was greatly concerned that a new Arab-Israeli war could lead to a superpower confrontation between the United States and the Soviet Union. America's European allies pressured the White House to begin talks on a comprehensive peace settlement.[10]

The administration initiated talks with the Soviet Union, Britain, and France, and separate (and more important) negotiations with the Soviets. Over the summer and fall, the State Department developed a framework of peace that followed the broad outlines of UN Resolution 242. The Israelis would be asked to give up the occupied territories. In return, the Arabs would agree to a permanent peace with Israel. But although the Sinai would be returned to Egypt in return for security guarantees for Israel, Moscow and Egypt rejected the proposal. Nasser claimed that Washington was trying to divide Egypt from the rest of the Arab world. The negotiations having failed, Secretary of State Rogers obtained permission from Nixon to state publicly the principles on which the United States had negotiated privately. In a speech on 9 December, the secretary presented what immediately came to be referred to as the Rogers Plan.[11]

Kissinger considered the plan a major mistake. It presumed that once the issue of the occupied territories was resolved, moderates would prevail over radicals in the Arab world. Such an assumption ignored the fact that Arab radicalism drew its strength from several sources, including opposition to Israel's very existence. Almost certainly, the Israelis would reject the proposal, which threatened their very security, while the radical Arab states would have grist for their propaganda mills. Even Nixon doubted the value of the Rogers Plan. "I knew that [it] could never be implemented," he later commented, "but I believed that it was important to let the Arab world know that the United States did not automatically dismiss its case regarding the occupied territories or rule out a compromise settlement."[12]

As the president and his national security adviser had predicted, the Israelis and all the Arab leaders except King Hussein of Jordan rejected the Rogers Plan. Israel maintained that the plan amounted to appeasement of the Arabs at Israeli expense.[13] Arab leaders were not yet ready to accept a proposal that required them to make peace with Israel. Fighting continued between Egyptian and Israeli forces along the Suez Canal, and Israeli jets conducted deep penetration raids, flying over Cairo and even bombing near the capital. In response, Soviet leader Kosygin sent Nixon a letter in January 1970 threatening to supply Egypt with SAM-3 missiles, its most sophisticated anti-aircraft system, if the bombing continued.[14]

Nixon was also upset by the raids, especially since they came at a time when the United States was trying to negotiate a peace agreement for the Middle East. He was further angered by a diplomatic incident involving French president Georges Pompidou while he was visiting the United States. In Chicago, the French leader was harassed by a group of Jewish war veterans because he had concluded an arms agreement with Libya. For the same reason, Mayor John Lindsay and Governor Nelson Rockefeller refused to greet him when he came to New York City. Although Nixon was disturbed by the bombings, he was almost as disturbed by what he considered "the unyielding and shortsighted" pro-Israeli sentiment in the United States. He decided in March to delay consideration of an earlier Israeli request for 50 Phantom fighter-bombers. But he also cautioned Kosygin that expanded arms shipments to Egypt could draw the Soviet Union and the United States deeper into the Mideast conflict.[15]

Despite Nixon's warning, the Soviets equipped Egypt with SAM-3 missiles. Even more ominously, they sent 1,500 military advisers to Egypt. In Kissinger's view, the Soviet action demanded a firm American response. "All experience teaches that Soviet military moves, which usually begin as tentative, must be resisted early, unequivocally, and in a fashion that gives Soviet leaders a justification for withdrawal," he later wrote. Instead of acting, though, Nixon vacillated. Preoccupied with the war in Southeast Asia and shaken by the violent reaction at home to news that American forces had been sent into Cambodia, the president failed to apply any kind of pressure on the Soviets.[16]

Although Israel suspended its deep penetration raids in early April, the Soviet military buildup in Egypt continued. Over the spring and summer, the Soviets increased the number of SAM sites from 22 to over 70 and began constructing sites along the canal. The SAM missiles soon began taking their toll on Israeli aircraft. In June and July, the Israelis lost one Skyhawk and five Phantom fighter-bombers. The Soviet Union also increased the number of its military personnel to between 12,000 and 17,000. Soviet crews manned the SAM sites, and Soviet pilots flew missions over Egypt.[17]

As the situation in the Middle East worsened, the differences in the views of Kissinger and the State Department became sharper. The national security adviser favored providing Israel with more military aid as a warning to the Soviets that the United States would not remain still while Moscow armed its client states. Attributing the Soviet military buildup to Israel's bombing of Egypt, the State Department argued that what was needed was not more arms for Israel but more Israeli flexibility. Rogers presented a new proposal, soon referred to as the Second Rogers Plan, which provided for a 90-day cease-fire along the canal and negotiations between Israel, Egypt, and Jordan (which the PLO was using as a base for raids into Israel) under the auspices of UN Special Representative Gunnar Jarring. Kissinger ridiculed the proposal, remarking that it amounted to ratification of the Soviet military presence in Egypt. But Nixon sided with his secretary of state, and at the end of July, Rogers seemed to win a major victory when Egypt, Israel, and Jordan agreed to a new cease-fire.[18]

It was a Pyrrhic victory, however. The Egyptians violated the agreement almost as soon as it was signed, moving more SAM-3s along the canal. But more importantly, a civil war in September followed Jordan's signing of the cease-fire agreement, which led to a major review of America's Mideast policy and a transfer of responsibility for the region to Kissinger. In Jordan, Palestinians had long been at odds with Hussein because of suspicions that he harbored a desire for peace with Israel and was willing to concede the Palestinian homeland to get it. But in the aftermath of the Six-Day War, the Palestinians felt betrayed even by Nasser, who was prepared to reach a political settlement with Israel, and by the Syrians, who espoused the Palestinian cause but would not allow guerrillas to operate against Israel from Syria.[19]

Deciding to take matters into their own hands, the Palestinian fedayeen became more militant, defiant of authority, and daring in their exploits. In Jordan, they operated much like an independent state, conducting their own affairs and even levying taxes, in near total disregard of the Amman government. From bases in Jordan and Lebanon, they continued to strike against Israel, and when the Israelis responded with a raid into the Jordan Valley in March 1968, they put up fierce resistance, inflicting heavy casualties on the Israelis. As a result, commando groups like al-Fatah were widely acclaimed, and even romanticized, within the Arab world. In February 1969, Yasir Arafat, the leader of al-Fatah, was elected chairman of the PLO. But the PLO was plagued by factional divisions, and the Popular Front for the Liberation of Palestine (PFLP), a group even more militant than al-Fatah, acted largely independently of the PLO and tried to provoke a conflict between Hussein and the fedayeen.[20]

King Hussein was reluctant to confront the PLO and other Palestinian groups, even after Palestinians tried to assassinate him in June, because of their strength in Jordan, the widespread support they enjoyed within the Arab world, and his own political vulnerability. But on 1 September, the fedayeen made another unsuccessful attempt on his life. Shortly thereafter, fighting broke out between the fedayeen and the Jordanian army. On 6 September, the renegade PFLP hijacked three commercial airliners and forced two of them to land at a Jordanian airstrip. (The other was flown to Cairo.) On 9 September, they hijacked a fourth plane, which they also flew to Jordan. On 12 September, they blew up the three empty planes. Four days later, Hussein declared martial law and ordered his army to suppress the Palestinian guerrillas.[21]

Hussein's action against the fedayeen created havoc in the Arab world. Iraq, which already had troops stationed in Jordan, declared its support for the Palestinians. So did the Algerians. Syria sent armored units to aid the fedayeen and massed tanks along the Jordanian-Syrian border. The Soviet Union also backed the Palestinians, referring to them as "progressive" nationalists seeking to free their homeland from its occupiers.[22]

The possibility that Hussein might be overthrown by the fedayeen had ominous implications as far as the White House was concerned. It would mean the victory of Arab radicals over Arab moderates and the loss of a friend in the Middle East to whom the White House looked to play a major role in ending the Arab-Israeli dispute. More importantly, it would also mean an unacceptable enhancement of Soviet power and prestige in the Middle East and the radicalization of the entire region. Almost certainly, Israel would not allow Jordan to fall under the control of the fedayeen or the Syrians without responding militarily, possibly escalating the crisis into a superpower confrontation between the United States and the Soviet Union.[23]

The administration decided, therefore, that it could not allow Hussein to be toppled. It also had to act on behalf of the 500 passengers, many Americans, who had been taken off the planes before they were blown up but who were now being held hostage by the Palestinians. Nixon was prepared to take direct military action if necessary to rescue the hostages and save the king. Following the hijackings, he put an airborne division at Fort Bragg on alert and sent the aircraft carrier *Independence* to the eastern Mediterranean just off the coast of Lebanon. Over the next two weeks, he ordered two other carriers and a helicopter carrier with 1,500 marines into the region. Twelve hundred marines who had just completed maneuvers off the island of Crete were told to stay in position.[24]

The president was determined, however, to confine the crisis to Jordan. For that reason, he strongly opposed the introduction of Israeli forces into Jordan, which could start another Arab-Israeli war. In a speech at Kansas State University on 16 September, he also warned the Soviets not to intervene in the fighting in Jordan. The next day, he raised the possibility of American intervention should Syria and Iraq take up arms on the side of the Palestinians. "We will intervene if the situation is such that our intervention will make a difference," he told the editors of the *Chicago Sun-Times*.[25]

The next week proved critical. By this time the Jordanian army had gained the upper hand against the fedayeen. In fact, in a 10-day period known as "Black September," the Jordanian army went on a rampage, destroying the refugee camps in and around Amman and hunting down and killing more than 3,000 Palestinians, many of them innocent civilians. Contrary to what the administration had feared, Iraqi forces stayed out of the fighting. But notwithstanding Soviet assurances that Syria would also stay out, on 20 September, 300 Syrian tanks crossed into Jordan. Believing that Moscow had purposely deceived the United States and was behind the Syrian invasion, National Security Adviser Kissinger concluded that the war in Jordan had become a contest between Washington and the Soviet Union for influence in the Middle East and that the United States needed to respond accordingly.[26]

For his response, Kissinger looked to Israel. He had been at odds with the president over the role the Israelis should play throughout the developing crisis. In contrast to Nixon, who strongly opposed Israeli military intervention, Kissinger maintained that the United States should support military action by Israel should Iraq or Syria move against Hussein. Kissinger also thought Washington should warn Moscow not to intervene against Israel. This would show moderate Arabs that the United States stood by its friends. Moreover, it would make clear to the radical Arab states that they could not resolve the Arab-Israeli dispute on the battlefield, and it would inform the Soviet Union that the United States would not permit the Middle East to fall under its control.[27]

On learning that Syrian tanks had moved into Jordan, Kissinger pressed his case with Nixon. "I had no doubt that this challenge had to be met," he later commented. "If we failed to act, the Middle East crisis would deepen as radicals and their Soviet sponsors seized the initiative."[28] This time the president agreed with him. Two days earlier, he had met with Israeli prime minister Golda Meir. After the meeting, he authorized $500 million in military aid for Israel and agreed to speed up the shipment to Israel of 18 Phantom jets. He now gave Israel the green light to launch air strikes against Syrian forces if necessary to save Jordan from defeat. The Israelis doubted that air strikes alone would be enough to stop the Syrians; ground forces, they maintained, would be needed as well. Reluctantly, Nixon consented to their employment provided Hussein also gave his consent. Although the king was willing to have Israel send its forces into Syria, he remained opposed to their use in Jordan, which would undermine his support even among loyal Jordanians. But Israel had already begun to mobilize, moving its forces toward the Golan Heights and preparing to launch an attack against Syrian forces in Jordan within 48 hours.[29]

But the crisis was resolved without Israeli intervention of any kind. For reasons that are still not entirely clear, the head of the Syrian air force, Hafiz al-Asad, did not provide air cover for the Syrian tanks in Jordan.[30] Hardened in his determination by the promise of American and Israeli support, Hussein committed his small air force against the tanks. Without air cover, they were easy targets.[31]

Meanwhile, Moscow responded to Washington's warnings and preparations for military action by applying considerable pressure on Damascus to withdraw its forces from Jordan. On 23 September, Syria complied after losing 120 tanks. Four days later, Nasser arranged a truce between the PLO and Hussein allowing the fedayeen to keep some of their northern strongholds. But the truce was temporary. Over the next year Hussein's army was able to drive the already weakened Palestinian forces from the country. Most took refuge in Lebanon, where they became an even more destabilizing force than they had been in Jordan.[32]

Jordan's civil war had a major impact on Nixon's Mideast policy. First, it seemed to undermine all the assumptions on which Secretary of State Rogers had based his approach to the Middle East. It also appeared to confirm Kissinger's views that Arab radicals would not come to the peace table until they were persuaded that it was in their best interest to do so and that the Soviet Union was behind most of the trouble in the Middle East. Throughout the crisis, the administration had acted on the assumption that Moscow was the puppeteer that pulled the strings of its client states. Syria had intervened in Jordan because the Soviets had willed it; Syria withdrew its tanks mainly because Moscow, alarmed by the United States' threats to use military force to save Hussein, ordered withdrawal.[33]

Yet the administration did not conclude that the United States should play a more active military role in the Middle East. Given the chorus of opposition to the Vietnam War in Congress and among the American people, that would have been political suicide. Indeed, a wail of protest had been heard from Capitol Hill after Nixon indicated that the United States might intervene in Jordan. Instead, Nixon began regarding Israel in much the same way as his predecessor Lyndon Johnson had—as a strategic ally and pillar of democracy in the region. In Nixon and Kissinger's view, Israel had proven its value as an ally. Although convinced that Moscow's intervention had been decisive in getting Syria to withdraw from Jordan, they were also persuaded that Israeli mobilization had been important.[34]

Reliance on Israel also fitted into a broader strategy the administration was developing for dealing with local and regional aggression. Instead of a policy predicated on the use of American forces, this new policy—often referred to as the Nixon Doctrine—provided for arming friendly regional forces and then having them assume the responsibility of military containment. Over the next 12 months, the United States supplied Israel with more than $600 million in arms. Jordan, which the White House also regarded as an important friend, received a lesser amount of economic and military assistance.[35]

Under the Nixon Doctrine, Israel's function was to combat Soviet influence and provide stability in the Middle East. This did not mean that the president and Kissinger were entirely satisfied with the status quo. Kissinger in particular believed that Israel had to be more flexible in negotiating with the Arab countries. He therefore argued against making the Israelis so militarily powerful and so secure that they would have no incentive to negotiate a settlement of the Arab-Israeli dispute.[36]

After the Jordanian civil war, the White House became preoccupied with other foreign policy matters, most notably ending the war in Vietnam, making a new opening to communist China, and reaching a strategic arms control agreement (SALT I) with the Soviet Union. Despite much talk in Washington and Moscow about a new detente between the United States and the Soviet Union, the White House still assumed that the Soviet Union determined the policies of the radical Arab states (Egypt, Syria, and Iraq). The administration thus ignored the fact that even such conservative and moderate leaders as Hussein and King Faisal of Saudi Arabia insisted that the Arab-Israeli dispute—the overriding issue in Washington's relations with the Arab world—could not be settled until the problems of the occupied territories and a homeland for the Palestinians were resolved. It also remained insensitive to the economic, social, and religious dimensions of Arab politics that were to become increasingly obvious over the next 20 years.[37]

During 1971 the State Department tried to arrange an interim agreement between Egypt and Israel providing for Israeli withdrawal from the west bank of the Suez Canal. But such initiatives lacked White House support, and as William Quandt, a member of the NSC staff, later observed, they only "raised the level of Arab frustrations while reinforcing the sense of complacency felt in Israel and in Washington."[38] Indeed, for the next two years, the administration refrained from undertaking any major new diplomatic effort to resolve the Arab-Israeli dispute.[39]

Since the end of the civil war in Jordan, major political changes had taken place in the Arab Middle East that altered forever the calculus of Middle East politics and made developments in the region one of the United States' paramount concerns. Of most immediate consequence was the death of Nasser, who suffered a fatal heart attack just one day after negotiating a truce between the fedayeen and the Jordanian government. Although the Egyptian leader had lost much of the luster he enjoyed among the Arab people following the Six-Day War in 1967, he had remained the most important figure in the Arab world.[40]

The new Egyptian leader, Vice President Anwar Sadat, seemed an unlikely prospect to fill the void created by Nasser's death. Lacking Nasser's charismatic personality, Sadat had been outside the mainstream of power in Egypt until 1969 when Nasser chose him as his vice president. He was allowed to become president by other members of Nasser's inner circle only because they believed he would be easy to control. Furthermore, there were others who viewed themselves as the rightful heir to Nasser's position as leader of the Arab world. Two of these were Colonel Muammar Qaddafi of Libya and al-Asad of Syria. Qaddafi had come to power in Libya in 1969 following a military coup against Libya's monarch, King Idris. In Syria, al-Asad assumed total control of the government in November 1970 after a successful coup against Salah Jadid, with whom he had nominally shared power.[41]

Those who anticipated that Sadat would be weak and easily overshadowed by other Arab leaders were wrong. Instead, Sadat moved quickly to establish his legitimacy as Egypt's new head of state and to stake out a claim as one of the Arab world's commanding figures. Perhaps better than any other Arab leader, Sadat understood the unenviable task he faced. In the last few years of Nasser's life, Egypt had become increasingly isolated within the Arab world. Attacked as pusillanimous by the Palestinians, Egypt was also ridiculed by such radical Arab states as Syria, Iraq, and now Libya for not being more aggressive in the struggle against Israel. Relying almost totally on the Soviet Union for weapons, Egypt still seemed defenseless against Israeli attack. Islamic fundamentalists also objected to Egypt's ties to the Soviet Union. Weakened by war, distrusted by the conservative monarchies of the Arab Middle East, despised by more radical Arab regimes, and dependent on a superpower whose ideology was anathema to the Islamic faithful, Egypt was a country whose ties with the rest of the Arab world badly needed mending.[42]

Even more pragmatic than Nasser, Sadat was willing to work with both moderate and radical Arab states. "My clear and declared policy was that Egypt could not distinguish one Arab country from another on the basis of so-called progressive and reactionary or republican and monarchical systems," he later wrote.[43] As Egypt's representative to Islamic conferences in the 1960s, he had cultivated good relations with a number of conservative and moderate Arab leaders, including King Faisal and King Hassan II of Morocco. As Egypt's new leader, he sought to develop similar relations with Qaddafi and al-Asad even though they were his rivals in the Arab world and called for a type of Arab socialism that conflicted with his more moderate political views.[44] But Arab solidarity was not an end in itself for Sadat. From the time he became Egypt's new leader, he was determined to end what had become Israel's de facto annexation of the occupied territories, preferably by diplomacy but by war against Israel if necessary. In contrast to other Arab leaders, he was motivated not so much by a desire to destroy the Jewish state as by a determination to regain for Egypt and the other Arab combatants in the Six-Day War the self-esteem and territories they had lost as a result of the conflict. Whether these aims were to be achieved through diplomacy or the resumption of hostilities, Sadat considered Arab unity essential.[45]

Largely through Sadat's efforts, by 1973 the Arab world enjoyed a degree of solidarity it had not had since the 1967 war. Egyptian and Syrian military commanders worked closely with each other in planning the resumption of war against Israel. Following a decision by Sadat in 1972 to expel almost all of the Soviet advisers in Egypt, Saudi Arabia agreed to provide Egypt with economic and military assistance, including 20 fighter-bombers it had purchased from Britain. Jordan, which had been diplomatically isolated because of its policies toward the Palestinian fedayeen, was allowed back into the fold. By the fall of 1973, Sadat had achieved enough of a united Arab front that he felt able to renew hostilities against Israel.[46]

Before deciding on a new war, however, the Egyptian president looked to the United States for help in getting Israel to withdraw from the occupied territories. That was one reason he decided to evict the Soviet advisers from Egypt despite the Friendship Treaty he had signed with Moscow just a year earlier. Although he was also dissatisfied with a sharp drop in the level and quality of military aid Egypt was receiving from the Soviet Union—due in large measure to Moscow's quest for detente with the United States—and, as a devout Muslim, found it distasteful to be closely tied to the leader of the communist world, he intended his action first and foremost as an overture to Washington.[47]

In February 1973, the Egyptian leader sent his security adviser, Hafiz Ismail, to the United States for talks with Nixon and Kissinger, but the discussions were unproductive. Ismail warned that Israel's continued occupation of Arab territories would mean another war. Nixon and Kissinger replied that before Israel would withdraw from the occupied territories, it would have to receive guarantees as to its security. Ismail rejected this proposal for a quid pro quo. As the Egyptian journalist Mohamed Heikal put it, Ismail was annoyed by the White House's efforts to reduce the Arab-Israeli dispute "to a simple equation between sovereignty and security." He was also displeased to read en route home to Cairo a *New York Times* report that Nixon had decided to sell Israel 36 Skyhawk and 48 Phantom jets.[48]

Convinced that the United States would not exert sufficient pressure for the Israelis to withdraw from the occupied territories, Sadat prepared for war. Although the preparations were undertaken with great secrecy, Sadat warned the White House repeatedly of renewed hostilities with Israel. During a summit meeting with Nixon in June, Soviet leader Brezhnev also warned of an impending conflict unless Washington and Moscow convinced Israel to give up the occupied territories. Notwithstanding Sadat's having unceremoniously kicked the Soviets out of Egypt a year earlier, the Egyptian leader, in need of arms, had patched up some of his differences with Moscow. He had even approved a five-year renewal of an agreement allowing the Soviet navy to use Egyptian ports. The Soviets had responded by resuming arms shipments to Egypt.[49] Yet Brezhnev did not want a resumption of hostilities in the Middle East, which could undermine his efforts at detente with the United States. "I could not sleep at night," Brezhnev even told Nixon in expressing his concern about the possibility of another Arab-Israeli conflict.[50] But while Nixon sensed the need for movement on the occupied territories, he was distracted by the developing Watergate scandal and the events leading to the forced resignation of his vice president, Spiro Agnew. And Kissinger simply did not take the Egyptian and Soviet warnings seriously. He later attributed his miscalculation to Sadat's diplomatic finesse. The Egyptian leader "was moving toward war, using an extraordinary tactic that no one fathomed," he later commented. "If a leader announces his real intentions sufficiently frequently and grandiloquently, no one will believe him." Kissinger had believed that time was working against Egypt, and that given Israel's military superiority and the cool relations between Moscow and Cairo, Sadat would have no other recourse but to seek a political settlement to the Arab-Israeli dispute.[51]

He was wrong. In September, Kissinger replaced Rogers at the Department of State. On 6 October, he faced his first major crisis as secretary of state when on Yom Kippur, the most sacred day in the Jewish religion, Egyptian forces crossed the Suez Canal and attacked Israeli forces on the canal's west bank. Simultaneously, Syrian armies struck against Israel's lightly defended fortifications on the Golan Heights. The Israelis were caught completely off guard. Despite having one of the world's best intelligence services, Israel had learned of the impending attack only 10 hours before it took place, hardly enough time to mobilize against it. The United States was also surprised, so certain was the White House that Sadat had been bluffing in warning about impending hostilities.[52]

Taking full advantage of the element of surprise and employing tremendous artillery and tank firepower, the Egyptians destroyed the Israeli defense line along the Suez Canal (the Bar-Lev Line), which had been thought to be impregnable, and advanced five miles into the Sinai. Syrian troops and tanks broke through Israeli defenses on the Golan Heights. As Israeli planes sought to destroy the bridgeheads the Egyptians had established across the canal, they were met by a massive barrage of SAM missiles, which in the first day of battle brought down 30 Skyhawk and several Phantom jets. Within the first three days of fighting, the Israelis lost about 60 aircraft, or about one-half the 120 Israeli planes that were downed during the conflict.

Most of Israel's air effort, however, was directed against Syrian forces on the Golan Heights, which posed the most immediate danger to Israeli territory and security. There, too, the Israelis suffered large losses, as Syrian air defenses shot down 30 Israeli aircraft in just the first afternoon of fighting. On the ground, Syrian forces also made impressive gains, forcing the Israelis from most of their defensive lines. On 7 October, Syria committed its armored divisions to the battle. As late as 9 October, four days into the fighting, the Syrians still held strategically important parts of the Golan Heights and nearly forced the Israeli Seventh Armored Brigade to withdraw from the battle, which would have allowed a major Syrian breakthrough.

By this time, though, Israel had fully mobilized its forces and gained mastery of the air, shooting down 70 Syrian aircraft in air-to-air combat. In control of the air, Israeli planes destroyed an estimated 400 of the more than 1,000 Syrian tanks involved in the fighting. Israeli ground forces recaptured the territory they had given up in the first four days of the battle. Israel also began strategic bombing, hitting at Syrian power stations and oil refineries and even attacking the headquarters of the Syrian air force and defense ministry in Damascus. By the end of the first week of the war, the Syrians were in retreat across the 1967 cease-fire line.

Aided by forces from Iraq and Jordan—which entered the war primarily out of fear of the Iraqis, who had been persuaded only with great difficulty to withdraw their troops from Jordan following its 1970 civil war[53]—the Syrians were able to stop the Israeli advance into Syria. When Damascus agreed to a cease-fire on 22 October, the Israelis had gained only about 300 square miles of Syrian territory, and the Arab forces on the eastern front were preparing to launch a five-division attack, which a military historian of the war, Edgar O'Ballance, believes "would have heavily taxed the Israelis."[54]

The Syrian withdrawal across the 1967 cease-fire line, however, allowed Israel to concentrate its military effort on the Egyptian front, where the fighting raged on. During the first week of the war, Egyptian forces continued to cross the Suez Canal, and on 14 and 15 October, Egyptian armored divisions, which had been brought across the canal just two days earlier, launched a major assault in hopes of seizing the strategic Sinai passes of Mitla and Giddi. But this proved to be a grave mistake, for Egyptian forces had been trained essentially for one operation—to cross the canal on a broad front, destroy the Bar-Lev line, and wait for a cease-fire. By moving eastward into the Sinai, away from Egypt's highly effective air defenses, Egyptian troops were subject to a pounding from Israel's superior air force. They were also met by four Israeli armored divisions. In the largest tank battle since World War II, fought over two days (14 and 15 October) and involving more than 2,000 tanks, Egypt lost an estimated 200 tanks and Israel about 60; both sides also suffered large losses in other armored vehicles and guns. Egypt failed to achieve any of its military objectives, and after the battle, the war shifted clearly in favor of the Israelis.

While fighting raged in the Sinai, the Israelis struck across the canal in order to destroy Egyptian defenses on the west bank and take advantage of a large gap between the Second and Third Egyptian Armies. By 19 October, the Israelis had five brigades and between 300 and 500 armored vehicles on the west bank. Shortly thereafter, they began encircling the Egyptian Third Army with its 20,000 men and 250 tanks. But by this time, Israel was coming under growing pressure from the United States to end the war.

Even after it had become apparent following the outbreak of hostilities on 6 October that a full-scale war was being fought and that the Egyptians and Syrians were inflicting heavy casualties on the Israelis, the White House and Pentagon had anticipated a decisive Israeli victory. "Every Israeli (and American) analysis before October 1973 agreed that Egypt and Syria lacked the military capability to regain their territory by force of arms," Secretary of State Kissinger later recounted. In his view, the United States' most important task was to warn the Soviet Union against getting involved in the fighting.[55] Indeed, an Israeli victory would make clear to the Arab states the futility of relying on the Soviet Union to come to their rescue and of seeking a military solution to the Arab-Israeli dispute. "If we played our hand well," Kissinger commented, "the Arab countries might abandon reliance on Soviet pressure and seek goals through cooperation with the United States." Washington would, therefore, support a cease-fire based on the 1967 cease-fire lines, but it would be in no hurry to have it implemented. It would also oppose Israeli conquest of any new territory, which would antagonize friendly Arab states and make a final Mideast peace settlement all the more unlikely.[56]

Not until 9 October did the White House gauge the full extent of what was taking place in the Middle East; in fact, just the day before, the CIA had erroneously reported that Israel had crossed the Suez Canal on both its northern and southern ends and had virtually recaptured the Golan Heights. But reality set in the next day when Israeli ambassador Simcha Dinitz informed Kissinger about the extent of his country's losses and requested an emergency supply of military equipment. That afternoon the secretary of state met with Nixon. They agreed to ship military supplies to Israel and to guarantee to replace Israeli losses of equipment.[57]

Either because of bureaucratic delays or as a subtle means of pressuring Israel into a cease-fire, the airlift to Israel was slow getting started.[58] But on 12 October, Israeli ambassador Dinitz delivered a note to the White House from Prime Minister Meir warning that Israel was in danger of losing the war unless the United States began a full-scale airlift of military equipment to Israel. Nixon responded affirmatively to Meir's urgent request and for the first time used American cargo planes to deliver goods to the Israelis.[59]

The American airlift of equipment to Israel resulted in an Arab boycott of oil to the United States. Despite the friendly relations that existed between Washington and Riyadh, Saudi Arabia had warned the Nixon administration on several occasions in 1973 that it would stop oil shipments to the United States if Washington continued to pursue a pro-Israeli policy. This marked a significant change in Saudi policy from just a year earlier when King Faisal rejected pressure from Sadat and other Arab leaders to brandish the oil weapon. Recalling the failure of the 1967 oil embargo and the significant losses in revenues that had resulted from his country's cutback in oil exports, Faisal had doubts about the impact of another boycott. The United States, he believed, would not need Persian Gulf oil until at least 1985. Ever fearful about the spread of Arab radicalism and the threat it posed to his own throne, he also looked to the United States to protect his interests.[60]

A year later, however, Faisal held a different view. Sadat was able to persuade him of the importance of Arab solidarity in forcing Israel, which Faisal hated as much as any Arab leader, to give up the occupied territories. He also concluded that the United States was already dependent on Persian Gulf oil, so that an oil embargo, coupled with cutbacks in oil production, might command a change in America's pro-Israeli policy. With the purchasing power of the dollar (the currency by which oil prices were set) deteriorating as a result of two recent devaluations, there was also an economic incentive to cut back oil production. "What is the point of producing more oil and selling it for an unguaranteed paper currency?" the Kuwaiti oil minister asked. The Saudis wondered the same thing.[61]

By reducing oil production, the oil-producing countries might also force a substantial increase in profits. In 1970, Libya had taken advantage of the world's growing oil consumption and of new entrants into the competition for Middle East oil production—most notably Occidental Oil, which in 1966 had discovered a massive new field in Libya—to force an increase in the profits it received for its oil: Libya simply insisted on an increase and then required Occidental and the other oil companies in Libya to cut their production until they agreed to its terms. When the Shah of Iran demanded an even higher share of the profits for his oil, a game of leapfrog began in which members of the Organization of Petroleum Exporting Countries (OPEC) were able to jack up oil prices and their share of profits. In 1973, it seemed to Saudi Arabia and other oil-producing countries that cutbacks in production tied to increases in prices might have the same result.[62]

Concerned about the possibility of an oil embargo, executives from ARAMCO and other oil companies with interests in the Middle East warned of the dire economic hardships it would cause and urged the White House to follow a more pro-Arab policy. Kissinger—who because of Nixon's preoccupation with the Watergate scandal now made most of the major foreign policy decisions—understood the risks involved in providing military assistance to Israel, but he could not chance an Israeli military defeat. On 19 October, the White House asked Congress for $2.2 billion in aid for Israel. The next day, King Faisal responded by announcing that Saudi Arabia was cutting its oil production and embargoing oil to the United States.[63]

By the time Faisal imposed the oil embargo, the war had turned decidedly in Israel's favor. Together these two developments persuaded Kissinger that it was time to promote a cease-fire agreement. Pressured by the Soviet Union and sensing that the tide of battle had turned, Sadat indicated on 18 October his acceptance of a cease-fire. But on the verge of surrounding Egypt's Third Army, Israel was in no hurry to stop the fighting. Kissinger cooperated with the Israelis to the extent that he stalled negotiations with the Soviet Union over joint sponsorship of a UN resolution calling for a cease-fire. But on 22 October, the Security Council adopted Resolution 338 mandating a cease-fire. The secretary of state was exultant. "[W]e had achieved our fundamental objectives," he later wrote. "We had created the conditions for a diplomatic breakthrough. We had vindicated the security of our friends. We had prevented a victory of Soviet arms. We had maintained a relationship with key Arab countries and laid the basis for a dominant role in postwar diplomacy."[64]

But even though Israel and Egypt agreed to a cease-fire, the fighting continued. Using an alleged Egyptian violation of the cease-fire agreement as a pretext, the Israelis completed their encirclement of the Egyptian Third Army and blockaded the city of Suez. For Washington and Moscow, the October War now entered its most critical phase. Kissinger was irate at the Israelis. Throughout the war, he had been guided by the same view that he had always held as a member of the Nixon administration—that Israel needed to be militarily strong but not so unassailable that it could dictate its own terms for the Middle East or act contrary to American interests. By its action, Israel violated that premise.[65]

On 24 October, Moscow responded to the resumption of fighting by calling for the United States and the Soviet Union to send a peacekeeping force to the Middle East. Brezhnev threatened to send in Soviet forces alone if Washington did not participate in a peacekeeping mission. The CIA reported that the Soviets had seven airborne divisions on alert. Under no circumstances was the United States prepared to allow the Soviets to introduce military forces into the Middle East. Another basic premise of Kissinger's Mideast policy had been to keep the Soviet Union out of the region.[66]

Accordingly, the White House issued DEFCON III (Defense Condition 3), placing all of America's military forces on alert worldwide, including its nuclear forces.[67] Kissinger also sent Brezhnev a letter signed by the president stating that sending Soviet troops to the Middle East would be a violation of an agreement on detente that Nixon and Brezhnev had signed during their meeting in June. Meanwhile, the Pentagon prepared to send American paratroopers to Egypt to confront Soviet forces if necessary.[68]

The military alert served its purpose. The Soviets backed down from their threatened military action. But the situation remained highly volatile, and Kissinger was determined not to allow Israel to undermine the diplomatic objectives he had already achieved by continuing the fighting. At a press conference on 25 October, he urged the warring parties to stop the conflict immediately, promising that after a cease-fire, the United States would "make a major effort to bring about a solution [to the Arab-Israeli conflict] that is considered just by all parties."[69] Shortly thereafter, the UN Security Council called for both sides to return to the 22 October lines as stated in UN Resolution 338 and provided for a UN observer force to oversee a cease-fire on this basis. Under intense pressure from Washington, Israel agreed to this latest cease-fire, finally ending the fourth Arab-Israeli war.[70]

The October War had a lasting impact, however, both within the Arab world and in Washington. On the one hand, it led to a restoration of Arab self-confidence, which made possible Anwar Sadat's dramatic gesture in 1977 of going to Israel in quest of peace. On the other hand, it resulted in greater American sensitivity to the Arab position in the Arab-Israeli dispute. More significantly, it forced the United States to reexamine some of the basic tenets of its Middle East policy, including the very perspective from which it approached regional problems.

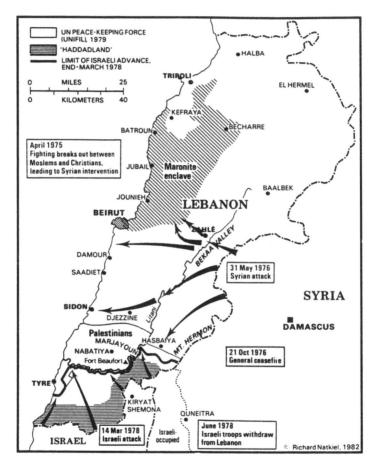

Lebanon
Courtesy Richard Natkiel

chapter 6

STEP-BY-STEP DIPLOMACY: 1974–1977

By almost defeating Israel in the first week of the October War, the Arab states in the Middle East had shattered the aura of Israeli military invincibility. No longer could Washington assume that Israel's military superiority over its Arab neighbors would ensure relative stability in the region. By successfully imposing an oil embargo against the United States, which increased the price of oil from about $5.12 a barrel in October 1973 to $11.65 by January 1974, the Arab world had also shown that Washington could no longer view it simply as a battlefield of the cold war.[1] To be sure, Soviet military support for Egypt and Syria during the war, the growing importance of Western access to Middle East oil that was emphasized by the oil embargo, and Moscow's threat on 24 October to send its own forces into the area increased the White House's determination to limit the Soviet presence in the region. But in the calculus of decision making in Washington, concern about Soviet intervention or communist subversion became much less pronounced after 1973.

At the same time, a new imperative was attached to resolving the Arab-Israeli dispute. Indeed, during his remaining three years in office—first under President Nixon and then, after Nixon's resignation in August 1974, under Gerald Ford—Secretary of State Kissinger probably spent more time mediating the Arab-Israeli dispute than dealing with any other foreign policy matter; in fact, during the first five months after the October War, he expended so much effort traveling between the capitals of the Middle East in quest of a military disengagement and an end to the oil embargo that a new term, "shuttle diplomacy," entered the lexicon to describe his well-publicized jaunts from city to city.

Yet shuttle diplomacy was deficient in dealing with the core questions of the Arab-Israeli dispute—Israel's existence as a nation, the occupied territories, and a Palestinian homeland. Without resolving these matters, there could be no permanent peace in the Middle East. But the combatants in the Yom Kippur War were no closer to settling these issues when President Gerald Ford left the White House in 1977 than they had been three years earlier when Richard Nixon was still president. As a result, Ford's successor, Jimmy Carter, began his presidency committed to another attempt at a comprehensive settlement rather than the step-by-step process Kissinger had pursued.

The secretary's first step following the 25 October cease-fire was to get Israeli and Egyptian forces to disengage. With the Egyptian Third Army surrounded on the east bank of the Suez Canal and Israeli forces still on the west bank, the chances of a new flare-up of fighting remained dangerously high. To prevent this, Kissinger flew to the Middle East in November for talks with Sadat, stopping first in Rabat and Tunis to visit Morocco's King Hassan and Tunisia's President Habib Bourguiba and finally landing in Cairo; this was the first time that the secretary had ever visited an Arab capital.[2]

Kissinger found Sadat both charming and conciliatory. Much to his surprise, the Egyptian president agreed quickly to a six-point plan guaranteeing the supply of nonmilitary items to the entrapped Third Army but did not insist on mutual withdrawal of Egyptian and Israeli forces to the 22 October lines as Kissinger had anticipated. Sadat also agreed to an exchange of prisoners-of-war (POWs) with Israel and accepted "in principle" the restoration of relations between Egypt and the United States, which had been broken during the June 1967 Six-Day War. Israel also gave its approval to the plan after insisting on an American-Israeli "Memorandum of Understanding" clarifying some of its details. An announcement that Israel and Egypt had reached an agreement was made from the White House on 9 November, and two days later, Israeli and Egyptian military negotiators, who had been meeting since 30 October at Kilometer 101, on the road between Cairo and Suez, formally signed the accord.[3]

On 12 December, Kissinger again traveled to the Middle East, this time to win support for a peace conference in Geneva. The cease-fire ending the October War had provided for such a conference "under Soviet and American auspices." The secretary never expected—never wanted—to achieve much at Geneva. As he later explained, "we strove to assemble a multilateral conference, but our purpose was to use it as a framework for an essentially bilateral diplomacy." He was determined to maintain complete control of the negotiating process.[4]

Once more, the secretary of state enjoyed considerable success. All the Arab leaders he talked with, including Algeria's radical leader Houari Boumedienne, Egypt's Sadat, Saudi Arabia's King Faisal, and Jordan's King Hussein, indicated support for the Geneva conference and his step-by-step diplomacy. Of particular importance was the approval of Syria's al-Asad, one of Israel's staunchest foes. Kissinger was meeting al-Asad for the first time on this trip, and he was deeply impressed by him. He found the Syrian leader tough and literal but also extremely intelligent, intense, and sardonically witty. Contrary to frequent reports about al-Asad's fanaticism, the secretary was also taken by his moderation. He even concluded that while the Syrian leader was heavily dependent on the Soviet Union for military equipment, he was "far from being a Soviet stooge." Although al-Asad told him that Syria would not send a representative to Geneva, he also made clear that he would not oppose the meeting and, more importantly, that he wanted a disengagement agreement with Israel and supported Kissinger's step-by-step approach to peace.[5]

As Kissinger had always intended, the meeting at Geneva was largely ceremonial. Represented at the conference were the United States, the Soviet Union, Egypt, Jordan, and Israel. Israel agreed to attend the meeting only after being given absolute assurance by the United States that the Palestinians would not be present or represented and only after warnings from President Nixon and Kissinger that it might lose American support if it failed to go to Geneva.[6]

As prearranged, the one-day gathering on 21 December adjourned after Arab and Israeli representatives delivered formula speeches listing their grievances and attacking each other. As a concession to the Soviets, Moscow and Washington appointed permanent representatives to Geneva to stay in contact with each other and to meet with the Arabs and Israelis at their request. But no one expected such a request to be made, and it never was. Bilateral diplomacy mediated by the United States was to be the road to peace. Although the conference had been jointly sponsored with the Soviet Union, it had been almost exclusively an American enterprise. The Soviets had deferred to Kissinger believing he would never be able to bring Arabs and Israelis to the same bargaining table. When he did succeed, negotiations began with Moscow largely excluded from the diplomatic loop.[7]

After the meeting, Kissinger sought to effect a disengagement of Egyptian, Syrian, and Israeli forces in the Sinai and on the Golan Heights. Reaching an Israeli-Egyptian agreement proved far easier than reaching an Israeli-Syrian agreement. Syria's al-Asad was far more passionate in his hatred for Israel and far less visionary or flexible than Sadat. The Egyptian leader had gone to war in 1973 as an unfortunate but necessary prelude to negotiations and peacemaking. Al-Asad had gone to war to regain territory and punish (if not destroy) Israel. Sadat had intended to fight a limited war to strengthen his negotiating hand. Al-Asad had wanted a more extended war aimed at retaking the Sinai and Golan Heights.[8]

Since Israeli forces still on the west bank of the Suez Canal were vulnerable to Egyptian attack, Israel had a vested interest in reaching an agreement with Egypt that would allow it to shift its troops across the canal. Israel could also withdraw from the area around the canal without endangering its security; indeed, Defense Minister Moshe Dayan had already prepared a plan of disengagement whereby Israel would withdraw to a point just west of the strategically important Giddi and Mitla Passes. In contrast, any Israeli concessions on the Golan, where Israel had already established a number of settlements and which overlooked Israel's Galilee region, posed an immediate and direct threat to Israeli security.[9]

With the Dayan Plan already on the table, the talks that Kissinger conducted with Egypt and Israel went relatively smoothly. Although Sadat wanted the Israelis to withdraw east of the Mitla and Giddi Passes, he gave in to Israel's demand that they remain west of the passes. The most contentious issue was Israel's insistence that both sides limit the size of their forces and weaponry in the areas under their control, including one small area south of the passes that Egypt had held even after the October War. To Sadat, the issue was almost moral. "It is difficult for me to sign a document which limits the forces in my own territory," he remarked. But while he refused to incorporate the force limitations into the final agreement, he went along with a proposal by Kissinger that they be defined in a separate letter from the secretary to both Egypt and Israel.[10]

On 18 January, Cairo gave its final consent to the disengagement agreement, which was officially signed that same day by Israeli and Egyptian commanders at Kilometer 101 and which has since become known as the Sinai One agreement. The Soviets complained bitterly about being left out of the negotiations, which, they also protested, had effectively short-circuited the Geneva process. Kissinger could not have agreed with them more.[11]

Unlike the negotiations between Israel and Egypt, concluding a disengagement agreement between Israel and Syria proved to be enormously difficult. It took Kissinger 34 days and 41 flights between Israel, Syria, and six other countries before reaching a Syrian-Israeli accord. Not since 1919 had a secretary of state been out of the country so long. The secretary haggled with al-Asad over Syrian territory taken in the Six-Day War. He renewed warnings to Israel that its failure to negotiate an agreement with Syria would threaten its support in the United States, and he endured great frustration as he negotiated tirelessly over the disengagement point between Syrian and Israeli forces in the area adjacent to the Syrian town of Kuneitra. But at the end of May, the secretary of state was able to complete an agreement for the Golan Heights. Similar in many ways to the arrangement worked out between Egypt and Israel, the Syrian-Israeli agreement provided for a United Nations buffer zone, other free zones, and troop and weapon limits for both sides. The new Israeli line on the Golan Heights was the same as the 1967 cease-fire line except that Israel gave up Kuneitra, which it had occupied since 1967.[12]

Kissinger's shuttle diplomacy won him the respect and admiration of most Arab leaders, including Sadat, Faisal, Hussein, and even al-Asad. "For the first time, I felt as if I was looking at the real face of the United States," Sadat later wrote about his initial meeting with Kissinger.[13] Although not always trusting the American secretary of state, the Arab leaders recognized—as Kissinger had always intended—that they could deal with Israel only through the United States.[14] Understanding the distrust the Arabs had for the friend of their enemy, the secretary of state assumed the role of honest broker, presenting the demands of each side in the Arab-Israeli dispute dispassionately, but with great sensitivity to their respective interests. Carrying out this responsibility brilliantly, he helped reduce the chances of war being resumed in the Middle East anytime soon.[15]

Kissinger also succeeded in getting the oil embargo imposed during the October War lifted. During his visit to Saudi Arabia in December, the secretary had discussed the embargo with King Faisal. The cutoff of oil from the Middle East was already beginning to have a calamitous impact on the United States. A barrel of oil was selling for as much as $17, and the Japanese, heavily dependent on Mideast crude, were bidding as high as $22.60 a barrel. Desperate shortages were being reported in parts of the United States, and panic buying had set in as businesses sought to stock up against future shortages. Fighting even broke out at gas stations as consumers waited as much as two hours in long lines to fill their tanks. A growing number of stations were posting signs saying they had no gas to sell. The oil shortage was also having a ripple effect on the entire economy, forcing up the price of most commodities. Almost overnight, America's confidence in its unlimited resources was shattered, and dire predictions were being heard about a permanent decline in the standard of living of most Americans.[16]

In his meeting with Kissinger, Faisal told the secretary of state that he was eager to end the embargo and to increase oil production. But he also said that since the oil weapon had been a joint Arab decision, he could not act without the approval of the other Arab states. Before he would agree to lift the embargo, he would also require that all of Jerusalem be returned to the Arabs.[17] But at a meeting in Algiers in February, a group of moderate Arab leaders, including Faisal, indicated they would lift the embargo against the United States after the conclusion of a Syrian-Israeli disengagement agreement. Later that month, Egyptian foreign minister Ismaili Fahmy and Saudi foreign minister Omar Saqqaf came to Washington where they too tried to link lifting the oil embargo to an agreement between Syria and Israel. But Kissinger resorted to his own linkage, indicating that he would not mediate an agreement unless the embargo was called off. In response, the Arab diplomats assured him that the embargo would be lifted by March. It was finally ended on 18 March.[18]

There is some question as to how significant the long-term effect of the oil embargo was on America's Middle East policy. According to the historian H. W. Brands, it had "relatively little effect" and may even have backfired. Brands contends that Americans, viewing the embargo as a form of Arab blackmail, became even more supportive of Israel than they had been before the October War.[19] There is considerable merit to this argument. Although the need for Middle East oil in the years after World War II had been an important concern for American policymakers, they had been more concerned with America's commitment to Israel and the growing Soviet influence in the region. After 1973, the United States continued to be Israel's staunchest ally, and limiting or eliminating Soviet influence throughout the world remained axiomatic to American foreign policy.

Following the October War and the oil embargo, however, the United States became far more understanding of the Arab position in the Arab-Israeli dispute and more critical of Israel. Concern about Soviet expansionism in the region also became less pronounced. At the same time, a new urgency developed in Washington about resolving the Arab-Israeli dispute; indeed, settling the dispute became one of the nation's highest priorities.

The prize of oil cannot alone explain these changes, which were, in any case, more shifts in emphasis than part of a fundamental reorientation of policy; that is, U.S. policy in the Middle East was never exclusively, or even primarily, a function of the region's vast oil resources. Arab success on the battlefield and the Soviets' diminished status in the Arab world after 1973 also greatly influenced American policymakers. After the October War, for example, Israel could no longer be regarded in quite the same way as it had been before the conflict; the war had exposed its military vulnerability. But by revealing for the first time just how dependent the United States had become on the region's vast oil supplies, the oil embargo was certainly important in altering the United States' approach to the Arab world.[20]

Because of his relentless pursuit of peace and his achievements in the Middle East (as well as a major breakthrough in America's relations with communist China), Kissinger became an international celebrity. His well-reported, glamorous lifestyle provided another dimension to a person whom many political observers regarded as one of the most brilliant and gifted diplomats in American history. He appeared on the cover of such magazines as *Time* and *U.S. News & World Report*. *Newsweek* even ran a cover story in which he was dressed as Superman and referred to as "Super K."[21] Indeed, his fame and celebrity, especially when contrasted with Nixon's public shame, made the president jealous of him. Determined to share Kissinger's glory and to strengthen his rapidly deteriorating political position at home by underscoring his own statesmanship, the president traveled in June to Egypt, Syria, Israel, and Jordan.[22]

Nixon's trip to the Middle East was symbolically significant since it was the first official visit by an American president to an Arab country in the region. It also generated considerable good will. In Egypt, the president was greeted by enthusiastic crowds estimated to number in the millions. Although his receptions in the other Arab countries were more subdued, they were also warm and friendly. Like Kissinger, the president was greatly impressed by al-Asad, whom he described as having "elements of genius." During his meeting with the Syrian leader, Nixon astonished some observers by seeming to suggest that Israel should withdraw from the Golan Heights. Following the meeting, Syria agreed to restore full diplomatic relations with the United States.[23]

Unfortunately for Nixon, his trip to the Middle East did little to help him at home. Two months after returning to Washington, he was forced to resign from office. His successor was Gerald Ford, who, prior to becoming Nixon's vice president in 1973, had been House minority leader. Ford was commonly perceived as knowing very little about foreign affairs. He later denied this charge, pointing out that, as a lawmaker on Capitol Hill, he had served on the House Defense Appropriations Committee for 20 years and had become well versed in foreign affairs. As vice president for eight months before entering the Oval Office, he had also had weekly foreign policy briefings from Kissinger and Kissinger's deputy, Brent Scowcroft.[24]

Nevertheless, Ford was far more interested in domestic issues than in foreign policy. Accordingly, he asked Kissinger, whom he much admired, to remain secretary of state. "It would be hard for me to overstate the admiration and affection I had for Henry," he later explained in his autobiography. "Our relationship began on solid, unshakable ground and grew even better with the passage of time." As a result, Kissinger enjoyed even greater latitude in formulating and carrying out foreign policy than he had under Nixon.[25]

The immediate problem facing the new administration was how to go beyond disengagement while also holding the Soviet Union at bay. As president, Ford was committed to Kissinger's strategy of limiting Soviet influence in the region even as the United States pursued its own step-by-step diplomacy. "Kissinger and I decided that we could accomplish more unilaterally by working with Israel and each of its Arab neighbors [than in working in concert with Moscow]," the president later commented.[26] But when he met with Andrei Gromyko, the Soviet foreign minister complained bitterly about Washington's exclusionary policy. Sadat and al-Asad also began to chafe over the limitations of the disengagement agreements, believing that Israel should make new territorial concessions.[27]

No Arab leader was more anxious or felt more pressure to have step-by-step diplomacy proceed than King Hussein of Jordan. Although he understood why Kissinger had given first priority to the disengagement of Arab and Israeli forces along two potentially explosive cease-fire lines, he felt it was imperative for Israel to return the West Bank to Jordan. Failure to do so, he feared, might mortally wound his government while strengthening a growing movement, even among moderate Arabs, to recognize the PLO as the legitimate representative of the Palestinian people. But the central dilemma of step-by-step diplomacy was precisely its failure to deal with the overarching issues Hussein felt needed to be addressed immediately.[28]

It was not that step-by-step diplomacy had been the wrong policy to pursue or that it lacked accomplishments. It had diminished the chances of war, and it had allowed the United States to outflank the Soviets in the Middle East. Moreover, there is no reason to believe that an alternative approach, such as employment of the Geneva process, would have been more successful in bringing peace to the Middle East. None of the principal actors in the Arab-Israeli dispute, including al-Asad, trusted the Soviets or were eager to have them return to the region in a major way. Sadat and King Faisal would have been almost as loath to sit at the bargaining table with the Soviets as with the Israelis. Even if they sat down together, it is unlikely that Israel and the Arab states would have been willing to make concessions they were not willing to make under step-by-step diplomacy.[29]

Nevertheless, step-by-step diplomacy amounted to diplomacy by avoidance; Kissinger had achieved his two disengagement agreements by purposely avoiding the issues that most divided Arabs and Israelis. Consequently, his shuttling between Mideast capitals may have done more long-term harm than short-term good, for it resulted in unrealistic expectations among some Arab leaders about Kissinger's ability to grapple with the essential issues of the Arab-Israeli dispute and to win concessions from Israel.

Step-by-step diplomacy had the additional consequence of deflecting American attention from Jordan. Along with Egypt, Jordan offered the most promise of reaching a lasting agreement with Israel. But because of its large Palestinian population, its government was more at risk over the Palestinian question and the occupied territories than the other Arab governments. Thus, King Hussein was anxious to start negotiations with Israel. In August, he flew to Washington, where President Ford and Secretary of State Kissinger reassured him that they would make the quest for a Jordanian-Israeli agreement one of their highest priorities.[30]

Resolution of the core issues in the Arab-Israeli dispute, however, was to be the final rather than the first step according to the strategy of step-by-step diplomacy. Almost certainly, Israel would oppose the concessions Hussein needed to satisfy Palestinians in his country and other Arab leaders. Failure to obtain an agreement would also embarrass Kissinger. The secretary of state decided, therefore, to concentrate on arranging a second disengagement agreement between Egypt and Israel, which would continue the momentum generated by the first agreement. Accordingly, he made only a halfhearted attempt to bring Jordan and Israel together. He began preliminary discussions with both countries but postponed further negotiations until after a meeting of Arab states at Rabat, Morocco, in October.[31]

The secretary of state thought that at the Rabat conference the Arab leaders would authorize Jordan to negotiate with Israel, but much to Kissinger's and Hussein's distress, the meeting instead recognized the PLO as the legitimate and sole representative of the Palestinian people and accorded it sovereignty over the West Bank; in return Saudi Arabia agreed to provide

Jordan $300 million in economic assistance. "I was distressed by the decision at Rabat," Hussein later told the journalist Edward F. Sheehan. "But I accepted it, and now Jordan cannot negotiate for the west bank unless authorized by the Arab leadership in council, including the P.L.O."[32]

Even Kissinger recognized the mistake he had made in waiting for the outcome of the Rabat summit, conceding that everyone "took the path of least resistance and brought about the worst possible outcome."[33] Moreover, his attempt to arrange a second disengagement agreement involving the further withdrawal of Israeli forces from the Sinai proved particularly difficult and frustrating. The negotiations were conducted over the better part of a year (from December 1974 to September 1975), were completely broken off during one period in March, led to unusually acrimonious exchanges between Kissinger, Ford, and Israeli leaders, and caused the administration at one point to reassess its entire policy toward the Middle East.[34]

The major issue in the negotiations concerned the Israeli demand for an Egyptian statement of nonbelligerency. In return, Israel was willing to make additional territorial concessions, including, by the end of the negotiations, the withdrawal of Israeli forces east of the Mitla and Giddi Passes and the return to Egypt of its oil fields at Abu Rudeis, which had been seized during the Six-Day War. Although Sadat was willing to negotiate with Israel on a number of issues and was even prepared to renounce the use of force against the Israelis, he insisted that Israel give up the two passes. He also remained adamantly opposed to issuing a statement of nonbelligerency, which would separate Egypt from the rest of the Arab world and turn it into an outcast among the Arab nations unwilling to end their war with Israel; largely for the same reason, Israel demanded such a statement.[35]

By March 1975 a new disengagement agreement appeared near. Israel no longer insisted on an Egyptian vow of nonbelligerency, accepting instead Sadat's pledge not to use force against Israel so long as the agreement was in effect. But without a statement of nonbelligerency, Israel refused to withdraw further than the crests of the Mitla and Giddi Passes.[36] Both Kissinger and President Ford were furious at Israel, holding it responsible for the impasse which followed. "We were in the position of becoming 'lawyers of Israel,' totally isolated and in a position to be blamed for lack of flexibility by Israel," the secretary of state told a cabinet meeting in March after returning from the Middle East.[37] The president felt the same way. Previously a strong supporter of the Jewish state, he had become increasingly annoyed at what he considered Israeli intransigence, which he believed could "radicalize the Arab countries" and result in a new Arab-Israeli conflict that "would almost certainly involve much heavier casualties and destruction than in 1973."[38]

Ford and Kissinger concluded that the time had come to make clear to the Israelis that the United States had options other than remaining tied to Israel. Following the breakdown of talks in March, therefore, the White House suspended negotiations on an Israeli request for $2.5 billion in military and financial assistance, including the purchase of F-15 fighter planes. It also undertook a complete reassessment of its policy in the Middle East.[39]

After conducting a month-long review of America's Middle East policy, during which some of the nation's most respected former diplomats and Middle East specialists were consulted, the White House concluded that there was no better alternative for the Middle East than to continue step-by-step diplomacy. Returning to Geneva and negotiating a comprehensive peace settlement based on guidelines worked out by the United States and the Soviet Union (the alternatives most frequently mentioned) were fraught with the same dangers that had led Kissinger to oppose multilateral talks and support step-by-step diplomacy in the first place.[40] The administration's "reassessment" of Mideast policy had also come under attack from Congress because it was directed against Israel. In the House, the Democratic leadership even withdrew a Senate resolution praising Kissinger's efforts in the Middle East. Both the House and the Senate raised questions about the administration's decision to sell Jordan HAWK and REDEYE anti-aircraft missile systems. The White House defended its action on the basis that "Jordan, alone among its neighbors, has no viable air defense system," but this point did not sit well with pro-Israeli lawmakers.[41]

Although the White House decided to maintain the policy it had been pursuing, months passed without much progress on a second Sinai agreement. At the beginning of June, President Ford met with Sadat in Salzburg, Austria, but while the talks were friendly, the Egyptian leader continued to insist on Israeli withdrawal from the Mitla and Giddi Passes and a return of the oil fields without offering the concession of a nonbelligerency statement. A week later, the president met with Israeli prime minister Yitzhak Rabin, who had replaced Golda Meir in 1974, but no progress was made toward resolving the issues holding up an agreement.[42]

Toward the end of the month, however, both Egypt and Israel began to show new flexibility. Sadat had too much invested in step-by-step diplomacy to see it fail, and his country was virtually destitute; he could hardly afford the chance of renewed war. The Israelis sensed an opportunity to bargain for increased American military aid. After two months of intense negotiations, during which Kissinger resumed shuttle diplomacy, at the beginning of September Egypt and Israel finally came to terms on a Sinai Two agreement, the main provisions of which called for Israel to give up the Mitla and Giddi Passes and return the oil fields at Abu Rudeis to Egypt. In return, Israel was allowed to maintain surveillance stations in the passes that would be manned by American and Israeli technicians. Egypt also agreed not to use force or impose naval blockades against Israel, to allow nonmilitary cargoes bound for Israel to pass through the Suez Canal, and to tone down anti-Israeli propaganda. A new buffer zone was also created between Egyptian and Israeli forces. Nothing was said about an Egyptian nonbelligerency statement.[43]

More significant than the agreement itself were the commitments the United States made to Israel in order to get it. Israel was promised more than $2 billion in American aid and a guarantee of oil to replace the production from the oil fields it was returning to Egypt. The United States also agreed to provide technicians for the monitoring stations inside the Giddi and Mitla Passes. Washington promised to consult with the Israelis if Israel was threatened by the Soviet Union, and the administration signed a separate agreement with Israel stating that it would not recognize or negotiate with the PLO until the PLO agreed to recognize Israel and abide by UN Resolutions 242 and 338. President Ford also sent a letter to Prime Minister Rabin in which he resolved "to continue to maintain Israel's defensive strength through the supply of advanced types of equipment, such as F-16 aircraft." Similarly, he promised that in the event of negotiations with Syria, the United States would "give great weight to Israel's position that any peace agreement with Syria must be predicated on Israel remaining on the Golan Heights."[44] In contrast to these side agreements with Israel, the United States merely promised Egypt to help it construct an early warning system in the buffer zone established by the agreement and to try to bring about further negotiations between Syria and Israel.[45]

Notwithstanding the concessions the United States made to Israel, the Sinai Two agreement represented another major achievement for Kissinger, who for months had labored against seemingly insurmountable obstacles. President Ford referred to the agreement as "one of the greatest diplomatic achievements of this century."[46] Yet it was also the last major accomplishment of step-by-step diplomacy. Internal divisions in the Arab world and continued Israeli refusal to give up the occupied territories or to deal with the Palestinian issue assured that step-by-step diplomacy, no matter how vigorously pursued by the United States, was no panacea for resolving the Arab-Israeli dispute and finally bringing peace to the Middle East.

One immediate result of the agreement was a return to the acrimony and hostility that had been the norm in Syria's relations with Egypt and the United States. Simply put, Syrian leader al-Asad felt abandoned by Cairo and betrayed by Washington. Relations between Cairo and Damascus had been cool since the October War. During the war al-Asad had expected Egypt to immediately move beyond the Bar-Lev Line after routing its Israeli defenders rather than to wait a week before trying to advance. Al-Asad believed that had Egypt moved more aggressively before the Israelis had a chance to mobilize their forces, the Syrian advance on the Golan Heights would not have been blunted and the war would have been won. In his view, Sadat had snatched defeat out of victory.[47]

As allies who together had planned and carried out a nearly successful attack against Israel, al-Asad expected Sadat to act in diplomatic concert with him. Instead, the Egyptian leader had unilaterally signed a second disengagement agreement with Israel. Worse, the agreement renounced the use of force, which in al-Asad's view amounted to perfidy. Likewise, it ignored completely Syrian claims to the Golan Heights. As for Washington, according to al-Asad, it had made promises it never intended to keep. "It seems to us now that the United States has three goals," al-Asad commented to Edward Sheehan following the signing of the Sinai Two agreement, "to strengthen Israel, to weaken the Arab nation, and to eliminate Soviet influence in the Middle East."[48] Other Arab leaders joined al-Asad in denouncing Egypt for giving up its struggle against Israel. As a result, Cairo became isolated in the Arab world.[49]

By this time, Syria had come under strong attack from neighboring Iraq because of its agreement with Israel over the Golan Heights. Although relations between the two countries had been poor since the 1966 split in the Ba'th Party, they had been patched up after al-Asad assumed power in 1970, and during the October War Iraqi forces had fought alongside the Syrians. But following the Golan Heights agreement, Iraq attacked Syria once more, making many of the same charges against al-Asad that the Syrian leader made against Sadat. Baghdad accused him of defeatism, cowardice, betrayal, and even treason. By the time of the Sinai Two agreement, relations between Damascus and Baghdad had become so bad that efforts by Saudi Arabia to mediate their differences failed, and both sides increased their forces along their common border.[50]

In the aftermath of the Sinai Two agreement, a new crisis also developed in Lebanon, which further divided the Arab world and underscored the fundamental weakness of step-by-step diplomacy based as it was on incremental gains rather than a comprehensive approach to peace. For two decades, the civil war that broke out in Lebanon in 1975 wreaked havoc with the Lebanese people and with diplomats seeking peace in the Middle East.

The irony was that since the short-lived civil war of 1958, when President Dwight Eisenhower had landed marines on the beaches of Beirut to prop up the anti-Nasserite government of Camille Chamoun, Lebanon had enjoyed a remarkable degree of peace and prosperity. Originally part of Greater Syria, Lebanon had been given its autonomy by the French after World War I. Following France's withdrawal from the Middle East after World War II, it had become an independent state. Although divided along religious, ethnic, and other lines, it seemed to stand out as an example of how people from vastly different backgrounds could live together harmoniously in a functioning democracy. Since 1943 an arrangement had existed by which the country's president was always a Maronite Christian and its prime minister a Sunni Muslim (the country's two predominant religious groups). This arrangement seemed to work well, and Lebanon prospered. Beirut became the commercial and financial center of the Middle East and one of the region's most cosmopolitan cities, with wide boulevards, handsome buildings, and fine restaurants.[51]

Surface appearances, however, masked underlying problems. Lebanon's parliament lacked a stable majority, and relations between the president, prime minister, and parliament grew increasingly strained. Political radicals, both Christian and Muslim, clashed with each other, with the government, and with other political groups bent on maintaining the status quo. The economy oscillated between high growth rates one year and stagnation the next. Economic distinctions between rich and poor became aggravated, and Beirut turned increasingly into a divided city with the eastern part largely Christian and relatively prosperous and the western part Muslim and poor. The influx of Palestinians into Lebanon following the Jordanian civil war added to the country's already considerable Palestinian population and to its growing social, political, and economic strains. Moreover, Palestinian militants acted independently of the state, much as they had done in Jordan. Palestinian refugee camps in southern Lebanon were used as bases from which to attack Israel. Israel responded by launching retaliatory raids into southern Lebanon.[52]

Lebanon's central government was incapable of dealing with these new developments. As a nation that the political scientist Itamar Rabinovich has rightly described as actually "a confederation of protonational communities, each of which claimed the ultimate allegiance of its members," Lebanon functioned as long as there was an interest among the different communities in maintaining the confederation. But by 1975 such a common interest no longer existed. Lebanon disintegrated, and Beirut became a battleground for the various Christians and Palestinian factions.[53]

Lebanon's disintegration invited intervention by neighboring Syria. As part of Greater Syria, Lebanon had strong historic, geographic, and familial ties to Syria that gave the Syrians a special stake in the country. Syrian support for Palestinian guerrillas in Lebanon was a major reason for the country's unraveling in the first place. Damascus feared an Israeli military move into Lebanon should the government completely collapse and Palestinian militants seize control of all or part of Lebanon. In that case, Syria's own claims as a regional power and its quest for leadership within the Arab world would also be at risk.[54]

Opposed to Lebanon's dissolution, al-Asad decided to intervene in the Lebanese civil war. In January he sent a Palestinian force based in Syria into the country in an effort to pressure the government into reforming itself. In making his decision, the Syrian leader anticipated a limited commitment of short duration, but as one authority on the intervention, Naomi Joy Weinberger, later commented, "Syria fell into the same trap as most interveners in miscalculating the potential costs of its commitment." Despite Syrian pressure, the Lebanese government failed to implement the changes that would have been necessary—if it were possible at all—to restore its legitimacy. In March, the Lebanese army fell apart.[55]

But al-Asad was no more successful in controlling the Palestinian militants, who welcomed the disintegration of the country, than he was in controlling the government. As the political situation in Lebanon deteriorated and he sought to prevent its irredeemable collapse, the Palestinian forces he had sent into Lebanon in January found themselves fighting Palestinians based in Lebanon, including his traditional ally, the PLO. Al-Asad's Palestinian forces met such heavy resistance that in May he committed a powerful Syrian column to the fighting.[56]

In order to prevent a Palestinian victory and Lebanon's dissolution, the United States gave its tacit approval to the Syrian intervention. In a meeting with Arab-American leaders in June, Secretary of State Kissinger explained the dilemma posed by the Palestinian problem in Lebanon. "The Lebanese Government," Kissinger remarked, "is trying to prevent Lebanon from becoming a battle-ground, but with 300,000 Palestinians in Lebanon and continuing raids across the border, it is impossible." The White House was persuaded that without Syria's intervention, Lebanon would have been taken over by "Lebanese left-wing forces . . . supported by the PLO and rejectionist Palestinians." Although the United States advised Damascus against sending regular army units into Lebanon, it privately agreed to a limited Syrian intervention. Largely for the same reasons, Israel did likewise, even though it warned Syria that it would move into Southern Lebanon if Syrian regulars intervened.[57]

Thus, by a curious twist of events, Syrian president al-Asad found himself in the awkward position of backing a government committed to maintaining the status quo against Palestinians whose cause he supposedly championed. He also found himself being tacitly supported by one country he distrusted (the United States) and another he had vowed to destroy (Israel). At the same time, he incurred the wrath of Arab public opinion and other Arab leaders for being on the wrong side in the Lebanese civil war. Syria's intervention therefore made for strange bedfellows, but then strange bedfellows were not atypical in Middle East politics.

By midsummer, the Syrian forces were able to turn the tide of battle in their favor. But the war in Lebanon so paralyzed the Arab world that Saudi Arabia sought to find a diplomatic solution to this internecine Arab conflict. By this time, Riyadh had joined most other Arab states in concluding that step-by-step diplomacy had not been productive or beneficial for them. Aware of pending elections in the United States, Saudi Arabia argued that the time had come to restore Arab unity so that Arab leaders would be in a stronger position to pressure the new administration in Washington into pursuing an approach to the Arab-Israeli dispute that was more favorable to the Arabs. The Saudis, therefore, convened a meeting of Arab leaders in October to resolve their differences and to find a peaceful solution to the Lebanese civil war. In response to pressure from Saudi Arabia, on whom

Syria was heavily dependent financially, al-Asad agreed to attend the Riyadh summit.[58]

The summit represented a significant victory for al-Asad. The leaders agreed to a cease-fire. But the armistice was to be maintained by a force of 30,000 troops composed mostly of Syrian forces. Although sporadic fighting continued for several weeks after the Riyadh meeting, a semblance of peace and order was restored to Lebanon. In reality, though, Lebanon had ceased to function as a state. The government's authority was limited to a small part of Beirut. Most of the country was controlled by rival Christian and Palestinian militias. Although Israel had been willing to allow Syria to end the Lebanese civil war to prevent Lebanon from being controlled by the Palestinians, it was not prepared to have a permanent Syrian and Palestinian presence on its northern border. For that reason, it had already begun to supply arms and equipment to Christian militias in southern Lebanon, with whom it was also developing a close political relationship.[59]

By the time Gerald Ford left office in January 1977 after losing his bid for reelection, step-by-step diplomacy had been discredited as a process for bringing peace to the Middle East. Despite some brilliant initial successes, it had failed to bring together in lasting fashion the major players in the Arab-Israeli dispute. Although there had been some success in Egyptian-Israeli negotiations, the chances of a permanent peace agreement between them still seemed remote. Even more farfetched was the likelihood of an agreement between Israel and its other Arab neighbors. Making matters worse was the political vacuum created by Lebanon's disintegration. As long as Syria remained in Lebanon and the Palestinians continued to use Lebanon as a base to carry out operations against Israel, Lebanon would be a tinder box ready to burst into flames.[60]

Step-by-step diplomacy had been predicated on avoiding the crucial issues of the Arab-Israeli dispute until the last stage in the negotiating process. "The step-by-step [approach] is more manageable [than an overall approach]," Kissinger explained in 1975, "since it avoids the toughest issues at the beginning, breaking them up into manageable segments, and takes away from the extremists the opportunity to break up peace efforts."[61] But the region's events were so volatile it was nearly impossible to choreograph the diplomacy of avoidance in the manner needed to assure its success, no matter how brilliantly it was pursued by Kissinger. Perhaps predictably then, Jimmy Carter took office intent on finding a comprehensive solution to the Middle East crisis, much as William Rogers had advocated before Kissinger had replaced him as secretary of state in 1971.

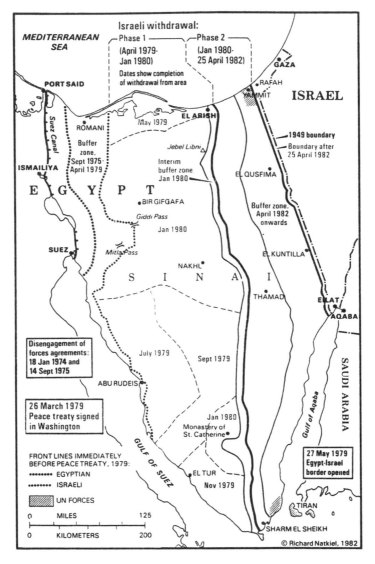

Israeli withdrawal from the Sinai
Courtesy Richard Natkiel

chapter 7

CARTER AND THE CAMP DAVID ACCORDS: 1977–1981

From the time Jimmy Carter took office in 1977, he made set-tling the Arab-Israeli dispute one of his highest priorities. During the 1976 presidential campaign, he had been warned by his advisers not to get involved in what they regarded as the Middle East quagmire. But as he later wrote, his concern about Israeli security, the rights of Palestinians, the possibility of Soviet influence in the region, and the West's dependence on Arab oil led him to ignore their counsel.[1]

Carter's campaign statements on the region had been unexceptional. Very early in his candidacy, he had urged Israel to withdraw from most of the occupied territories, and he had later endorsed the establishment of a Palestinian state on the West Bank. But in an obvious effort to court the Jewish vote, he had increasingly emphasized the importance of strengthening ties with Israel and had come out in support of Israel's demands for "defensible borders," a term generally understood to mean continued occupation of the areas taken in 1967. He had also stated that he would not recognize the PLO or "other government entities representing the Palestinians" until he was convinced that they acknowledged Israel's right to exist.[2]

Once in office, Carter decided to wield American influence to resolve the Arab-Israeli conflict even if it meant placing himself at odds with Israeli leaders and the American Jewish community. Rejecting the step-by-step approach pursued by former secretary of state Henry Kissinger, the president preferred to achieve a comprehensive settlement by reconvening the 1973 Geneva conference. That strategy was risky. First, there were logistical problems; it was doubtful that such a gathering could be arranged by year's end. In the meantime, moderate Arabs might not be able to withstand pressure from more radical groups to renew military action against Israel. Second,

Egypt would want to send its own delegation to Geneva in order to negotiate bilaterally with Israel, while its arch rival, Syria, would hold out for a single Arab delegation in order to keep Egypt from reaching a separate agreement with the Israelis. But the most intractable problem concerned the status of the PLO at a Geneva conference. Would the PLO try to send its own delegation to Geneva, or would it accept membership in a pan-Arab delegation? More to the point, would Israel permit PLO representation under any circumstances? To explore these issues and to prepare the groundwork for a Geneva conference, President Carter sent his secretary of state, Cyrus Vance, in February 1977 to the Middle East.[3]

The new president had chosen Vance as his secretary of state because he wanted a good diplomat and administrator in that position. A former secretary of the army and deputy secretary of defense under Presidents Kennedy and Johnson, Vance would transact the nation's business abroad. He was also expected to be a tough and competent manager and a good team player. But from the time he took office, Carter intended to take charge of his own foreign policy. Major foreign policy decisions would originate from the Oval Office, not the Department of State, which, as a Washington outsider, the president distrusted. Assisting the president would be his National Security Adviser, former Columbia professor Zbigniew Brzezinski, whom the president regarded as a conceptualizer and first-rate thinker.[4]

Vance and Carter were encouraged by the reception the secretary of state received during his trip to the Middle East, especially from Egyptian president Anwar Sadat. According to Vance, Sadat "showed more flexibility on the question of peace" than any other Arab leader he met. But even Syrian president al-Asad, whom Vance described as "the hardest" of the Arab leaders, appeared willing to make some compromises, indicating, for example, that he might be prepared to accept something less than full autonomy for the Palestinians. As for Israel, Prime Minister Yitzhak Rabin said his country might compromise on borders (although it would never return to the pre-1967 lines). He even suggested that Israel might tolerate the presence of Palestinians at a Geneva conference if they came as part of the Jordanian delegation. Most importantly, every leader Vance met endorsed the goal of holding a meeting at Geneva before the end of 1977.[5]

The optimism of February soon faded, however. In March, Rabin came to Washington, the first of the Mideast heads of state to call on Carter. Over the next three months, other Mideast leaders, including Sadat, Crown Prince Fahd of Saudi Arabia (who had assumed an administrative role after King Faisal was assassinated in 1975), and King Hussein of Jordan visited the White House. In May, Carter flew from London, where he had been attending an economic summit, to Geneva in order to meet al-Asad. But these talks were mostly unproductive. Contrary to what he had indicated earlier, Rabin now told the president that he would oppose a Geneva conference if the PLO or other Palestinian representatives were present. He also stated that he would not agree to total withdrawal from the West Bank or Golan Heights or permit the establishment of an independent state on the West Bank. Discussions with other Mideast leaders were not much more fruitful. Although Carter was clearly charmed by Sadat's good-natured friendliness and had great admiration for him, even their talks produced no significant breakthrough.[6]

Meanwhile, relations with Israel began to sour. Israeli leaders reacted angrily to remarks Carter made on several occasions in favor of some form of Palestinian homeland or entity, and they were afraid the president was trying to impose his own peace settlement on the Middle East. With a May election approaching, they were also worried that Carter's meeting with al-Asad would play into the hands of the hard-line Likud Party headed by Menachem Begin. As they feared, on 23 May Israelis gave the Likud Party a stunning victory in the national elections.[7]

On 19 July, Prime Minister Begin arrived in Washington for meetings with the president. Carter had been shocked to learn that Begin would be Israel's new leader. A hard-liner whom *Time* labeled a "superhawk," Begin referred to the West Bank and Gaza Strip as "liberated territories, part of the land of Israel" and even called the West Bank by its biblical names of "Judea and Samaria."[8] In the president's view, Begin's election did not bode well for the peace process. But Carter was pleasantly surprised by his two days of talks with the Israeli leader. Begin proved to be an intelligent, courteous, and even charming figure, who listened attentively both to the president's reassurances that he would not impose a peace plan on Israel and to his objections about the building of Israeli settlements in the occupied territories. In response, the prime minister expressed his desire for a Geneva conference. He also stressed that all issues were negotiable at Geneva and that the deliberations should be based on United Nations Resolutions 242 and 338 calling for the withdrawal of Israeli troops from the occupied territories in return for Arab recognition of the state of Israel.[9]

While the Carter-Begin talks did much to dispel the president's fears about Begin's inflexibility, major differences still existed between the Israeli prime minister and the American president. Begin interpreted UN Resolutions 242 and 338 to mean withdrawal of Israeli forces from "some" occupied territories; Carter construed the resolutions to mean from "all" the territories. Under no circumstances would Begin give up the West Bank, parlay with the PLO, begin talks in Geneva with a combined Arab-Palestinian delegation, agree to a Palestinian homeland, or stop the construction of Israeli settlements in the occupied territories. Soon after returning to Israel, the prime minister announced plans for a large number of new settlements on the West Bank. Despite Carter's best efforts, his talks with Begin had failed to make any progress toward resolving the Mideast crisis.[10]

But Carter did not allow Begin's actions to interfere with his goal of reconvening the Geneva conference on the Middle East, which had been dormant since 1973. On 19 September, Israeli foreign minister Moshe Dayan met with President Carter and Secretary Vance in the Oval Office and promised that Israel would delay settlements in the occupied territories for at least a year. Dayan even indicated that Israel might accept Palestinians at Geneva as part of a pan-Arab delegation. Leaving the White House after the meeting, Dayan said a Geneva meeting could be set up by year's end.[11]

On 1 October, however, the administration took a step that even the secretary of state later acknowledged was counterproductive. It issued a joint communique with the Soviet Union formally calling for a new Geneva conference. Vance believed that as one of the cosponsors of the conference, the Soviets had to be involved in summoning the meeting and establishing the agenda. But the joint statement produced a storm of protest in Israel and in the United States.[12]

Critics of the communique objected to it on three grounds. Most importantly, they protested a reference in the statement to "the legitimate rights of the Palestinian people." Since these were code words used by the PLO to justify their struggle against Israel, Washington had in the past always referred to Palestinian "interests" rather than "rights." Second, the communique made no reference to UN Resolution 242 recognizing Israel's right to exist in secure borders. Finally, it seemed to invite the Soviet Union, which had been thrown out of the Middle East in 1973, back into the region, something that most Americans, as well as Israelis, were anxious to prevent.[13]

As a result, the Geneva meeting never took place. The largest stumbling block remained PLO representation. Israel would not attend a Geneva meeting with the PLO; Syria would not go without it. As the movement toward Geneva became deadlocked once more, President Carter and Egyptian president Sadat grew increasingly frustrated. On 21 October, Carter wrote Sadat a personal letter asking the Egyptian leader for help. On 2 November, Sadat replied by proposing a conference in East Jerusalem that would be attended by the disputants and permanent members of the UN Security Council—an idea Carter believed was "doomed to failure."[14]

Much to Carter's surprise, when he heard from Sadat the next time, in the second week in November, the Egyptian president informed him he would be going to Israel. Earlier Sadat had let Begin know, through Secretary Vance, that he was eager to meet with the Israeli leader, and Begin had invited him to come to Jerusalem. Distressed by the lengthy and tedious negotiations over calling a Geneva conference and doubting the likely success of such a gathering, the Egyptian leader accepted, hoping it might break the stalemate.[15]

Sadat's dramatic three-day trip to Jerusalem and his address to the Knesset drew worldwide attention. Thousands of Israelis, many waving Egyptian flags, turned out to welcome their former enemy. In his hour-long speech to the Knesset, Sadat captured the poignancy of the moment when he said he had come to Israel not to sign a peace treaty but to break down "the barriers of suspicion, fear, illusion, and misrepresentation" that for so many years had kept his country and Israel from even talking about peace.[16] Sadat's actions, however, incurred the wrath of much of the Arab world. As Carter and Vance had feared, Sadat's visit to Israel also ended whatever likelihood remained of a Geneva meeting. Returning home, the Egyptian president invited "all the parties to the [Mideast] conflict" to Cairo in order "to prepare for a Geneva conference." But not one of the Arab states—not even such moderate states as Tunisia, Morocco, the Sudan, or Saudi Arabia—came to Cairo. Instead, representatives from such anti-Sadat nations as Iraq, Algeria, and Libya gathered in Tripoli, where they formed a "rejectionist" front and condemned the Egyptian leader.[17]

Sadat responded by announcing that he would negotiate alone if other Arab leaders did not join him. To bolster his position in the Arab world, he sent Begin an urgent message asking him to make some positive statement on the Palestinian question and the occupied territories. The Israeli leader's reply was disappointing. Instead of communicating directly with Sadat, Begin came to Washington with an offer to withdraw Israeli forces from the Sinai in two stages over a three- to five-year period. He also proposed granting Palestinians home rule in the West Bank and Gaza Strip for a five-year period, during which Israel would "hold in abeyance" its claim to sovereignty over the region. Israel would retain responsibility for public order and the right of military access throughout this time. After five years, Israel would decide whether to continue or modify the arrangement.[18]

Carter and Vance found the plan not only unacceptable but also dangerous. "I expressed my concern that his proposal was inadequate and that the inadequacy of it might cause the downfall of Sadat," the president recorded in his diary after conferring with Begin. He and Secretary Vance believed Begin's proposal for home rule was an unsatisfactory substitute for Israeli withdrawal and Palestinian self-determination. They were also disturbed that there was no role provided for the Arab states and no clear indication whether Palestinian refugees and exiles would be allowed to return to their former homes. Finally, they wanted the five years proposed by Begin to be a transition period leading to a plebiscite of Palestinians living on the West Bank and Gaza and a peace treaty between the Palestinians and Israel—in contrast to Begin's proposal that the term be an experiment in autonomy, which, if successful, might be made permanent.[19]

On the eve of the new year, therefore, fundamental differences remained between Egypt and Israel. As if to underscore the gap separating the two countries, talks between Begin and Sadat that began on Christmas Day were unproductive. Meeting with their advisers at the Egyptian town of Ismailia near the Suez Canal, Begin and Sadat could not agree on anything other than forming two committees to discuss political and military matters. Most of their time was spent arguing over Sadat's demands that Israel leave the occupied territories and grant Palestinian self-determination.[20]

In the meantime, Carter embarked on a nine-day trip at the end of December that included visits to Saudi Arabia, Egypt, and Iran (where he met with Jordan's King Hussein). His conversations with Arab leaders offered little reason for optimism. Sadat was still angry that Begin had not been more forthcoming during their recent talks. Although Carter had hoped to involve Hussein in the peace process begun by Sadat, the king made it clear he would not participate in negotiations until Israel withdrew from the occupied lands and agreed to Palestinian autonomy. The Saudis basically concurred.[21]

Israel also pursued a hard line. In an interview, Israeli prime minister Begin revealed how distant a Mideast accord truly was. When asked if there were any conditions under which Israel could accept Palestinian self-determination, he replied there were not. When questioned about the new Israeli settlements on the West Bank and Sinai Peninsula, he answered by referring to the "rights of Jews to acquire land and settle in Judea, Samaria, and Gaza."[22]

The administration concluded that the United States needed to become more involved in the negotiating process if Sadat's peace initiative was to succeed. Accordingly, the president decided to invite the Egyptian and Israeli leaders to Washington. Sadat would come first, so that Carter could reaffirm his support for Sadat's overtures and develop a common strategy for dealing with Israel's intransigence. This would give the appearance that the administration was siding with Egypt against Israel, but as Brzezinski later commented, "the bilateral Egyptian-Israeli talks were leading nowhere. Sadat now needed American help desperately in order to obtain an accommodation."[23]

The Egyptian president arrived in the United States on 3 February. In his discussions with Carter, he criticized Begin's "ridiculous" position regarding Israeli settlements in the Sinai and Palestinian self-determination, and he repeated his conviction that the Israeli prime minister did not want peace. He also expressed his disappointment that Washington was not playing a more instrumental role as mediator. Convinced that his initiative would collapse unless the United States compelled Israel to make concessions, he wanted Washington to resume its central place in negotiating a Mideast peace.[24]

Carter agreed, but little progress was made over the next three months in obtaining an agreement between Israel and Egypt, much less in arriving at a comprehensive settlement. Indeed, as weeks passed without success Carter became less concerned about a broad accord and more interested in a separate treaty between Egypt and Israel. But even this more limited objective began to seem beyond reach, partly because of worsening relations between Jerusalem and Washington. On 8 February, the day Sadat left the United States, Carter held a briefing for American Jewish leaders in which he accused Israel of being the biggest obstacle to a Mideast peace because of its position on the settlements issue. On the same day, Secretary of State Vance stated in a press conference that Israeli settlements in the Sinai were illegal, diminished the chances for peace, and should be dismantled. Prime Minister Begin lashed out at the administration, accusing it of taking sides against Israel. When he learned that the White House had decided to sell fighter planes to Saudi Arabia and Egypt (part of a deal that also included the sale of jet fighters to Israel), he blasted the proposal as a threat to Israel's national security.[25]

The Israeli leader arrived in the United States for his visit with Carter on 20 March. Zbigniew Brzezinski described the president's two days of talks with the Israeli leader as "generally unpleasant."[26] The president was clearly in a fighting mood. Although he had been appalled by a PLO attack along the Israeli coast on 11 March in which 35 people were killed, he told Begin that Israel had overreacted: its retaliatory invasion of southern Lebanon had left more than 1,000 dead and 100,000 homeless. He also insisted that under UN Resolution 242, Israel would have to remove its forces from the occupied lands, including the West Bank. After five years, during which neither Israel nor Jordan would lay claim to the West Bank, the Palestinians living there would then have the right to decide for themselves whether to affiliate with Israel or Jordan or to continue under the so-called interim government.[27]

The president tried to reassure Begin that the United States would not permit the establishment of an independent Palestinian state on the West Bank. He also endorsed a modification of the West Bank's western boundary in order to give Israel greater security. But the Israeli prime minister refused to soften his stance on any issue he discussed with Carter. The president was so frustrated and angered by his talks with Begin that, after they were over, he did not even walk the Israeli leader to his waiting limousine. Meeting with congressional leaders, Carter stated that negotiations had reached an impasse, for which Begin was responsible.[28]

The administration's strategy for a Mideast settlement seemed in ruins. It had been based on close collaboration with Sadat and separate negotiations with Begin, in the hope that Israel would soften its position on the occupied territories. The result was not compromise but impasse. Over the first six months of 1978, Carter tried to restart the negotiations, but to no avail. Begin refused to guarantee the residents of the West Bank and Gaza eventual autonomy even after Sadat agreed to allow Israel to maintain security forces in these territories during a transitional period. The Israeli leader's position had not altered one dot since December: limited home rule for the West Bank and Gaza Strip for three to five years, after which Israel would review the arrangement and evaluate how it was working.[29]

Afraid of renewed conflict in the Middle East, Carter sought to bridge the chasm between Egypt and Israel. At the beginning of July, Vice President Walter Mondale visited Israel and traveled to Alexandria where he conferred with Sadat. Both Begin and Sadat agreed to a personal request from Carter to send their foreign ministers to London later that month for a meeting arranged and presided over by Vance. But the London session did not produce any concrete proposal for resolving the core issues separating Israel and Egypt. Then a secret meeting in Vienna between Sadat, Shimon Peres (the leader of Israel's opposition Labor Party), and Israeli defense minister Ezer Weizman backfired. Although Begin had given his approval for the discussions, the Israeli cabinet censured Peres and Weizman for allegedly negotiating without authority and for using the peace process to further their own ambitions. Sadat was angry and retaliated by ordering out of Egypt the Israeli military mission that had remained there since official talks had been broken off in February.[30]

For Vance and his staff, the London episode confirmed that the United States would have to change its role in the search for a Mideast accord. "We felt that there was no use in continuing to try to mediate [an] Egyptian-Israeli agreement on the general principles of peace," the secretary later remarked. Instead Vance began to think in terms of an American proposal for a comprehensive settlement that would include an Egyptian-Israeli peace and an autonomy plan for the West Bank.[31]

After Sadat's expulsion of the Israeli mission, Vance and President Carter decided that the secretary of state should go to the Middle East once more. Despite a vitriolic public exchange between Sadat and Begin, Sadat still seemed anxious to continue the negotiating process. "I think we have now reached important and crucial crossroads, and that it would be useful at this juncture, to ponder over what has happened since my visit to Jerusalem," he wrote Carter on 26 July.[32] Faced with a cabinet sharply divided over the occupied territories, Begin also seemed to welcome a new American initiative. Although the president and Vance originally conceived of Vance's Mideast trip as a "rescue mission" to breathe new life into the negotiations, Carter decided to make the bold move of inviting both Begin and Sadat to a summit at Camp David. The president had concluded that the only way an agreement between Israel and Egypt could be reached was to bring the principals together for as long as it took to work out their differences. Once that was achieved, the door would be open to a general Mideast settlement.[33]

The Camp David summit was a gamble for the president. Although Begin and Sadat accepted Carter's invitation almost immediately, the chances were that they would not see eye to eye on anything. Failure of the Camp David talks would only add to the growing public perception of an ineffectual president. In addition, the meeting violated a cardinal rule of summitry. Heads of state did not come together until after agreements had been worked out at lower levels of government, so that summits were largely ceremonial.

Vance and Brzezinski thought the president's main task should be to persuade Begin to make concessions on the Palestinian question, but Carter believed that he should concentrate on achieving an Egyptian-Israeli accord without linking it to progress on this perennial stumbling block. Consequently, he directed the American team accompanying him at Camp

David to "assume as our immediate ambition" a peace agreement between Egypt and Israel.[34]

Sadat and Begin arrived at Camp David on 5 September and were housed in separate cottages. The talks got off to an inauspicious start.[35] There was little chemistry between Carter and Begin, whom the president described as rigid, unimaginative, and more concerned with particulars than with the larger picture of a Middle East settlement. Even his first session with his good friend Sadat did not go well, as Carter was disappointed by Sadat's insistence that no agreement was possible until Israel withdrew from all the occupied lands.

In coming to Camp David, the Egyptian leader was at a disadvantage. Although Begin could leave the summit at any time without penalty, the Egyptian leader had incurred the wrath of the other Arab nations and risked his own political future by his peace initiative; he could not return home empty-handed. He hoped that Carter could force Begin into easing Israeli demands. But Sadat underestimated the Israeli leader's ability to resist pressure even in face-to-face talks with the American president. Because Begin was a stickler for detail, he was also far less ready to compromise on specific issues than Sadat, who became bored by particulars and preferred to deal in more general terms.[36]

At first, the president met with the two leaders together. But because they did not get along, he soon began conferring with them separately, thinking he might be able to break down the mistrust and animosity that had developed between them. But no progress was made until 12 September, when Carter presented Sadat with a four-page proposal for an Egyptian-Israeli peace treaty, the key sentence of which provided for restoration of "full Egyptian sovereignty . . . in the Sinai." The Egyptian leader considered the draft largely acceptable, but the next day, Begin flatly rejected it and stated that he would never agree to the removal of Israeli settlements from the Sinai.

The critical moment in the summit had arrived. Carter had brought Begin and Sadat to the pastoral surroundings of Camp David with the idea that the two key leaders would come to trust and work with each other. Instead, they were not even on speaking terms. Then Sadat announced on 15 September that he was preparing to leave immediately for Egypt. Informed that the Egyptian delegation to Camp David was already packing its bags, Carter hurried to Sadat's cottage and warned him that the American people would hold the Egyptian leader responsible for the failure of the summit. Relations between the United States and Egypt would deteriorate, peacekeeping efforts would end, and his own administration would be discredited. Shaken by the force of Carter's argument, Sadat agreed to continue the negotiations.

Events then moved quickly. Israeli defense minister Weizman raised the possibility that Israel might give up its airfields in the Sinai if the United

States would help build new airfields in the Negev Desert. The president indicated he would go along with such a deal provided Israel relinquished its settlements in the Sinai. Under tremendous pressure from even his own cabinet, Begin relented. On 17 September, during the twelfth day of negotiations, he told Carter that within two weeks he would have the Knesset vote on whether or not the settlements should be removed and that he would abide by its decision. Carter persuaded Sadat to accept this arrangement. The major obstacle to a Sinai agreement had now been removed.

Less successful were concurrent negotiations on the other disputed issues, most notably the Palestinian problem and the Israeli occupation of the West Bank and Gaza. Egypt wanted an Israeli commitment to withdraw from the territories by a specified date and to grant the Palestinians in the West Bank and Gaza autonomy; Begin refused. Instead, he and Sadat finessed the matter by agreeing to an ambiguous "framework for peace," which Carter had prepared a week earlier when the summit seemed about to collapse. This second accord provided for a transitional period of no more than five years during which Egypt, Israel, and Jordan would determine the final status of the territories but assure the inhabitants of the two areas "full autonomy" and a "self-governing authority." Their negotiations would also be predicated on the principles of UN Resolution 242—though the pact did not spell out what that actually meant.

After 13 days, Carter was able to announce publicly that a consensus had been reached at Camp David calling for the signing of a peace treaty between Egypt and Israel and providing the basis for a Mideast settlement—a prize that had eluded peacemakers for more than 30 years. The signing of the Camp David Accords at a White House ceremony carried by all the major television networks represented the high point of the Carter presidency. The summit was widely hailed as a shining triumph, and Carter was singled out for plaudits.

But even as the president was being acclaimed, some observers expressed reservations about the pacts. Several commentators pointed out that nothing was said in the "framework for peace" about the building of new Israeli settlements on the West Bank and Gaza. In addition, the Camp David agreements assumed that Jordan and the Palestinians living in the occupied lands would participate in the negotiations. Yet King Hussein had stated several times that he would not enter the peace process until Israel returned the West Bank and East Jerusalem, a condition the Israelis would never accept.[37] Furthermore, the two accords signed at Camp David were replete with ambiguous terms and provisions, which would make future talks extremely difficult. For example, the negotiators were expected to consider "resolution of the Palestinian problem, in all its aspects," as well as "other outstanding issues" concerning the West Bank and Gaza. But the documents did not specify what these other "aspects" or "outstanding issues" were.[38]

In fairness to Carter, he had clearly accomplished his primary purpose at Camp David: to establish a basis for future negotiations. The Egyptian-Israeli accord was possible precisely because it did gloss over many of the most acrimonious issues blocking peace in the Middle East. Once these two enemies had agreed to a conciliatory framework, Carter hoped the other moderate Arab nations, particularly Saudi Arabia, would join the peace process. When that happened, he believed, the remaining obstacles to a Mideast settlement could be resolved. Perhaps the president was naive to think peace was attainable in that troubled region, but what better alternative was there?

Yet the Camp David agreements were dangerously vague and were based almost as much on faith as on a hard assessment of Mideast politics. By papering over key differences between Egypt and Israel, they set up a diplomatic minefield that could very well explode in Carter's face. Amity required that the Arabs and Israelis proceed with more care and goodwill than they had previously displayed, but beyond the jubilation of the moment, there was hardly any reason to expect such a change in behavior. Despite their public professions, Sadat and his chief aides were keenly disappointed by the results of Camp David. Foreign Minister Mohamed Ibrahim Kamel, who had opposed going to Camp David, even resigned from office. Egypt had obtained an Israeli commitment to withdraw from the Sinai and surrender its rich oil fields, but Israel had remained silent about the other occupied territories and the Palestinians. Sadat returned to Egypt, therefore, with little that would entice other Arab leaders to a conference table with Israel.[39]

By December, the fragility of the Camp David Accords became apparent. Although Egyptian and Israeli negotiators had set 17 December as the deadline for a peace agreement between their two nations, talks soured very quickly after Israel announced the construction of new settlements on the West Bank. In an effort to meet the target date, Secretary Vance traveled to the Middle East and engaged in six days of shuttle diplomacy between Cairo and Jerusalem. But nothing came of this activity; in fact, Israeli leaders accused the White House of taking Egypt's side in the negotiations.[40]

By early 1979, the Mideast peace process had broken down completely. In a lengthy memorandum to Carter, his senior adviser, Hamilton Jordan, described the depression enveloping the White House as a result of the Middle East stalemate. "Not only have the Israeli-Egyptian negotiations taken much of our time, energy, and resources," he told the president, "the recent growing concern that all that has been accomplished might somehow be lost has had a very negative effect on the attitude and morale of our foreign policy team."[41]

Yet as Carter realized, Egypt and Israel remained anxious to come to terms. Both Begin and Sadat understood that failure to sign a peace treaty would strengthen the hands of the hard-line Arab states (Syria, Iraq, and

Libya) that had denounced the Camp David agreements. The problem was how to get both sides talking again. The president considered another summit, but he and Vance concluded that the risks of failure were too great. Instead, they held a series of high-level talks at Camp David with Egyptian foreign minister Mustapha Khalil and Israeli foreign minister Moshe Dayan. When these efforts also proved unproductive, Carter invited Begin to the United States for further negotiations.[42]

The first session between the two leaders was so acrimonious that the president canceled a second one scheduled for that afternoon. But the next day, the atmosphere improved considerably. Perhaps chastened by the hasty impasse, the Israeli leader became less confrontational and more flexible on several key points. One issue was whether an Egyptian-Israeli peace treaty would take precedence over defense agreements Egypt had with other Arab nations. The Israelis held it would, Egypt maintained it would not. Carter resolved the problem by stipulating in the draft treaty that the agreements would not supersede Egypt's other treaties nor would these other agreements supersede the Egyptian-Israeli pact.[43]

The Israeli leader also seemed amenable to language proposed by Carter that would once more skirt the critical issue of linkage between a treaty and Palestinian autonomy. The formula Carter suggested implied linkage by stating that the treaty was part of the "framework for a comprehensive peace treaty signed at Camp David." Begin also indicated a willingness to go along with ambiguous phrasing recommended by the president calling for a "goal" rather than a "timetable" of 12 months for arriving at an agreement on Palestinian autonomy but leaving unanswered what would happen if the "goal" was not achieved. After consulting his cabinet, Begin informed Carter than the proposals were acceptable to Israel. Now the president had to sell them to Sadat.[44]

To finalize a pact, Carter visited Egypt and Israel at the end of March 1979. After further discussions with Sadat and Begin, Carter announced the conclusion of an Egyptian-Israeli peace treaty. Both sides had compromised. Egypt dropped its insistence on stationing personnel in the Gaza Strip preliminary to agreement on the fate of Palestine and also accepted the Israeli wording on a timetable for Palestinian autonomy. Israel gave up the demand that Cairo guarantee to sell Israel oil from the Sinai fields being returned to Egypt. Israel also promised to remove its forces from the western half of the Sinai within nine months, as Sadat had requested. In return, Cairo would exchange ambassadors with Jerusalem one month after that phase of the withdrawal was completed.[45]

Carter had achieved another diplomatic coup to match the Camp David Accords. Once more, he was greeted with a tremendous outpouring of public acclaim—hailed as a statesman who had gone the extra mile and grasped the impossible. But like the Camp David Accords, the Egyptian-Israeli agreement was reached only by avoiding the two crucial obstructions to a meaningful peace in the Middle East: Palestinian autonomy and Israeli withdrawal from the occupied territories. Arab reaction to the treaty was swift and negative. Jordan's King Hussein, whose support was essential to any settlement involving the West Bank, held an emergency meeting of his cabinet and then called for implementation of economic measures against Egypt. From Saudi Arabia, which could have attempted to topple Sadat by denying Egypt the financial support on which it depended, there was cryptic silence. Although some commentators interpreted this as acquiescence to the pact, no evidence corroborated that view. In fact, Sadat had become so isolated in the Arab world, and his political future so mortgaged to a comprehensive Mideast settlement, that any further diplomatic tremors could unravel the Egyptian-Israeli agreement.[46]

At this juncture, developments in the Iranian Revolution intervened. The revolution in Iran, which led in 1979 to the overthrow of the Shah of Iran and the establishment of the fundamentalist Islamic government of the Ayatollah Ruhollah Khomeini, spiritual leader of Iran's Shi'ite majority, is beyond this book's coverage. Nevertheless, the revolution had a profound impact on the United States, especially in its relations with the Arab states of the Middle East. By virtually shutting down Iran's oil fields, the revolution contributed to a second round of skyrocketing oil prices (the first having occurred during the Yom Kippur War), which would last until 1985 and drive the cost of oil to as much as $31.75 a barrel.[47]

The Iranian Revolution also shocked the more conservative and moderate Arab leaders, such as those in Egypt, Saudi Arabia, Kuwait, and the other principalities of the Arabian Peninsula, who worried about the stability of their own regimes. Conversely, the revolution was greeted with wild abandon by Shi'ites, other Islamic fundamentalists, and Palestinians who identified with Khomeini's shrill attacks on Western values, influence, and interests in the Middle East, especially Washington's support of Israel. Iran became a center for terrorist activity directed against Israel and more moderate regimes in the Middle East, as the Khomeini government sought to spread Islamic revolution throughout the region. The net effect of the revolution was to limit Washington's leverage in the region and to further complicate the peace process that the Camp David agreement was intended to promote. [48]

The Iranian Revolution also changed the strategic balance in the Middle East. Since Richard Nixon's administration, the Shah of Iran had been allowed—indeed, encouraged—to purchase a vast amount of American military equipment because he was considered a valuable, almost indispensable, ally. Vance described the country's strategic importance as follows: "Iran was seen as the major force for stability in the oil-rich Persian Gulf. Its military strength ensured Western access to gulf oil and served as a barrier to Soviet expansion. Its influence in [OPEC] made it important to the United States." Following the Iranian Revolution, however, this pillar of American interests was no longer there.[49]

Over the next 12 months, America's troubles in Iran and neighboring states went from bad to worse. In November 1979, militant Iranians claiming to be students seized the American embassy in Tehran and took 60 American hostages, precipitating a crisis that was to last more than a year, consume Carter's administration, and help defeat his bid for reelection in 1980.[50] In December, the Soviet Union sent 85,000 troops into Afghanistan in an unsuccessful effort to prop up a Marxist government against Afghan insurgents.[51]

At the same time as the Soviet Union was invading Afghanistan, much of the Islamic world, including the vital Persian Gulf, was being thrown into turmoil. The fervor of Islamic revolution that had begun in Iran appeared to be spreading throughout the region. In Saudi Arabia, a small but fanatic Muslim sect seized the Grand Mosque in Mecca, Islam's holiest shrine, holding hundreds of pilgrims hostage. After two weeks of bloodshed during which as many as 200 pilgrims and 300 guerrillas may have died, Saudi forces finally regained complete control of the shrine. But in Pakistan, 20,000 Muslim rioters stormed and burned the American embassy in Islamabad after rumors circulated that the United States and Israel had been responsible for the Saudi raid on the rebels in the Grand Mosque.[52]

With much of the Middle East in upheaval, Carter feared that unless he took a firm stand against the invasion of Afghanistan, the entire region would be vulnerable to Soviet attack. "A successful takeover of Afghanistan," he later wrote, "would . . . pose a threat to the rich oil fields of the Persian Gulf area and to the crucial waterways through which so much of the world's energy supplies had to pass."[53] Delivering his State of the Union address on 23 January 1980, he issued what became known as the Carter Doctrine. "Let our position be absolutely clear," he told a joint session of Congress. "An attempt by any outside force to gain control of the Persian Gulf region will be regarded as an assault on the vital interests of the United States of America, and such an assault will be repelled by any means necessary, including military force."[54]

Until the Iranian Revolution and the Soviet invasion of Afghanistan, the president had very rarely framed his policy for the Middle East in terms of the need for oil or concern about Soviet influence in the region. Not that these were unimportant matters for Carter. America's growing dependence on Mideast oil was one reason he had placed such emphasis on developing and enacting a national energy program. Until the revolution, he had also lobbied hard with the Shah of Iran, who was the leading advocate of higher oil prices, to keep prices stable.[55] Similarly, the administration had always been alert to Soviet activity in the region. It was especially worried that another Arab-Israeli war might drag the two superpowers into the fighting on opposite sides—as had almost happened in 1973. As National Security Adviser Zbigniew Brzezinski later wrote, "a new war would likely generate a major U.S.-Soviet confrontation, more intense and direct than the one that almost came to a head in 1973."[56]

But during Carter's first three years in office, oil and the Soviet danger do not appear to have been his overriding concerns with respect to the Middle East. This was understandable because during this time, oil prices remained fairly stable,[57] and the Soviet presence in the region appeared far less threatening than it had been prior to the Yom Kippur War of 1973. Indeed, the historian Robert O. Freedman has correctly pointed out that there had been "a serious deterioration of the Soviet position in the Arab world" since 1973. Former secretary of state Henry Kissinger had effectively driven the Soviets to the sidelines, and the "anti-imperialist" coalition that Moscow had supported in the region had collapsed.[58] As a result, Carter's first impulse as president had been to involve the Soviets more in the peace process by reconvening the Geneva conference that Kissinger had so effectively scuttled. Rather than concerns about oil or the Soviet menace, the most pressing issue during the first three years of Carter's administration was the Arab-Israeli dispute independent of other concerns. Indeed, Carter's deeply held religious beliefs and his veneration for the Holy Land made ending the Arab-Israeli conflict and bringing peace to the Middle East almost a moral imperative for him.

In his last year in office, however, Carter perceived the Middle East differently. Because by this time, he believed America's most vital interests were at risk, he issued the Carter Doctrine. To show that he was serious about using force if necessary, the president proposed to Congress that all men between the ages of 18 and 26 be required to register for a future draft. He also asked for five annual increases of 5 percent in real military spending rather than the 3 percent that had been his goal since 1977, and he requested $400 million in military and economic aid to Pakistan, which bordered Afghanistan. Furthermore, he announced that his administration would negotiate with countries near the Persian Gulf for the use of naval and air facilities and expand the American military presence in the Indian Ocean.[59]

Notwithstanding this display of military bravado, Carter's policy for the Arab Middle East, like much of his foreign policy, was in shambles by the time he left office in 1981. Even his crowning achievement, the 1978 Camp David agreement, had reached a dead end. Despite repeated affirmations by both Egypt and Israel of their solid commitment to the Camp David peace process, they had made little progress in resolving the Arab-Israeli dispute. The immediate problem remained Palestinian autonomy in the West Bank and Gaza Strip. Although the Camp David Accords called for an agreement on self-rule by 26 May 1980, Israeli prime minister Begin held steadfastly to a definition of Palestinian autonomy limited largely to municipal affairs. Under no circumstances would he permit Palestinian self-determination, which was what Sadat intended. President Carter tilted toward the Egyptian position, believing that the Palestinians were entitled to "full autonomy."[60]

At the end of March 1980, the president sent Sol Linowitz, a seasoned negotiator, to the Middle East with instructions to develop a package of proposals on the Palestinian question acceptable to both Egypt and Israel. But Linowitz's mission was a failure. Although Israel agreed to view the May date as a "positive incentive" for deciding the autonomy issue rather than a fixed deadline, Begin refused the American request to suspend the building of new settlements on the West Bank until after 26 May. Egyptian foreign minister Khalil responded that Israel would have to declare a moratorium on new construction before Cairo would agree even to an extension of the deadline.[61]

In addition to dispatching Linowitz to Egypt and Israel, Carter invited Sadat and Begin to Washington for separate talks on the full panoply of Middle East concerns. But those negotiations also proved largely unproductive. Sadat agreed to ignore the May cutoff and even said that if Israel assented to a formula for Palestinian autonomy, he would be willing to declare publicly that there should be no separate Palestinian state. But Begin would not budge from his frequently declared positions on either Palestinian independence or the building of Israeli settlements in the occupied territories. All the president achieved was Begin's acquiescence to nonstop talks between Egypt and Israel during the 40 days before 26 May.[62]

The true significance of the Carter-Begin discussions was the president's recognition of the fundamental weakness of the Camp David Accords. Perhaps for the first time, he understood that the terms contained in the documents—such as "autonomy," "security," "Palestinian rights," and even "West Bank"—had different connotations for each of the parties involved in the Arab-Israeli strife. The issue, however, was not semantics but the foundation of a final agreement. For Israel that meant security; for the Palestinians, their legitimate rights as a people; for Egypt, its credibility and influence within the Arab world. Under these circumstances, there was scant room for compromise. As a result, weeks of talks between Egyptian and Israeli negotiators bore no fruit.[63]

Two weeks before the 26 May target date, Sadat broke off the sessions after Begin stated that security in the West Bank and Gaza "must remain exclusively in Israel's hand." During the two months that negotiations were suspended, Begin lost considerable public support even in Israel for his hardline approach to the Palestinian problem and the occupied territories. Nevertheless, the Israeli prime minister remained defiant. At the beginning of August, the Knesset passed a measure making an undivided Jerusalem the capital of Israel, even though U.S. Ambassador Samuel Lewis had warned Begin that the United States might not be able to conduct face-to-face meetings with him if he moved his offices to East Jerusalem.[64] With Begin resistant to outside pressures, Carter increasingly distracted by the Iranian hostage crisis and his own campaign for reelection, and little hope of further progress in the bilateral talks between Egypt and Israel, the peace process that had begun at Camp David a year earlier simply ran out of time. Following Carter's defeat in November by former California governor Ronald Reagan, the president held a farewell meeting with Begin, which he had earlier hoped would be a prelude to another Begin-Sadat summit. But now it was purely ceremonial.

When asked after leaving office to state the major accomplishments of his administration, Carter placed high on his list the Camp David agreement. Certainly it was a significant achievement. However limited and ultimately disappointing to the Egyptians, the agreement did lead to the evacuation of the Sinai Peninsula by Israel and the reestablishment of diplomatic and economic relations between Cairo and Jerusalem. Furthermore, future efforts to resolve the issue of Palestinian autonomy on the West Bank and Gaza Strip would be predicated on the formula negotiated at Camp David. Even more importantly, the Camp David Accords changed the equation of Middle East politics and diplomacy forever. Without Egypt's participation, another Arab-Israeli conflict was highly unlikely. But the accords were hardly the great success story that so many had anticipated when, for the first time, an Arab leader joined an Israeli leader in signing a peace agreement.

chapter 8

REAGAN AND LEBANON: 1981–1984

The dominant characteristics of the United States' relations with the Arab Middle East since the end of World War II have been consistent frustration and persistent failure. For every American president since Harry Truman the Middle East became an impenetrable riddle locked in an apparently unresolvable puzzle. Each president sought a resolution of the Arab-Israeli dispute; each failed. Jimmy Carter enjoyed partial success with the signing of the Camp David Accords. But the fact that an agreement that skirted the major issues preventing a permanent settlement was greeted with national euphoria only underscores the limited achievements of American peacemaking in the Middle East.

Yet the United States' efforts at peacemaking continued under Ronald Reagan, with similar results. Indeed, in its dealing with the Middle East, the Reagan White House had much in common with earlier administrations. Like most of his predecessors, Reagan took office committed to strong ties with Israel. "I've believed in many things in my life," he later remarked, "but no conviction I've ever held has been stronger than my belief that the United States must ensure the survival of Israel."[1] But like earlier presidents, Reagan became increasingly frustrated by what he regarded as Israeli truculence in resolving its dispute with its Arab neighbors.

Like most of his predecessors—and certainly far more than Carter—Reagan also approached the Middle East from the perspective of the cold war, never fully understanding the internal dynamics of Middle East politics. Rather, he viewed the region as another battleground in Washington's ongoing struggle against Soviet expansionism. "The rainbow of ancient antagonisms in the Middle East," he said later, "produced an instability that the Soviet Union spent decades and billions seeking to exploit."[2] Viewing the Middle East as a battleground of the cold war, Reagan committed American forces to a peacekeeping mission in Lebanon. These troops were withdrawn following the suicide car bombing of a military barracks at the Beirut airport that caused a huge loss of American lives.

The situation in Lebanon was not the only major Middle East crisis during the Reagan administration. The Iranian Revolution and the Soviet invasion of Afghanistan occupied more of the president's attention than did developments in Lebanon. But events in Lebanon were pivotal in America's relations with the Arab Middle East and were pressing throughout Reagan's eight years in office.

In 1977, soon after Jimmy Carter took office, Kamal Jumblatt, the leader of a small Muslim sect called the Druze and a widely respected social reformer with a large following among Lebanese Muslims, was assassinated; this led to Muslim reprisals against Maronite Christians. During the rest of the Carter presidency, there was also fighting between two rival Christian militias, the Tigers led by Danny Chamoun and the more prominent right-wing Phalangists headed by Bashir Gemayel. In July 1980 Chamoun was killed, probably by persons loyal to Gemayel. Clashes also took place between Syrians and Phalangists, who in 1976 had welcomed Syrian intervention in Lebanon against left-wing Palestinians and Lebanese Muslims but who now wanted Syrian forces out of their country.[3]

Yet for the most part, the situation in Lebanon remained relatively stable during Carter's presidency. The Syrians acted as peacekeepers, the cease-fire negotiated in 1976 held, and Gemayel established hegemony over the Maronite Christians, who controlled the small coastal strip between Beirut and the northern Lebanese city of Tripoli. Israel forged a military relationship with Major Saad Haddad, whose Christian-led militia provided a security zone for Israel in southern Lebanon in return for Israeli arms and money.[4]

Basically satisfied with the status quo, the administration relegated Lebanon to a secondary position in its agenda for the Middle East. To the extent that the White House concerned itself with Lebanon, it supported the government of Elias Sarkis, viewed the Phalangists as reactionaries, and hoped that the Palestinians would become integrated into the Lebanese political system. Its main interest, however, was in preventing any developments in Lebanon that might hinder or undermine the peace process elsewhere in the Middle East.[5]

Although largely ignored by the United States, the crisis in Lebanon lingered, and the problems that had been responsible for the country's civil war continued to fester. Indeed, Syria's decision to withdraw some of its forces from Lebanon (largely to save money) and to redeploy the others added to the country's political instability. Lebanon was further destabilized by Syria's decision following the Camp David Accords to mend fences with the PLO, which controlled most of southern Lebanon and used its many refugee camps as bases for guerrilla attacks against settlements in northern Israel. In March 1978, Israel responded by sending its forces into Lebanon. In the conflict that followed, 2,000 Lebanese and Palestinians were killed and an estimated 200,000 displaced from their homes.[6]

Three months later, Israel withdrew its troops. But it found the situation in Lebanon increasingly unacceptable. Not without justification, it considered Syria the agent provocateur, encouraging the Palestinians in their attacks on Israel. At the end of April 1981, Israel shot down two Syrian helicopters flying over Lebanon's Bekaa Valley. Syria, which had recently signed a treaty of friendship and cooperation with the Soviet Union, responded by deploying Soviet surface-to-air missiles in the valley.[7] Afraid of a full-scale Syrian-Israeli war and fearful of a confrontation with Moscow, the Reagan administration sent a highly respected diplomat, Philip C. Habib, to the Middle East.[8]

Habib was able to negotiate a cease-fire between Syria and Israel.[9] But fighting broke out the next month between Israelis and Palestinians along the Lebanon-Israel border after an Israeli air raid on the suspected headquarters of the PLO in Beirut, which left 300 killed and 800 wounded. With the help of Saudi Arabia, Habib was able to arrange another cease-fire, this time between the Israelis and the PLO. But demand grew in Israel for a full-scale invasion of Lebanon. Leading the call was Israel's minister of defense, Ariel Sharon, a hard-line former general who was committed to the complete elimination of the PLO. On 6 June 1982, Israel attacked Lebanon in an assault it called Operation Peace in Galilee.[10]

The Reagan administration knew about the impending invasion. Secretary of State Alexander Haig had learned about Israeli plans to invade Lebanon as early as October 1981 while attending the state funeral of Egyptian president Anwar Sadat, who had been slain while reviewing a military parade. Notwithstanding Sadat's enormous popularity in the West, there had been growing discontent with the Egyptian leader for a variety of reasons, including his signing the Camp David Accords, his close ties to the United States, his lavish lifestyle, his suppression of militant Islamic groups, and Egypt's troubled economy and isolation within the Arab world. His assassins were members of one such group, al-Jihad (Sacred Struggle).[11]

At Sadat's funeral, Prime Minister Menachem Begin told Haig of his plan to move Israeli forces into Lebanon. There were other private and public warnings as well. Although Haig cautioned Begin that he would be acting without the support of the United States and he and the president issued similar warnings prior to the invasion, the administration's overall policy was acquiescence in Israel's plans. On 26 May 1982, the secretary of state made a major speech in Chicago in which he called for "international action" to end the Lebanese civil war; most analysts interpreted the speech as giving Israel the green light to invade Lebanon.[12]

Yet the administration was of two minds with respect to its Mideast policy. Reagan remained strongly committed to Israel, and other officials in his administration, including Secretary of State Haig who viewed the Middle

East from the prism of the cold war, believed that radical Arab states like Syria were agents of Soviet expansionism and that the United States should draw still closer to Israel. Haig even defended Israel against its critics, complaining at one time that "acts of terrorism against Jews aroused less indignation than Israeli acts of reprisal."[13]

Other leaders in the administration, however, including Defense Secretary Caspar Weinberger and National Security Adviser William Clark, argued the need to placate moderate Arab regimes in the region by moving away from America's traditional pro-Israeli policy and by adopting a more balanced approach to the Arab-Israeli dispute.[14] As a result of an acrimonious dispute with Israel over the sale of AWACS to Saudi Arabia, which Israel's advocates almost blocked on Capitol Hill, even President Reagan began to have second thoughts about unequivocal support of Israel. Although the sale of the AWACS had been negotiated by the Carter administration over the objection of Israel, Reagan went ahead with it. He had been told by the Pentagon that it would not materially alter the balance of power in the Middle East. Because of Saudi Arabia's oil and its status as a bastion of anticommunism, Reagan also wanted to strengthen ties with the Riyadh government. Furthermore, he thought the AWACS sale had great symbolic importance. "I . . . wanted to send a signal to our allies and to Moscow," he later remarked, "that the United States supported its friends and intended to exert an influence in the Middle East not just limited to our support of Israel."[15]

What angered the president was not so much Israel's opposition to the sale of the AWACS, which was well-known and understandable, but Israeli prime minister Menachem Begin's public lobbying against it. In February 1981, just a month after Reagan took office, Israeli foreign minister Yitzhak Shamir visited Washington. In conversations with Haig, Shamir indicated that Israel would mute its opposition to the sale; in return it was promised 15 F-15 jet fighters at a cost of $300 million. During his visit to Washington later that summer, Begin also said that while he opposed the AWACS agreement with Saudi Arabia, he would not campaign actively against it. But he then proceeded to denounce the sale both in a speech to a joint session of Congress and in subsequent television interviews. The president was furious. Using the full weight of his office and taking advantage of his own personal popularity and powers of persuasion, he was able in October to gain Senate approval for the sale by the narrow vote of 52 to 48.[16]

Reagan was also upset that the Israeli leader had ordered the bombing in June 1981 of an Iraqi nuclear plant housing a French-built reactor believed capable of producing a nuclear weapon. Although Reagan noted in his diary that he "sympathized with Begin's motivation [and] had no doubt that the Iraqis were trying to develop a nuclear weapon," he was annoyed that Israel had acted without consulting the United States or France. "We could have done something to remove the threat," he recorded in his diary but did not elaborate on.[17] Pictures of the mass destruction and human suffering caused by Israel's air raid on Beirut the next month also deeply troubled the president, as did a decision by Israel in December to extend Israeli law to the Golan Heights, thereby effectively annexing it.[18]

The divided counsel within the administration over its Middle East policy and the president's own growing reservations about Israel were reflected in the White House's response to Israel's invasion of Lebanon.[19] On the one hand, Reagan and his secretary of state, believing that the cease-fire between the PLO and Israel was bound to collapse, saw the invasion as an opportunity both to bring about a solution to the Lebanese crisis and perhaps even to begin a new effort at resolving the Arab-Israeli dispute. Accordingly, the president remained silent for three days after learning that Israel had launched a major assault into Lebanon. Furthermore, he responded to a note from Soviet leader Leonid Brezhnev accusing the United States of prior knowledge of the invasion by remarking that Moscow had to share much of the responsibility for the present crisis because it had not used its influence "on Syria and [the PLO]" to stabilize the situation in Lebanon.[20]

On the other hand, Weinberger and Clark were concerned about the anti-American feeling Israel's attack on Lebanon would generate in the Arab world and the danger it posed to such moderate and pro-American countries as Egypt, Jordan, and Saudi Arabia. The corollary to these developments, Weinberger maintained, would be increased Soviet influence in the region. Such arguments resonated with Reagan.[21] Earlier in the year, Egypt's new president, Hosni Mubarak, had accepted a Soviet offer to send technical advisers to Egypt to help in its industrial development. Mubarak's decision made Reagan wonder whether the Egyptian leader "was planning to revert to a Nasser-style relationship with Moscow." Although Mubarak reassured Reagan during his visit to Washington in February that this was not the case, the president interpreted the Egyptian leader's statement as a warning not to take the support of Egypt or any other moderate Arab state for granted.[22]

At the time that Israel invaded Lebanon, Prime Minister Begin told Washington that Israeli forces would advance only 40 kilometers (24 miles) into Lebanon, thereby putting PLO artillery out of range of Israeli settlements, and that he had no desire to seize "even one inch" of Lebanese territory; Israel's purpose was merely to force the PLO away from Lebanon's border with Israel "so that all our civilians in the region of Galilee will be set free of the permanent threat to their lives."[23] But despite a UN Resolution calling for a cease-fire and the withdrawal of Israeli forces from Lebanon, by 13 June the Israelis had moved to the outskirts of Beirut and had trapped the PLO inside the city. Israeli forces had also encountered and defeated Syrian troops in the central and eastern parts of Lebanon, while Israeli jets shot down more than 20 Syrian planes and destroyed the Syrian surface-to-air missiles in the Bekaa Valley of eastern Lebanon.[24]

Israel's rapid advance and the looming threat of an all-out war between the Israelis and Syrians were more than the administration had bargained for. It was sympathetic to Israel's determination to drive the PLO out of Lebanon, and it feared anarchy if Israel simply withdrew its forces from Lebanon. But it was also concerned about the political consequences of allowing Israel to tighten its grip on Beirut and eradicate the PLO. Pressure mounted on the United States from Arab leaders and even from America's European allies to order Israel out of Lebanon. The president urged Israel once more to halt hostilities. Even Haig remarked that "the Israelis had cast off restraint entirely." The White House considered a plan proposed by Haig whereby all "foreign forces" (Syrian, Palestinian, and Israeli) would withdraw from Lebanon and an effective Lebanese government would be reestablished which would be able to ensure the security of Israel's northern border.[25]

Haig later explained, "the strategy was to use the shock of the Israeli attack to force the PLO out of Beirut, to make the feuding Lebanese understand at last that their collective peace and security could be achieved only through unity, and, finally, to reinforce the incentives for both Syria and Israel not to prolong their adventures in Lebanon." Although the plan was modified over the next several weeks to include a multinational peacekeeping force that would guarantee the safe evacuation of the PLO from Lebanon, it was the basis on which the PLO finally agreed to leave the country at the end of August.[26]

The agreement did not come easily, however, and caused a serious rift in Israeli-American relations and public exposure of the Reagan administration's internecine warfare, which hampered the development of a coherent Middle East policy and left Haig one of its victims. The secretary of state first outlined his plan on 12 June in draft instructions to Habib, a copy of which he sent to Reagan. When the president did not respond, Haig sent the instructions to Habib, who was scheduled to meet in Damascus with Syrian president Hafiz al-Asad. The next day Haig received an angry call from National Security Adviser Clark, who told the secretary he had acted without proper authority. Already engaged in a simmering dispute with Clark over who ran foreign policy, Haig insisted on a meeting with the president. Employing a tactic he had used before, Haig threatened to resign unless Reagan reaffirmed his authority over foreign policy. The president urged him not to resign but otherwise remained silent.[27]

Two weeks later, the secretary had another disagreement with Clark over relations with Europe and sanctions against Moscow. Once more, Haig threatened to resign unless the president gave him a vote of confidence and the reassurances he wanted. This time Reagan accepted Haig's resignation. To replace him, he appointed George Shultz, an economist and business leader who had served in several cabinet-level posts during the Nixon administration and had been widely rumored at the time of Reagan's election to be his choice for secretary of state. The president asked Haig to remain in his post until Shultz was confirmed by the Senate.[28]

Meanwhile, the PLO had to be persuaded to leave Lebanon for Haig's plan to succeed. In the secretary's view, this was best accomplished by making the Israeli military knot around the PLO in Beirut so tight that the PLO would have to withdraw from the country or face total destruction; this would involve the threat of an Israeli move into West Beirut, where most of the Palestinians were located, unless the PLO agreed to a swift and unconditional evacuation.[29]

Haig was infuriated, therefore, when other voices at the White House signaled that the administration opposed an Israeli move into West Beirut. Contrary to rumors at the time, this was not part of a White House conspiracy to undermine Haig's strategy. In June, Israeli naval guns and artillery began a massive bombardment of West Beirut, which left hundreds of civilians killed or wounded and outraged the president and his advisers. At a 21 June meeting with Begin, who was in Washington on a state visit, the president made known his displeasure with Israel, and Begin and Weinberger got into a shouting match over Israel's actions. But instead of relenting, Israel increased its artillery attack against Beirut. Reagan and his advisers were so angry at Israel that even Haig warned the Israelis to desist or risk being abandoned entirely by the United States.[30]

The mixed signals coming from the White House about the Israeli move into West Beirut encouraged the PLO to remain where they were.[31] The confused signals also destroyed whatever credibility Haig still had as the nation's chief diplomat and made it appear—not inaccurately—that American foreign policy was being conducted without anyone at the helm. The president wanted to be rid of Haig. Secretary of State-designate Shultz was increasingly uncomfortable that he had to operate through Haig, who was reluctant to relinquish authority. While meeting with Reagan over the July Fourth holiday, Shultz offered to call Haig and tell him it was time to give up the reins of power. With the president's approval, Shultz made his call, and Reagan confirmed it when Haig insisted that he hear it from the president himself.[32]

Meanwhile, Israel, which had no desire to add to its already heavy casualties by moving into West Beirut and engaging in house-by-house combat with the PLO, told the White House on 25 June that it was ready to accept a cease-fire and endorsed the plan first proposed by Haig: that is, the withdrawal of the PLO and all foreign armies from Lebanon. To Reagan's surprise, Israel asked the United States to assume responsibility for negotiating the PLO's pullout, even though it had always been America's policy, at Israel's request, not to conduct business with the PLO until it recognized Israel's right to exist.[33]

During the next week, PLO leader Yasir Arafat danced a diplomatic minuet indicating, on the one hand, that the PLO was ready to leave Lebanon but holding out, on the other, for favorable terms, including a political presence in Beirut, a symbolic military presence in the country, and guarantees for the safe evacuation of his forces. In response, President Reagan agreed to include American troops in a peacekeeping force, which would guarantee the PLO's safety as it left Lebanon. But the problem of finding a new home for the PLO remained. Either because they feared the political instability the PLO's presence would create or because they were worried about becoming a homeland for the 400,000 Palestinians living in Lebanon, none of the Arab states wanted to accept the PLO. The Israelis also made negotiations difficult by sporadically shelling Beirut.[34]

By the second week of July, it appeared that an end to the fighting in Lebanon was in sight. The PLO agreed to leave Lebanon in return for a political office in Beirut and a military force of 600 men in the northern Lebanese city of Tripoli. Saudi Arabia had been trying to find a home for the PLO, and Damascus indicated to it that the PLO could reside in Syria and that Syrian forces would be withdrawn from Lebanon upon the Beirut government's request. When this happened, Israel would also have to withdraw its forces.[35]

The cessation of hostilities that seemed so near, however, proved to be a vanishing shadow, and what was already a major disaster for Lebanon turned into a horrible and unremitting human tragedy with many villains and no heroes. The new secretary of state believed it was imperative that the PLO leave Lebanon as soon as possible. Prior to being named to his position, Shultz had been president of the Bechtel Corporation, an engineering and construction company with large interests in the Middle East. As a result, he had been unfairly labeled by some members of Congress as an "Arabist," a charge he vigorously denied at his confirmation hearings. In truth, his views on the Middle East were more nuanced than that, and as secretary of state, he himself spoke critically of "Arabists" in the State Department who were more optimistic than he about Arab moderation in matters involving Israel. But he had been deeply offended by Israel's invasion of Lebanon and its shelling of Beirut, a city he had visited several times and much admired. Certainly, he was not nearly as friendly to Israel as his predecessor.[36]

More to the point, though, Shultz took office on 16 July committed to bringing about a comprehensive peace for the Middle East. On his first full day as secretary of state, he called together a group of Middle East experts to secretly develop a plan for resolving the Arab-Israeli dispute. Although he later commented that he "was determined not to be pinned down by the Beirut crisis," he recognized that the chances of a lasting peace would be increased by a successful resolution of the conflict in Lebanon, which in his view meant the peaceful evacuation of the PLO from Beirut. "If we can remove the PLO fighters from Beirut peacefully, get them somewhere else, and avoid an explosion in Beirut, we will have accomplished something very important for the long-run cause of peace," he had remarked to lawmakers during his confirmation hearings.[37]

Unfortunately, Syria backed away from its promise to accept the PLO, which had been made under pressure from its financial benefactor, Saudi Arabia, and the search for a home for the PLO started once more. At the end of July, it appeared that the PLO might be dispersed among several Arab countries, including Egypt, Jordan, Syria, and the Sudan, but this arrangement also fell through. Meanwhile, Israel resumed its artillery barrage of Beirut. From the Lebanese capital, Habib, who was still trying to negotiate the evacuation of the PLO, reported the worst shelling of the war. By August, television was showing nightly scenes of the horrible damage and terrible human suffering being inflicted by the Israeli guns and aircraft. Israeli forces also moved into the southern suburbs of Beirut and seized control of the airport.[38]

The president and his secretary of state were enraged. On 1 August, a day referred to by the media as "Black Sunday," Israeli foreign minister Shamir arrived in Washington. The next day, he met with the two American leaders. Visibly shaken, the president told Shamir that if Israel invaded West Beirut, "it would have the most grievous consequences for our relationship." Reagan strongly implied that the United States would cut off all military aid to Israel. Meeting separately with Shamir, Shultz also warned Israel to stop its attack against Beirut so Habib could continue to negotiate the evacuation of the PLO.[39]

Despite American pressure, Israel continued its attack. On 4 August, Israeli armored units moved into West Beirut. Shultz, Vice President George Bush, and most of Reagan's other advisers urged the president to take stern measures against Israel. But while the president sent Begin a letter warning that the relationship between Israel and the United States was "at stake," he still refused to stop military assistance to Israel.[40] On 12 August, Habib reported from Beirut that the Israelis had launched a massive air, naval, and ground assault against West Beirut. Habib urged the White House to do something to stop the attack, remarking that the United States was being blamed for it and that Beirut was being destroyed. Moscow urged an emergency meeting of the UN Security Council. Shultz believed that America's reputation in the Middle East was being compromised. President Reagan telephoned Begin and again warned that relations between the United States and Israel were at risk. "I used the word 'Holocaust' deliberately and said the symbol of his country was becoming 'a picture of a seven month old baby with its arms blown off,'" the president recorded in his diary afterwards.[41] Twenty minutes later, Begin responded to Reagan's latest warning by agreeing to stop Israel's attack on West Beirut, which had apparently been launched at Sharon's orders and without the knowledge of the prime minister.[42]

The cumulative effect of Israel's military action and the United States' efforts to restrain the Israelis while searching for a diplomatic solution to end the fighting in Beirut was an agreement toward the end of August for the evacuation of the PLO from Lebanon. The pounding it had sustained at the hands of the Israelis made the PLO desperate to leave Beirut. At the same time, the United States was able to persuade Arab leaders, who had failed to come to the assistance of the PLO even though they championed its cause, that they had a responsibility to find it a new home.

A number of problems had to be worked out, including finding a new residence for the PLO and determining the responsibilities of the multinational force (MNF) that was to assure its safe evacuation. Although plans had already been formulated to take the entire organization to Yemen, Saudi Arabia, which regarded the PLO as a threat to its own security, made clear that it did not want the Palestinian organization on the Arabian Peninsula. But after further negotiations, Arab leaders agreed to disperse the PLO to several countries, including Algeria, Syria, North and South Yemen,[43] and Tunisia, where the PLO eventually established its headquarters. As for the MNF, which was composed of French, Italian, and American forces, the French and Italians had the primary responsibility for the PLO evacuation. At the insistence of Defense Secretary Weinberger, the 800 American marines assigned to the MNF were confined to Beirut's port area, so they would not be at risk. The first contingent of the PLO left Beirut overland for Syria on 27 August. By 1 September, when the evacuation was completed, more than 15,000 Palestinians and Syrians had left Lebanon.[44]

But the evacuation of the PLO was the end of the first act rather than the concluding scene of the Lebanese crisis. On 23 August, even before the evacuation had gotten underway, Bashir Gemayel was elected Lebanon's new president. The Reagan administration and the Israelis anticipated that, with the PLO gone and Gemayel installed as president, political stability would be restored to the war-torn country. With the war in Lebanon apparently over, the time seemed favorable to launch a new peace initiative for the Middle East. Shultz had wanted the president to announce a new plan, which his group at the State Department had been working on since July, as soon as the fighting ended in Lebanon. The president was also eager to get the peace process started again.[45]

On 2 September, Reagan delivered a televised address from the Oval Office in which he described a plan that built on the Camp David agreement of 1979 but was far more specific. Rejecting an independent Palestinian state, he nevertheless called for Palestinian autonomy on the West Bank and Gaza, which would be loosely federated with Jordan. Israel would be expected to relinquish most of the occupied territories in return for secure and defensible borders and Arab recognition of its right to exist. Jerusalem would remain undivided subject to later determination as to its final status. All this would be worked out through negotiations in which Jordan would represent the Palestinian people (although Palestinians might serve on its delegation). Also, there would be a five-year transition period before the Palestinians became fully autonomous.[46]

The address, which was widely hailed as the most imaginative new proposal for Middle East peace since the Camp David Accords, reflected Shultz's abiding concern, expressed at his confirmation hearings, to address the plight of the Palestinians. It also reflected his distrust of the PLO. By delegating to Jordan responsibility for representing the Palestinians, the plan amounted to a tacit rejection of the 1974 Rabat conference, which had recognized the PLO as their sole representative. Nevertheless, moderate Arab leaders welcomed what became known as the Reagan Plan.[47]

In Israel, Prime Minister Begin called the plan totally unacceptable since it meant giving up the West Bank. According to Defense Secretary Weinberger who met with the Israeli leader after visiting the MNF in September, Begin "harangued" him for nearly four hours about the inequities of the president's proposal, stating that Israel needed the West Bank for its own security and would never yield it to Jordan. The Israeli cabinet also voted to reject the plan.[48]

Arab leaders responded to Reagan's peace initiative by holding a summit meeting on 21 September in Fez, Morocco, where they offered their own peace proposals. These called upon Israel to give up the occupied territories, reaffirmed the PLO as the legitimate representative of the Palestinian people, and advocated the establishment of an independent Palestinian state with Jerusalem as its capital. This was familiar ground, and even Jordan supported creating an independent Palestinian state, which was, of course, beyond the pale as far as Israel was concerned.[49]

But in what Secretary of State George Shultz called a "gigantic step for the Arabs," the leaders at the Fez summit recognized Israel's right to exist as a nation, and they encouraged the United States to move forward with the peace process. Despite Israel's immediate rejection of Reagan's peace plan and the major divide between the president's proposals and those offered at the Fez summit, the White House hoped that the president's peace initiative might provide the basis for subsequent negotiations.[50]

Unfortunately, developments in Lebanon doomed the plan even before it could receive serious consideration in Middle East capitals. The presence of the PLO had not been the only reason for Lebanon's problems over the last decade. After the PLO left Lebanon, the country remained badly divided along almost every demographic line. In particular Shi'ite Muslims, who constituted Lebanon's largest religious group and lowest economic class, had been aroused to militant action by the Ayatollah Khomeini's successful revolution in Iran. The Druze, whose stronghold was the Shuf Mountains overlooking Beirut, had been fighting the Maronite Christians off and on for more than two centuries. There also remained major factional divisions among the Christians. Even the Phalangists were divided in their support of Gemayel.[51]

Contrary to American and Israeli expectations, therefore, the situation in Lebanon actually deteriorated following the evacuation of the PLO. On 14 September, Bashir Gemayel was killed by a bomb that exploded while he was addressing a group of his followers in Beirut. Israel responded the next day by moving its forces back into West Beirut. Ostensibly, their purpose was to prevent civil war from breaking out in the city. But *New York Times* journalist Thomas Friedman, who was in Beirut at the time, believes their real purpose was "wiping out the PLO as a military and political threat." Israeli forces also surrounded Palestinian refugee camps in Beirut's southern suburbs.[52]

On 18 September, Phalangist militia attacked two of these camps, Sabra and Shatila, and slaughtered an estimated 800 to 1,000 men, women, and children while Israeli troops did nothing to stop them. The world was outraged when it learned of the massacres and saw graphic pictures of the murder and plunder. Even in Israel, there was disbelief and anger that such indiscriminate killing could have taken place under the eyes of Israeli soldiers. In response the Begin government undertook a formal investigation that led eventually to Sharon's resignation as minister of defense.[53]

The United States, which had already strongly protested Israel's occupation of Beirut, responded to the massacres by demanding that the Israelis withdraw their forces from Beirut immediately. At the same time, President Reagan ordered the American marines who had left Lebanon after the PLO evacuation to return to the country. He asked France and Italy to have their forces return as well. In addition, he requested that Arab leaders try to get the Syrians to withdraw their forces stationed in Lebanon. His hope was that the reconstituted MNF would keep the peace and that once the estimated 50,000 Syrian troops were out of the country, he could persuade Israel to withdraw its forces.[54]

At first Reagan's strategy seemed to work. Israel agreed to a phased withdrawal of its forces from West Beirut. On 20 September, Bashir Gemayel's older brother, Amin, was elected overwhelmingly by Lebanon's parliament as the nation's new president, a measure of the desire of Lebanese lawmakers to unite and end the bloodshed in their country. Reagan was hopeful that Amin Gemayel would be able to bring peace to the region. The MNF was also reconstituted and moved back into Beirut. Although terrorism and killing by competing Muslim and Christian factions continued, the level of violence subsided.[55]

Unfortunately, Amin Gemayel, who lacked Bashir's charisma and political astuteness, very quickly alienated many of the groups that had supported his brother. Also, the Syrians and Israelis refused to withdraw their forces from Lebanon. Complicating matters was the widespread influence the PLO continued to exert in Lebanon and among Palestinians at large. Although the White House and most Middle East experts had expected the PLO's embarrassing exit from Lebanon to mark its exit as a political force in the Middle East, they were wrong. The Sabra and Shatila massacres breathed new life into the PLO and its leader, Yasir Arafat. Indeed, the abandonment of the PLO by most Arab leaders and the killings of Palestinians at Sabra and Shatila created a new bond between Arafat and the Palestinian people.[56]

Consequently, Israel's purpose in invading Lebanon—to rid itself of the PLO—backfired. Similarly, the premise of Reagan's plan for peace in the Middle East—that Jordan rather than the PLO would represent the Palestinian people—was undercut.[57] To make matters worse, Syria allowed elements of the Iranian Revolutionary Guard to establish a headquarters in the Bekaa Valley, from which it maintained contact with a radical Shi'ite faction in Lebanon known as the Hezbollah (Party of God).

But these developments were not yet apparent as 1982 gave way to 1983. What was apparent was the intensified hostilities in the Lebanese civil war, the incompetence of Amin Gemayel, and his inability to stop the fighting in his country. In April 1983, the conflict in Lebanon took a dramatic new turn for the United States after a van full of explosives blew up outside the American embassy in Beirut, destroying much of the structure and killing 63 people, including 17 Americans.[58]

The destruction of the American embassy brought into sharp relief the ongoing conflict within the administration over the extent of America's military commitment in Lebanon. On the one hand, Defense Secretary Weinberger, supported by the Joint Chiefs of Staff, opposed the use of American forces, especially as part of a multinational peacekeeping operation. The Pentagon believed that such a peacekeeping operation placed American troops seriously at risk, particularly if they were expected to intercede between much larger Syrian and Israeli forces. On the other hand, the secretary of state favored maintaining a military presence in Lebanon, arguing that the United States could not permit a group of terrorists to drive it out of the country; the NSC staff wanted to increase the size of the American force in Lebanon. President Reagan sided with his secretary of state.[59]

In May, Shultz went to the Middle East in an effort to resolve the Lebanese crisis. He intended to procure an agreement between Lebanon and Israel for the withdrawal of Israeli troops from Lebanon, which he could then use to gain a similar agreement between Damascus and Beirut. After shuttling between various Middle East capitals, he was able to announce that such a pact had been reached. In return for an Israeli withdrawal, Lebanon agreed to end its state of war with Israel that dated to 1948. Although it was not yet prepared to establish formal diplomatic relations with Israel, it also approved a provision allowing Israel to open a liaison office in Lebanon. In addition, Lebanon agreed to not allow itself to be used as a staging area for an attack against Israel and gave its consent to various security arrangements in southern Lebanon, including limits on its own military presence there, permission for Israel to patrol the region, and acquiescence to the authority of Major Saad Haddad, Israel's surrogate in the area.[60]

The problem with this agreement, however, was that Israel insisted that it be contingent on Syria's withdrawal of its forces from Lebanon, which Syria had no intention of doing. For Syrian president al-Asad, the last five years had been a period of extreme frustration and setbacks. The wartime relationship he had forged with Egypt in 1973 was in ruins, and the Camp David Accords destroyed the hope he had had early in the Carter administration of a major shift in America's Middle East policy. By trading the Sinai for an Egyptian peace, Israel had pried Egypt from the Arab camp and neutralized its strongest military foe. Israel had also gained worldwide approval as a peacemaker even though, in al-Asad's view, the agreement reached at Camp David actually increased the likelihood of an Israeli attack on Syria.[61]

Because of his intervention against the PLO in Lebanon, al-Asad had earned the contempt of most of the Arab world. Indeed, the war in Lebanon was a particularly wrenching experience for the Syrian leader. His claim that Syria was a regional power with a special interest in Lebanon had been successfully challenged by Israel, a country he believed was his competitor in a contest for control of the entire Levant (Lebanon, Jordan, and Palestine). His assertion of regional leadership had gone largely unacknowledged by most other Arab states, including Egypt, Saudi Arabia, Jordan, and Iraq, each of which had reasons for wanting to prevent Syria from becoming more powerful than it already was by recognizing al-Asad's claims of special entitlements in the Levant.[62]

In addition, al-Asad had to worry about a challenge from Iraq. A brief Iraqi-Syrian reconciliation in 1978 following the Camp David agreement had gone awry, and the two countries had reverted to their traditional hostile relationship. Al-Asad had also recently suppressed, with unusual ruthlessness, an internal challenge to his leadership by the fundamentalist group known as the Muslim Brotherhood. The climax to this rebellion occurred in February 1982 in the central Syrian city of Hamah where, for three weeks, Syrian forces battled Islamic rebels for control of the city. After the fighting ended, the Syrian troops, apparently on al-Asad's orders, murdered an estimated 5,000 to 10,000 Muslims and razed whole neighborhoods.[63]

Feeling surrounded by enemies, al-Asad was in no mood—and saw no reason—to withdraw his forces from Lebanon, especially as part of an agreement brokered by the United States, which he thoroughly distrusted. Quite the contrary, he was prepared to stand alone against Israel if necessary, and he was already rebuilding his military machine with some of the Soviet Union's most sophisticated military technology, including its most advanced surface-to-air missiles. In 1980, he had patched up relations with the Soviet Union, which had been another casualty of Syria's intervention against the PLO in Lebanon. In response to the developing relationship between Egypt and the United States and al-Asad's courting of Moscow, the Kremlin signed a security treaty with Syria in October 1980. Although Soviet leader Brezhnev made some weapons available to Syria, he failed to come to Syria's aid during the war in Lebanon for fear of risking a confrontation with the United States. But Brezhnev died in November 1982, and his successor, Yuri Andropov, soon vastly increased the size and improved the quality of the weaponry it shipped to Syria.[64]

Thus, rather than withdrawing his forces from Lebanon, al-Asad joined in a concerted campaign with Lebanese Shi'ites, Druzes, Palestinians, and others to force the Israelis out of Lebanon and overthrow Gemayel. Their strategy was to make the Israeli presence in Lebanon so costly in terms of casualties that Israel would withdraw from the country, leaving Gemayel an easy prey.[65]

The strategy worked. Throughout the spring and summer, Israeli casualties mounted as Israeli forces fell victim to snipings, ambushes, car bombings, and other terrorist tactics. As the casualty lists grew, so did the opposition in Israel to its occupation of Lebanon. Stunned by Israeli losses, disheartened by the opposition, and distraught over the recent death of his wife, Begin ordered a withdrawal of Israeli troops from the Shuf Mountains overlooking Beirut to the Awali River south of the city. Before long he resigned from office and went into seclusion.[66]

With the Israelis gone, the Druzes reclaimed their former stronghold and instituted a terrible revenge against their opponents, who were no longer protected by Israeli troops. The MNF became involved in the fighting, providing logistical support for the Lebanese army. The Druzes responded in July by shelling the Beirut airport, where the American forces were stationed. The marines also became targets for other groups fighting the government.[67]

Despite increased pressure from the Pentagon, the president and his secretary of state remained determined to keep American forces in Lebanon. On 11 September, Reagan approved the use of gunfire from American ships and air strikes against the Druzes. But this only resulted in intensified bombardment of the Beirut airport from the well-protected Druze positions in the Shuf Mountains. As the shelling continued and the casualties mounted, the American public and lawmakers on Capitol Hill became increasingly critical of the president. "The people just don't know why we're there," Reagan acknowledged at the end of September after looking at his job ratings in public opinion polls.[68]

But the blow that finally led to the withdrawal of American forces—and shortly thereafter of the entire MNF—occurred on 24 October when a truck loaded with dynamite and probably driven by a Shi'ite fundamentalist got past armed sentries and smashed into the U.S. Marine headquarters and barracks at the airport, where it exploded, killing 241 marines. Almost at the same hour, a second car bomb blew up a building two miles away killing 58 French paratroopers.[69]

Reagan, supported by the State Department, vowed once more that terrorists would not force the United States out of Lebanon or the Middle East, remarking that Americans needed to "be more determined than ever that [terrorists] cannot take over that vital and strategic part of the world."[70] In December, he ordered a retaliatory mission against the headquarters of the Iranian Revolutionary Guard in the Bekaa Valley. But the attack backfired. Syrian missiles shot down two American bombers. One pilot was killed and another airman was captured but later released. In contrast, the damage done by the bombing was quickly repaired.[71]

By this time, opposition from the Pentagon and on Capitol Hill to the American presence in Lebanon had become so strong that it was only a matter of time before the president would have to order American forces to leave the country. Opposition grew following the release of a government report at the end of the month on the 24 October bombing, which was highly critical of the American military presence in the country. Furthermore, in February 1984 the Lebanese army disintegrated following an incident involving the killing of a Shi'ite militiaman, and the Gemayel government collapsed. Under these circumstances, the president had no alternative but to order the withdrawal of the American marines to naval vessels offshore. In issuing the order, Reagan maintained that he was merely redeploying American forces and taking them out of harm's way. The United States, he said, would assist in the reconstitution of the Lebanese government. But most Washington observers understood that the United States was withdrawing from Lebanon. Soon its partners in the MNF would do the same.[72]

Critics of America's policy in Lebanon have maintained that in seeking a solution to the Lebanese civil war—and, indeed, to the larger Middle East crisis—Secretary of State Shultz made the mistake of ignoring Syria, whose cooperation was essential to the peace process. In his defense, Shultz has argued that he did try "to create leverage on Assad [sic]," albeit indirectly, through other Arab countries. He also believes that the debacle in Lebanon was not the result of American inattention to Syria but of the failure to back diplomacy with force. Israel should have withdrawn from Lebanon in a more measured way, he argues, and the United States should have stayed its military course as part of the MNF. Instead, Defense Secretary Weinberger "was reluctant to contemplate or cooperate with even a limited application of military force to bolster our diplomacy. As a result, the crucial combination of strength and diplomacy required for success was not available."[73]

It is difficult to understand, though, how any policy in Lebanon could have worked without al-Asad's cooperation. For al-Asad, the stakes were simply too great to withdraw from Lebanon, especially since he could employ Palestinian and Lebanese terrorists and militias to inflict punishment on Israeli forces and the MNF at a minimum risk or cost to Syria. Moreover, his treaty with Moscow and the Soviet weaponry he was receiving by 1983 strengthened his resolve to control events in Lebanon.

Indeed, the importance of Shultz's statement about American failure in Lebanon lies not so much in his analysis as in what it reveals about his views on Syria and about divisions within the administration. It shows that, as his critics have maintained, Shultz believed that peace could be achieved in Lebanon without a diplomatic dialogue with Syria. It also makes clear that the administration remained badly divided over the course to follow in Lebanon.[74] These were far more important reasons for America's failure there than an American lack of will or an Israeli loss of will to back diplomacy with military force.

Yet given the sectarian divisions within Lebanon, the country's geostrategic importance both to Syria and Israel, Syria's regional hegemonic claims, and the ongoing Arab-Israeli dispute, one can legitimately ask if any policy pursued by the United States would have been significantly more successful than Reagan's in fitting together the pieces of the Lebanese puzzle.

chapter 9

IN THE PURSUIT OF PEACE: 1984–1989

The United States' experience in Lebanon during Reagan's first three years in office left the White House totally frustrated. The administration was determined not to get its hands singed again by becoming too embroiled in Middle East politics, at least not until the Arab states and Israel displayed more flexibility in seeking a resolution of the Arab-Israeli dispute. "We're not going to chase you until you catch us," Secretary of State George Shultz told Arab and Israeli leaders. Yet Shultz was unprepared to place the Middle East on the back burner of the administration's foreign policy. Without efforts at a peace agreement, a diplomatic vacuum would be created, which, he believed, Arab terrorists and radical Arab and Israeli leaders (the former abetted by the Soviet Union) would rush in to fill. Such a vacuum would pose an unacceptable threat to the national interests of the United States.[1]

Thus, there were ongoing efforts to end the Arab-Israeli dispute. But complicating these peace initiatives were the increased level of terrorism in the Middle East and the expansion of a war between Iraq and Iran that had begun in 1980, both of which contaminated the diplomatic environment. Because terrorism and the Iran-Iraq War also threatened American interests in the Persian Gulf, they posed major problems during Reagan's second administration and were still unresolved when the president turned over the reins of power to his successor, George Bush, in 1989.

The United States remained wedded to the idea that Jordan should represent the Palestinians in the peace process. But King Hussein understood far better the realities of Middle East politics than Washington did. Having forced the PLO from Jordan in 1971 after it had attempted on several occasions to overthrow his government and regarding the PLO as a major contributor to political instability in the Middle East, he would have been happy to see the Palestinian organization vanish as a major political force in the region. But with more than a million Palestinians living in Jordan, whose loyalty was to Yasir Arafat rather than to him, he understood that the PLO had to be part of any peace process. He also realized the danger he faced from Syria should he venture too far ahead of the rest of the Arab world in seeking a negotiated peace with Israel.[2]

A survivor who had watched one American president after another make promises and undertake initiatives that they did not keep or could not fulfill, Hussein was also skeptical about attaching too much importance to the latest peace initiative under Ronald Reagan, especially following America's pullout from Lebanon. He understood that he was politically vulnerable internally and externally, and he had doubts about the depth of America's commitment to a Middle East peace, particularly one that might require the United States to deal directly with the PLO.[3]

Another Arab leader whose support the United States sought for a new peace initiative but who shared many of Hussein's views was Egypt's Hosni Mubarak. Mubarak had come to power following Anwar Sadat's assassination in 1981. At the time Sadat was murdered, his regime faced considerable opposition from Egyptians disturbed by Egypt's deviation from Arab unity. While most Egyptians had responded enthusiastically to Sadat's peace initiatives with Israel in 1978, his support had dwindled because of Egypt's ostracism by most other Arab nations and the failure of the Palestinian autonomy talks following the Camp David Accords.[4]

Mubarak understood and shared the growing desire in Egypt for renewed political legitimacy within the Arab world. He did not reject his predecessor's peace initiative with Israel; to the contrary, he tried to engage other Arab states in the peace process. But because he also sought to reestablish Egypt's leadership position within the Arab world, his conduct toward other Arab leaders was more modulated and his rhetoric more reasoned and less recriminatory than Sadat's. He also designed a foreign policy that the historian Joseph P. Lorenz has described as "put[ting] Egypt squarely into the Arab mainstream on matters of Arab-wide importance." This included coolness toward Israel, especially before 1982 when it seemed that the Israelis might not return the Sinai to Egypt as provided by the 1979 Egyptian-Israeli peace treaty.[5] It also involved cooperation with Jordan in military and strategic matters, increased consultation with Saudi Arabia regarding the defense of the Persian Gulf, and support for Iraq in its war with Iran. It did not include public backing for Reagan's peace initiative.[6]

Without the strong endorsement of the two most moderate Arab leaders, Reagan's proposals for peace, which had already been undercut by the war in Lebanon, were doomed. Hussein, who at the 1982 Fez summit had objected to the call for the establishment of an independent Palestinian state, tried unsuccessfully to get PLO leader Arafat to agree to Palestinian representation on a Jordanian negotiating team as provided for under the Reagan plan. On several occasions, he indicated that he might enter into negotiations with Israel without the PLO. But in an interview in March 1984, the Jordanian leader criticized the United States for its pro-Israeli policies and rejected negotiations with the Israelis. Similarly, Mubarak told the United States that only the PLO could negotiate on behalf of the Palestinian people. By the spring of 1984, therefore, the Reagan peace initiative was dead.[7]

But its failure did not end America's efforts at peacemaking. On 11 February 1985, Arafat and King Hussein reached an agreement providing for the inclusion of Palestinians in a Jordanian-Palestinian delegation to negotiate with Israel. Arafat also accepted the principle of a Jordanian-Palestinian confederation rather than the establishment of an independent Palestinian state. On this basis, Hussein called for an international conference on the Middle East. Secretary of State Shultz was opposed to such a gathering, believing new problems would arise over its composition, location, and agenda. Instead he wanted direct negotiations between Jordan and Israel. But he welcomed the agreement between Arafat and Hussein as a major diplomatic breakthrough, and he believed he could persuade Hussein to agree to direct talks with Israel on the basis of the agreement.[8]

Once more, Shultz was disappointed. For the next 12 months, he tried to get the Jordanian leader to agree to bilateral talks with Israel. He even proposed a complex plan that provided for an international conference leading to direct negotiations. The Jordanian delegation at these talks would be allowed to include members of the PLO provided the PLO was willing to recognize Israel's right to exist (that is, to accept UN Resolution 242) and to denounce terrorism. But despite the 11 February agreement, the PLO would not accept the American conditions. Hussein indicated on several occasions—as he had when the White House was promoting the Reagan plan—that he might negotiate with Israel without the PLO. But he remained committed to an international conference that would include the PLO and continue even after bilateral talks with Israel began. These were conditions that were unacceptable to Israel and to the United States. The end to this latest peace initiative came in February 1986 when Hussein announced that he was giving up his effort to develop a joint strategy with Arafat.[9]

In making his announcement, Hussein blamed the PLO for the failure of negotiations, accusing it of inflexibility and duplicity. The PLO was guilty on both counts. Its 11 February agreement with Jordan, on which hopes of a major break in the diplomatic logjam had been predicated, was an effort by Arafat to mask problems inside the PLO and the PLO's weakened position within the Arab world. Arafat's popularity among Palestinians represented not so much an acclamation of his leadership as the fact that he symbolized the Palestinian cause. Within the PLO there was growing opposition to his leadership. In 1983 a Syrian-backed mutiny had broken out led by Colonel Sad Abu Musa, who accused Arafat of establishing a corrupt and self-indulgent bureaucracy that was increasingly indifferent to the sufferings of the Palestinian people and incapable of carrying on the revolutionary struggle for a Palestinian homeland.[10]

Arafat put down the revolt, but it left him politically vulnerable. The PLO leader ended the insurrection by tying the rebels to a Syrian plot against the Palestinian people. Although Arafat exaggerated the extent of the plot, Syrian leader Hafiz al-Asad considered Arafat a dangerous nuisance at best and a threat to Syria's ambitions in the Levant at worst. He also personally disliked the PLO leader, whom he regarded as untrustworthy and a charlatan. In 1983, he came to the rescue of PLO dissidents in the Lebanese city of Tripoli who were fighting PLO forces loyal to Arafat. Following the shelling of the Arafat loyalists by Syrian artillery, the PLO leader, who had come to Tripoli to be with his men, had to endure another humiliating evacuation from Lebanon under French protection.[11]

Badly weakened politically and fearing that the PLO might be ignored even by other Arab leaders, Arafat negotiated his 1985 agreement with Hussein as a way of keeping alive diplomatically. "Arafat had to keep contact with the West Bankers, and make sure that King Hussein did not try to make a deal with them and the Israelis that might exclude the PLO," the journalist Thomas Friedman later explained. But Arafat's real purpose was to undermine the negotiating process, not embrace it. And he succeeded.[12]

The United States also had to bear responsibility for the failure of negotiations. Although Shultz agreed to a joint Jordanian-Palestinian negotiating team that might include the PLO, he was never enthusiastic about the idea, and President Reagan remained strongly opposed to including PLO members in the negotiating process.[13] Accordingly, the conditions the White House insisted upon for PLO inclusion virtually assured its exclusion. But King Hussein would have been hard pressed by Palestinians in Jordan and by other Arab leaders to negotiate without some form of PLO representation. Similarly, the United States was willing to accept an international conference only if it were preliminary and subordinate to direct talks between Jordan and Israel. But Hussein would have been in great danger, particularly from Syria, had he entered bilateral talks with Israel. The Jordanian leader remembered well the Arab response to the peace treaty between Egypt and Israel; since Jordan was a much weaker state than Egypt, Hussein was far less able than Anwar Sadat to resist pressures against his regime.[14]

Like Hussein, Reagan was not entirely a free agent. He had to take into account Israeli opposition to an international conference at which Israel would be under intense pressure by the other participants to agree to a comprehensive peace that included giving up the occupied territories and establishing an independent Palestinian state. Nor was Israel prepared to negotiate with the PLO even as part of a Jordanian-Palestinian delegation. Given the constraints under which Hussein and the White House operated, it is not surprising, therefore, that this latest effort at peacemaking failed.[15]

Complicating matters were a wave of state-supported terrorism and the Iran-Iraq War, which had begun in 1980 following Iraq's invasion of Iran but which had turned decidedly in Iran's favor by 1986. Although terrorism was familiar in the Middle East, it took on a new dimension when terrorists began receiving support from the three most radical Middle East regimes—those in Syria, Libya, and Iran. On 14 June 1985, hijackers, believed to be members of Hezbollah, seized TWA flight 847 bound from Athens to Rome with 153 passengers aboard and forced it to fly to Beirut, where they released 19 women and children. After refueling, the hijackers forced the plane to go to Algiers, where they freed additional women and children but then ordered the pilot to fly back to Beirut.[16]

The hijackers demanded that Israel release 700 Shi'ites who had been taken prisoner during its invasion of Lebanon and that Kuwait free 17 members of a militant Shi'ite organization (al-Dawa) who in 1983 had been captured after attacking the American and French embassies in Kuwait.[17] The hijackers said that if their demands were not met, they would kill the remaining passengers. To show they meant business, they shot an American sailor, Robert Stethem, in the back of the head and dropped his body onto the tarmac at the Beirut airport. The skyjacking became a media event as live pictures were broadcast of Stethem's body on the ground and of the remaining passengers pleading with Israeli and Kuwaiti authorities to give in to the hijackers' demands. Perhaps because al-Asad feared an American military strike (this was the view later expressed by Secretary of State Shultz),[18] Syria was able, with the help of Iran, to gain the release of the remaining passengers on 30 June after Israel indicated it would release the Shi'ite prisoners in exchange.[19]

Other well-publicized terrorist incidents included the seizure in October of the Italian cruise ship, the *Achille Lauro*, and the murder of one of its American passengers, Leon Klinghoffer, an invalid confined to a wheelchair. In separate incidents in Beirut, suspected Palestinian and militant Shi'ite groups also seized seven American hostages whom they threatened to execute if their demands (usually involving the release of prisoners) were not met.[20]

At the end of 1985, 20 people, including 5 Americans, were killed in attacks at airports in Vienna and Rome. In April 1986, a number of Americans were badly wounded after a bomb exploded at a nightclub in West Berlin killing two persons. These three incidents were thought to be the work of terrorists backed by Libyan leader Muammar Qaddafi.[21] Qaddafi had been a constant thorn in Washington's side since coming to power in a bloody coup in 1969 that overthrew the pro-Western government of King Idris. Espousing a doctrine that combined pan-Arabism and socialism, he forced the closing of the strategically important Wheelus Air Force Base, played a major role in driving up the price of oil at the end of the 1960s and beginning of the 1970s, and sought to overthrow the governments in neighboring Egypt and Chad.[22] Although the United States at first adopted a policy of trying to accommodate Qaddafi, his often erratic behavior, frequent attacks on the United States and the West, and support of terrorism, pushed Libya, as far as Washington was concerned, into the ranks of other international outcasts, like North Korea, Cuba, Vietnam, and most recently, Iran.[23] In 1981, Navy F-14s shot down two Libyan fighters in a dispute involving the Gulf of Sidra, which the United States maintained was international waters and Libya claimed was part of its territorial waters. In March 1986, Libya fired missiles at U.S. ships involved in naval exercises in the Gulf of Sidra, which were intended to challenge renewed Libyan claims to the gulf. The United States responded by attacking two Libyan missile sites and sinking three Libyan patrol boats.[24]

Following the bombing of the Berlin nightclub, President Reagan decided to retaliate against Libya as a warning to all nations supporting terrorism, an action Secretary of State Shultz had been urging and Defense Secretary Weinberger had been resisting.[25] On 14 April, Reagan went on television to announce that American naval and air forces had attacked a number of terrorist facilities in Libya, including the barracks of Qaddafi's elite guards at Benghazi and the international airport at Libya's capital of Tripoli. Qaddafi responded by threatening a worldwide campaign of terrorism. The degree of terrorist activity attributed to Libya actually dropped after the attack. Nevertheless, state-supported terrorism and the holding of hostages in Lebanon were ongoing issues in the dialogue of Middle East diplomacy, further complicating the search for peace in the region.[26]

The Iran-Iraq War also confounded the administration. As with its response to the Lebanese civil war and state-supported terrorism, it was divided over what policy to pursue toward Iran and Iraq. Some White House officials, including National Security Adviser Robert MacFarlane and CIA Director William Casey, believed that the United States should seek to establish ties with moderate elements in Iran. In their view, the country was too important strategically and its oil resources too valuable to the West to be ignored by the United States. The elderly Ayatollah Khomeini, already in ill health, would not live many more years, and once he died, MacFarlane and Casey believed, moderate elements in Iran would be in a position to seize power. The United States should, therefore, begin to cultivate good relations with these groups.[27]

Most administration officials, including Secretaries Shultz and Weinberger, however, continued to view Iran as an outcast nation like Libya, in that it supported terrorism and fostered revolution in the Middle East. In their view, an Iranian victory in the Iran-Iraq War would be disastrous to the chances of peace and stability in the region and pose an immediate threat to the vital Persian Gulf. Accordingly, they tilted in favor of Iraq and launched an effort, known as Operation Staunch, to get all nations to stop shipping weapons to Iran. To "permit or encourage a flow of Western arms to Iran," Shultz wrote in response to MacFarlane's proposal to sell arms to Iran, "is contrary to our interest both in containing Khomeinism and in ending the excesses of this regime."[28]

Besides contributing to political instability and uncertainty in the Middle East, state-sponsored terrorism and the Iran-Iraq War also had major impacts on inter-Arab relations. Except for Syria, the Arab states supported Iraq in its war against Iran. Iraq, which had been largely isolated and feared by more moderate regimes like Saudi Arabia and Egypt, now began to receive considerable financial assistance from the Saudis and Kuwaitis, who were more concerned about the threat from the Ayatollah Khomeini's revolutionary brand of Islamic fundamentalism than they were from Iraq's radical regime. In contrast, Syria supported Iran against its longtime Ba'th rival, Iraq. Following Hussein's attack on the PLO, Syria and Jordan had also reached a new accommodation; in effect, Jordan cast aside its rapprochement with the PLO in favor of Syria, causing Arafat to realize that his worst fears were nearly coming true. Hussein closed PLO offices in Jordan, and Egypt closed the PLO office in Cairo. At the Arab summit in Amman in 1987, Egypt was formally welcomed back into the Arab fold and once more assumed a central position in the Arab world.[29]

The immediate effect of these developments was a more moderate and pragmatic Arab approach to the Arab-Israeli dispute that included a greater willingness to negotiate a settlement recognizing Israel's right to exist in peace with secure boundaries. At the same time, the revelation in 1987 of the so-called Iran-Contra affair[30] led to a shakeup in the Reagan administration that increased Secretary of State Shultz's influence and resulted in greater coherence in the formulation of foreign policy. Together, these changes led to Shultz's third effort to bring peace to the Middle East.[31]

Despite the failure of his last peace initiative, Shultz remained committed to direct negotiations between Jordan and Israel and to Palestinian autonomy without an independent Palestinian state. "I had become more convinced than ever," he later wrote, "that the most promising way to approach the Palestinian-Israeli conflict lay in some form of shared, overlapping, or interwoven sovereignties across Israel, the West Bank, and Jordan." As in the past, he was also willing to accept Palestinians in the Jordanian delegation and an international conference, provided it was brief, ceremonial, and preliminary to bilateral negotiations. Furthermore, he believed that a major breakthrough had occurred when King Hussein and Israeli foreign minister Shimon Peres met secretly in London and reached an agreement for negotiations very much along the lines he favored, namely, an international conference, which after a short session, would divide into committees for subsequent bilateral negotiations.[32]

But Peres, a moderate, had acted without the approval of Israeli prime minister Yitzhak Shamir, a hard-liner who rejected the London agreement. He also refused when Shultz offered to come to the Middle East to begin the peace process. Instead, the Israeli leader held his own secret meeting with

Hussein in London, which proved to be a disaster. After the meeting, Hussein told Shultz that Shamir was "hopeless" and that it would be impossible to work with him.[33]

Not ready to give up, Shultz presented Reagan with a proposal, suggested to him by Peres, that at the forthcoming summit between the president and Soviet leader Mikhail Gorbachev, the president raise the possibility of a meeting under U.S.-Soviet auspices between Hussein, Peres, and representatives from Syria, Egypt, and Lebanon to launch direct negotiations. The United States remained leery about a Soviet presence in the Middle East, while the Soviet Union still sought to limit America's military and political influence in the region. It continued, for example, to supply arms to Syria and Libya. It also drew closer to the PLO and backed an uprising against Israeli rule in the West Bank and Gaza known as the intifada.[34] Nevertheless, Soviet policy was more reactive than proactive. In fact, Gorbachev did not give Syria all the military hardware it wanted. He also warned the Syrians that their conflict with Israel would have to be solved politically rather than militarily, and he moved toward restoring diplomatic relations with Israel, which had been broken during the June 1967 Arab-Israeli war.[35]

Even though American policy had been to exclude the Soviets from matters involving the Middle East, the secretary of state believed that the Soviet Union's recent constructive policy in the region and the thawing in the cold war since Gorbachev came to power in 1985 justified involving Moscow in the peace process. But King Hussein, who by now thoroughly distrusted Shamir and thought Syrian president al-Asad would reject the U.S.-Soviet initiative, said he would not attend the conference if it were held. For Reagan, who had grown weary of the Middle East, that was enough to squash the proposal. Like Shultz's earlier peace initiatives, this one was stillborn.[36]

By this time, the White House's attention was distracted by the Iran-Iraq War, which was spilling into the Persian Gulf and posing an immediate military threat to Saudi Arabia and the small but oil-rich country of Kuwait that bordered on both Iraq and Saudi Arabia. In January 1987, Iran launched a major offensive into southern Iraq that brought its forces south of the Iraqi city of Basra, close to the gulf. Iran also launched naval attacks against neutral shipping bound for the gulf Arab states through the narrow Strait of Hormuz at the southern end of the Persian Gulf and mined the gulf in an effort to stop tanker shipments of oil from the Arabian Peninsula. But it made Kuwait its principal target, mining Kuwaiti shipping channels and aiming highly effective Chinese Silkworm surface-to-surface missiles at Kuwait from the captured Iraqi peninsula of Al Faw.[37]

In response, Kuwait asked Washington to reflag 11 Kuwaiti tankers so they would be under the protection of the U.S. Navy. Strong opposition existed in the United States to the Kuwaiti request. America's relations with Kuwait, which had achieved its independence from Britain in 1961, had never been good. Because the Soviets would sell the Kuwaitis military equipment and Washington would not, Kuwait had developed friendly relations with Moscow. Moreover, placing Kuwaiti shipping under American protection increased the likelihood of a military confrontation with Iran, which most lawmakers on Capitol Hill vehemently opposed.[38]

Administration officials, however, worried about the ramifications of not assisting Kuwait. Moscow had already informed Kuwait that it would provide protection to some Kuwaiti tankers, and Washington's refusal to do the same would afford the Soviet Union a unique opportunity to increase its naval presence in the gulf area. "I was quite sure that if we did not respond positively to the Kuwaitis," Defense Secretary Weinberger later commented, "the USSR would quickly fill the vacuum, and that the Gulf states, already concerned for a number of reasons about American reliability, would not be able to deny basing and port facilities to their new protector."[39]

Conversely, agreeing to the Kuwaiti request would be an opportunity for the United States to enhance its reputation among the gulf sheikhdoms, which had been tarnished by its failure to support the Shah of Iran during the Iranian Revolution. Several gulf states, including Kuwait, Saudi Arabia, and especially Bahrein, had significant Shi'ite populations believed loyal to the Ayatollah Khomeini. As a result, they feared the same type of internal uprising that had toppled the Iranian regime. American credibility, therefore, would be greatly enhanced by American assistance to Kuwait.[40]

Finally, the reflagging of Kuwaiti tankers would be a way for the United States to send a warning to Iran that it considered America's vital interests at stake in the Persian Gulf. Although some opponents of reflagging argued that the United States did not depend on Kuwaiti oil, in fact a large percentage of Kuwait's oil was handled by American-owned companies. More importantly, Kuwait was a major oil producer, and because oil was a fungible commodity (that is, it was interchangeable and indistinguishable from oil found elsewhere) any interruption in the world's overall supply of oil would affect the supply and price of oil everywhere.[41]

Therefore, despite significant opposition on Capitol Hill, the White House agreed to the reflagging request in May. By midsummer, the United States was routinely escorting Kuwaiti tankers in the Persian Gulf. Other nations joined with the United States and the Soviet Union in providing protection to reflagged oil tankers.[42] The participation in these operations by the United States and these other countries had its military cost. In May, Iraq mistakenly launched a missile attack against the USS *Stark*, killing 37 American sailors. Baghdad immediately apologized and agreed to pay compensation and damages to the families of those whose lives had been lost. But the incident led both to increased opposition on Capitol Hill to America's involvement in the Persian Gulf and to a growing demand, rejected by the White House, that it abide by the War Powers Act of 1973, which limited the president's power to engage in military action abroad without congressional consent.[43]

Of greater concern to the administration than Iraq's attack on the *Stark*, which was clearly an accident, was Iran's mining of the Persian Gulf, its deployment of Silkworm missiles, and the use of small but very fast naval patrol boats to attack shipping in the gulf. In July, a mine caused considerable damage to the *Bridgeton*, a Kuwaiti tanker that the United States had reflagged. Over the summer, a number of other ships were also damaged by Iranian mines, and at least one vessel, a service ship, was sunk and five of its crew were lost. The United States, Kuwait, and Saudi Arabia conducted a joint minesweeping operation that limited the destruction caused by the mines. Britain, France, Belgium, Italy, and the Netherlands also contributed minesweepers to the operation. But the next year, as the war heated up once more, Iran laid new mines. In April 1988, the USS *Roberts*, a guided-missile frigate, struck a mine, which injured 10 sailors and did considerable damage to the ship. In response, the United States attacked two Iranian oil platforms in the gulf, effectively knocking them out. Meanwhile, small Iranian boats conducted hit-and-run attacks, and Iran fired Silkworm missiles at Kuwaiti shipping and Kuwaiti oil installations; together, they did considerable damage.[44]

Overall, though, the reflagging operation, which was carried out by a number of nations, was highly successful, and the Iranian threat to gulf shipping was largely contained. Indeed, the Middle East expert William Quandt believes that the success of the reflagging operation may have been one reason Iran agreed in 1988 to a cease-fire in its eight-year war with Iraq. In Quandt's view, the operation also contributed to increased American prestige in the Middle East, which he points out, "had sunk to a low point after the Iran-Contra revelations."[45]

As the Iran-Iraq War drew to a close, Shultz undertook one final effort at peacemaking. The impetus for this last effort by the secretary of state was an uprising against Israeli rule by young Palestinians living in the West Bank and Gaza Strip. Although the uprising, known by the Arabic term "intifada," at first involved little more than rock-throwing against Israeli soldiers patrolling the occupied territories, it came to have as much impact on the Arab-Israeli dispute as any event in the Middle East since the Camp David Accords of 1978. Because of Israel's harsh response to the intifada, which resulted in almost daily killing and maiming of young Palestinians, world opinion turned against Israel, even among American Jews who had been among Israel's strongest supporters.[46]

The Palestinian question took on renewed importance, and the PLO, having been relegated to secondary status in the Arab world, was suddenly given new life and respectability as a result of the intifada, even though it had not been involved with the uprising. At their summit in Amman, Arab leaders had made the Iran-Iraq War their main order of business, the first time the Palestinian question had not been the top agenda item since the Arab League was formed in 1945. But that changed with the intifada, and once again Arafat became the recognized spokesman—and conscience—of the Palestinian cause. Unable to cope with the new form of warfare against its rule, Israel began to rethink and redefine its position on dealing with the PLO.[47]

Secretary of State Shultz, who at first mistakenly interpreted the intifada to mean the PLO's loss of leadership of the Palestinian cause, believed the uprising represented a fresh opportunity to rekindle the peace process, particularly since Israel had in the past indicated a willingness to negotiate with Arab residents of the West Bank and Gaza who were not members of the PLO. "The intifada," he later remarked, "bore promise of a new generation of Palestinians, with new leaders trying to take hold of their own affairs."[48]

Responding quickly to the changing dynamics of Mideast politics, Shultz developed a timetable for Palestinian self-rule in the West Bank and Gaza, which provided for negotiations to begin on Palestinian autonomy in April 1988 and for elections to be held for a Palestinian self-governing authority by January 1989. He also proposed to begin talks on the occupied territories in December 1988. The two sets of negotiations would be "interlocked"; that is, they would overlap, so that Arab leaders and the Palestinians would know that the autonomy talks would not be a substitute for negotiations on the occupied territories, which they had always regarded as a sina qua non of any peace initiative. Yet the negotiations would follow separate tracks, so that Palestinian autonomy could be achieved before a final settlement was reached on the occupied territories. This would satisfy the Israeli policy of separating the issues of Palestinian autonomy and the occupied territories. It would also respond to Israel's desire, in the wake of the intifada, to change conditions in the West Bank and Gaza by granting the Palestinians autonomy. Finally, it would speed up the negotiating process.[49]

Almost immediately, Shultz's new initiative ran into resistance. Hussein still insisted on an international conference in which the PLO had to play a central role. Shamir, who thought Shultz's proposal was a disguised effort to arrange such a meeting, would not negotiate with the PLO under any circumstances. Al-Asad insisted on the return of the Golan Heights before he would negotiate with Israel on other matters. The PLO, seizing the opportunity to reestablish its leadership of the Palestinian movement, warned Palestinians against negotiating with the Israelis.[50]

Despite being frustrated by the response to his proposal, Shultz continued to pursue it, engaging in March in a round of shuttle diplomacy between Mideast capitals and returning to the Middle East again in June. Although Arab and Israeli leaders encouraged Shultz to continue his efforts, nobody committed to his plan. Then King Hussein announced at the end of July that Jordan was cutting its ties to the West Bank, which meant it would no longer pay the salaries of local Palestinian officials or represent or speak for the

Palestinian people on the West Bank. Using the United States as an intermediary, Hussein informed Israeli foreign minister Shimon Peres that his action was intended to force the PLO to moderate its position on peace with Israel, since the eyes of the world would be focused on it. But because America's policy was to not negotiate with the PLO until it recognized Israel's right to exist and Shultz's solution to the Palestinian question relied on a federation of the West Bank and Gaza Strip with Jordan, Hussein's action killed the Shultz initiative.[51]

Yet for reasons that are not entirely clear, although they were probably related to the PLO's tentative and tenuous position within the Arab world, the PLO modified its position. In September, it let the White House know that it was ready to recognize Israel's right to exist on the basis of UN Resolution 242 and to end its violence against Israel. The administration was reluctant to respond to the PLO overture for fear that if news were leaked to the press that the United States was talking with the PLO, it could hurt Vice President George Bush's presidential campaign. But the PLO pressed the United States for a reply, and the day after Bush's election on 9 November, it requested a visa for Yasir Arafat to come to the United States to address the United Nations. It also announced a week later the establishment of an independent Palestinian state "on our Palestinian territory, with holy Jerusalem as its capital" but also hinted at recognition of Israel.[52]

Shultz turned down Arafat's request for a visa, citing continued acts of PLO terrorism. But by now the tide of world opinion, even in the United States, was turning decidedly in favor of dealing with the PLO. Former president Jimmy Carter had urged the administration to grant Arafat a visa, and even President-elect Bush told National Security Adviser Colin Powell that he disagreed with Shultz's decision. The *New York Times* and the *Washington Post* also criticized the secretary of state. The UN moved its session of the General Assembly to Geneva so that Arafat could speak to the body.[53]

Shultz responded to his critics by saying that, before changing his position on dealing with the PLO, he wanted a public statement from Arafat accepting UN Resolution 242 and renouncing terrorism. That came on 14 December, and having no other choice, a still skeptical Shultz announced, with the president's approval, that the United States was ready to engage in a "substantive dialogue with PLO representatives."[54]

Surprisingly, reaction in the Arab world to Shultz's statement was mixed, in part because it had been expected, in part because the Israelis were still not prepared to deal with the PLO, and in part because some Arab diplomats regarded the announcement as a scheme by the United States to diffuse the impact of the intifada, thereby taking the pressure of world opinion off Israel. Nevertheless, there was no denying that a real breakthrough had taken place in the Arab-Israeli dispute. It would now be up to the Bush administration to seize the opportunity it had inherited from the Reagan administration.[55]

chapter 10

BUSH AND THE PERSIAN GULF WAR: 1989–1991

Few American presidents have come to the Oval Office with more experience in foreign affairs than George Bush. As a former ambassador to the United Nations, U.S. envoy to the People's Republic of China, director of the Central Intelligence Agency, and vice-president under Ronald Reagan, he had spent most of his public career dealing with foreign affairs. But it was far from clear what policy he would pursue in the Middle East. Unlike Europe and the Soviet Union, which he had studied for years, the Middle East was something of a mystery to him. Before entering public life, Bush had been a successful Texas oilman, and this background, along with the many acquaintances he had made with Arab leaders while at the UN and CIA and as vice-president, suggested that he would be sensitive to the Arab view of the Arab-Israeli dispute. During Israel's invasion of Lebanon in 1982, he had urged the White House to adopt a tough stance toward the Israelis. Certainly the American Jewish community and Israeli leaders feared he would pursue a much less friendly policy toward Israel than his predecessor.[1]

Yet in 1988 the Republican Party had adopted one of the most vigorously pro-Israeli platform planks in recent times, stating, for example, that Jerusalem should never be a divided city and should remain Israel's capital. Candidate Bush also courted the Jewish vote with strongly pro-Israeli remarks. He reaffirmed the United States' commitment to Israel's security and called for an end to the Arab-Israeli dispute on the basis of UN Resolutions 242 and 338.

To a far greater extent than Reagan, Bush intended to be in charge of the nation's foreign policy. "He wanted to be the player, the guy who made as many of the calls as possible," observed the journalist and author Bob

Woodward. A World War II veteran, Bush accepted the Munich analogy that appeasement of aggression results in further aggression. This had a direct impact on his response to the invasion of Kuwait by Iraq in 1990.[2]

Bush's secretary of state was James Baker. A former chief of staff and treasury secretary during the Reagan administration and Bush's campaign manager in 1988, Baker owed his present position more to his considerable political skills and 35-year friendship with Bush than to his knowledge of world affairs. With respect to the Middle East, he did not think the United States should act prematurely or be too visible in trying to bring Arab and Israeli leaders to the negotiating table. At the same time, he was anxious to build on the momentum created by the opening of a dialogue between Washington and the PLO at the end of the Reagan administration.[3]

Shortly after Bush took office, the new administration asked Israel for its views on restoring the peace process. Considering this an opportunity to establish the terms for the next round of Mideast negotiations, Israeli prime minister Yitzhak Shamir proposed elections of non-PLO Palestinians on the West Bank and Gaza, followed by talks on Palestinian autonomy. Although Baker welcomed Shamir's offer of direct negotiations with Palestinians, he soon became frustrated by what he regarded as Israel's continued recalcitrance on the issue of the occupied territories. In May 1989, he spoke before the American-Israel Public Affairs Committee (AIPAC), the principal pro-Israeli lobbying group in Washington. In a sharply worded address, he called upon the Israeli government to "lay aside once and for all the unrealistic vision of a greater Israel." Even though previous administrations, including Reagan's, had occasionally rebuked Israel publicly, his remarks were widely interpreted as representing a major departure in American-Israeli relations. Commenting on his speech, Thomas Friedman pointed out the next day that his address lacked "many of the usual laudatory emotional references to Israel as a beleaguered and strategic American ally which were standard during the Reagan years."[4]

For almost a year, Baker coaxed and cajoled the Israeli government and Palestinians to hold talks on autonomy for the West Bank and Gaza. But just as the secretary appeared on the verge of success, Bush held a press conference in which he attacked Israel's construction of additional settlements in East Jerusalem for newly arriving immigrants from the Soviet Union. Whether the president's comments—which seemed to conflict with his own party's platform in 1988—were simply a blunder, as much of the media suggested, or a deliberate ploy to force Shamir and his Likud Party to embrace Baker's initiative, as the Israeli prime minister believed, is not clear.[5] What was certain was the president's growing frustration with Shamir. In particular, he was angry at Israel's refusal to guarantee that a $400 million housing loan from the United States would not be used to build new settlements in the occupied territories.[6]

Bush's comments elicited a sharp reaction both in the United States and in Israel. Prior to the press conference, King Hussein of Jordan had stated that new Jewish settlements for Soviet émigrés in Jerusalem and the West Bank would drive out Palestinians, who would then settle in his kingdom and cause him trouble. Shamir accused the White House of being more attentive to Hussein's concerns than to Israel's security needs. Bush's remarks also torpedoed the peacemaking effort begun by Baker a year earlier. The upshot of the press conference was a rejection by the Shamir government of the Baker plan.[7]

Bush's remarks also angered the American Jewish community and pro-Israeli forces on Capitol Hill and probably contributed to the collapse of Shamir's "unity" government, a weak coalition of Shamir's Likud Party and the Labor Party, whose leader, Shimon Peres, announced that he was pulling out of the government following its rejection of the Baker plan. This development was not entirely unwelcome at the White House, where it was hoped that new elections in Israel would bring the more moderate Labor Party to power. Instead, the election resulted in a standoff between Labor and Likud. Shamir then formed a new and even more hard-line government by gaining the support of small, ultraorthodox parties and excluding Laborites from the ruling coalition.[8]

Chastened by the negative reaction among American Jews and in Israel to Bush's remarks on new settlements in East Jerusalem, the White House sought to reassure Israel that it had no intention of weakening the U.S.-Israeli relationship. The president and secretary of state wrote letters to Israel's supporters in Congress and to Jerusalem's mayor, Teddy Kollek, assuring them that the administration had not changed its policy toward Israel. Although avoiding the troublesome question of whether Jerusalem should be Israel's capital, Bush told Kollek that the city's status "should be decided by negotiations," presumably between Israel and Arabs. But Bush's assurances were not enough to head off the formation of a more rightist government in Israel headed by Shamir.[9]

Meanwhile, talks between the United States and the PLO, which had been going on in Tunis for 18 months, were abruptly halted after the Palestinian Liberation Front (a PLO-associated group led by Abu Abbas) attempted on 31 May a seaborne infiltration of Israel on the beaches near Tel Aviv. The terrorists were intercepted by Israeli forces, and in the fire-fight that followed 4 of them were killed and 12 captured. One prisoner said that they had been ordered to attack international hotels and kill as many civilians as possible. Bush demanded that the PLO denounce the raid and expel Abu Abbas from the PLO's executive committee. Although Yasir Arafat disassociated himself from the attack and condemned attacks on civilians in principle, he failed to meet the president's conditions. Already under pressure from Congress to suspend or end negotiations with the PLO, Bush announced on 21 June that he was "suspend[ing] the dialogue between the United States and the PLO" pending a more satisfactory response from Arafat. For the moment, further peacemaking efforts in the Middle East were put on hold.[10]

Overtaking the Arab-Israeli dispute as Bush's chief concern in the Middle East, however, was the invasion of Kuwait by Iraq on 2 August 1990. Despite undeniable evidence that Iraq was mounting a huge military force on its border with Kuwait, including artillery and armored vehicles, few within the administration had anticipated the attack until just a few days before it began. When it came, it threw the administration into turmoil and caused confusion as to the White House's policy in the Persian Gulf. But it also resulted in Bush's finest hour as president.

Throughout the summer, Iraq's leader, Saddam Hussein, had been making threatening gestures in the Persian Gulf. The Iraq-Iran War had been extremely costly for Iraq, forcing it to borrow as much as $80 billion. Saddam maintained that the Arab powers should forgive their loans to Iraq since Iraq had spilled its blood to defend them from Iran's aggression. He focused his attention on Kuwait, which for more than half a century had been a bone in the throat of Baghdad. (Kuwait had loaned Iraq an estimated $20 billion.) In 1923, after granting Iraq statehood, the British had defined the Kuwait-Iraq border in a way that gave Kuwait more territory in the north than Kuwaiti rulers had historically controlled. Britain also purposely limited Iraq's access to the Persian Gulf to the much disputed Shatt al-Arab waterway, which flowed 50 miles between the port city of Basra and the gulf.[11]

Iraq disputed the border imposed by the British, and in 1961, after Britain granted Kuwait its independence, Baghdad claimed all of Kuwait as its own. Britain and the Arab League sent military and naval units to Kuwait to defend the country against an anticipated Iraqi invasion. Iraq did not attack Kuwait, but it refused to recognize the new country until 1963. Even then, Iraqi officials and propaganda continued to claim Kuwait as part of Iraq.[12]

Following the Iran-Iraq War, Saddam accused the Kuwaitis of stealing oil from Iraq's Rumaila oil field by slanting wells downward from Kuwait's small corner of the field into Iraqi territory. He also charged Kuwait with driving down the price of oil (the principal source of Iraqi income) by producing more than its quota of oil as established by the Organization of Oil Exporting Countries (OPEC). He demanded that Kuwait cut back its oil production, forgive its loans to Iraq, and hand over the $2.4 billion which, he said, it had stolen from the Rumaila field. In addition, he wanted possession of Kuwait's Warba and Bubiyan islands in order to improve Iraq's access to the Persian Gulf, especially since the Shatt al-Arab waterway was partially blocked by wreckage from the Iran-Iraq War.[13]

Although U.S. intelligence had detected the marshalling of Iraqi forces and weaponry along Iraq's border with Kuwait in July, most experts thought that Saddam's purpose was merely to pressure (or blackmail) Kuwait into meeting his demands. Such an analysis seemed borne out by the fact that only nine days before the invasion, the Iraqi leader had assured Egyptian president Hosni Mubarak that he did not intend to invade Kuwait. Meanwhile, the Kuwaitis had agreed to negotiations with Baghdad about their border dispute and had stated that they would stop pressing for an increase in their OPEC oil-production quota, which Iraq wanted cut. OPEC had agreed to raise the price of its oil from $18 to $21 a barrel.[14]

Most of the world was stunned, therefore, when Iraq crossed into Kuwait with a massive force and, in a matter of hours, took control of the sheikhdom. In justifying its invasion, Baghdad proclaimed that it had come to "liberate" Kuwait from the tyranny of the emir of Kuwait, Sheikh Jabir al-Ahmad al Sabah, who fled with his family to Saudi Arabia. Although Iraq established a new government of "young revolutionaries" and promised to begin a rapid withdrawal of its forces from Kuwait (it even had the media videotape Iraqi tanks preparing to leave), no one, least of all other Arab states, doubted that Iraq's purpose was to incorporate Kuwait into Iraq.[15]

In the Arab world a great amount of uncertainty and division existed as to how to respond to Iraq's seizure of Kuwait. Kuwait's wealth (including overseas assets of more than $100 billion), which the ruling family had flaunted, made it a target of resentment. Arab radicals also believed Kuwait was too closely tied to the West, and many of them viewed Saddam as the reincarnation of Nasser, welcoming his invocation of pan-Arabism and inveterate hostility to Israel. Defending his buildup of military forces, Saddam had argued that only by gaining military parity with Israel could the Arab world compel the Israelis to recognize Palestinian rights. He was also the only Arab leader in 1990 to unequivocally champion the Palestinian cause. Accordingly, he enjoyed the enthusiastic backing of the Palestinian people. The PLO, Libya, and newly united Yemen indicated their strong support for the Iraqi leader. In Libya and Yemen as well as in Jordan, Algeria, Tunisia, Lebanon, and the Sudan, thousands of demonstrators took to the streets to show their support of Saddam.[16]

In contrast, the leaders of Saudi Arabia, Egypt, and most other Arab states strongly opposed Iraq's invasion of Kuwait. For Saudi Arabia's conservative regime, Saddam presented a real and immediate danger. Saudi forces would be far outnumbered by Iraq's military machine should they be attacked. Although Saddam stated that he did not intend to invade Saudi Arabia, there were plenty of reasons to believe otherwise, including both that the Iraqi force sent into Kuwait was far bigger than was needed to seize that tiny and largely undefended country and that Iraq positioned its troops along the Kuwait-Saudi border. Egypt was also frightened by the prospect of Iraqi dominance of the Middle East, which clashed with its own historical aspirations. The same was true of Iraq's long-standing rival, Syria, whose president, Hafiz al-Asad, not only feared Iraq's growing power but despised Saddam.

Yet the Saudis, who would almost certainly have to seek American help in a military conflict with Iraq, had always been reluctant to allow foreign military personnel into the country. Accordingly, they were hesitant to challenge Iraq head-on. Egypt was also reluctant to act alone and groped for an Arab solution to the Iraqi invasion. That was also the position of King Hussein of Jordan, who was highly vulnerable to Iraqi pressure and could hardly come out in opposition to Baghdad given that the majority of his country's population was Palestinian.[17]

In the United States, President Bush responded angrily to Iraq's invasion of Kuwait. The White House had pursued good relations with Saddam, even blocking an attempt by Congress to impose economic sanctions against Iraq after it had used poisonous gas against Kurds in northern Iraq. But while the administration had indicated to Saddam (through the American ambassador to Iraq, April Glaspie) that it did not intend to become involved in Iraq's border dispute with Kuwait, Bush was outraged at what he called Saddam's "naked aggression." Remarking that "this will not stand," he froze $30 billion in Kuwaiti and Iraqi assets in the United States and worked the telephones in an attempt to build a coalition of Arab and European opposition to Iraq. He also ordered three aircraft carrier task forces to the region and stated that, to protect vital American interests, he was prepared to assist "Saudi Arabia in any way we possibly can."[18]

The president's efforts met with great success. The UN Security Council imposed a complete trade embargo on Iraq and demanded an immediate and unconditional withdrawal of Iraqi forces from Kuwait.[19] British prime minister Margaret Thatcher, who had first encouraged Bush to take a strong stand against Saddam during a brief meeting with the president on 2 August in Aspen, Colorado, stated that she stood solidly behind the president. After receiving a visit from Secretary of State Baker whom Bush had sent to the Middle East, Turkey agreed to stop the flow of Iraqi oil through a pipeline in its territory and to allow 14 U.S. F-111 fighter-bombers already positioned in Turkey to be used to protect Saudi Arabia.[20]

Even the Soviet Union, Iraq's biggest supplier of arms, cut off further arms shipments to Iraq and joined the United States in voting for the UN resolutions authorizing a trade embargo and the means to enforce it. By the time of Iraq's invasion of Kuwait, the cold war conflict between Washington and Moscow, which had shrouded most international politics for nearly half a century, was nearing its historic conclusion. This did not mean that Soviet policy was always in tandem with American policy or that Mikhail Gorbachev's efforts at reconciliation with the West were uniformly well-received within the walls of the Kremlin; far from it, as the 1991 botched coup against Gorbachev would make clear. Conservative hard-liners within the Soviet Union harshly attacked Gorbachev for such recent events as the tearing-down of the Berlin Wall, the reunification of Germany, and the collapse of the Warsaw Pact. Soviet military leaders also remained concerned about an expanded and permanent American military presence in the Persian Gulf.[21]

But while Gorbachev sought to link a resolution of the crisis over Kuwait to a settlement of the Arab-Israeli dispute as Saddam wanted,[22] he was also committed to avoiding international conflict, behaving as a responsible participant in the world community, solving regional disputes peacefully, and focusing his attention on interests more immediately vital to him than the Middle East, including fostering perestroika (domestic restructuring) and glasnost (openness to outside competitiveness). Accordingly, the Soviet Union surprised its erstwhile ally Iraq by being willing to support a trade embargo against it.[23]

Particularly impressive, though, was Saudi Arabia's response to the embargo, because it risked Saddam's wrath by joining Turkey in shutting down an Iraqi oil pipeline extending from the Iraqi city of Basra to the Saudi port of Yanbu on the Red Sea. Saudi Arabia also agreed to the basing of American forces in the country after Defense Secretary Richard Cheney showed King Fahd satellite photographs proving that Saddam had lied when he said his troops were pulling out of Kuwait. At an Arab League summit, a majority of Arab countries rejected an Iraqi proposal to link the withdrawal of Iraqi forces from Kuwait to the withdrawal of Israeli forces from the occupied territories. They also rejected Saddam's call for a jihad (holy war) against the coalition Bush was putting together. Instead, they voted to send Arab forces to Saudi Arabia. Syria announced that it would send at least 9,000 soldiers, a fully mechanized division, and as many as 270 tanks to help stop Saddam. Egypt agreed to deploy as many as 24,000 troops. The United Arab Emirates, Bahrain, and Qatar, which since becoming independent from Britain in 1971 had guarded their independence and avoided being dragged into the maelstrom of world politics, gave permission for American warplanes to use their territory. The Saudis, gulf states, and Kuwait's government in exile agreed to bankroll most of the military buildup. In addition, Riyadh gave up to $500 million in economic aid to Syria and $800 million to Egypt.

Despite Bush's leadership in rallying much of the world against Iraq, the administration itself was badly divided and uncertain as how to respond to Saddam's invasion of Kuwait. Its most immediate concern was that Iraq might attack Saudi Arabia. Defending the Saudis would pose a logistical nightmare even if Saddam put off his invasion for a month or two; if Iraq attacked immediately, there seemed no way, short of employing nuclear weapons, that an American force large enough to defend the Saudis could be assembled in time. The United States had theoretically been preparing to defend the Persian Gulf since President Jimmy Carter pledged in 1980 to use military force if necessary to prevent an outside force from gaining control of the gulf. But because Saudi Arabia and neighboring states had refused to permit American bases in the region, the closest base east of Turkey was on the island of Diego Garcia, 2,600 miles out in the Indian Ocean. Available supplies at Diego Garcia were sufficient to outfit only one division of 16,000 marines for 30 days. Furthermore, there were only 10,000 U.S. military personnel in the gulf region, almost all naval forces.[24]

The Pentagon estimated that it would take at least 60 days to transport just two divisions and between 90 and 120 days to move 100,000 ground troops to the gulf. These troops could be facing an Iraqi army of more than half a million men equipped with the latest military hardware, including biological and chemical weapons, which Iraq had been willing to use in its war against Iran. Moreover, most military experts regarded forcing Iraq out of Kuwait as unthinkable for the immediate future given the size and disbursement of Iraqi forces in that small country. According to General Norman Schwarzkopf, the commander of the U.S. Central Command (CENTCOM), which was responsible for the Middle East and Southwest Asia, it would take between 8 and 12 months to transport sufficient troops and equipment to drive the Iraqis from Kuwait.[25]

Yet by the end of August, the most dangerous period had passed as far as the United States was concerned. By this time, the first contingent of armed forces from the United States, the Ready Brigade of 2,300 troops from the 82nd Airborne Division, had arrived in Saudi Arabia. Other reinforcements were on the way, including marines and army airmobile and armored units. About 200 American warplanes, including F-15 fighters, had landed in bases in Saudi Arabia. They were backed up by the F-111s in Turkey, 50 huge B-52 bombers in Diego Garcia, and 60 aircraft on the three carrier task forces. The entire operation, known as Desert Shield, provided for 125,000 American troops to be sent to the region over the next two months supplemented by smaller forces from the Arab countries and the United States' western European allies.[26]

Iraq, in other words, had lost the opportunity for an early knockout blow of Saudi Arabia. While it was by no means certain that Iraq would be defeated if it launched an invasion, chances of that happening improved with each passing day. Instead of attacking Saudi Arabia, Saddam responded to the military buildup against him by taking foreign nationals in Iraq and Kuwait as hostages (he referred to them as "guests of Iraq") and threatening to use them as human shields if Iraq were attacked. He also ordered the closing of foreign embassies in Kuwait City since, he claimed, Kuwait was now the nineteenth province of Iraq. In September, Iraqi forces entered the Canadian, Dutch, and Belgian embassies and the residence of the French ambassador, where they took four French citizens captive. Although they were later released, French president François Mitterrand was so enraged by Iraq's action that he ordered a large French military force, including several thousand troops and tanks, to Saudi Arabia.[27]

The purpose of the coalition that Bush had assembled in Saudi Arabia remained a major question. Was it there to prevent the Saudis from being overrun by Iraq or to drive Iraq out of Kuwait? The president did not provide a clear answer. Although hindsight has shown his determination to force Iraq out of Kuwait even if that required military action, he failed to communicate his purpose adequately either to America's allies or to Congress. At one point, he stated that, in sending forces to Saudi Arabia, he intended to draw a "line in the sand" along the Saudi border, making it plain to Baghdad that crossing the line would mean war with the United States and its allies. But at other times he declared that he would accept nothing short of Iraqi withdrawal from Kuwait. Sometimes, he even seemed to suggest that he would not be satisfied until Saddam was driven from power and Iraq's warmaking ability, including its nuclear- and missile-production facilities, was totally destroyed. Speaking from the Oval Office in the morning of 8 August, he asserted that the United States sought "the immediate, unconditional and complete withdrawal of all Iraqi forces from Kuwait." But two days later, he remarked that the mission of American forces was "wholly defensive" and that they would not be used to liberate Kuwait. Apparently reversing course again, the president delivered a stinging attack against Saddam a few days later in which he strongly suggested that he intended to drive Iraq from Kuwait.[28]

The president's ambivalence caused considerable consternation at the Pentagon. As it appeared increasingly unlikely that Iraq was going to attack Saudi Arabia, General Schwarzkopf wanted to know whether the military buildup should continue and what America's military mission was. The chairman of the Joint Chiefs of Staff, Colin Powell, who had expressed reservations about sending American forces to the Middle East, was deeply disturbed at the military cost necessary to drive Iraq out of Kuwait. He was also annoyed that he had not been consulted by the president before Bush's 8 August remarks. According to Bob Woodward, it seemed to Powell "almost as if the President had six shooters in both hands and he was blazing away."[29]

Bush's failure to clearly articulate America's purpose in Saudi Arabia also caused rifts within the coalition and difficulty on Capitol Hill. While the coalition partners agreed on the need to keep Iraq from conquering Saudi Arabia and thereby gaining control of about 40 percent of the world's oil supply, they were not unanimous over whether to use military force to drive Iraq out of Kuwait. Even among those who believed that Iraq had to leave Kuwait, there was significant opposition to using military power, especially on the part of those who, like the Soviet Union, argued that economic sanctions would work if given enough time. This was a view also shared by many Washington lawmakers.[30]

In October, Israeli police killed at least 19 persons and wounded a score of others during a Palestinian demonstration in the West Bank and Gaza. The incident, which was the bloodiest day of the intifada, was a keen embarrassment for the White House and the coalition. Arabs did not need to be reminded that the United States was Israel's strongest supporter. It also became increasingly difficult for Arab leaders to justify their stand against Iraq's invasion of Kuwait as long as Israel held on to the occupied territories. Saddam's effort to link Iraq's evacuation of Kuwait to Israel's evacuation of the occupied territories was having its impact on the Arab world.[31]

For a time after the military buildup began, it appeared that a diplomatic solution to the Kuwaiti crisis might be achieved. Saddam pulled back some of his forces from the Kuwait-Saudi border. In interviews with Western reporters and journalists, including one with CBS's news anchorman Dan Rather in which Saddam dressed in a civilian suit rather than in his usual military uniform (presumably to show that he was a man of peace rather than war), he indicated that he was receptive to new ideas on how to resolve the crisis. Furthermore, he did not close down the foreign embassies in Kuwait as he had threatened to do, and he ordered Iraqi ships not to challenge a naval blockade the UN had imposed on Iraq on 25 August to enforce economic sanctions.[32]

In an interview with *Time* magazine, Egypt's leader, Hosni Mubarak, urged a diplomatic solution to the crisis even as he feared that the Middle East was moving toward war. "We can avoid war. It is not that difficult," he remarked. "War is a tragedy, a disaster."[33] Moscow also made clear its opposition to the use of military force. In September, the president met with Soviet leader Gorbachev. Although the two men issued a joint statement saying that Iraq's aggression "must not be tolerated," Gorbachev insisted that the gulf crisis could be settled peacefully.[34]

Worried about the fragility of the coalition he had put together, Bush also seemed amenable to negotiations. In October, he indicated support for a peace initiative begun by Jordan's King Hussein. But Saddam was unwilling to withdraw from Kuwait, and for the president, that remained the bottom line of any solution to the crisis. Increasingly he spoke about the opportunity, now that the cold war was over, for a "new world order," which he never defined but which, he argued, would be stillborn if aggressors like Saddam went unpunished. As Iraq systematically looted Kuwait and strengthened its forces along its border with Saudi Arabia, Bush became persuaded that by the time economic sanctions worked (if they would work at all), Kuwait would be destroyed as a nation.[35]

In contrast, Chairman Powell of the Joint Chiefs of Staff believed that economic sanctions were working and should be given a chance. Powell tried to enlist Defense Secretary Cheney and Secretary of State Baker in his effort to persuade the president to change his mind about sanctions. But Cheney remained noncommittal, and while Baker also preferred economic pressure to military confrontation, he either did not press his case with Bush or failed to budge the president. Two months into the crisis, National Security Adviser Brent Scowcroft told Powell that the president was "more and more convinced that sanctions are not going to work."[36]

Determined to liberate Kuwait from Iraq and increasingly skeptical about the value of economic sanctions, Bush announced in November, after the midterm elections, that the forces in Saudi Arabia would be expanded to 380,000 "to ensure that the coalition has an adequate offensive military option." Although polls showed that the American people continued to back the president, they also revealed that as the United States appeared to be drifting toward war, support for his policies eroded rapidly. The president was building up American forces in Saudi Arabia to convince Saddam that he would be driven out of Kuwait if he did not leave and to be ready for military action if he remained. But to the extent that Bush tried to frighten the Iraqi leader, he also scared the American people.[37]

On Capitol Hill, some lawmakers began to question the president's authority to order such a huge military buildup without congressional approval, while others warned against going to war simply to free Kuwait, which they maintained was a feudal autocracy. Still other critics accused Bush of preparing for war so that the United States would not have to pay a few cents more for a gallon of gasoline. Those who made this charge ignored the stakes involved in having ready access to much of the world's energy supplies. They also failed to produce hard evidence that oil, rather than Iraqi aggression, was what motivated Bush.[38]

Nevertheless, such charges resonated among the American people, and even the president was forced to admit that his support was waning because he had not explained his goals clearly. But in an interview with the Cable News Network (CNN), he also acknowledged that there was "a ticking of the clock toward war." Part of the reason for this, he said, was precisely because public support for his policies was dropping![39]

Bush also continued to face opposition within the coalition to his massive buildup of American forces. Both Egypt's Mubarak and Turkey's prime minister, Turgut Ozal, urged that economic sanctions be given several more months to work. Toward the end of November, the White House decided to seek, as part of its campaign to pressure Saddam out of Kuwait, a UN resolution authorizing military action against Iraq. Almost immediately the resolution ran into trouble over its wording. While France and the Soviet Union were agreeable to the resolution, they were reluctant to give the United States the blanket authority it sought; rather, they wanted further consultation before military force was deployed against Iraq. In a meeting with Bush, German chancellor Helmut Kohl also called for more negotiations with Saddam before resorting to war.[40]

Saddam tried to play on the antiwar sentiment being heard at the UN and elsewhere by pursuing a carrot-and-stick policy. On the one hand, he agreed to release the hostages he had been holding since August; provided Iraq was not attacked, they would be freed in stages beginning on Christmas day and ending by 25 March 1991. On the other hand, he coupled this conciliatory gesture with an announcement that Iraq was sending 250,000 military reservists to Kuwait and with new warnings about how costly a war against Iraq would be. His policy backfired. Instead of increasing the antiwar opposition at the UN, his defiant position on Kuwait helped assure passage on 29 November of the American resolution authorizing the use of force if Iraq did not withdraw from Kuwait by 15 January.[41]

The president's biggest problem was now on Capitol Hill, where some Republicans and a growing number of Democrats, including Sam Nunn of Georgia, the powerful chairman of the Senate Armed Services Committee, were speaking out against going to war. Following passage of the UN resolution, Saddam played his hostage card one last time by announcing the immediate release of the hostages and by apologizing for having taken them in the first place. This was enough to convince some lawmakers that the White House should give diplomacy another chance. "Saddam's pledge to release hostages is pretty good evidence that you don't have to pull the trigger to get his attention," commented Democratic Senator Christopher Dodd of Connecticut. Other lawmakers continued to argue that economic sanctions needed more time to work. Even Bush's director of the CIA, William Webster, testified that over time sanctions could cripple Iraq.[42]

In response to the growing opposition to war, Congress decided to vote on its own war-power resolutions. Bush also decided to seek congressional authorization for the use of force. He did not doubt his constitutional right to employ America's military power in the Persian Gulf. "I feel I have the constitutional authority" to go to war and "Saddam Hussein should be under no question on this," he remarked on 9 January 1991, just one week before hostilities began.[43] The Justice Department informed him that he could use military force without congressional approval, just as President Harry Truman had done in 1950 during the Korean War. But he was concerned that going into battle against the expressed wishes of the Congress might create a constitutional nightmare. He also agreed with most of his advisers that it would be wrong to risk American lives without having the nation fully committed to the war effort. He did not want a repeat of the Vietnam War. On 8 January, therefore, a day before he reiterated his belief that he did not need Congress's consent, he sent a letter to Capitol Hill asking for congressional authorization to use military force against Iraq.[44]

The 15 January deadline in the UN war-powers resolution had been intended in part to mollify congressional and other critics of Bush's policy by giving Iraq "a last chance" to leave Kuwait peacefully. Stating that he was still willing to "go the extra mile for peace," the president even agreed to send Secretary of State Baker to Iraq to meet with Saddam and extended an invitation to Iraq's foreign minister, Tariq Aziz, to meet with him at the White House. The Iraqi leader responded that he would send Aziz to Washington but that he could not meet with Baker before 12 January. Bush rejected the proposal, maintaining that a meeting so close to the 15 January would only provide Saddam with an opportunity to stall. But as Bush's critics and other commentators pointed out, there was really nothing to negotiate other than the terms of Iraq's withdrawal from Kuwait. "On this question," Bush remarked, "I've got it boiled down very clearly to good vs. evil. . . . I think what's at stake here is the new world order." That made the issue of Iraqi withdrawal nonnegotiable.[45]

In the final month before the war, there was much speculation that a negotiated settlement would be worked out involving some face-saving concessions to Iraq (perhaps including territorial concessions) in return for its withdrawal from Kuwait. But nothing happened. In the hope of dividing Arab leaders and undermining the coalition against him, Saddam tried to manipulate the crisis by linking it once more to the Arab-Israeli dispute and appealing to Arab unity. He indicated that he might be willing to withdraw his forces from Kuwait in return for Israeli withdrawal from the occupied territories. But Arab unity had always been honored more in rhetoric than in reality, and although Saddam succeeded in causing strains within the coalition, it held together.[46]

In the United States, a final showdown took place between Capitol Hill and the White House as the vote drew near on the war-powers resolution. But once more Iraq played into Bush's hands. Although Bush had turned down a 12 January meeting between Baker and Saddam, he proposed that the secretary of state and Iraqi foreign minister Aziz meet at Geneva sometime between 7 and 9 January. Iraq accepted the offer, but the meeting at Geneva on 9 January was counterproductive. Aziz refused to accept a letter from the president to Saddam in which Bush warned that Iraq and the United States were on the brink of war and that failure to leave Kuwait would be calamitous for Iraq.[47]

Despite Aziz's refusal to transmit Bush's letter to Saddam, the vote in the Senate on the war authorization resolution was very close. The House approved the resolution by a vote of 250 to 183, but in the Senate it passed by a margin of only 52 to 47. The singular failure of the Baker-Aziz meeting had shifted the burden of intransigence from Bush to Iraq and made it difficult for many senators to vote against the president. Absent the failed Geneva meeting and Aziz's unwillingness to forward Bush's message to Saddam, the vote might have gone the other way.[48]

The road of diplomacy had ended. On 16 January the road of war began, and Operation Desert Shield gave way to Operation Desert Storm. On the day after the UN deadline expired, American aircraft and cruise missiles launched from naval vessels in the Persian Gulf struck at communication and transportation targets in and around Baghdad. This was part of a military plan against Iraq that had been in preparation since August. The plan was divided into four stages. The first three involved an air campaign designed to sever communications between Kuwait and Baghdad, wipe out Iraq's air force and defense systems, destroy its transport, munitions, and supply facilities, and attack Iraqi forces on the ground.[49]

Only when Iraq's infrastructure had been rendered sufficiently useless would the final stage of the operation, a ground attack, begin. Initially the ground phase had called for a strike into Kuwait against Iraq's most entrenched forces. But Defense Secretary Cheney rejected the plan because he thought it made no sense to attack what was believed to be an overwhelming Iraqi force. Instead, he favored a flanking operation. The new plan, known as "the enhanced option," reflected Cheney's input. Instead of striking at the center of Iraq's lines, it provided for a wide flanking movement in which coalition forces, heavily reinforced with tanks and other armored vehicles, would cross into Iraq 200 miles west of Kuwait. They would then move rapidly eastward hitting Saddam's much vaunted Republican Guard in southern Iraq and striking at Iraqi forces withdrawing from Kuwait.[50]

The entire military operation worked brilliantly. Following the first night's raid against Baghdad, which was carried live over television from the Baghdad hotel room of CNN correspondents Bernard Shaw and Peter Arnett, public euphoria swept the United States in anticipation of a short and largely bloodless war. The euphoria was quickly dispelled as cloud cover over Iraq made it difficult to launch new strikes. Even after the weather cleared and the air campaign began again, it became apparent that severing the Iraqi command-and-control system would be difficult. As it seemed that the air campaign would not be sufficient to force Iraq to surrender, necessitating a ground war, concern mounted in the United States about the possible casualty count in such a war.[51]

The air campaign continued for three weeks with great effectiveness, thereby challenging the view of many military analysts that wars could not be won from the air. Americans were able to see almost daily pictures of Iraqi targets being taken out by laser-directed bombs, some of which had the ability to burrow deep beneath the ground. Iraqi air defenses proved a sham, and most of the once-feared Iraqi air force was either destroyed on the ground or fled to nearby Iran. To the surprise of some commentators, moreover, Iraq did not use any of the chemical or biological weapons it had in its arsenal and had used against Iran.

Before the war began, Saddam had made it clear that if he were attacked, he would launch missiles against Israel. This caused the White House considerable concern because Israel's policy had always been to retaliate after being attacked. The administration feared—and Saddam hoped—that if this happened, the Arab members of the coalition might break away, worried about the domestic consequences of fighting on the same side as Israel against another Arab country. Keeping his word, Saddam launched SCUD missiles against Haifa and Tel Aviv, killing and wounding a number of

Israelis. In all, Iraq sent between 30 and 40 SCUDs against Israel. But pressed by the United States and understanding the possible consequences of retaliation, Israel refrained from responding, even though Iraq attacked Israel and Saudi Arabia with missiles from mobile launchers that proved extremely difficult to locate and destroy.[52]

As the air campaign continued, the Pentagon grew more confident that the conflict would be short rather than long. Still, the war plan called for a ground offensive against Iraq beginning around the third week of hostilities. The offensive started on 24 February. By this time, coalition forces had grown to over half a million, and more than 250,000 men and 1,000 tanks had been deployed to the west along the Iraq-Saudi border, their movement hidden by the air campaign. To confuse Iraqi defenders as to where the expected offensive would take place, coalition forces conducted feints along the border. Thousands of American marines at sea also prepared for an amphibious invasion that never took place. But because the Iraqis believed that the coalition might strike from the gulf, they diverted six divisions to defend against such an attack.

The entire ground operation lasted 100 hours. Coalition forces easily breached the famed Hussein Line and moved into Kuwait to fool the Iraqis into believing that the main attack would be toward Kuwait City. Far to the west, though, the real battle took place when the armored and airborne forces of the Seventh and Eighteenth Corps advanced against the Iraqi Republican Guard. The initial attack went so well that General Schwarzkopf accelerated his battle plan by 15 hours. Although there were pockets of resistance, along the whole battle line Iraqi defenses crumbled faster than anyone had anticipated. Iraqi artillery fired only sporadically or not at all for fear of being destroyed from the air. The massive air campaign had terrified Iraqi forces. Thousands of Iraqi troops simply put down their arms and surrendered to coalition forces.

By 26 February, Iraqi forces in Kuwait had been routed, and the highway out of Kuwait City had become clogged with more than a thousand trucks fleeing north into Iraq. The road itself became known as the "highway of death," as the convoy became an easy target for coalition aircraft. To the west, the Republican Guard, supported by a massive force of armored vehicles, put up significant resistance, and the toughest battle of the war was fought on the night of 26–27 February when the Seventh Corps launched a major attack against three mechanized divisions of the Republican Guard. The tank battles which took place were the largest since World War II, involving 3,500 tanks on the coalition side alone. But by the evening of 27 February, the Republican Guard had been routed and was fleeing northward in full retreat.

The war came to an end on 28 February when President Bush ordered a cease-fire following peace overtures from Baghdad. Some critics believe that Bush should not have ended the war until the remaining Iraqi forces, especially the Republican Guard, had been completely destroyed and Saddam toppled from power. But the carnage, which was covered extensively by the media, was so great, especially along "the highway of death," that the president felt he had no choice but to agree to a termination of hostilities.[53]

Following the end of the war, the United Nations adopted Resolution 686, requiring Iraq to renounce all ambitions on Kuwait and to agree to a number of other steps, including the destruction of its nuclear, biological, and chemical warfare capabilities.[54] On 3 March 1991, General Schwarzkopf met with Iraqi military leaders who agreed to the terms of the resolution, thereby formally bringing an end to the Gulf War.[55]

The Persian Gulf War had been a resounding success for the United States and its coalition partners, making heroes of the military commanders who had led the coalition. Most notable among these were the chairman of the Joint Chiefs of Staff, Colin Powell, who had held firm to his conviction that if the United States was going to fight a war in the Middle East, it had to do so with whatever forces and equipment were needed to win decisively, and CINC Commander Norman Schwarzkopf, who had helped develop and then had brilliantly executed the plan that won the war. But no one came out of Desert Shield and Desert Storm with greater glory than President Bush.

From the beginning of the crisis following Iraq's invasion of Kuwait, Bush had held firm to his conviction that Kuwait had to be liberated. He had pieced together a coalition that just a few months earlier would have been virtually inconceivable. At home, he had also overcome considerable opposition, especially on Capitol Hill, to war against Iraq. Despite stresses and strains within the coalition and domestic opposition, he had achieved a quick and decisive military victory. Less than two years before the next presidential elections, his reelection seemed almost a certainty.

Despite the acclaim he received, Bush was not without his critics. In a sharp attack on the president's policies during the Kuwait crisis, historian Jean Edward Smith summarized in 1992 many of the criticisms of Bush. Among these were the president's personal animus toward Saddam which affected Bush's judgment ("Bush personalized the crisis," Smith commented), his inflated view of his authority as commander in chief, his disinterest in seeking a peaceful solution to the crisis, the autocratic nature of the Kuwaiti regime (and, for that matter, of the other Arab members of the coalition), the legitimacy of some of Iraq's grievances against Kuwait, and finally, the fact that nothing much had happened as a result of the war ("Saddam Hussein remains in power, and the Baathist regime appears as firmly entrenched as ever," Smith noted,) except that "the United States finds itself deeply embroiled in the muddled affairs of the Middle East."[56]

There is much truth to many of these arguments, and it is hard to deny Smith's fundamental point—that the Persian Gulf War was "George Bush's war." It will be many years before the war's full impact on the Middle East is known. But on one point, Smith is clearly wrong. Contrary to what he wrote in 1992, the conflict produced major changes in the dynamics of Middle East politics, which together with the intifada uprising and the end of the cold war, resulted in the most significant breakthrough in the Arab-Israeli dispute since the establishment of Israel in 1948. By greatly limiting Iraq's military power and political influence in the Middle East, increasing America's military and political credibility in the region, isolating the PLO, underscoring the injustices of oppressed people, revealing Israel's military vulnerability, and furthering Soviet-American cooperation, the Persian Gulf War fostered the climate and helped to create the framework that made this breakthrough possible.

chapter 11

IN THE AFTERMATH OF WAR: 1991–1994

Whether President George Bush would have been able to put together the coalition to fight the Iraqis without the end of the cold war is impossible to say. But it seems highly unlikely. Soviet cooperation rather than traditional cold war opposition allowed the administration to engage in coalition building and to exert its military power in the Middle East without fear of a Soviet military response.

The end of the cold war also meant that Soviet clients in the Middle East, including Iraq, Syria, and the PLO, could no longer look to Moscow for military and economic assistance. This did not result in a quick or easy resolution of the Arab-Israeli dispute, especially given Israel's reluctance to deal with the PLO or relinquish the occupied territories. But together with the intifada and the changes in the Middle East brought about by the Persian Gulf War, it vastly increased the chance of a negotiated settlement.

Indeed, by the time Bush left office in 1993 after being defeated in his reelection bid by the Democratic candidate, Governor Bill Clinton of Arkansas, Palestinian and Israeli negotiators were meeting to discuss the provisions of an agreement for Palestinian self-rule. This resulted in a historic meeting at the White House in September 1993 between PLO chairman Yasir Arafat and Israeli prime minister Yitzhak Rabin watched over by Clinton. As the president looked on, the two leaders, arch enemies all their adult lives, signed documents in which Israel recognized the PLO as the legitimate representative of the Palestinian people and agreed to allow Palestinians in the Gaza Strip and the town of Jericho on the West Bank to begin the process of self-government. In return, the PLO recognized Israel's right to exist in peace. Following the signing ceremony, a reluctant Rabin, coaxed by Clinton, shook hands with Arafat.

In the months that followed the White House meeting, the peace process seemed to falter as disagreement developed between Israeli and Palestinian negotiators over the specifics of the agreement and as opposition spread both among Palestinians and Israelis to the accords. In February 1994, most of these obstacles were overcome, and a new agreement was signed in Cairo spelling out the details of the transition to Palestinian self-government. A massacre of Palestinians at a mosque in Hebron later that month by a fanatic Israeli settler, Baruch Goldstein, once more threw the peace process into turmoil. But in May, talks between Israel and the PLO over the extension of Palestinian autonomy throughout the West Bank, which had been suspended following the Hebron massacre, were resumed, as were other negotiations between Israel and Jordan.

A number of dangerous and unresolved problems still leave the future of the Middle East cloudy and uncertain at best. But toward the end of July, these Israeli-Jordanian talks culminated in another historic agreement signed at the White House, this time by Rabin and Jordan's King Hussein, which normalized relations between their two countries. This has provided reason for cautious optimism that the Arab-Israeli dispute, which has been the central issue in the United States' relations with the Arab Middle East for most of the period since 1945, might finally be settled.

Although planning for Desert Shield and Desert Storm had extended over six months, the White House had given surprisingly little attention to what would happen after Saddam was driven from Kuwait. In testimony before Congress in December 1990, Defense Secretary Richard Cheney acknowledged that "everybody has been so busy dealing with the crisis at the moment that there hasn't been much effort put into that longer-range focus yet."[1]

But the war had a major impact on the Middle East. The massive deployment of American and European troops in Saudi Arabia fueled anti-Western sentiment among Islamic fundamentalists and Palestinians, which was one reason Saudi Arabia had been reluctant to play host to American forces before the war and was anxious to have most of them leave after the fighting was over. Saddam's efforts to manipulate his conflict with coalition forces into one between the "haves" and the "have nots" also highlighted the enormous economic and social gaps within the Arab world. In the process, it threatened to fuel extremism and undermine existing Arab regimes in the region. Furthermore, the Gulf War made available to the Arab members of the coalition substantial amounts of the United States' most sophisticated military technology, which posed a threat to the precarious military balance of power between Israel and the Arab states.[2]

The end of the war also raised a number of questions about the future of Iraq. The possibility that Iran might take advantage of Iraq's defeat and Saddam's humiliation by positioning itself among Iraq's Shi'ite population in a post-Saddam power struggle and building a new regional order in the gulf was one reason Bush administration officials were not anxious to see Saddam toppled from power and Iraq's military capability completely liquidated. "If Iraq is totally out of the picture," remarked William Quandt of the Brookings Institution, "there is no counterbalance to Iran."[3] But Syria and Turkey also had designs on Iraq. Syria's leader Hafiz al-Asad had long claimed to be the sole legitimate leader of the Ba'th Party, and Turkey had historic claims to Iraq's oil-rich Mosul province in the north. Furthermore, Kurds in northern Iraq and Shi'ites in southern Iraq were in open rebellion against Baghdad. The political instability in Iraq and the potential for even more serious problems elsewhere in the Middle East were so great that some officials at the State Department, Pentagon, and CIA suggested that the United States could win the war but lose the peace.[4]

But the forces of change resulting from the war offered opportunity as well as danger. A widespread sense of good feeling because of the coalition's victory raised the possibility that Arab and Israeli leaders might be willing to sit down at the bargaining table, resolve their differences, and live at peace with one another. Some commentators even maintained that Saddam's defeat had buried forever the idea of an Arab military solution to the Palestinian problem. At the same time, Saddam's effectiveness in identifying himself with the cause of the Palestinian people forced world leaders to focus on the plight of the Palestinians with a renewed sense of urgency.[5]

As leader of the coalition and the world's only remaining superpower, the United States was in a stronger position to advance the cause of peace than at any time since the signing of the Camp David Accords a decade earlier. Even al-Asad, America's inveterate foe in the Middle East for a quarter century, seemed interested in some kind of rapprochement with the United States. His cultivation of America's goodwill suggested that he—and other Arab leaders—might be prepared to accept Israel's right to exist in peace.[6]

To what extent the PLO and those Arab regimes that had backed Saddam would go along with or participate in a new peace effort was still unclear. But the PLO had lost its purse strings because it backed Iraq, and its future was tied to whatever role it might be offered or could play in subsequent Arab-Israeli negotiations. Although Jordan had also supported Iraq during the war, King Hussein's most fervent wish was to resolve the Palestinian question in a way that did not imperil his country or threaten his throne. Other Arab regimes that had backed Iraq, such as Libya, Yemen, and the Sudan, were largely marginal players in the region's politics. Libya, of course, was still a major oil producer and had a large military force. It also supported terrorism. But in recent years, Qaddafi had remained relatively quiescent. Certainly Libya had kept a low profile during the Persian Gulf War, as had the Sudan and the Yemeni republic, which voted against the UN resolution authorizing war against Iraq but complied with the economic sanctions imposed by the UN.[7]

The most immediate problem facing the White House after the Persian Gulf War was the civil war that had erupted in Iraq, with rebellions against

Saddam's rule in both the country's northern and southern regions. In contrast to the decisiveness he displayed throughout Desert Shield and Desert Storm, Bush appeared weak and ineffective as he tried to respond to the Iraqi civil conflict. In the north, Iraq's Kurdish population had long sought the establishment of an autonomous Kurdish state. Although Saddam had ruthlessly put down a Kurdish rebellion in 1988, Kurds hoped his defeat would lead to autonomy or even independence, and they looked to the United States for support.[8] The Shi'ites in the south, who had always objected to the fact that Sunni Muslims controlled the country even though Shi'ites were in the majority, also saw an opportunity to break away from Iraq or to overthrow the government in Baghdad and create an Islamic republic.[9]

The civil war raging in Iraq put the administration in a difficult position. It could not intrude with force without contributing to the very dismemberment of the country that it opposed. Furthermore, it did not want to get into a Vietnam-like situation by becoming involved in a protracted civil war. Moreover, Saudi Arabia wanted neither a Shi'ite government in Baghdad, which would presumably be closely tied to Tehran, nor the spread of Shi'ite nationalism to its own minority Shi'ite population. Similarly, Kurdish autonomy in northern Iraq posed a threat to Turkey with its substantial Kurdish population. Yet as Bush's critics pointed out, the president had spent eight months encouraging the Iraqis to overthrow Saddam. Having fostered rebellion and vilified Saddam, how could he simply turn his back on those who looked to Washington for support?[10]

But that is what the administration did. In the south, Saddam's Republican Guard ruthlessly suppressed and massacred Shi'ite dissidents without an American response. In the north, Kurdish fighters actually controlled part of the region for a short time. When it became apparent that the United States was not going to rescue them from stronger government forces, hundreds of thousands of Kurds, frightened and fearing for their lives, fled their homes and journeyed by foot into the mountains separating Iraq and Turkey.[11]

As reports circulated in the United States about events in Iraq, the president faced his first serious criticism since the end of the war. He was reproached both by his traditional political foes, including those who had opposed the Gulf War, and by others who had only recently praised his leadership. Not helping matters was the fact that, after Bush warned Iraq not to fly its airplanes near coalition forces, American fliers shot down three Iraqi aircraft in northern Iraq, 250 miles from the nearest coalition forces. This led to speculation that the White House was really trying to tip the balance in Iraq's civil war against the Baghdad government. But the speculation was put to rest when the administration resisted pressure two weeks later to shoot down Iraqi helicopters being used by Saddam to suppress the rebellion.[12]

To help the cold and starving Kurds in the mountains of northern Iraq, where an estimated 500 to 1,000 Kurds were dying each day, Bush ordered a massive relief mission in April. Under pressure from Turkish president Turgut Ozal and British prime minister John Major, he also agreed to the establishment of enclaves for the Kurds, guarded by American, British, and French troops, which would be off-limits to Iraq's military forces. But he made this decision reluctantly, and only after being reassured by his advisers that it would not delay the return home of American forces from Desert Storm. "I am not going to involve any American troops in a civil war in Iraq," he told reporters. Because of the administration's determination to limit America's involvement in Iraq's civil strife, the president was accused by some of his critics of pursuing an immoral policy.[13]

Over the spring and summer, criticism of the president's policy mounted. Between March and September, Secretary of State Baker made eight trips to the Middle East in what appeared to be a largely unsuccessful attempt at shuttle diplomacy. The secretary offered no plan for ending the conflict, preferring instead to have the disputants develop their own proposals. But this seemed to result only in diplomatic drift. At the beginning of June, the administration presented a plan for Middle East arms control, but the Pentagon turned back a State Department proposal for a one-year moratorium on arms sales, and the United States continued to negotiate arms deals with Saudi Arabia and Egypt. In Israel, Defense Secretary Cheney promised Israeli leaders 10 F-15 fighters and $210 million in aid for its Arrow anti-missile program. White House efforts to establish security arrangements for the Persian Gulf also foundered, and plans for economic development languished.[14]

Six months after Bush had declared victory over Saddam, it appeared that his administration still lacked a well-defined postwar policy for the Middle East. To the extent that there was a plan it appeared aimless, inconsistent, and largely unproductive.[15] Yet while the president and his secretary of state had no grand design for the Middle East, they regarded the successful conclusion of the Persian Gulf War as an opportunity to end the deadlock in the Arab-Israeli dispute. America's "commitment to peace in the Middle East does not end with the liberation of Kuwait," the president had stated soon after the fighting stopped.[16] And while he and Baker offered no American proposal for breaking the deadlock in the peace process other than a suggestion by Bush that Israel be willing to trade land for peace, they were eager to convene an international conference on the Middle East. During his trips to the region, the secretary of state received tentative commitments from Egypt, Saudi Arabia, Syria, Jordan, Lebanon, and Israel to attend a meeting cosponsored by the Soviet Union sometime in the fall. Saudi Arabia and Kuwait also indicated their acceptance of Israel by agreeing to end their secondary boycott against that country (boycotting any firm that traded with Israel) and by renouncing the UN resolution that equated Zionism with racism.[17]

Neither Syria nor Israel were especially anxious to participate in an international conference. Syria had always resisted any talks with Israel until the Israelis agreed to withdraw from the occupied territories. Syrian leader al-Asad agreed to negotiations largely because he wanted good relations with the United States now that it was the only superpower and had shown its willingness to use military force to protect its interests in the Middle East. He also understood that the only way Syria could hope to recover the Golan Heights was to negotiate for them, and he feared that if he remained outside the peace process, Syria might lose the financial support it was receiving from the Persian Gulf states. No longer could he look to the Soviet Union, which was disintegrating, for military and economic aid. Indeed, Soviet president Mikhail Gorbachev lectured al-Asad on the need to make peace with Israel, warning him that Moscow would not support Syrian military efforts to resolve the conflict.[18]

Although Israeli prime minister Yitzhak Shamir agreed in principle to an international meeting, he remained opposed to the whole peace process being promoted by Washington. Not only would Israel be required to give up land for the less tangible concession of peace, but it could be outvoted at an international meeting. The Israeli leader gave his conditional consent to the meeting because he did not want to antagonize Washington and because he concluded that Israel's interests would be better protected by being involved in the peace process than by being outside of it.[19]

Even though Baker gained early agreement for an international conference from both Arab and Israeli leaders, working out the actual details of the meeting proved troublesome and frustrating. As in earlier efforts at negotiations, the two thorniest questions were over Israeli settlements on the West Bank and Gaza and Palestinian representation at the meeting. Shamir remained defiant on the settlements issue. His government continued to build housing in the occupied territories for the thousands of Soviet Jews who, in the era of glasnost, were being allowed to emigrate to Israel.[20]

Shamir's refusal to curtail construction of new settlements infuriated Bush, who disliked the Israeli leader and considered his action a personal affront. Furthermore, Arab leaders made the White House's response to the new settlements a test of its credibility as an honest broker. They were not disappointed. Still enjoying overwhelming support at home because of the Persian Gulf War, the president convinced Congress in September to withhold $10 billion in loan guarantees to Israel for 120 days—a "pause for peace," he said, to avoid jeopardizing the Middle East peace process. Almost as importantly, he spoke out against the settlements and publicly attacked the pro-Israeli lobby on Capitol Hill.[21]

The question of Palestinian representation at an international conference also proved difficult, although not nearly as much as in the past, when the Arab states had insisted on a PLO presence in the negotiations. Israel held to its familiar position that under no circumstances would it meet with representatives of the PLO. Nor would it engage in discussions with Palestinians who carried Jerusalem residence cards or lived outside the occupied territories. These demands were consistent with Israel's position that the establishment of an independent Palestinian state or a change in the status of Jerusalem were not negotiable and that any changes in the status of the West Bank and Gaza would have to be transitional.[22]

Fortunately for the peace process, Egypt, Syria, Saudi Arabia, and the other gulf states no longer designated the PLO as the sole legitimate representative of the Palestinian people. Moreover, Palestinians in the occupied territories, who previously had been unprepared to act without the approval of the PLO, were now willing to assume a leadership role. Nevertheless, Palestinian leaders warned that any attempt by Israel to determine the composition of a Palestinian delegation would undermine the chances of their attending the conference. After much negotiation, a formula was worked out that largely met the Israeli conditions. But it was also widely understood that the Palestinian representatives at the meeting would be chosen from a list approved by the PLO and that the PLO would be unofficially represented.[23]

The four-day conference met in the Crystal Pavilion in Madrid, Spain, beginning on 30 October. Madrid was chosen as the meeting site because, having had to contend with its own Basque terrorists, Spain was thought to be able to provide better security than most countries. Also, there was symbolic significance to holding the conference in a country where Arabs and Jews had once lived peacefully together. Because the Soviet Union had cohosted the 1973 Geneva meeting on the Middle East and was still a major power, it also cohosted this conference. But no one doubted that the United States was the driving force behind the conference and would be its guiding hand. Indeed, after some perfunctory opening remarks by Soviet leader Gorbachev, the Soviets largely disappeared from the scene. Their role was minor and largely supportive of the United States. No longer could Arab leaders look to the Soviet Union to defend their interests as they had in the past.[24]

President Bush joined Gorbachev in opening the Madrid Conference. In his brief remarks, Bush stated that the purpose of the gathering was "not simply to end the state of war in the Middle East" but to achieve a real peace that would include treaties on a wide range of matters from diplomatic relations to tourism and cultural exchanges. Realistically, he acknowledged, this might take several years, but the United States was prepared to "play an active role in helping the [peace] process succeed."[25]

At Madrid, there were two forums, one public and the other private. The public forum amounted to little more than statements of long-held grievances and recriminations by both Arab and Israeli delegates. The rhetorical clashes that took place were heated and vituperative. The exchange between Israeli prime minister Shamir, whose very presence indicated the importance he attached to the conference, and Syrian foreign minister Farouk al-Sharaa was particularly vicious. But much of this was also maneuvering and posturing (taking a maximalist position), intended to assuage domestic opponents of the conference, who could watch the televised proceedings. The real negotiations were to take place in bilateral meetings between Israel and the various Arab states, which would begin in Madrid but continue after the conference had been adjourned. There would also be ongoing multilateral negotiations on issues that crossed national boundaries such as arms control, refugees, and economic development. Negotiations between Israel and the Palestinians would be based on the framework first agreed to at Camp David in 1978—that is, an interim agreement on self-government for five years followed by negotiations on the permanent status of the West Bank and Gaza.[26]

The Madrid Conference was far from a rousing success. Arab delegates were genuinely disappointed that Shamir did not offer proposals based on the principles of UN Resolutions 242 and 338 (territory for peace). The Israeli delegation was equally unhappy that the Arab representatives were not more forthcoming in recognizing Israel's genuine security concerns. Secretary Baker expressed his own disappointment at the "unwillingness of the parties to take confidence-building steps." A number of procedural questions also marred the conference, including disagreements over the venues for the talks that would follow the conference. No new proposals for peace were put on the table or developed at Madrid.[27]

Nevertheless, the conference represented a milestone in the Arab-Israeli dispute. For instance, the meetings between the Israeli and Jordanian/Palestinian delegations went surprisingly well. Afterward, both the Israelis and Palestinians expressed optimism about the prospects for future negotiations, which they said would take place in about two or three weeks. The Palestinians even made clear that their talks with Israel would not be impeded by the other bilateral negotiations taking place, such as those between Syria and Israel, which promised to be the most difficult.[28]

Although the Syrians termed their first round of talks with the Israelis disastrous, the very fact that they were sitting down with the Israelis in face-to-face meetings would have been unthinkable just a year earlier. Even Syrian foreign minister al-Sharaa, who two days earlier had been vitriolic in his denunciation of Israel, left Madrid sounding upbeat. "Have you ever seen a conference with so much interest all over the world?" he asked reporters. "I think that this is a driving force that should never stop."[29] The Madrid Conference had initiated a process that had a momentum of its own, making it unwise for its participants to avoid it.[30]

Yet it took 21 months and 11 rounds of negotiations before a real breakthrough occurred in the peace talks. During the second round, held in Washington from 10 to 18 December 1991, Israeli, Jordanian, and Palestinian delegates vainly tried to decide the format for subsequent talks. Separately, Syria and Israel held chilly discussions with negligible progress. In the third round in January, the Israeli delegates came under heavy pressure from right-wing politicians at home who wanted to pull out of the negotiations. The fourth round, held the next month, ended in disarray after Israel rejected a Palestinian proposal for elections in the West Bank, Gaza, and East Jerusalem. But in the fifth round at the end of May, Israel proposed holding municipal elections in the West Bank and Gaza and turning over the administration of 14 hospitals to the Palestinians. Palestinians wanted to move directly to electing a self-governing authority, but they neither accepted nor rejected the Israeli plan.[31]

Before the next round of talks at the end of August, Israel held new parliamentary elections in which the Likud coalition, which had controlled the government for most of the time since 1977,[32] was soundly defeated by the Labor opposition. Israel's new leader, Yitzhak Rabin, was far more prepared than his predecessor to negotiate with Arab leaders. Shortly after taking office, he traveled to Egypt, where he held friendly talks with President Hosni Mubarak. After returning home, he canceled plans for new settlements in the West Bank, although he allowed existing construction to continue.[33]

As another indication of a new era in Israeli politics, at the sixth round of peace negotiations beginning at the end of August, Israel talked openly for the first time about the possibility of withdrawing from part of the Golan Heights. Rabin even offered to meet with Syrian leader al-Asad in Damascus to discuss Syrian-Israeli relations, but al-Asad was not ready to engage in a summit with the Israelis.[34] But Rabin had limits on how much he would compromise on the Golan. At the seventh round beginning on 21 October, Israel reiterated its willingness to talk about pulling out of the Golan Heights, but its negotiators made it clear that they were not prepared to yield the entire strategic plateau. Nor were they receptive to the Palestinians' call for a similar Israeli commitment to yield ground on the West Bank, Gaza, and East Jerusalem.[35]

As a result, the Palestinians sent a scaled-down delegation to the eighth round of negotiations in December. They also demanded that the United States apply more pressure on Israel to make concessions on the issue of Palestinian self-rule. But the negotiations hit a snag when Palestinians killed six Israeli paratroopers, and Israel responded by deporting more than 400 Palestinians from the West Bank and Gaza to southern Lebanon, where they lived in makeshift camps and endured a harsh winter.[36]

The next round of negotiations in April 1993 opened on a more hopeful note. Israel revoked its objection to Faisal Husseini, a key East Jerusalem PLO activist, participating in the talks. Israel also repatriated 30 Palestinians expelled between 1967 and 1987 and offered to take back some of those deported in December. But the discussions ended in disarray after the Palestinians rejected an American proposal on Palestinian self-government—Washington's first direct attempt to bridge the gap between Israeli and Palestinian negotiators.[37]

By the time the tenth round of talks began on 15 June, it appeared that this latest attempt at a negotiated peace, which had begun on an optimistic note in Madrid over a year earlier, had reached the same dead end as earlier peace efforts. Washington proffered a new document to help identify Israeli-Palestinian differences, but both sides were unhappy with it. Israel reported that separate talks it had been conducting with Syria and Lebanon were also at a stalemate. Syrian president al-Asad said he would offer Israel "full peace" for "full withdrawal" of Israeli forces from the Golan Heights. But he declined to spell out what he meant by "full peace," and the Israelis were unwilling to discuss "full withdrawal" until he did.[38]

Making matters worse, a new round of fighting between Israelis and Iranian-backed Palestinians (the Hezbollah) broke out in July when the Palestinians fired Katyusha rockets from southern Lebanon against Israeli settlements. Israel responded by bombarding southern Lebanon in the heaviest attack since the Israeli invasion in 1982.[39]

Furthermore, a split developed within Palestinian ranks, as PLO leader Arafat came under increasing criticism from other Palestinian leaders, who accused him of making major concessions to Israel, and in particular of putting aside Palestinian claims to East Jerusalem without any Israeli concessions in return. Three of the Palestinian delegates to the peace negotiations submitted their resignations in protest, saying that they had not been consulted by Arafat. Although the rift was healed,[40] the resignations were indicative of the high level of frustration and sense of futility that had enveloped the negotiating process by the late summer of 1993.[41]

By this time, however, secret negotiations between Israel and the PLO that had been going on in Oslo, Norway, for more than a year were nearing completion. The "Oslo connection" resulted from a chance meeting in April 1992 between Yossi Bellin, then an opposition Labor member of the Knesset, and Terje Rod Larsen, head of a Norwegian institute studying conditions in the occupied territories. Larsen offered to put Bellin in touch with senior Palestinian officials. Following the Labor Party's election victory in July, Bellin was appointed Israel's deputy foreign minister, and Larsen returned to Israel where he renewed his offer. In September, a senior Norwegian diplomat proposed that Norway become the secret passage between Israel and the PLO.[42]

In the ensuing months, representatives of Israel and the PLO met at various locales in and around Oslo, where they painstakingly put together a set of principles for a proposed agreement that included mutual recognition of Israel and the PLO and limited self-government for Palestinians living on the West Bank and Gaza Strip. As the talks neared completion, Israeli foreign minister Peres flew to Norway to help wrap things up.[43]

The Declaration of Principles (D.O.P.) reached at Oslo at the end of August represented the most significant breakthrough in the Arab-Israeli dispute since the Camp David Accords of 1978. It provided for a three-part peace process. The first part called for Palestinian self-rule that would go into effect initially in Gaza and the small town of Jericho on the West Bank before being extended to the rest of the West Bank. There would be an elected Palestinian council that would govern Palestinians in the West Bank and Gaza for a transition period of no more than five years, after which the final status of the territories would be determined. The council, which would be elected within nine months after the signing of the agreement, would have jurisdiction over such matters as education, taxation, health, and social welfare. The Palestinians would also be allowed to have their own police force. The second part of the peace process involved making decisions and establishing procedures relating to the actual governance of Gaza and Jericho under Palestinian authority. The final part had to do with the exchange of mutual recognition agreements.[44]

Both in the Middle East and the United States, response to news of the D.O.P. was overwhelming surprise, even disbelief, that two such bitter foes as Israel and the PLO could reach a peace agreement. Most Israelis, Palestinians, and Arab leaders welcomed or at least accepted the agreement, which promised to give Israel the security and recognition it wanted, the Palestinians the territory and self-rule—however limited—they had always sought, and Arab leaders the peace they desired. For Arab and Israeli extremists, however, the Oslo accord was a cruel blow, which depending on one's perspective, either denied Palestinians their birthright or threatened Israeli security and settlements.[45]

The United States had played only a small role in the secret negotiations taking place in Norway and in the bilateral negotiations that followed the 1991 Madrid meeting. President Clinton was far more interested in domestic matters than foreign policy. The attention he paid to foreign policy was devoted more to events in the Balkans following the disintegration of Yugoslavia and America's ties with the former Soviet Union than to the Middle East. Secretary of State Warren Christopher's most significant contribution to the peace process was, with the help of Syrian president al-Asad, brokering an end to the fighting that had taken place during the summer along Israel's northern border with Lebanon.[46]

Nevertheless, President Clinton played host on 13 September 1993 to the historic meeting between PLO chairman Arafat and Israeli prime minister Rabin, who had come to Washington for the signing ceremony. Before reporters, television cameras, and 2,500 guests, including former presidents Jimmy Carter and George Bush, whom Clinton had invited to the South Lawn of the White House, Mahmoud Abbas, the foreign policy aide for the PLO, and Israeli foreign minister Shimon Peres signed the D.O.P.[47]

Though the accord reached between Israel and the PLO was historic, the issues left for the second phase of the peace process still had to be worked out. Although Israeli forces had to withdraw from the Gaza Strip and Jericho within four months of the signing of the agreement, the extent of the troop withdrawal and which spheres Israel and the Palestinians would control remained unclear. Similarly, the precise responsibilities of the Palestinian police force, including its relationship with Israeli forces, had yet to be decided, and the agreement was vague on how Israel would protect Israeli settlers, particularly when they were outside their settlements. Indeed, the precise municipal boundaries of Jericho still had to be determined.[48]

All these issues represented diplomatic minefields, and disagreement on any one of them could delay, if not undermine, the entire peace process, especially given the ammunition they offered opponents of the agreement. Nor was there any reason to suppose that Arab and Israeli extremists would cease using force and terrorism to achieve their objectives.

What was surprising, therefore, was not the delay in implementing the agreement or the opposition to it that grew among both Israelis and Arabs as its provisions became better known and its opponents rallied to defeat it. Rather, it was the progress along several fronts that was being made prior to 25 February 1994, when Baruch Goldstein, an Israeli physician from Brooklyn, New York, and a resident of the ultra right-wing settlement of Kiryat Arba on the West Bank, entered a mosque in the nearby town of Hebron and killed more than 40 Palestinians and wounded several hundred more. The carnage stopped only after he was beaten to death by worshipers who had overcome their initial terror.[49]

Prior to the Hebron massacre, the chances for ending the Arab-Israeli dispute and resolving a number of related issues had seemed better than at any time since the establishment of Israel in 1948. The September agreement had been accompanied by an announcement from Jordan that both Amman and Jerusalem had decided, for the first time, upon an agenda for negotiations, which called for agreements on water resources, boundary disputes, the plight of the 1.5 million Palestinian refugees in Jordan, and the dismantling of weapons of mass destruction. The fact that separate, direct talks between the PLO and Israel were taking place meant that Jordan could push ahead in its negotiations with Israel unencumbered by the Palestinians.[50]

A new relationship between Syria and Israel also appeared to be commencing. In January, President Clinton flew to Geneva where he met privately for five hours with Syrian president al-Asad. After their meeting, they held a joint news conference. Speaking to the press, al-Asad declared, "We want a genuine peace which secures the interests of all sides and renders to all their rights. If the leaders of Israel have sufficient courage to respond to this kind of peace, the new era of normal, peaceful relations among all shall dawn." But al-Asad kept his language purposely vague and general. For example, he did not define what he meant by "normal relations." There was also the ongoing problem that as a precondition for establishing full peace with Israel, al-Asad insisted on Israeli withdrawal from the Golan Heights, while Israel made an unequivocal commitment by al-Asad to full peace and normal relations a precondition for withdrawal. In addition, al-Asad failed to offer new security assurances to Israel if it withdrew from the Golan Heights, a point that disturbed Prime Minister Rabin, who had earlier indicated a willingness to give back large parts of the Golan—though not all of it—if it meant a genuine peace treaty with Syria.[51]

Nevertheless, most observers agreed that Syria, faced with a flat economy and needing aid and trade from the West, was committed to improving relations with the United States and that al-Asad realized that to achieve this he had to reach some kind of accord with Israel. Certainly President Clinton felt this way. Speaking to reporters while returning from his meeting with al-Asad, Clinton termed the meeting a significant step forward. "I think he has reached a conclusion that it is in the interest of his people, his administration, and his legacy to make a meaningful and lasting peace," the president remarked.[52]

Most of the issues delaying implementation of the September agreement had been resolved prior to the Hebron massacre. Warning that he would be overpowered by Islamic militants if he did not get what he wanted, Arafat was able to secure a number of major concessions from Israel. For example, the Israelis, who had always insisted on retaining full control over external security, agreed to allow the Palestinians to share duties at border crossings, including having a separate Palestinian wing at the border terminals for travelers heading to Gaza or the West Bank. The Palestinian flag would be flown at these terminals. Israel also agreed to rely on the Palestinian police rather than on its own security forces for capturing terrorists fleeing from Israel into the Gaza Strip or Jericho, and it nearly doubled its original offer on the size of the autonomous region around Jericho. Enough progress had been made on these and other issues that on 9 February, just two weeks before the Hebron massacre, Arafat and Peres met in Cairo where they signed a second accord paving the way for implementation of the D.O.P.[53]

The Hebron massacre, however, threw the entire peace process into jeopardy. Palestinians in the West Bank and Gaza took to the streets in violent protest against the massacre. Prime Minister Rabin and other Israeli leaders condemned the killings as a lunatic act committed by a madman and promised a crackdown on Israeli extremists. At the same time, Rabin warned that "the only way to end [the bloodshed] or to give peace a chance [was] by achieving an agreement in which we start to implement the D.O.P."[54] But some Israeli settlers on the West Bank characterized Goldstein as a hero and organized antipeace marches in defiance of the Israeli prime minister.[55]

Meanwhile, PLO leader Arafat stated that he would not resume negotiations with Israel until the UN approved a resolution to put an armed force into Gaza and Jericho. He also canceled a ceremony in Gaza City planned to mark the transfer of a police station from Israeli to Palestinian control. Arafat was himself seriously weakened as a result of the Hebron massacre. Although his authority had been declining since at least the start of the intifada in 1987, he was still a hero to most Palestinians, and he enjoyed a resurgence of popularity and power because of his association with an agreement that, for the first time, promised the Palestinian people the semblance of autonomy and statehood. But the killings at Hebron provided powerful ammunition for Palestinian extremists, like the Popular Front for the Liberation of Palestine and the Islamic fundamentalist organization known as Hamas, which opposed the peace accord with Israel and promised to avenge the killings at Hebron.[56]

Yet the Hebron massacre did not lead to Arafat's demise or have any lasting impact on the agreement signed in Washington in September, other than, perhaps, to speed up the peace process. Just as he had done after the Jordanian civil war in 1970, the Lebanese civil war in 1982, and the Persian Gulf War in 1991, Arafat survived politically. Notwithstanding the growing opposition to the PLO chairman, even within the PLO, there was simply no other figure so closely associated with the Palestinian cause as Arafat; in a real sense, he remained the symbol—the only symbol—of Palestinian nationalism. He also remained committed to the Declaration of Principles agreed to in Washington six months earlier. Accordingly, while he called Israel's pledge to crack down on leading Jewish militants on the West Bank inadequate, he agreed in May to the resumption of negotiations with Israel after the United Nations condemned the Hebron massacre and Israel agreed to allow a small, lightly armed international force to enter the occupied territories and help restore normal life in Hebron.[57]

The September agreement also offered Israel the best hope of resolving a problem that, since the intifada, had become increasingly costly diplomatically, politically, financially, and morally, to say nothing about the 33 Israelis who lost their lives in the West Bank and Gaza between the signing of the declaration in September and the Hebron massacre in February. Anxious to resume negotiations, Rabin indicated his intention to speed up the peace process by reducing the transition period before the final status of the West Bank and Gaza was determined, and in May, Israeli soldiers finally began withdrawing from the Gaza Strip and Jericho.[58]

This did not mean that the transition to Palestinian self-rule went smoothly and without incident. To the contrary, it continued to be marred by disagreement over the transfer of power, by clashes between Israelis and Palestinians on the West Bank, and by a wave of international terrorism, believed to be the work of the Hezbollah and other extremist Palestinian groups seeking to wreck the Mideast peace process. On 16 May, for example, a Palestinian resident of Gaza City was accidentally shot when Israeli soldiers clashed with Palestinian gunmen. The next day, Israeli settlers and soldiers in Hebron shot and wounded at least 10 Arabs. Twenty-four hours later, Islamic militants retaliated by killing two Israeli settlers just south of the town.[59]

Such random killings of Israelis continued into the summer. In July, members of Hezbollah ambushed Israeli troops in south Lebanon, and other terrorists, also believed to be members of Hezbollah, destroyed a Jewish community center in Buenos Aires and planted a bomb on a commuter plane in Panama, killing 21 passengers, most of them Jewish businessmen. "There is no doubt in my mind," said Prime Minister Rabin, "we face a wave of extreme Islamic radicals terrorist movements."[60]

Nevertheless, the transfer of power on the West Bank and Gaza to the Palestinians went forward. Shortly after the resumption of negotiations in May, Israel finally concluded a self-rule agreement with the PLO. As part of that agreement, Israeli and Palestinian security forces began patrolling together in Jericho. On 19 May, Israeli soldiers completed their evacuation of the Gaza Strip. On 29 May, Arafat appointed a 14-member governing board for the Gaza Strip and Jericho. In June, a joint command center, where Palestinian and Israeli flags flew side-by-side, was established at Jericho. On 10 June, Israel freed 180 Palestinian prisoners, some of them convicted killers serving life sentences. A week later, it freed an additional 170 prisoners. (But it failed to meet the deadline of mid-June for releasing 5,000 Palestinian prisoners as part of its self-rule agreement with the PLO.) By the end of June, the Gaza Strip and Jericho had passed to Palestinian rule. To celebrate the event, Arafat went to Gaza, where he kissed the ground after disembarking from his plane and, in an emotional speech, referred to the formerly occupied territory as "the first free Palestinian land."[61]

The transition of power to the Palestinians in Gaza and Jericho was only part of the larger ongoing effort being promoted by the Rabin government and the Clinton administration to bring an end to the nearly half-century-old Arab-Israeli dispute. In May, Israel offered once more to withdraw from the Golan Heights over a period of five to eight years in return for peace and normal relations with Syria. To promote such a Syrian-Israeli agreement, Secretary of State Christopher engaged in an exhausting round of negotiations with al-Asad in Damascus.[62]

Meanwhile, talks between Israel and Jordan, which had broken off following the Hebron massacre in February, were resumed in Washington. At the end of June, Jordan's King Hussein told American officials that he was willing to take major steps toward normalizing relations with Israel irrespective of progress in Israel's negotiations with Syria or other Arab countries. In making this statement, he broke with the notion of Arab solidarity in dealing with Israel that had been honored by all other Arab countries except Egypt. "As far as we are concerned," he remarked to reporters, "this is a matter involving Jordan itself and has nothing to do with, nor is it tied to, movements on any other tracks." In early August, he and Israeli prime minister Rabin came to the White House, where they concluded the second historic Arab-Israeli agreement in less than a year. As President Clinton watched, they signed documents ending their 46-year state of war and providing for the normalization of relations between their countries. In sharp contrast to Rabin's meeting with Arafat the previous September, the Israeli's meeting with Hussein was, by all accounts, warm and friendly.[63]

It is still uncertain how successful the latest initiatives at ending the Arab-Israeli dispute will be. Despite the opening of a dialogue between Israel and Syria and encouraging indications that al-Asad might be amenable to an agreement with Israel over the Golan Heights, he has refused to attend a summit with Israeli leaders. Israeli intelligence chiefs told the cabinet at an annual briefing in March 1995 that al-Asad was in no hurry to reach an agreement with Israel based on a partial Israeli pullout from the Golan Heights.[64] Israel's refusal to compromise on the status of East Jerusalem, which both Muslims and Jews consider a holy shrine but which Israel has vowed never to give up, poses another, even more serious, obstacle to the resolution of the Arab-Israeli conflict.

Relations between Egypt and Israel have also grown increasingly strained. Since the signing of the 1993 peace accord with the PLO, Israel has established profitable economic and financial ties with a number of Arab states, including Jordan, Morocco, Tunisia, and several Persian Gulf countries. It has also sought to establish a new regional order that is more Middle Eastern than Arab—an order in which Israel would be the dominant economic power. But this has resulted in considerable mistrust among the Egyptian ruling elite, who resent Israel's decision to bypass Egypt by dealing directly with other Arab countries and who regard Israel as a threat to their own influence in the region. Egypt has even tried to link the normalization of economic relations between Arabs and Israelis to a comprehensive peace settlement. Egyptian president Hosni Mubarak has also made clear his displeasure at Israel's refusal to open up its nuclear facilities to international inspection at a time when Egypt is under considerable pressure from the United States to sign the 1968 Nuclear Nonproliferation Treaty. Economic stagnation, a rising tide of Islamic fundamentalism, and increased political instability and insecurity in Egypt have also led Mubarak to distance himself politically from Israel (and the United States), thereby threatening the entire Middle East peace process.[65]

The situation in Lebanon, which continues to be used as a base for Shi'ite guerrillas financed by Iran, also remains a problem. In June, Israeli planes launched one of their bloodiest attacks in years against Lebanon, flying deep into the Bekaa Valley, where they bombed and strafed training bases for guerrilla activities, killing several dozen Palestinian recruits in retaliation for their launching of Katyusha rockets against Israeli towns in northern Israel. Israel also sent tanks and artillery to its northern border ready to move into Lebanon if the attacks were resumed.[66]

Palestinian extremists in the Gaza Strip and the West Bank continue their efforts to undermine the fragile autonomy agreement between the PLO and Israel. In October 1994, an Israeli soldier, Nashon Waxman, was kidnapped by Hamas on the West Bank and later killed in a raid by Israeli forces on the kidnappers' hideout. Two weeks later, Palestinian terrorists bombed a bus in Tel Aviv, killing 23 people, including the bomber. In January 1995, two Palestinian bombers killed 20 young Israelis at Beit Lid, north of Tel Aviv. The kidnapping, bombings, and other incidents involving the killing of at least 59 Israeli citizens since the spring of 1994 by Hamas has heightened Israeli unease about Palestinian self-rule, weakened the Rabin government, and led to a growing demand in Israel for sterner measures against the Palestinians. Israel has sealed off its borders to tens of thousands of Palestinian workers from the Gaza Strip and West Bank and has begun to replace them with workers from Romania, Bulgaria, Thailand, and China. It has also refused to withdraw the Israeli Defense Forces (IDF) from the major cities on the West Bank.[67]

Israel might have taken even sterner measures had the Rabin government not sought to avoid weakening Arafat even more by making him look powerless against Israeli reprisals. Nevertheless many Palestinians living in the terribly impoverished Gaza Strip and on the West Bank regard Arafat as a traitor for signing an agreement with Israel. The Palestinian leader has made matters worse by isolating himself from the Palestinian people. PLO officials in the Gaza Strip have already been accused of corruption and of violating the civil rights of Palestinian citizens. A leading Palestinian spokesman, Hanan Ashrawi, has even formed a private commission to look into these violations. Meanwhile, Hamas and other extremist groups continue to gain support among the Palestinian people as Palestinian frustration grows over Israel's delay in widening Palestinian self-rule beyond Gaza and Jericho to include more land in the West Bank.[68]

Leading scholars and experts on the Middle East disagree as to the future of a Palestinian state. Although William Quandt, now at the Brookings Institution, maintains that a "Palestinian state is slowly being born" in the Gaza Strip and Jericho and that "Palestinian democracy" is both attainable and desirable, Amos Perlmutter of American University takes a less benign view, arguing that a "Palestinian state ruled by Arafat and his PLO cronies will likely be authoritarian, noninclusive and undemocratic" and that elections "will only bring the Islamic fundamentalists to power." Indeed, Perlmutter claims that the D.O.P. "is for all intents and purposes dead" and that Arafat is largely irrelevant.[69]

Strong opposition also continues in Israel to relinquishing more of the occupied territories. Following Arafat's visit to Gaza, massive antigovernment demonstrations, led by right-wing critics of Israel's agreement with the PLO, took place in Jerusalem. Seeking to capitalize on this opposition to Rabin, Ariel Sharon, Israel's hawkish former defense minister who was instrumental in getting Israel to invade Lebanon in 1982, has declared his candidacy for prime minister and has been outspoken in his condemnation of the Israeli prime minister. Several political pundits have even predicted that in the next parliamentary elections Rabin will be defeated and the Likud returned to power.[70]

Moreover, to the extent that the struggle with Israel has bound the Arab world together and moderated some of its historic divisiveness, a resolution of that conflict can only mean an increase in inter-Arab rivalry and confrontations, which would pose new problems in the Middle East.

Yet Arabs and Israelis have embarked upon a course from which they are unlikely to depart. For almost 50 years, the prime political fact of life in the Middle East was the Arab-Israeli conflict. As Thomas Friedman has pointed out, "the illegitimacy of Israel [defined] the limits of the permissible." This is no longer the case. According to the Middle East historian Fouad Ajami, "for years, generations of Arabs were told that there can be no democracy because of the struggle with Israel; there can be no development because of the struggle with Israel. Israel was the great alibi of Arab political life." But that alibi is gone.[71]

In the United States, the agreements reached between Israel, the PLO, and Jordan have reoriented the Clinton administration toward the Middle East. Although the administration had taken no part in the secret negotiations leading to the 1993 D.O.P. agreement and had shown little interest in the region, that changed dramatically after the pact was signed, as evidenced by the president's Geneva meeting with al-Asad in January and Secretary of State Christopher's subsequent efforts at mediating a Syrian-Israeli agreement on the Golan Heights. In contrast to the president's travails with respect to such places as Bosnia, Somalia, and Haiti, the White House signing ceremonies of September 1993 and August 1994 have stood out as major achievements for the Clinton administration.

So has the president's decisive response in October 1994 to Iraq's movement of 70,000 elite troops toward its border with Kuwait. Although Saddam's purpose in massing this force near the Kuwait border is unclear,[72] the administration interpreted it as a test of its resolve to protect Kuwait from another Iraqi invasion. It responded by sending 36,000 troops and more than 100 warplanes to the Persian Gulf area (bringing the total number of American planes and helicopters in the region to about 650) and putting another 155,000 ground troops on alert. "We will not allow Saddam Hussein to defy the will of the United States and the international community," President Clinton declared in an address from the Oval Office.[73]

The crisis ended almost as suddenly as it began. On 10 October Iraq announced that it was withdrawing its troops from the Kuwait border, and two days later, American intelligence confirmed the withdrawal of Iraqi forces towards Basra. The same group of nations that had opposed Iraq's invasion of Kuwait in 1990 also joined together to support the American president, although France and Russia questioned the continuation of economic sanctions against Iraq, and French leaders speculated publicly on whether Clinton was motivated to act as much for domestic political reasons (to increase his standing in public opinion polls) as out of concern about another Iraqi invasion of Kuwait. Saudi Arabia and six other Gulf states agreed to pay the cost of the American operation. Reversing his stand during the Gulf War, even Jordan's King Hussein condemned the Iraqi troop movements.[74]

In addition to reorienting the Clinton administration toward the Middle East, the agreements that Israel signed with the PLO and Jordan in 1993 and 1994 have also given the United States added flexibility in dealing with Israel and the Arab world. The disintegration of the Soviet Union and its final collapse in August 1991 had already allowed the United States considerable leeway. The Middle East was no longer a battleground of the cold war because the cold war was over. But the cold war had been only one concern, albeit a major one, in determining American policy in the Middle East. Another had been the growing dependency of the United States and its allies on Middle East oil. But while the West's oil needs had always been an important consideration for American policymakers, they had never been the deciding issue.

Washington's commitment to Israel's security had always been far more important. This put America's Middle Eastern allies, such as Saudi Arabia and Egypt, on the defensive and limited the United States' ability to maneuver among the Arab powers. But with the acceptance and recognition of Israel by the PLO and the threat to Israel's existence consequently minimized, there will be less need for Arab leaders to distance themselves from the United States and more opportunity for cooperative ventures between Washington and Arab capitals.

CHRONOLOGY

1917   2 November

            Balfour Declaration.

1920   Levant awarded as mandate to France.

1922   22 July

            League of Nations confirms British mandate for Palestine.

1924   Hashemite family driven from Arabian Peninsula. Ibn Saud becomes King of Saudi Arabia.

1943   Lend-Lease aid extended to Saudi Arabia.

1945   14 February

            President Franklin D. Roosevelt meets with Saudi King Ibn Saud while returning from Yalta Conference.

            22 March

            Arab League formed.

            13 November

            U.S. and Britain agree to form commission to examine problem of European Jews and Palestine.

1946   22 March

Britain and Transjordan sign treaty ending British mandate.

7 May

Britain and France complete withdrawal from Syria.

22 July

Irgun bombs King David Hotel in Jerusalem.

1947   14 February

London conference on Palestine ends without agreement. Palestine question referred to United Nations.

12 March

Truman Doctrine.

29 November

UN votes for partition of Palestine.

5 December

U.S. places embargo on arms shipments to Middle East.

8 December

Arab League pledges to help Palestinian Arabs resist partition of Palestine.

1948   14 May

Establishment of State of Israel. U.S. grants Israel de facto recognition.

15 May

First Arab-Israeli War begins.

1949   6 January

Israel and Egypt announce cease-fire.

31 January

U.S. grants Israel de jure recognition.

11 March

Israeli-Transjordan armistice.

1 June

Transjordan renamed Hashemite Kingdom of Jordan.

20 July

Israeli-Syrian armistice.

14 August

Military coup in Syria.

1950   23 January

Jerusalem becomes official capital of Israel.

13 April

Arab League signs mutual defense treaty.

25 May

Tripartite Agreement regarding security in the Middle East.

21 November

Britain rejects Egyptian demand for immediate withdrawal from Suez Canal Zone.

1951   2 January

ARAMCO agrees to share profits with Saudi Arabia.

22 July

Jordan's King Abdullah assassinated.

27 October

Egypt formally notifies Britain that 1936 Treaty of Alliance and 1899 agreement on joint administration of the Sudan are abrogated.

1952   18 January

British troops and Egyptians battle for four hours at Port Said.

23 July

Egyptian King Farouk flees country following military coup.

11 August

Crown Prince Hussein named King by Jordan's parliament.

7 September

General Muhammad Naguib assumes leadership of Egypt.

18 September

Lebanon's parliament elects Camille Chamoun president.

7–8 October

Egypt renounces 1936 treaty and 1899 Condominium Agreement with Great Britain.

1953   12 February

Britain and Egypt sign treaty providing for independence of Sudan in three years.

29 November

The Sudan's first general elections result in victory for those seeking union with Egypt.

1954   25 February

            Egyptian president Naguib resigns after Egyptian legislature
            refuses to give him absolute power.

            26 February

            Army overthrows government in Syria.

            17 April

            Colonel Gamal Abdel Nasser becomes Egyptian premier.

            11 June

            Egypt and Saudi Arabia agree to a unified military com-
            mand.

            27 July

            Britain signs pact with Egypt ending 72-year occupation of
            Egypt.

1955   Turkey, Iraq, Britain, Pakistan, and Iran sign Baghdad
            Pact.

            21 May

            Soviet Union decides to sell arms to Egypt.

            27 September

            Czech arms deal with Egypt announced.

            19 October

            Egypt, Syria, and Jordan decide to unify military com-
            mands.

            22 November

            Baghdad Pact countries form Middle East Treaty
            Organization.

19 December

Jordan's pro-Western premier quits in dispute over joining Baghdad Pact.

26 December

Egyptian, Jordanian, and Saudi Arabian forces placed under Egyptian commander.

1956   1 January

Sudan proclaimed independent republic.

13 January

Syria and Lebanon sign mutual defense pact against Israel.

21 April

Egypt signs military pact with Saudi Arabia and Yemen.

31 May

Jordan and Syria sign military agreement.

23 June

Nasser named Egyptian president.

27 July

Egypt nationalizes Suez Canal.

2 August

Britain mobilizes forces on Suez.

3 August

Syrian president Shukri el-Kuwatly deposed by Syrian military.

14 August

U.S. creates Middle East Emergency Committee.

26 August

Nasser agrees to five-nation mission to discuss Suez.

14 September

Egypt takes control of Suez Canal.

29–31 October

Israeli, French, and British forces attack Egypt.

6 November

Britain and France agree to a cease-fire in Egypt.

6–20 November

Eisenhower applies pressure on British, French, and Israeli troops to withdraw.

30 November

U.S. puts into operation emergency oil plan.

22 December

Last British and French troops withdraw from Egypt.

1957   19 January

Egypt, Saudi Arabia, and Syria agree to replace British aid to Jordan.

1 March

Israel agrees to remove troops from Gaza Strip.

9 March

Eisenhower Doctrine signed into law.

13 March

Anglo-Jordanian treaty ends. Britain to withdraw in six months.

13 April

Syria attacks Jordan.

29 June

Hussein accepts $10 million in U.S. foreign aid.

5 September

U.S. announces plans to send arms to Jordan, Lebanon, Turkey, and Iraq.

11 November

Palestinian refugees demonstrate in Damascus and call for death of King Hussein.

1958   1 February

Egypt and Syria form United Arab Republic.

4 February

Jordan and Iraq form union.

1 May

Nasser visits Moscow.

22 May

Lebanon accuses Egypt of fomenting revolution in Lebanon.

29 June

Heavy fighting breaks out again in Lebanon.

14 July

Iraqi army deposes King Faisal II.

15 July

Eisenhower sends 5,000 U.S. marines into Lebanon.

17 July

British troops land in Jordan at King Hussein's request.

19 July

United Arab Republic and Iraq sign mutual defense treaty.

31 July

General Fuad Chehab elected president of Lebanon.

2 August

Hussein dissolves union with Iraq.

22 September

Lebanon's pro-West regime resigns.

23 October

Soviet Union agrees to lend Egypt money to build Aswan Dam.

25 October

Last U.S. troops leave Lebanon.

1959   24 March

Iraq pulls out of Baghdad Pact.

14 August

Jordan and United Arab Republic reopen diplomatic relations.

1960   27 March

Iraq announces plans to train Palestinians for a war against Israel.

14 September

Organization of Petroleum Exporting Countries (OPEC) formed.

1961   16 March

               Saudi Arabia ends pact on U.S. bases at Dharan.

               19 June

               Britain relinquishes control of Kuwait.

               1 July

               British troops land in Kuwait in response to Iraqi threats.

               28 September

               Syrian military revolts against Egyptian domination of
               United Arab Republic.

               5 October

               Nasser gives up claims to Syria.

               31 December

               Lebanon crushes right-wing army coup.

1962   12 February

               New Syrian regime seeks aid from Soviet bloc.

               27 March

               Syrian regime ousted by army and replaced with new junta.

               2 June

               Iraq orders departure of American ambassador after U.S.
               accredits ambassador from Kuwait.

               17 October

               King Saud of Saudi Arabia names Prince Faisal as premier.

               6 November

               Saudi Arabia breaks ties with United Arab Republic.

15 November

Yemen declares war on Saudi Arabia.

1963   8 March

Syria has eighth revolt since 1945.

17 April

Iraq, Syria, and Egypt form new United Arab Republic.

19 July

Syria executes 12 pro-Nasser rebels after failed coup.

18 November

Civilian Ba'thist government overthrown in Iraq.

22 November

President John F. Kennedy assassinated.

1964   17 January

13 Arab nations agree to prohibit Israel from diverting Jordan River to irrigate Negev Desert.

28 March

Saudi king Saud loses power to Faisal.

28 April

Syria cancels pact of military union with Iraq.

8 May

Khrushchev visits Cairo.

24 May

Soviet Union extends loan of $227 million to United Arab Republic.

2 November

Crown Prince Faisal proclaimed King of Saudi Arabia.

1965   12 February

West Germany halts military shipments to Israel.

1 March

Cairo signs $100 million aid pact with East Germany.

27 May

Israel raids Jordan, alleging retaliation for Jordanian border strikes.

24 August

Faisal and Nasser sign agreement ending civil war in Yemen.

1966   3 January

U.S. and UAR sign $55-million aid agreement.

2 April

U.S. agrees to sell jets to Jordan.

21 June

President Lyndon Johnson meets with King Faisal.

15 August

Israel downs two Syrian MiGs over Sea of Galilee.

20 November

Arab League votes to boycott Ford and Coca-Cola.

24 November

Rioters in Jordan protest King Hussein's policy of moderation with Israel.

11 December

Arab League votes to put troops in Jordan against Israel.

1967   7 April

Israel downs six Syrian MiGs.

18 May

At Nasser's request, UN forces leave Israeli-Egyptian border.

5 June

War breaks out between Israel and Egypt.

6 June

Egypt closes Suez Canal; breaks ties with U.S. Kuwait and Iraq cut off oil shipments to U.S.

7 June

Israel occupies Old Jerusalem; Jordan accepts UN cease-fire resolution.

8 June

Israel attacks U.S.S. *Liberty*.

9 June

Nasser resigns; resignation rejected. Israeli forces drive deep into Syria.

19 June

Soviet Union breaks diplomatic relations with Israel.

11 July

Israel and Syria accept UN cease-fire.

21 October

Egypt sinks Israeli destroyer *Elath* off coast.

24 October

Israel strikes Egyptian oil refinery.

22 November

UN Resolution 242 approved.

26 November

Cairo bars Soviet military bases in Egypt.

28 November

People's Republic of South Yemen established after Britain declares independence of South Arabia.

1968   16 January

Britain announces withdrawal east of Suez.

17 July

Fourth coup in ten years deposes Iraq's government.

27 December

U.S. agrees to sell Israel 50 F-4 jets.

28 December

Israel attacks Beirut airport.

1969   28 January

Iraq executes nine Iraqi Jews for espionage.

3 February

Yasir Arafat acknowledged as leader of PLO.

12 February

Israel downs Syrian MiG-21.

26 March

Israeli air raid against Jordan kills 18.

2 July

Israel downs three Egyptian MiG-21s in dogfight.

8 July

Israel downs seven Syrian MiG-21s.

10 July

Border clashes between Egypt and Israel.

3 August

Israel announces plans to keep Golan Heights, Gaza Strip, and most of Sinai Peninsula.

11 August

Israeli jets strike against Lebanon in retaliation for alleged terrorist acts.

12 August

Syria breaks off diplomatic relations with Jordan following border clashes.

26 August

UN condemns Israel for attack against Lebanon.

1 September

Libyan king Idris ousted by Colonel Qaddafi.

11 September

Israel downs 11 Egyptian planes in raid over Suez Canal.

25 October

Three hundred members of PLO move into Lebanon.

2 November

Cease-fire reached with PLO in Lebanon.

6 November

Nasser threatens "fire and blood" against Israel.

1970   28 January

Israeli jets attack Cairo suburb.

2 February

Israel and Syria clash in worst fighting since Six-Day War.

14 April

Civil war in Yemen between republican and royalist forces ends.

12 May

Israeli forces move into Lebanon; withdraw after 32 hours.

12 June

Cease-fire between Jordan and Palestinian guerrillas.

3 July

Nasser accepts three-month cease-fire on Israeli-Egyptian border.

9 August

Israel bombs guerrilla bases in Lebanon.

1 September

Hussein escapes assassination attempt.

7 September

Arab terrorists take 150 hostages from New York–bound jets and hold them in Jordan desert.

9 September

Arab guerrillas hijack British jet and bring it to Jordan.

12 September

Three jets blown up in Jordan.

19 September

Syria invades Jordan.

26 September

Jordan and PLO agree to cease-fire.

28 September

Nasser dies of heart attack.

5 October

Anwar Sadat named new Egyptian president.

23 October

U.S. agrees to sell Israel 180 tanks.

13 November

Hafiz al-Asad seizes control of Syria in coup.

27 November

Syria joins pact linking Libya, Egypt, and Sudan.

1971   3 February

OPEC decides to set oil prices without consulting buyers.

2 April

Western oil companies sign five-year oil pact with Libya.

27 May

Egypt and Soviet Union sign fifteen-year friendship treaty.

12 August

Syria severs ties with Jordan in support of PLO.

18 September

Egypt and Israel exchange fire over Suez Canal.

7 December

Libya nationalizes British Petroleum Company.

1972   -5 February

U.S. agrees to sell Israel 42 F-4 Phantom jets and 90 A-4 Skyhawks.

31 March

U.S. agrees to sell Jordan 24 F-5 Phantom jets.

6 April

Egypt severs diplomatic relations with Jordan.

9 April

Soviets sign anti-Zionist pact with Iraq.

13 June

Israeli, Egyptian planes clash over Mediterranean Sea.

21 June

Israeli armor hits southern Lebanon.

18 July

Egypt expels Soviet advisers.

2 August

Sadat and Qaddafi agree to unified political leadership.

5 September

Eleven Israeli Olympians killed in Munich.

15 October

Israel launches its first unprovoked attack against Palestinian bases in Syria and Lebanon.

1973   21 February

Israel shoots down Libyan passenger jet by accident.

7 May

Martial law proclaimed in Lebanon as fighting between Palestinian guerrillas and army resumes.

21 April

UN denounces Israeli raids on Lebanon.

12 September

Egypt reopens relations with Jordan.

13 September

Israel takes claim for downing of 13 Syrian MiGs over Mediterranean.

6 October

Outbreak of Yom Kippur War.

10 October

Israel announces abandonment of Bar-Lev Line. Egyptian forces cross Suez Canal. Syrian army pushed back to 1967 cease-fire line.

15 October

U.S. begins resupplying arms to Israel.

17 October

Sadat proposes immediate cease-fire, but fighting continues.

21 October

Imposition of Arab oil embargo against U.S.

22 October

UN Resolution 338 calls for cease-fire and Israeli withdrawal from lands seized in 1967 war. Cease-fire takes effect on Egyptian-Israeli border, but fighting still continues.

25 October

Nixon puts U.S. military on world alert.

29 October

Syria accepts cease-fire.

7 November

U.S. announces resumption of ties with Egypt.

11 November

Israel and Egypt sign cease-fire agreement.

1974   17 January

Secretary of State Henry Kissinger's "shuttle diplomacy" results in Egyptian-Israeli accord on separation of Suez forces, opening of Suez Canal.

4 March

Israel completes its Suez front pullback.

13 March

Arab nations end oil embargo against U.S.

19 April

Syria and Israel fight first air battle since end of Yom Kippur War.

16 May

Israeli planes strafe Palestinian refugee camps following Maalot massacre.

29 May

Syria and Israel agree to truce on Golan Heights.

12 June

Nixon begins tour of Middle East.

14 June

U.S. and Egypt sign friendship treaty.

16 June

Syria resumes relations with U.S.

29 September

Egypt and Syria recognize PLO as the sole representative of the Palestinian people.

28 October

Rabat conference: Arab leaders call for independent Palestinian state.

22 November

PLO given "observer" status at UN.

1975

6 January

Saudi Arabia purchases 60 F-5 jets from U.S.

9 January

Saudi Arabia pledges to use its oil wealth in struggle against Israel.

18 February

Soviet Union sells MiG-23 fighters to Egypt.

25 March

King Faisal of Saudi Arabia is assassinated.

13 April

Right-wing Lebanese raid bus, kill 22 Palestinians.

15 April

Palestinians fight Christian militia in Beirut.

5 June

Suez Canal reopens after eight-year closure.

13 July

Israeli planes strike largest Palestinian refugee camp in Lebanon; Arabs retaliate with rockets.

1 September

Israel and Egypt sign interim peace pact.

11 September

Egypt closes PLO radio station. Israeli jets raid targets in southern Lebanon.

16 September

Beirut torn by civil war.

26 October

Sadat becomes first Egyptian president to visit U.S.

10 November

U.S. declares Zionism racist.

2 December

Israeli jets hit Palestinian refugee camps in Lebanon.

1976   12 January

PLO given speaking rights at UN.

22 January

Beirut factions reach peace agreement.

14 March

Sadat ends 1971 friendship pact with Soviet Union.

8 May

Elias Sarkis elected president of Lebanon.

1–8 June

Syria sends armed forces into Lebanon, cutting off Beirut.

12 August

Lebanese Christians seize Tell Zaatar Palestinian camp after two-month siege.

21 November

Syrian troops seize key ports in Beirut.

1977   24 February

Jordan and PLO agree to form "link."

6 March

Israeli Prime Minister Yitzhak Rabin arrives in U.S. for talks with President Jimmy Carter.

3 April

Sadat arrives in U.S. for talks with Carter.

13 April

Egypt accuses Libya of plotting against Sudan.

9 May

Carter and Syrian president al-Asad meet in Geneva.

18 May

Menachem Begin becomes Israeli premier.

24 May

Saudi Crown Prince Fahd praises Carter for supporting idea of Palestinian homeland.

10 July

King Hussein and President Sadat agree to an "explicit link" between Jordan and PLO.

16 July

Sadat announces he is willing to accept Israel as Middle East nation.

21–24 July

Egypt engages in major border clash with Libya.

9 November

Israeli jets raid Lebanon.

21 November

Sadat addresses Israeli Knesset.

16 December

Begin agrees to return Sinai to Egypt.

1978   11 March

Palestinians kill 30 Israelis on bus.

14 March

Israel sends 22,000 troops into southern Lebanon.

24 March

Syria announces ban on aid to PLO in Lebanon.

30 April

Begin arrives in U.S. to meet with Carter.

13 June

Israel withdraws last of its forces from southern Lebanon.

26 June

Pro-Soviet faction seizes control of South Yemen.

1 July

Twenty-two killed in Lebanon in clash between Syrian forces and Christian militia.

22 July

Israel refuses to give up El Arish and Mount Sinai.

23 July

Sadat rejects further meeting with Israelis.

3 August

Israeli jets strike in Lebanon in retaliation for terrorist attack in Tel Aviv.

14 August

Israeli cabinet approves additional settlements on West Bank.

29 August

Syrian troops complete sweep of militia strongholds in northwest Lebanon.

5–18 September

Camp David Summit.

18 September

Carter announces Camp David Accords.

5 November

Arab League asks Egypt to renounce accord with Israel.

10 December

Begin and Sadat share Nobel Peace Prize.

1979   16 January

Shah of Iran forced to leave country.

1 February

Ayatollah Khomeini returns to Iran.

24 February

Border war breaks out between North and South Yemen.

7 March

U.S. sends military aid to North Yemen.

20 March

Sadat and Begin sign Egyptian-Israeli peace treaty.

27 March

Arab League condemns Egypt for signing peace treaty.

2 April

Begin visits Egypt.

26 April

Israel and PLO agree to UN truce in Lebanon.

27 June

Israeli and Syrian planes clash over Lebanon.

24 September

Israel downs four Syrian planes over Lebanon.

4 November

Students seize U.S. embassy in Tehran.

20–24 November

Gunmen occupy Grand Mosque in Mecca. Saudi troops defeat them.

1 December

Two thousand storm U.S. embassy in Libya.

26 December

Soviets send troops into Afghanistan.

1980   1 February

Syria withdraws peacekeeping force from Lebanon.

19 August

Five hundred Israeli troops launch preemptive strike into Lebanon.

20 September

Iraq-Iran War begins.

1981   20 January

Iran releases U.S. hostages.

26 April

Israeli jets attack Lebanon.

28 April

Israel downs two Syrian helicopters over Lebanon.

8 May

Syria announces that it will keep its missiles in the Bekaa Valley in Lebanon.

24 June

Israelis destroy Iraqi nuclear reactor.

17 July

Israeli jets kill 123 in shelling of PLO targets in Lebanon.

17 September

Sadat expels 1,000 Russians from Egypt.

6 October

Sadat assassinated.

14 December

Israel annexes Golan Heights.

1982   31 January

Israel agrees to four-nation peace force in Sinai.

10 March

U.S. bans Libyan oil imports, accusing Libya of continuing to support terrorism.

6 June

Major Israeli force invades Lebanon.

10 June

Israel bombs outskirts of Beirut, warns Syrians to evacuate city.

11 June

Israel and Syria announce cease-fire.

13 June

Saudi King Khalid dies; Crown Prince Fahd to succeed.

14 June

Israeli tanks cut off Moslem West Beirut.

6 July

President Ronald Reagan agrees to contribute U.S. troops to peacekeeping mission in Beirut.

11 July

Israelis engage in artillery duel with PLO in West Beirut.

25 July

PLO leader Arafat signs declaration accepting Israel's right to exist.

27 July

Israeli jets devastate West Beirut.

5 August

Israel rejects U.S. appeal for Beirut pullback.

19 August

Israel agrees to end Beirut siege.

21 August

PLO begins leaving Beirut.

14 September

Lebanese President-elect Bashir Gemayel assassinated.

15 September

Pope John Paul II holds audience with Arafat.

17 September

Sabra and Shatila massacres.

18 September

Begin tells Knesset borders with Arab countries secure for first time.

1983   8 January

Israeli inquiry places "indirect" blame on Israeli leadership for Beirut massacre.

11 January

Ariel Sharon resigns as Israeli defense minister.

15 January

Lebanese army takes control of East Beirut from Christian Militia.

18 April

U.S. embassy in Beirut bombed.

21 June

PLO rebels seize eight Arafat positions in Beirut.

24 July

Iraq accuses U.S. of giving weapons to Iran.

17 September

U.S. ships bomb Syrian areas in Lebanon.

23 October

213 marines killed in truck bombing in Beirut.

12 December

Car bomb kills seven at U.S. embassy in Kuwait.

20 December

PLO forces leave Tripoli, Lebanon.

1984   18 January

Malcolm H. Kerr of American University in Beirut killed by
terrorists.

14 February

Druze drive Lebanese government troops from vital mountain area.

16 February

Lebanon abrogates 1983 withdrawal pact with Israel.

21 February

U.S. Marines in Beirut moved to ships.

22 February

U.S. and Britain send ships to Persian Gulf following Iranian
offensive offshore.

16 May

Iran attacks three Kuwaiti and Saudi oil tankers in Persian Gulf.

21 August

Egypt charges Libya with mining Mideast waters.

28 August

Israeli jets attack PLO bases in Bakaa Valley.

20 September

Beirut bomb kills 23 at U.S. embassy.

1985   24 February

Israeli forces besiege nine villages in Lebanon.

8 March

Car bomb kills 62 in Beirut.

17 March

Cabinet in Lebanon resigns as Shi'ites take West Beirut. Iran and Iraq fight heaviest battle yet.

20 May

Israel frees 1,500 Palestinians in exchange for release of three Israeli soldiers.

10 June

Thomas Sutherland becomes eighth American kidnapped in Beirut by Palestinians. Israeli forces begin withdrawal from Lebanon.

30 June

Hijacked hostages on TWA plane freed in Beirut by Hezbollah after 17 days.

3 July

Israel frees 300 Shi'ite prisoners.

15 September

Reverend Benjamin Weir released in Lebanon after sixteen months in captivity.

7 October

Arabs hijack Italian liner *Achille Lauro*.

30 December

Palestinian terrorists attack El Al Israeli airline ticket counters in Rome and Vienna.

1986   8 January

Reagan freezes Libyan assets in U.S.

24 March

U.S. and Libyan forces clash in waters off Libyan coast.

5 April

Terrorists bomb Berlin nightclub popular with American soldiers.

15 April

U.S. bombs military targets and home of Qaddafi in Libya.

23 May

Car bomb kills 11 in Christian East Beirut.

2 November

U.S. hostage David Jacobsen freed in Beirut.

6–25 November

Irangate revelations.

1987   11 April

               Israel and Jordan agree in London to international confer-
               ence on Middle East.

               24 April

               Israeli Prime Minister Yitzhak Shamir rejects London agree-
               ment.

               9 December

               Start of intifada movement.

1988   4 March

               Secretary of State George Shultz offers new peace proposal
               for Middle East.

               31 July

               Jordan relinquishes all ties to the West Bank.

               19 October

               PLO accepts UN resolutions 242 and 338 as basis for inter-
               national conference.

               14 December

               PLO renounces all forms of terrorism, recognizes Israel's
               right to exist.

               16 December

               U.S. begins talks with PLO in Tunis.

               22 May

               Secretary of State James Baker publicly urges Israel to with-
               draw from occupied territories.

1990   20 June

               President George Bush suspends talks with PLO.

16 July

U.S. intelligence shows Iraq mobilizing near border with Kuwait.

2 August

Iraq invades Kuwait.

3 August

Bush freezes Iraqi and Kuwaiti assets, imposes embargo on most trade with Iraq.

8 August

Bush announces U.S. military buildup in Saudi Arabia and Persian Gulf.

9 August

Arab leaders appeal to Iraq to withdraw from Kuwait. Operation Desert Shield begins.

11 September

In speech before Congress, Bush calls for a "new world order."

29 November

UN Security Council authorizes use of force to expel Iraqi forces from Kuwait. Secretary of State James Baker sets January 15, 1991, deadline for Iraq to leave Kuwait.

1991   9 January

Baker meets with Iraqi foreign minister Tariq Aziz in Geneva in futile effort to avoid war.

12 January

Congress authorizes military action against Iraq.

16 January

Persian Gulf War (Operation Desert Storm) begins.

11 February

Bush announces end of Persian Gulf War.

29 May

Bush administration proposes regional arms control for Middle East.

30 October

Madrid Peace Conference opens.

1992   23 June

Likud Party suffers stunning defeat in Israel.

21 October

Israel indicates willingness to negotiate on Golan Heights.

1993   28 August

Declaration of Principles on Middle East Peace Process agreed on in Oslo, Norway.

13 September

PLO Chairman Arafat and Israeli Prime Minister Rabin sign Declaration of Principles at White House meeting.

1994   9 January

President Bill Clinton meets with Syrian president al-Asad in Geneva.

25 February

Hebron massacre.

18 May

Israel concludes self-rule agreement with PLO.

19 May

Secretary of State Warren Christopher announces no breakthrough after four days of diplomacy between Syria and Israel.

21 May

Two Israeli soldiers killed by Arab militants in Gaza Strip.

22 May

Israel abducts guerrilla leader from Lebanon. PLO denounces killing of Israeli soldiers.

29 May

Arafat appoints 14-member governing board for Gaza Strip and Jericho. Israeli planes attack Hezbollah training camp in Bekaa Valley.

6 July

Arafat installs provisional government in Jericho.

17 July

Arab police clash with Israeli army during Gaza riot.

18 July

Twenty-six killed in bombing of Argentine Jewish Center.

25 July

Hussein and Rabin sign agreement at White House ceremony ending 46-year state of war between Israel and Jordan.

30 July

Hezbollah ambushes Israeli troops in southern Lebanon.

8–11 October

Clinton orders troops and planes to Persian Gulf after Iraq moves troops toward Kuwait border.

12–15 October

Iraq retreats. Kidnapping of Israeli soldier leads Israel to halt talks with PLO.

1995

17 February

Rabin and Arafat meet to step up self-rule on West Bank.

22 February

Arafat meets with PLO executive committee in response to growing Palestinian frustration at pace of self-rule.

NOTES AND REFERENCES

INTRODUCTION

1.   William L. Cleveland, *A History of the Modern Middle East* (Boulder: Westview Press, 1994), xiii.

2.   L. Carl Brown, *International Politics and the Middle East: Old Rules, Dangerous Games* (Princeton: Princeton University Press, 1985), 7.

CHAPTER 1

1.   For the diplomacy of oil after World War II, including British-American rivalry in Saudi Arabia and elsewhere, consult Aaron David Miller, *Search for Security: Saudi Arabian Oil and American Foreign Policy* (Chapel Hill: University of North Carolina Press, 1980), 122–72; Michael B. Stoff, *Oil, War and American Security: The Search for a National Policy on Foreign Oil, 1941–1947* (New Haven: Yale University Press, 1980); Irving H. Anderson, *Aramco, the United States and Saudi Arabia: A Study of the Dynamics of Foreign Oil Policy, 1933–1950* (Princeton: Princeton University Press, 1981); Daniel Yergin, *The Prize: The Epic Quest for Oil, Money, and Power* (New York: Simon & Schuster, 1991), 393–430; and William Roger Louis, *The British Empire in the Middle East, 1945–1951* (Oxford: Clarendon Press, 1984), 173–204.

2.   The quotes are from Miller, *Search for Security*, 101–2.

3.   Peter L. Hahn, *The United States, Great Britain, and Egypt, 1945–1956: Strategy and Diplomacy in the Early Cold War* (Chapel Hill: University of North Carolina Press, 1991), 25–27; Melvyn P. Leffler, *A Preponderance of Power: National Security, the Truman Administration, and the Cold War* (Stanford: Stanford University Press, 1992), 77–81, 112–13. On the northern tier, see also Bruce R. Kuniholm, *The*

Origins of the Cold War in the Near East: Great Power Conflict and Diplomacy in Iran, Turkey, and Greece (Princeton: Princeton University Press, 1980).

4. Louis, *The British Empire in the Middle East*, 226–64; Peter Mansfield, *The British in Egypt* (New York: Holt, Rinehart and Winston, 1971), 271–89; Habibur Rahman, "British Post–Second World War Planning for the Middle East," *Journal of Strategic Studies*, 5 (December 1982): 511–29; Hahn, *The United States, Great Britain, and Egypt*, 38–63.

5. There is a large literature on the Palestine issue and the establishment of the state of Israel. The discussion that follows relies heavily on Steven L. Spiegel, *The Other Arab-Israeli Conflict: Making America's Middle East Policy, from Truman to Reagan* (Chicago: University of Chicago Press, 1985), 16–49.

6. *Foreign Relations of the United States* (1945), 8:1–9. (Hereafter cited as *FRUS*.)

7. Ibid., 237–39.

8. On Bevin, see especially Louis, *The British Empire in the Middle East*, 1–6, 383–96.

9. Walter Laqueur and Barry Rubin, eds., *The Israel-Arab Reader: A Documentary History of the Middle East* (New York: Penguin Press, 1991), 85–94.

10. Quoted in Louis, *The British Empire in the Middle East*, 419.

11. T. G. Fraser, *The USA and the Middle East since World War 2* (New York: St. Martin's Press, 1989), 25–34.

12. Bruce Maddy-Weitzman, *The Crystallization of the Arab State System, 1945–1954* (Syracuse: Syracuse University Press, 1993), esp. ix–xiv, 175–81.

13. *FRUS*, 1947, 5:1263–64.

14. Ibid., 1948, 5:1005–7.

15. Compare, for example, Leffler, *A Preponderance of Power*, 237–42; and Michael Cohen, *Palestine and the Great Powers, 1945–1948* (Princeton: Princeton University Press, 1982), 379–96 with Robert Donovan, *Conflict and Crisis: The Presidency of Harry S. Truman, 1945–1948* (New York: W. W. Norton & Co., 1977), 318–30, 369–87; and David McCullough, *Truman* (New York: Simon & Schuster, 1992), 595–620. See also J. Snetsinger, *Truman, the Jewish Vote and the Creation of Israel* (Stanford: Hoover Institute Press, 1974); Zvi Ganon, *Truman, American Jewry, and Israel, 1945–48* (New York: Holmes and Meier, 1979); and Spiegel, *The Other Arab-Israeli Conflict*, 39, 46–49.

16. *FRUS*, 1948, 5:1415.

17. Ibid., 1513.

18. "Possible Developments from the Palestinian Truce," 31 August 1948, Box 1, Folder "NSC-CIA-Memoranda, 5/21/48–8/31/48," Records of the National Security Council, CIA File, Papers of Harry S. Truman, Harry S. Truman Library, Independence, Missouri.

19. Brown, *International Politics and the Middle East*, 43.

20. Quoted in Louis, *The British Empire in the Middle East*, 335.

21. Ibid., 575–82; Mansfield, *The British in Egypt*, 285–89.

22. "Tripartite Declaration Regarding Security in the Near East" in *The Arab-Israeli Conflict: Readings and Documents*, ed., John Norton Moore (Princeton: Princeton University Press, 1977), 988–89; Hahn, *The United States, Great Britain, and Egypt*, 82–92, 101–02.

23. Louis, *The British Empire in the Middle East*, 707–20; Hahn, *The United*

States, Great Britain, and Egypt, 93–94; D. A. Farnie, *East and West of Suez: The Suez Canal in History, 1854–1956* (Oxford: Clarendon Press, 1969), 691–99.

24. Dean Acheson, *Present at the Creation: My Years in the State Department* (New York: W. W. Norton & Co., 1969), 562–66; *FRUS*, 1952–54, 6:732–38; Gail E. Meyer, *Egypt and the United States: The Formative Years* (Cranburg, N.J.: Associated University Presses, 1980), 24; Peter Hahn, "Containment and Egyptian Nationalism: The Unsuccessful Effort to Establish the Middle East Command, 1950–53," *Diplomatic History* 11 (Winter 1987): 23–40.

25. Hahn, *The United States, Great Britain, and Egypt*, 109–54.

26. United Nations Statistical Office, *World Energy Supplies, 1951–1954* (New York: United Nations Statistical Office, 1956); Burton I. Kaufman, *The Oil Cartel Case: A Documentary Study of Antitrust Activity in the Cold War Era* (Westport, Conn.: Greenwood Press, 1978), 72–73.

27. Senate Subcommittee on Monopoly of the Select Committee on Small Business, *The International Petroleum Cartel: Staff Report to the Federal Trade Commission* (Washington, D.C.: Government Printing Office, 1952), 33.

28. Kaufman, *The Oil Cartel Case*, 38–47.

29. Burton I. Kaufman, "Mideast Multinational Oil, U.S. Foreign Policy, and Antitrust: The 1950s," *Journal of American History* 63 (March 1977): 945–46.

30. Truman to McGranery, 12 January 1953 in Senate Subcommittee on Multinational Corporations of the Committee on Foreign Relations, *Report, Multinational Oil Corporations and U.S. Foreign Policy*, 94th Cong., 1st sess., (Washington, D.C.: Government Printing Office, 1975), v–vi.

CHAPTER 2

1. "A Report to the National Security Council," 14 July 1953, Box 5, Office of the Special Assistant for National Security Affairs, NSC Series, Policy Papers Subseries, Truman Papers.

2. Shimon Sharir, "The Collapse of Project Alpha," in *Suez 1956: The Crisis and Its Consequences*, eds. William Roger Louis and Roger Owen (Oxford: Clarendon Press, 1989), 73–100. See also Steven Z. Freiberger, *Dawn Over Suez: The Rise of American Power in the Middle East, 1953–1957* (Chicago: Ivan R. Dee, 1992), 107–32, 133, 149, 152, 213; Diane B. Kunz, *The Economic Diplomacy of the Suez Crisis* (Chapel Hill: University of North Carolina Press, 1991), 39–45.

3. "A Report to the National Security Council," 14 July 1953, Box 5, Office of the Special Assistant for National Security Affairs, NSC Series, Policy Papers Subseries, Truman Papers; Hahn, *The United States, Great Britain, and Egypt*, 155–56; Robert Stephens, *Nasser: A Political Biography* (New York: Simon & Schuster, 1971), 132.

4. Ibid.; Donald Neff, *Warriors at Suez: Eisenhower Takes America into the Middle East* (New York: Simon & Schuster, 1981), 55.

5. Anthony Eden, *Full Circle: The Memoirs of Anthony Eden* (Boston: Houghton Mifflin Co., 1960), 70–71, 244–45, 274–77; Victor Rothwell, *Anthony Eden: A Political Biography, 1931–57* (New York: Manchester University Press, 1992), 127–32; Selwyn Lloyd, *Suez: A Personal Account* (London: Jonathan Cape, 1978), 60–61.

6. William J. Burns, *Economic Aid and American Policy toward Egypt, 1955–1981* (Albany: State University Press of New York, 1985), 14–16.

7. Hahn, *The United States, Great Britain, and Egypt*, 165–69, 183–85.

8. Memorandum of Discussion at the 147th Meeting of the National Security Council, 1 June 1953, *FRUS, 1952–1954*, 9:379–86.

9. The quote is from Freiberger, *Dawn Over Suez*, 91.

10. Anthony Nutting, *Nasser* (New York: E. P. Dutton, 1972), 7–8, 14–15, 67–68, 304–7, 477–81; Stephens, *Nasser*, 111–13, 141–42.

11. "Progress Report on 'United States Objectives and Policies with Respect to the Near East' (NSC 5428)," 17 May 1956, Box 12, White House Office, Office of the Special Assistant for National Security Affairs, NSC Series, Policy Papers Subseries, Dwight D. Eisenhower Papers, Dwight D. Eisenhower Library, Abilene, Kansas.

12. Nutting, *Nasser*, 74–90; Stephens, *Nasser*, 144–45, 148–51, 173–75.

13. Nutting, *Nasser*, 94–95, 139.

14. Ibid., 90–101.

15. Burton I. Kaufman, *Trade and Aid: Eisenhower's Foreign Economic Policy, 1953–1961* (Baltimore: Johns Hopkins University Press, 1982), 58–73.

16. Ibid.

17. Robert R. Bowie, "Eisenhower, Dulles, and the Suez Crisis," in *Suez 1956: The Crisis and Its Consequences*, eds. William Roger Louis and Roger Owen (Oxford: Clarendon Press, 1989), 190–91; Eden, *Full Circle*, 388–92; Rothwell, *Anthony Eden*, 185–86; Burns, *Economic Aid and American Policy toward Egypt*, 44–74.

18. Dwight D. Eisenhower, *Waging Peace, 1955–1960: The White House Years* (New York: Doubleday, 1965), 30–32.

19. Stephen E. Ambrose, *Eisenhower*, 2 vols. (New York: Simon & Schuster, 1984), 2:329–30; Hahn, *The United States, Great Britain, and Egypt*, 200–203.

20. Stephens, *Nasser*, 193–94.

21. Keith Kyle, "Britain and the Suez Crisis, 1955–1956," in *Suez 1956: The Crisis and Its Consequences*, eds. William Roger Louis and Roger Owen (Oxford: Clarendon Press, 1989), 109–15, 123; Maurice Vaisse, "France and the Suez Crisis," in ibid., 131–36; Eden, *Full Circle*, 422–26.

22. Robert Murphy, *Diplomat Among Warriors* (Garden City: Doubleday, 1964), 383; Bowie, "Eisenhower, Dulles, and Suez," 198–213.

23. Diane Kunz, "The Economic Diplomacy of the Suez Crisis," in *Suez 1956: The Crisis and Its Consequences*, eds. William Roger Louis and Roger Owen (Oxford: Clarendon Press, 1989), 219–31.

24. Eisenhower to Anderson, 30 July 1957, papers accompanying Dillon Anderson interview, Dwight D. Eisenhower Library, Abilene, Kansas.

25. Freiberger, *Dawn Over Suez*, 189–209; Ambrose, *Eisenhower*, 2:358–75.

26. According to most recent writers on the Suez crisis, however, Eden knew all along that Eisenhower would be opposed to Britain's seizure of the canal. See, for example, Bowie, "Eisenhower, Dulles, and Suez," 213; Freiberger, *Dawn Over Suez*, 161–67; Ambrose, *Eisenhower*, 2:330–34, 350–52, 358–60. But Eden biographer Victor Rothwell makes the point that "Eisenhower's forthright warnings against the use of force had to be set against Dulles's equivocations." Rothwell, *Anthony Eden*, 207.

27. Ambrose, *Eisenhower*, 2:381–83, 388.

28. Malcolm H. Kerr, *The Arab Cold War: Gamal 'Abd al-Nasir and His Rivals, 1958–1970* (London: Oxford University Press, 1971).

29. Uriel Dann, *King Hussein and the Challenge of Arab Radicalism: Jordan, 1955–1967* (New York: Oxford University Press, 1989), 34–65.

30. Patrick Seale, *The Struggle for Syria: A Study of Post-War Arab Politics, 1945–1958* (London: I. B. Tauris & Co., 1986), 186–282.

31. Eisenhower, *Waging Peace*, 262; Seale, *The Struggle for Syria*, 254–60, 283–306.

32. Eisenhower, *Waging Peace*, 197–202; David W. Lesch, *Syria and the United States: Eisenhower's Cold War in the Middle East* (Boulder: Westview Press, 1992), esp. 5–13, 190–214; Nutting, *Nasser*, 211; Stephens, *Nasser*, 263–64.

33. Minutes of the 427th Meeting of the National Security Council, 9 July 1959, Box 10, NSC Series, Eisenhower Papers. On Iraq, see also Edith and E. F. Penrose, *Iraq: International Relations and National Development* (Boulder: Westview Press, 1978), 199–237; Christine Moss Helms, *Iraq: Eastern Flank of the Arab World* (Washington, D.C.: Brookings Institution, 1984), 59–77; Marion Farouk-Sluglett and Peter Sluglett, *Iraq Since 1958: From Revolution to Dictatorship* (London: KPI Limited, 1987), 38–50.

34. Dann, *King Hussein and the Challenge of Arab Radicalism*, 56–65; Eisenhower, *Waging Peace*, 135, 194–95.

35. Eisenhower, *Waging Peace*, 269.

36. Minutes of the 368th Meeting of the National Security Council, 3 June 1958, Box 10, NSC Series, Eisenhower Papers.

37. Burns, *Economic Aid and American Policy toward Egypt*, 118.

38. Nutting, *Nasser*, 293–97.

39. Ibid., 297–99; Minutes of the 366th Meeting of the National Security Council, 22 May 1958, Box 10, NSC Series, Eisenhower Papers.

40. "The Situation in Iraq—Comments and Questions," 16 August 1959, Box 13, NSC Series, Briefing Notes Subseries, Eisenhower Papers; Minutes of the 410th Meeting of the National Security Council, 1 October 1959, Box 11, ibid.

41. "Note by the Executive Secretary to the National Security Council on U.S. Policy Toward the Near East," 17 June 1960, Box 29, NSC Series, Policy Papers Subseries, ibid.

42. Yergin, *The Prize*, 505.

43. Walter B. Smith to Attorney General Herbert Brownell, 27 April 1953, Department of Justice, Record Case 60-57-140. Senate Committee on Foreign Relations, *Committee Print, The International Petroleum Cartel, The Iranian Consortium and U.S. National Security.*, 93rd Cong., 2nd sess., (Washington D.C.: Government Printing Office, 1974), 63, 65.

44. By 1960, the Justice Department had reached agreement with Exxon and Gulf. In 1963, Texaco settled with the government. But Mobil and Standard Oil of California (SOCAL) failed to reach an agreement, and in 1968, the Justice Department decided to drop its case against them, satisfied it had gained as much relief as it was likely to achieve. Kaufman, *The Oil Cartel Case*, 93–101.

45. Fugate to Kirkpatrick, November 10, 1960, Department of Justice, Record Case 60-57-140.

CHAPTER 3

1. Quoted in Mordechai Gazit, *President Kennedy's Policy toward the Arab States and Israel: Analysis and Documents* (Tel Aviv: Shiloah Center for Middle Eastern and African Studies, 1983), 14.

2. Quoted in Douglas Little, "The New Frontier on the Nile: JFK, Nasser, and Arab Nationalism," *Journal of American History* 75 (September 1988): 502.

3. On this point, see especially Spiegel, *The Other Arab-Israeli Conflict*, 94–95.

4. George Lenczowski, *American Presidents and the Middle East* (Durham: Duke University Press, 1990), 73–74.

5. Arthur Schlesinger Jr., *A Thousand Days: John F. Kennedy in the White House* (Boston: Houghton Mifflin Co., 1965), 473.

6. Little, "The New Frontier on the Nile," 501–5.

7. William J. Burns, *Economic Aid and American Policy toward Egypt*, 121–34; Gazit, *President Kennedy's Policy toward the Arab States and Israel*, 15–22.

8. Robert Stephens, *Nasser*, 446–47; Burns, *Economic Aid and American Policy toward Egypt*, 127–28.

9. "The President's Conversation with the United Arab Republic Ambassador," 4 May 1961, Box 127, President's Office File, Presidential Papers of John F. Kennedy, John F. Kennedy Library, Boston, Massachusetts.

10. Quoted in Burns, *Economic Aid and American Policy toward Egypt*, 129. See also George Lenczowski, *Soviet Advances in the Middle East* (Washington, D.C.: American Enterprise Institute for Public Policy Research, 1972), 86–88.

11. Patrick Seale, *The Struggle for Syria*, 307–26; Walter Z. Laqueur, "Syria: Nationalism and Communism," in *The Middle East in Transition*, ed. Walter Z. Laqueur (Freeport, N.Y.: Books for Libraries Press, 1971), 325–36; Gabran Majdalany, "The Arab Socialist Movement," in ibid., 335–37; Lenczowski, *Soviet Advances in the Middle East*, 101–11.

12. Stephens, *Nasser*, 330–43; Nutting, *Nasser*, 245–54, 262–70.

13. Walter Laqueur, *The Struggle for the Middle East: The Soviet Union in the Mediterranean, 1958–1968* (New York: Macmillan, 1969), 67–68.

14. On this matter, see chapter 10.

15. John S. Badeau, *The Middle East Remembered* (Washington, D.C.: Middle East Institute, 1993), 190–91.

16. Ibid., 190–91; Burns, *Economic Aid and American Policy toward Egypt*, 132.

17. Spiegel, *The Other Arab-Israeli Conflict*, 95–99.

18. Quoted in ibid., 106.

19. Dana Adams Schmidt, *Yemen: The Unknown War* (New York: Holt, Rinehart and Winston, 1968), 36–47; Little, "The New Frontier on the Nile," 510–11; Glen Balfour-Paul, *The End of Empire in the Middle East: Britain's Relinquishment of Power in Her Last Three Arab Dependencies* (Cambridge: Cambridge University Press, 1991), 76–78.

20. John S. Badeau, *The American Approach to the Arab World* (New York: Harper and Row, 1968), 127.

21. Ibid., 129; Gazit, *President Kennedy's Policy toward the Arab States and Israel*, 22.

22. Badeau, *The American Approach to the Arab World*, 130; Uriel Dann, *King Hussein and the Challenge of Arab Radicalism*, 125.

23. George Ball to Badeau, 27 September 1962, Box 127, National Security Files, Presidential Papers of John Fitzgerald Kennedy; Edward Weintal and Charles Bartlett, *Facing the Brink: An Intimate Study of Crisis Diplomacy* (New York: Charles Scribner's Sons, 1967), 39–41.

24. Spiegel, *The Other Arab-Israeli Conflict*, 103.

25. Badeau, *The American Approach to the Arab World*, 135–38; J. B. Kelly, *Arabia, the Gulf and the West* (New York: Basic Books, 1980), 8–15.

26. Kennedy and Hart quoted in Little, "The New Frontier on the Nile," 514.

27. Paul-Balfour, *The End of Empire in the Middle East*, 76–80; Gazit, *President Kennedy's Policy toward the Arab States and Israel*, 23–24.

28. Schlesinger, *A Thousand Days*, 474; Badeau, *The American Approach to the Arab World*, 136–39.

29. Badeau, *The American Approach to the Arab World*, 140.

30. Quoted in Little, "The New Frontier on the Nile," 517.

31. Ibid., 517–19.

32. Weintal and Bartlett, *Facing the Brink*, 43–44.

33. Mohamed Hassanein Heikal, *The Cairo Documents: The Inside Story of Nasser and His Relationship with World Leaders, Rebels, and Statesmen* (Garden City: Doubleday, 1973), 216–18.

34. Little, "The New Frontier on the Nile," 521–22.

35. Heikal, *The Cairo Documents*, 222–23; Badeau, *The American Approach to the Arab World*, 142–43.

36. For this and the next two paragraphs, see Malcolm H. Kerr, *The Arab Cold War*, 27–95; Joseph P. Lorenz, *Egypt and the Arabs: Foreign Policy and the Search for National Identity* (Boulder: Westview Press, 1990), 32–33; Eberhard Kienle, *Ba'th v. Ba'th: The Conflict between Syria and Iraq* (London: I. B. Tauris & Co., 1990), 13–15; Dann, *King Hussein and the Challenge of Arab Radicalism*, 118–24, 127–37; Marion Farouk-Sluglett and Peter Sluglett, *Iraq Since 1958*, 83–95; Patrick Seale, *Asad of Syria: The Struggle for the Middle East* (Berkeley: University of California Press, 1988), 81–90; Edith and E. F. Penrose, *Iraq*, 297–315; Stephens, *Nasser*, 389–405; Nutting, *Nasser*, 323–37.

37. Quoted in Little, "The New Frontier on the Nile," 523.

38. Jon D. Glassman, *Arms for the Arabs: The Soviet Union and War in the Middle East* (Baltimore: Johns Hopkins University Press, 1975), 22–26; Burns, *Economic Aid and American Policy toward Egypt*, 140.

39. Glassman, *Arms for the Arabs*, 25–26.

40. Gazit, *President Kennedy's Policy toward the Arab States and Israel*, 33–36, 40–41; Burns, *Economic Aid and American Policy toward Egypt*, 141.

41. Ibid. See also Spiegel, *The Other Arab-Israeli Conflict*, 108–9.

42. Burns, *Economic Aid and American Policy toward Egypt*, 140–44.

43. Quoted in ibid., 146.

44. Little, "The New Frontier on the Nile," 526.

CHAPTER 4

1. The fifth and largest of the areas, the Sinai Peninsula was eventually returned to Egypt by 1982.

2.   I discuss this point in Burton I. Kaufman, "Foreign Aid and the Balance of Payments Problem: Vietnam and Johnson's Foreign Economic Policy," in *The Johnson Years*, vol. 2, *Vietnam, the Environment, and Science*, ed. Robert A. Divine (Lawrence: University Press of Kansas, 1987), 79–81. See also Philip Geyelin, *Lyndon B. Johnson and the World* (New York: Frederick A. Praeger, 1966), 30.

3.   Burns, *Economic Aid and American Policy toward Egypt*, 150.

4.   Heikal, *The Cairo Documents*, 225–26. See also Burns, *Economic Aid and American Policy toward Egypt*, 150–51.

5.   Lyndon Baines Johnson, *The Vantage Point: Perspectives of the Presidency, 1963–1969* (New York: Holt, Rinehart and Winston, 1971), 297; Spiegel, *The Other Arab-Israeli Conflict*, 121; Merle Miller, *Lyndon: An Oral Biography* (New York: G. P. Putnam's Sons, 1980), 477–78.

6.   Geyelin, *Lyndon B. Johnson and the World*, 141–58.

7.   Itamar Rabinovich, *Syria under the Ba'th, 1963–66: The Army-Party Symbiosis* (Jerusalem: Israel Universities Press, 1972), 101–2; Dann, *King Hussein and the Challenge of Arab Radicalism*, 136–37; Stephens, *Nasser*, 442–50.

8.   Dann, *King Hussein and the Challenge of Arab Radicalism*, 137; Stephens, *Nasser*, 451 and 454; Jillian Becker, *The PLO: The Rise and Fall of the Palestinian Organization* (London: Wiedenfeld and Nicolson, 1984), 35–40; Janet Wallach and John Wallach, *Arafat: In the Eyes of the Beholder* (New York: Carol Publishing Group, 1990), 110–11.

9.   Dann, *King Hussein and the Challenge of Arab Radicalism*, 452; Donald Neff, *Warriors for Jerusalem: The Six Days That Changed the Middle East* (New York: Simon & Schuster, 1984), 33; Kerr, *The Arab Cold War*, 106–7, 114–16; Wallach and Wallach, *Arafat*, 110–12; Alan Hart, *Arafat: Terrorist or Peacemaker?* (London: Sidgwick and Jackson, 1987), 160–71.

10.   Stephens, *Nasser*, 452–53; Rabinovich, *Syria under the Ba'th*, 102–3, 209–14; Kerr, *The Arab Cold War*, 98–105.

11.   Stephens, *Nasser*, 412–27; Kerr, *The Arab Cold War*, 106–14.

12.   Dann, *King Hussein and the Challenge of Arab Radicalism*, 147–48.

13.   Neff, *Warriors for Jerusalem*, 32, 37–39; Wallach and Wallach, *Arafat*, 120–22.

14.   Geoffrey Kemp, "Strategy and Arms Levels, 1945–1967," in *Soviet-American Rivalry in the Middle East*, ed. J. C. Hurewitz (New York: Praeger, 1969), 22–24; Jon D. Glassman, *Arms for the Arabs*, 26–32.

15.   Circular telegram to Chiefs of Mission in Arab states from Phillip Talbot, 18 March 1965, Box 116, National Security File, Country File, Lyndon Baines Johnson Papers, Lyndon Baines Johnson Library, Austin, Texas.

16.   "Outgoing telegram, Department of State," 18 March 1965, Box 17, National Security File, NSC History, Middle East Crisis, ibid.; "Recommendations on Near East Arms," n.d., ibid. See also Harry N. Howard, "The Soviet Union in Lebanon, Syria, and Jordan," in *The Soviet Union and the Middle East: The Post-World War II Era*, eds. Ivo J. Lederer and Wayne S. Vucinich (Stanford: Hoover Institution Press, 1974), 150; Spiegel, *The Other Arab-Israeli Conflict*, 132–35.

17.   Glassman, *Arms for the Arabs*, 27–28.

18.   Neff, *Warriors for Jerusalem*, 84; Spiegel, *The Other Arab-Israeli Conflict*, 132–34.

19.   Trevor N. Dupuy, *Elusive Victory: The Arab-Israeli Wars, 1947–1974* (New

York: Harper and Row, 1978), 231, 337; Lenczowski, *Soviet Advances in the Middle East*, 149–50; Neff, *Warriors for Suez*, 193–94.

20. Dupuy, *Elusive Victory*, 231–33; Patrick Seale, *Asad of Syria*, 116–18.

21. Edgar O'Ballance, *The Third Arab-Israeli War* (Hamden: Archon Books, 1972), 37–48.

22. Glassman, *Arms for the Arabs*, 36.

23. J. B. Kelly, *Arabia, the Gulf and the West* (New York: Basic Books, 1980), 25–46.

24. Johnson, *The Vantage Point*, 288. See also Ishaq I. Ghanayem and Alden H. Voth, *The Kissinger Legacy: American Middle East Policy* (New York: Praeger, 1984), 22.

25. Burns, *Economic Aid and American Policy toward Egypt*, 150; Stephens, *Nasser*, 457.

26. Burns, *Economic Aid and American Policy toward Egypt*, 163–70.

27. Nutting, *Nasser*, 384–86; Stephens, *Nasser*, 458–59.

28. "Memorandum of Conversation," 13 January 1965, Box 159, National Security File, Country File Subseries, Johnson Papers.

29. Kelly, *Arabia, the Gulf and the West*, 264.

30. Rabinovich, *Syria under the Ba'th*, 180–208.

31. Nutting, *Nasser*, 386–89; Kerr, *The Arab Cold War*, 122–28.

32. Dann, *King Hussein and the Challenge of Arab Radicalism*, 147–51.

33. Neff, *Warriors for Jerusalem*, 34–36.

34. Ibid., 39–41; Walter Laqueur, *The Road to War: The Origin and Aftermath of the Arab-Israeli Conflict, 1967–8* (Baltimore: Penguin Books, 1968), 71–72.

35. Dann, *King Hussein and the Challenge of Arab Radicalism*, 155; Neff, *Warriors for Jerusalem*, 41–46.

36. Neff, *Warriors for Jerusalem*, 47–49.

37. Nutting, *Nasser*, 388–89.

38. Kerr, *The Arab Cold War*, 114.

39. Stephens, *Nasser*, 466–67.

40. Except where otherwise noted, the account of the events preceding the Six-Day War that follows is based on an unpublished history prepared for the National Security Council. See "United States Policy and Diplomacy in the Middle East Crisis, May 15–June 10, 1967," unpublished manuscript, National Security File, NSC History, Middle East Crisis, Johnson Papers. (Hereafter cited as USPD/MEC.) See also Hal Kosut, ed., *Israel and the Arabs: The June 1967 War* (New York: Facts on File, 1968), 1–65; Laqueur, *Road to War*, 97–267; Neff, *Warriors for Jerusalem*, 55–172; Michael Bar-Zohar, *Embassies in Crisis: Diplomats and Demagogues behind the Six-Day War* (Englewood, N.J.: Prentice Hall Inc., 1970).

41. Quoted in USPD/MEC, 7–8.

42. William B. Quandt, *Peace Process: American Diplomacy and the Arab-Israeli Conflict since 1967* (Washington, D.C.: Brookings Institution, 1993), 26.

43. Ibid.

44. Ibid., 28.

45. Ibid., 30.

46. Memorandum for the President from Walt Rostow, 23 May 1967, Box 1, National Security File, Meeting Notes File, Johnson Papers.

47. Johnson, *The Vantage Point*, 292.

48. Memorandum of Conversation between the President and Eban, 30 May 1967, Box 12, National Security File, NSC History, Middle East Crisis, Johnson Papers.

49. Walt Rostow to the President, 28 May 1967, Box 17, ibid.

50. Nutting, *Nasser*, 388–401; Stephens, *Nasser*, 470–77.

51. Quoted in Stephens, *Nasser*, 481.

52. W. W. Rostow to the President, 2–3 June 1967, Box 18, National Security File, NSC History, Middle East Crisis, Johnson Papers.

53. Walt Rostow to the President, 28–29 May 1967, Box 17, ibid.; Abba Eban, *Personal Witness: Israel through My Eyes* (New York: G. P. Putnam's Sons, 1992), 406–8; Michael Brecher, *Decisions in Israel's Foreign Policies* (New Haven: Yale University Press), 413–33.

54. Memorandum for the Secretary of Defense from the Joint Chiefs of Staff, 2 June 1967, Box 18, National Security Council File, NSC History, Middle East Crisis, Johnson Papers.

55. Stephens, *Nasser*, 481–86.

56. Quandt, *Peace Process*, 45–48.

57. Stephens, *Nasser*, 487.

58. For the military history of the war, see O'Ballance, *The Third Arab-Israeli War*, 49–265; Dupuy, *Elusive Victory*, 245–340.

59. Dann, *King Hussein and the Challenge of Arab Radicalism*, 160–62.

60. A list of the telephone calls between the two leaders can be found in Box 1, National Security File, NSC History, Middle East Crisis, Johnson Papers.

61. Memorandum for Mr. W. W. Rostow from Nathaniel Davis, 6 June 1967 and Memorandum for Mr. Rostow, 7 June 1967, Box 18, ibid.

62. "The Middle East Crisis: Preface," 20 December 1968, Box 17, ibid.

63. Johnson, *Vantage Point*, 298–99.

64. USPD/MEC, 107, 111.

65. Memorandum for Mr. W. W. Rostow from Nathaniel Davis, 6 June 1967 and Rostow to the President, 6 June 1967, National Security File, NSC History, Middle East Crisis, Johnson papers.

66. King Hussein still retained operational control of his forces. Nevertheless, as Samir A. Mutawi points out, Hussein's decision to place his troops under Egypt's leadership "was disastrous for the Jordanians" both militarily and in terms of the response it evoked from Israel. On these points, see Samir A. Mutawi, *Jordan in the 1967 War* (Cambridge: Cambridge University Press, 1987), esp. 16, 108, 122–62.

67. Stephens, *Nasser*, 503–8.

68. CIA Intelligence Report, 10 June 1967, Box 20, National Security File, NSC History, Middle East Crisis, Johnson Papers; Johnson, *Vantage Point*, 302–4; Quandt, *Peace Process*, 51–52.

69. Incoming Telegram, Department of State, 26 June 1967, Box 22, National Security File, NSC History, Middle East Crisis, Johnson Papers; Robert W. Stookey, *America and the Arab States: An Uneasy Encounter* (New York: John Wiley and Sons, 1975), 208–9; Stephens, *Nasser*, 494, 503–9.

70. W. W. R. to President, 8 June 1967, Box 18, National Security File, NSC History, Middle East Crisis, Johnson Papers.

71. Nutting, *Nasser*, 425–32.

72. "Memorandum for the Record" by Harold Saunders, 7 June, 1967, Box 18, National Security File, NSC History, Middle East Crisis, Johnson Papers.

73. The Israelis immediately apologized for the attack, which left 34 American crewmen dead and 164 wounded, saying it was a terrible accident. But the commander of the *Liberty*, James M. Ennes, Jr., and many other commentators believe the attack on the *Liberty* was committed purposely to stop American intelligence gathering, which might harm Israel. See James M. Ennes, Jr., *Assault on the* Liberty: *The True Story of the Israeli Attack on an American Intelligence Ship* (New York: Random House, 1979) and Dupuy, *Elusive Victory*, 31–32. But for the opposing view, see O'Ballance, *The Third Arab-Israeli War*, 265–67.

74. Stookey, *America and the Arab States*, 209; Spiegel, *The Other Arab-Israeli Conflict*, 158.

75. On the Israeli government's postwar views, see especially Don Peretz, "Israeli Policies toward the Arab States and the Palestinians since 1967," in *The Arab-Israeli Conflict: Two Decades of Change*, eds. Yehuda Lukacs and Abdalla M. Battah (Boulder: Westview Press, 1988), 26–29. See also Amos Elon, *The Israelis: Founders and Sons* (New York: Holt, Rinehart and Winston, 1971), 28–32.

76. CIA Assessment of Kosygin's UN Speech of 19 June 1967, Box 18, National Security File, NSC History, Middle East Crisis, Johnson Papers; Rostow to the President, 19 June 1967, ibid.

77. Quandt, *Peace Process*, 55.

78. Brecher, *Decisions in Israel's Foreign Policy*, 447–48; Dupuy, *Elusive Victory*, 344.

79. Kerr, *The Arab Cold War*, 131–33; Seale, *Asad of Syria*, 144–45; Stephens, *Nasser*, 520–21.

80. Stephens, *Nasser*, 522–23; Nutting, *Nasser*, 434–37.

81. Yergin, *The Prize*, 554–58.

82. Dupuy, *Elusive Victory*, 348–49; Glassman, *Arms for the Arabs*, 68; Stephens, *Nasser*, 516.

83. Quandt, *Peace Process*, 55–56.

84. The full text of UN Resolution 242 can be conveniently found in Quandt, *Peace Process*, 435–36.

85. Prior to approval of the resolution, however, the United States had signed a memorandum of understanding with Britain which stated that the text "referring to withdrawal must similarly be understood to mean withdrawal from occupied territories of the UAR, Jordan, and Syria." This suggests that, in return for peace, Washington intended for Israel to withdraw from all the occupied territories with some minor modifications for security purposes. Certainly the administration led King Hussein to believe this is what it had in mind. According to Donald Neff, a historian of the Six-Day War, the United States' position had been made clear to the Arab states by the first week in November. "It would support adjustments to the armistice lines, but still it was assumed that they would entail only minor bits of land and that Israel's withdrawal would be nearly complete in return for peace." Neff, *Warriors for Jerusalem*, 341. See also Quandt, *Peace Process*, 56–57.

86. Quandt, *Peace Process*, 56–58.

87. Glassman, *Arms for the Arabs*, 65–69; Quandt, *Peace Process*, 58; J. C. Hurewitz, "Origins of the Rivalry," in *Soviet-American Rivalry in the Middle East*, ed. J. C. Hurewitz (New York: Praeger, 1969), 3–5.

CHAPTER 5

1. Richard Nixon, *The Memoirs of Richard Nixon* (New York: Grosset and Dunlap, 1978), 249–50.

2. Ibid., 478.

3. Henry Kissinger, *White House Years* (Boston: Little, Brown & Co., 1979), 341.

4. Ibid., 26–27; Nixon, *The Memoirs of Richard Nixon*, 339.

5. Nixon, *The Memoirs of Richard Nixon*, 477. See also Kissinger, *White House Years*, 348.

6. Kissinger, *White House Years*, 29–30, 350–51, 354–55; Edward R. F. Sheehan, *The Arabs, Israelis, and Kissinger: A Secret History of American Diplomacy in the Middle East* (New York: Thomas Y. Crowell, 1976), 15–18; Walter Isaacson, *Kissinger: A Biography* (New York: Simon & Schuster, 1992), 209–11, 286.

7. Kissinger, *White House Years*, 344–45, 350–57. See also Ghanayem and Voth, *The Kissinger Legacy*, 36–37.

8. Stephens, *Nasser*, 517–19.

9. Speech of Nasser, 6 November 1969 cited in Glassman, *Arms for the Arabs*, 73.

10. Nixon, *The Memoirs of Richard Nixon*, 477.

11. Kissinger, *White House Years*, 373–77; Stephens, *Nasser*, 516–19; Glassman, *Arms for the Arabs*, 64–73; Quandt, *Peace Process*, 72–83.

12. Nixon, *The Memoirs of Richard Nixon*, 479. See also Ghanayem and Voth, *The Kissinger Legacy*, 40–44, 66–67.

13. Shlomo Aronson, *Conflict and Bargaining in the Middle East: An Israeli Perspective* (Baltimore: Johns Hopkins University Press, 1978), 89–90; Peretz, "Israeli Policies toward the Arab States and the Palestinians since 1967," 26–27.

14. Kissinger, *White House Years*, 560–62; Stephens, *Nasser*, 526–29; Glassman, *Arms for the Arabs*, 71–75.

15. Nixon, *The Memoirs of Richard Nixon*, 479–81; Stephen E. Ambrose, *Nixon: The Triumph of a Politician* (New York: Simon & Schuster, 1989), 335; Glassman, *Arms for the Arabs*, 75.

16. Kissinger, *White House Years*, 569; Glassman, *Arms for the Arabs*, 75–77; Quandt, *Peace Process*, 86–87.

17. Glassman, *Arms for the Arabs*, 77–79. See also Foy D. Kohler, Leon Goure, and Mose L. Harvey, *The Soviet Union and the October 1973 Middle East War: The Implications for Detente* (Miami: University of Miami Press, 1974), 32–36.

18. Kissinger, *White House Years*, 571–82; Quandt, *Peace Process*, 88–91.

19. Hart, *Arafat*, 235–83; Wallach and Wallach, *Arafat*, 141–42.

20. Becker, *The PLO*, 64–73; Kerr, *The Arab Cold War*, 133–40; Hart, *Arafat*, 255–71; Wallach and Wallach, *Arafat*, 141–51.

21. Becker, *The PLO*, 74–77; Wallach and Wallach, *Arafat*, 151–52; Hart, *Arafat*, 284, 317–19.

22. Kerr, *The Arab Cold War*, 147–50; Glassman, *Arms for the Arabs*, 82; Freedman, *Soviet Policy toward the Middle East since 1970*, 37–38.

23. Nixon, *The Memoirs of Richard Nixon*, 482; Kissinger, *White House Years*, 594–97; Quandt, *Peace Process*, 94–95, 100–103; Aronson, *Conflict and Bargaining in the Middle East*, 132–33.

24. Nixon, *The Memoirs of Richard Nixon*, 484–85; Kissinger, *White House Years*, 610–11; Ghanayem and Voth, *The Kissinger Legacy*, 78–80.

25. *Chicago Sun-Times*, 18 September 1970. See also Kissinger, *White House Years*, 612; Quandt, *Peace Process*, 100–103.

26. Kissinger, *White House Years*, 617–19; Ghanayem and Voth, *The Kissinger Legacy*, 78–81; Isaacson, *Kissinger*, 293.

27. Kissinger, *White House Years*, 611–12.

28. Ibid., 618.

29. Ibid., 624–26; Nixon, *The Memoirs of Richard Nixon*, 485; Quandt, *Peace Process*, 105–7; Isaacson, *Kissinger*, 299–304.

30. The reason most commonly given for al-Asad's failure to provide air cover for the Syrian tanks has to do with a power struggle underway in Syria between al-Asad and his rival in the Ba'th Party, Salah Jadid, who allegedly had sent the tanks into Jordan. In this interpretation, al-Asad's purpose in not providing protection for the tanks was to discredit Jadid. But al-Asad's biographer, Patrick Seale, maintains that at the time of the Jordanian crisis, al-Asad was already "master of Syria in all but name" and that the tanks could not have been sent into Jordan without his approval. Al-Asad intervened, according to Seale, in order to save the Palestinians from being massacred. But his intervention was "reluctant and circumscribed." Since he had no great regard for the Palestinians and did not want them to take Amman, he refused to escalate the fighting by committing his air force to protect the Syrian tanks. Patrick Seale, *Asad of Syria*, 157–59. Compare with Naomi Joy Weinberger, *Syrian Intervention in Lebanon: The 1975–76 Civil War* (New York: Oxford University Press, 1986), 76; and Quandt, *Peace Process*, 112.

31. Henry Brandon, *The Retreat of American Power* (New York: Delta Books, 1974), 137–38; Glassman, *Arms for the Arabs*, 82–83.

32. Itamar Rabinovich, *The War for Lebanon, 1970–1983* (Ithaca: Cornell University Press, 1984), 34–36; Becker, *The PLO*, 93–98.

33. Kissinger, *White House Years*, 626–29; Quandt, *Peace Process*, 107–12.

34. Ibid.; Nadav Safran, *Israel: The Embattled Ally* (Cambridge: Belknap Press, 1978), 455–56.

35. Sheehan, *The Arabs, Israelis, and Kissinger*, 20–21; Safran, *Israel*, 456.

36. Kissinger, *White House Years*, 571–76.

37. Raymond Garthoff, *Detente and Confrontation: American-Soviet Relations from Nixon to Reagan* (Washington, D.C.: Brookings Institution, 1985), 86–87; Quandt, *Peace Process*, 117–18.

38. Quandt, *Peace Process*, 115.

39. Aronson, *Conflict and Bargaining in the Middle East*, 154–55.

40. Kerr, *The Arab Cold War*, 153–56; Stephens, *Nasser*, 55–59.

41. Joseph P. Lorenz, *Egypt and the Arabs*, 36–39; Raphael Israeli, *Man of Defiance: A Political Biography of Anwar Sadat* (London: Wiedenfeld and Nicolson, 1985), 53, 59–61; Mohamed Heikal, *The Road to Ramadan* (New York: Quadrangle/New York Times Book Co., 1984), 123–33; Seale, *Asad of Syria*, 162–63; Kissinger, *White House Years*, 1276–77.

42. Raymond William Baker, *Sadat and After: Struggles for Egypt's Political Soul* (Cambridge: Harvard University Press, 1990), 79; Heikal, *The Road to Ramadan*, 68–113; Lorenz, *Egypt and the Arabs*, 33–34.

43. Anwar el-Sadat, *In Search of Identity: An Autobiography* (London: Collins, 1978), 239.

44. Lorenz, *Egypt and the Arabs*, 40–41; Israeli, *Man of Defiance*, 84–93.

45. Heikal, *The Road to Ramadan*, 204–6; Seale, *Asad of Syria*, 185; Henry Kissinger, *Years of Upheaval* (Boston: Little, Brown & Co., 1982), 226.

46. Walter Laqueur, *Confrontation: The Middle East and World Politics* (New York: Quadrangle/New York Times Book Co., 1974), 12–18; Lorenz, *Egypt and the Arabs*, 41–45; Israeli, *Man of Defiance*, 83–93.

47. Freedman, *Soviet Policy toward the Middle East since 1970*, 68–72, 82–87; Heikal, *The Road to Ramadan*, 120, 166–84; Laqueur, *Confrontation*, 12–18.

48. Heikal, *The Road to Ramadan*, 200–203. See also Sheehan, *The Arabs, Israelis, and Kissinger*, 23–25. Kissinger, *White House Years*, 1300; Kissinger, *Years of Upheaval*, 214–16, 226–27.

49. Freedman, *Soviet Policy toward the Middle East since 1970*, 110–15, 118, 122–23; Kissinger, *White House Years*, 1284–85.

50. Quoted in Stephen Ambrose, *Nixon: Ruin and Recovery, 1973–1990* (New York: Simon & Schuster, 1991), 176. See also Nixon, *The Memoirs of Richard Nixon*, 885; Garthoff, *Detente and Confrontation*, 331–32, 364–68.

51. Kissinger, *White House Years*, 1290; Kissinger, *Years of Upheaval*, 206; Ambrose, *Nixon: Ruin and Recovery*, 176.

52. The military history of the October War that follows is based on Edgar O'Ballance, *No Victory, No Vanquished: The Yom Kippur War* (San Rafael: Presidio Press, 1978); Dupuy, *Elusive Victory*, 387–617; Frank Gervasi, *Thunder over the Mediterranean* (New York: David McKay Co., 1975), 381–407.

53. On this point see Farouk-Sluglett and Sluglett, *Iraq since 1958*, 133–37.

54. O'Ballance, *No Victory, No Vanquished*, 217.

55. Kissinger, *Years of Upheaval*, 455–58.

56. Ibid., 468.

57. Nixon, *The Memoirs of Richard Nixon*, 922–24; Kissinger, *Years of Upheaval*, 488–92.

58. In his memoirs, Kissinger has vehemently denied the charge, which became a heated political issue after the war, that the United States purposely delayed the airlift in order to pressure Israel into agreeing to a cease-fire. His position has been supported by Abba Eban, who was Israel's foreign minister at the time. Kissinger, *Years of Upheaval*, 496, 515; Abba Eban, *Abba Eban: An Autobiography* (New York: Random House, 1977), 515–16; Eban, *Personal Witness*, 534–35. But Israel's defense minister in 1973, Moshe Dayan, suggests otherwise. Moshe Dayan, *Story of My Life* (New York: William Morrow & Co., 1976), 511–13. For a middle position, see Aronson, *Conflict and Bargaining in the Middle East*, 184–85.

59. Kissinger, *Years of Upheaval*, 507–16.

60. Heikal, *The Road to Ramadan*, 265–66; Kissinger, *Years of Upheaval*, 593–94; Nixon, *The Memoirs of Richard Nixon*, 1012; Yergin, *The Prize*, 594; Philip Terzian, *OPEC: The Inside Story* (London: Zed Books, 1985), 164–65.

61. The quote is from Yergin, *The Prize*, 595; Heikal, *The Road to Ramadan*, 268–77. On Saudi Arabia's response to the war, see also Aronson, *Conflict and Bargaining in the Middle East*, 180–81; Laqueur, *Confrontation*, 210–52.

62. Yergin, *The Prize*, 577–85; Kaufman, *The Oil Cartel Case*, 104–6.

63. Yergin, *The Prize*, 606–9; Quandt, *Peace Process*, 163–64.

64. Kissinger, *Years of Upheaval*, 532–44; Israeli, *Man of Defiance*, 120–21; Quandt, *Peace Process*, 168–71.

65. Kissinger, *Years of Upheaval*, 552–54, 568–81; Isaacson, *Kissinger*, 524–29.

66. Kissinger, *Years of Upheaval*, 581–87; Garthoff, *Detente and Confrontation*, 374–78. On Soviet policy during the war see also Kohler, Goure, and Harvey, *The Soviet Union and the October 1973 Middle East War*, 57–68; and Freedman, *Soviet Policy toward the Middle East since 1970*, 141–90.

67. In his memoirs, Nixon contends that he was responsible for issuing the military alert. Nixon, *The Memoirs of Richard Nixon*, 939. But two authorities on U.S.-Soviet relations and U.S. policy toward the Middle East during the Nixon administration, Raymond Garthoff and William Quandt, who differ in several other important respects, agree that Kissinger was largely responsible for issuing the alert. So does Kissinger's biographer, Walter Isaacson. Garthoff, *Detente and Confrontation*, 378–79; Quandt, *Peace Process*, 174; Isaacson, *Kissinger*, 529–33.

68. Kissinger, *Years of Upheaval*, 586–91; Garthoff, *Detente and Confrontation*, 378–80; Quandt, *Peace Process*, 175–76.

69. The quote is from Quandt, *Peace Process*, 176.

70. Kissinger, *Years of Upheaval*, 590–99; Garthoff, *Detente and Confrontation*, 380–85.

CHAPTER 6

1. Yergin, *The Prize*, 625.

2. Kissinger, *Years of Upheaval*, 621–24, 629–32.

3. Ibid., 636–54; Sheehan, *The Arabs, Israelis, and Kissinger*, 49–51, 80–81; Isaacson, *Kissinger*, 539–42; Ghanayem and Voth, *The Kissinger Legacy*, 126–28.

4. Kissinger, *Years of Upheaval*, 747–50, 755–59.

5. Ibid., 755–81; Seale, *Asad of Syria*, 230–34.

6. Kissinger, *Years of Upheaval*, 789–92; Quandt, *Peace Process*, 195–96; Sheehan, *The Arabs, Israelis, and Kissinger*, 102–6.

7. Kissinger, *Years of Upheaval*, 792–98; Sheehan, *The Arabs, Israelis, and Kissinger*, 85, 106; Isaacson, *Kissinger*, 544–45; Seale, *Asad of Syria*, 236; Eban, *Personal Witness*, 552–53.

8. Seale, *Asad of Syria*, 197.

9. Kissinger, *Years of Upheaval*, 800–803; Dayan, *Story of My Life*, 553–70.

10. Kissinger, *Years of Upheaval*, 803–29; Sheehan, *The Arabs, Israelis, and Kissinger*, 106; Aronson, *Conflict and Bargaining in the Middle East*, 212–16, 228–29; Israeli, *Man of Defiance*, 143–44.

11. Kissinger, *Years of Upheaval*, 829–46; Sheehan, *The Arabs, Israelis, and Kissinger*, 89; Aronson, *Conflict and Bargaining in the Middle East*, 230–31; Freedman, *Soviet Policy toward the Middle East since 1970*, 147–55.

12. Seale, *Asad of Syria*, 239–46; Kissinger, *Years of Upheaval*, 935–45, 957–74, 1032–36, 1042–110; Quandt, *Peace Process*, 203–15; Aronson, *Conflict and Bargaining in the Middle East*, 232–43; Sheehan, *The Arabs, Israelis, and Kissinger*, 115, 118–28; Ghanayem and Voth, *The Kissinger Legacy*, 137–43.

13. el-Sadat, *In Search of Identity*, 291.

14. Kissinger, *Years of Upheaval*, 665–66.

15. Isaacson, *Kissinger*, 550–59.

16. Yergin, *The Prize*, 613–19.

17. Kissinger, *Years of Upheaval*, 664.

18. Ibid., 664–65, 945–51, 978; Nixon, *The Memoirs of Richard Nixon*, 987; Ambrose, *Nixon: Ruin and Recovery*, 294, 311.

19. H. W. Brands, *Into the Labyrinth: The United States and the Middle East, 1945–1993* (New York: McGraw-Hill, 1994), 140.

20. On these points see Michael A. Palmer, *Guardians of the Gulf: A History of America's Expanding Role in the Persian Gulf, 1883–1992* (New York: Free Press, 1992), 97–98.

21. Sheehan, *The Arabs, Israelis, and Kissinger*, 129. For Kissinger's cultivation of the press, see also Isaacson, *Kissinger*, 573–86.

22. Ambrose, *Nixon: Ruin and Recovery*, 348.

23. Nixon, *The Memoirs of Richard Nixon*, 1013; Seale, *Asad of Syria*, 248–49; Ambrose, *Nixon: Ruin and Recovery*, 348, 355–61; Quandt, *Peace Process*, 215–17.

24. Gerald R. Ford, *A Time to Heal: The Autobiography of Gerald R. Ford* (New York: Harper and Row, 1979), 128–29.

25. Ibid.

26. Ibid., 183.

27. Seale, *Asad of Syria*, 250–51; Kissinger, *Years of Upheaval*, 940–45, 1034–36, 1050.

28. Seale, *Asad of Syria*, 252–54; Kissinger, *Years of Upheaval*, 1037–38. See also Eban, *Personal Witness*, 560, 575–76.

29. Quandt, *Peace Process*, 219; Freedman, *Soviet Policy toward the Middle East since 1970*, 156–58.

30. Sheehan, *The Arabs, Israelis, and Kissinger*, 148.

31. Quandt, *Peace Process*, 224–26; Sheehan, *The Arabs, Israelis, and Kissinger*, 148–49; Seale, *Asad of Syria*, 251–55.

32. Sheehan, *The Arabs, Israelis, and Kissinger*, 149–50; Quandt, *Peace Process*, 226–27; Wallach and Wallach, *Arafat*, 160; Hart, *Arafat*, 405–6.

33. Isaacson, *Kissinger*, 630–31.

34. Quandt, *Peace Process*, 229–43.

35. Israeli, *Man of Defiance*, 151–53; Sheehan, *The Arabs, Israelis, and Kissinger*, 154–59.

36. Israeli, *Man of Defiance*, 153; Sheehan, *The Arabs, Israelis, and Kissinger*, 159–65.

37. Cabinet Meeting of 26 March 1975, Box 294, Folder "Handwritten Notes," Ron Nessen Files, Gerald R. Ford Papers, Gerald R. Ford Library, Ann Arbor, Michigan.

38. Meeting with Rep. Sidney R. Yates, 13 May 1975, Box 6, Congressional Relations Office, Max L. Friedersdorf Files, ibid.

39. Ford, *A Time to Heal*, 244–47; Sheehan, *The Arabs, Israelis, and Kissinger*, 165–67.

40. Quandt, *Peace Process*, 237–38.

41. Max Friedersdorf to the President, 24 March 1975, Box 33, Presidential Handwriting File, Ford Papers; Friedersdorf to the Honorable Thomas Morgan, 25 June 1975, Box 27, Philip Buchan Files, 1974–77, ibid.; Israeli, *Man of Defiance*, 153–54.

42. Sheehan, *The Arabs, Israelis, and Kissinger*, 176–77.

43. Israeli, *Man of Defiance*, 154–56; Sheehan, *The Arabs, Israelis, and Kissinger*, 179–90.

44. A copy of the letter can be found in Michael Widlanski, ed., *Can Israel Survive a Palestinian State?* (Jerusalem: Institute for Advanced Strategic Political Studies, 1990), 120–21.

45. Lorenz, *Egypt and the Arabs*, 53; Sheehan, *The Arabs, Israelis, and Kissinger*, 178, 190–94.

46. Isaacson, *Kissinger*, 635. See also Burns, *Economic Aid and American Policy toward Egypt*, 184.

47. Seale, *Asad of Syria*, 197–99, 207–15, 220–22; Lorenz, *Egypt and the Arabs*, 46–47.

48. Sheehan, *The Arabs, Israelis, and Kissinger*, 197; Seale, *Asad of Syria*, 239–42.

49. Seale, *Asad of Syria*, 259–61; Lorenz, *Egypt and the Arabs*, 48–52, 59–60.

50. Kienle, *Ba'th v. Ba'th*, 61–94; Amatzia Baram, "Ideology and Power Politics in Syrian-Iraqi Relations, 1968–1984," in *Syria under Assad: Domestic Constraints and Regional Risks*, eds. Moshe Ma'oz and Avner Yaniv (London: Croom Helm, 1986), 128–33; Seale, *Asad of Syria*, 262–63.

51. Rabinovich, *The War for Lebanon*, 27–31.

52. Rabinovich, *The War for Lebanon*, 22, 34–43; Weinberger, *Syrian Intervention in Lebanon*, 116–27; Wallach and Wallach, *Arafat*, 159, 221–23.

53. Rabinovich, *The War for Lebanon*, 22, 43–44; Weinberger, *Syrian Intervention in Lebanon*, 84–112; Wallach and Wallach, *Arafat*, 223–24, 226–27; Hart, *Arafat*, 417–19.

54. Rabinovich, *The War for Lebanon*, 47–49; Weinberger, *Syrian Intervention in Lebanon*, 4–5. See also Itamar Rabinovich, "The Changing Prism: Syrian Policy in Lebanon as a Mirror, an Issue and an Instrument," in *Syria under Assad: Domestic Constraints and Regional Risks*, eds. Moshe Ma'oz and Avner Yaniv (London: Croom Helm, 1986), 179–81.

55. Weinberger, *Syrian Intervention in Lebanon*, vii, 8; Rabinovich, *The War for Lebanon*, 48–49.

56. Weinberger, *Syrian Intervention in Lebanon*, 8–27; Rabinovich, *The War for Lebanon*, 49–54; Moshe Ma'oz and Avner Yaniv, "On a Short Leash: Syria and the PLO," in *Syria under Assad: Domestic Constraints and Regional Risks*, eds. Moshe Ma'oz and Avner Yaniv (London: Croom Helm, 1986), 192–200; Wallach and Wallach, *Arafat*, 227–28; Hart, *Arafat*, 421–25.

57. Memorandum of Conversation, 26 June 1975, Box 31, White House Central Files, Subject File, Ford Papers; Meeting of the National Security Council, 7 April 1976, Box 9, Richard Cheney Files, ibid.; Rabinovich, *The War for Lebanon*, 49.

58. Rabinovich, *The War for Lebanon*, 53–56.

59. Ibid., 56–57; Ze'ev Schiff and Ehud Ya'ari, *Israel's Lebanon War* (New York: Simon & Schuster, 1984), 9–18.

60. Rabinovich, *The War for Lebanon*, 57–58.

61. Memorandum of Conversation, 26 June 1975, Box 31, White House Central Files, Subject Files, Ford Papers.

CHAPTER 7

1.   Jimmy Carter, *Keeping Faith: Memoirs of a President* (New York: Bantam Books, 1982), 279, 315–16; Jimmy Carter, *The Blood of Abraham: Insights into the Middle East* (Boston: Houghton Mifflin Co., 1986), 10–11.

2.   *The Presidential Campaign, 1976*, 3 vols. (Washington, D.C.: Government Printing Office, 1978), 1:709–14.

3.   Carter, *Keeping Faith*, 274–77; Cyrus Vance, *Hard Choices: Critical Years in American Foreign Policy* (New York: Simon & Schuster, 1983), 164–68; Thomas Parker, *The Road to Camp David: U.S. Negotiating Strategy towards the Arab-Israeli Conflict* (New York: Peter Lang, 1989), 99–100; Aronson, *Conflict and Bargaining in the Middle East*, 331–35; Safran, *Israel*, 564–66.

4.   Carter, *Keeping Faith*, 51–55.

5.   Vance, *Hard Choices*, 168–71; Parker, *The Road to Camp David*, 100–103.

6.   Carter, *Keeping Faith*, 279–88; Vance, *Hard Choices*, 171–79; Parker, *The Road to Camp David*, 103–4; Quandt, *Peace Process*, 260; Safran, *Israel*, 568–69; Robert Slater, *Rabin of Israel* (New York: St. Martin's Press, 1993), 271–73; Yitzhak Rabin, *The Rabin Memoirs* (London: Weidenfeld and Nicolson, 1979), 228–35.

7.   Carter, *Keeping Faith*, 288–90.

8.   *Time*, 109 (30 May 1977): 22. See also Eric Silver, *Begin: A Biography* (London: Wiedenfeld and Nicolson, 1984), 167–68.

9.   Carter, *Keeping Faith*, 290–91; Carter, *The Blood of Abraham*, 42; Vance, *Hard Choices*, 179–84; Moshe Dayan, *Breakthrough: A Personal Account of the Egypt-Israel Peace Negotiations* (New York: Alfred A. Knopf, 1981), 18–21; Parker, *The Road to Camp David*, 105–6; Ned Temko, *To Win or to Die: A Personal Portrait of Menachem Begin* (New York: William Morrow & Co., 1987), 201–2; Quandt, *Peace Process*, 262–63; William B. Quandt, *Camp David* (Washington, D.C.: Brookings Institution, 1986), 66–67, 69–84.

10.   Carter, *Keeping Faith*, 291; Vance, *Hard Choices*, 184–86; Dayan, *Breakthrough*, 21–25; Temko, *To Win or to Die*, 206.

11.   Dayan, *Breakthrough*, 55–64; Zbigniew Brzezinski, *Power and Principle: Memoirs of the National Security Adviser, 1977–1981* (New York: Farrar, Straus, & Giroux, 1985), 106–10; Parker, *The Road to Camp David*, 107–8.

12.   Vance, *Hard Choices*, 191–92; Carter, *Keeping Faith*, 293; Quandt, *Camp David*, 122–24; Garthoff, *Detente and Confrontation*, 580–81; Parker, *The Road to Camp David*, 108–9.

13.   Vance, *Hard Choices*, 192–95; Carter, *Keeping Faith*, 293–94; Dayan, *Breakthrough*, 67–72; Quandt, *Camp David*, 124–34; Quandt, *Peace Process*, 267–69.

14.   Carter, *Keeping Faith*, 293; Quandt, *Camp David*, 143–45.

15.   Quandt, *Camp David*, 146–47; Dayan, *Breakthrough*, 75–77; Silver, *Begin*, 171–72. On Sadat's views about the likely failure of a Geneva conference see also Raymond A. Hinnebusch, Jr., *Egyptian Politics under Sadat: The Post-Populist Development of an Authoritarian-Modernizing State* (Cambridge: Cambridge University Press, 1985), 66–67.

16.   *Time*, 110 (28 November 1977): 28–47; Silver, *Begin*, 174–76.

17.   Carter, *Keeping Faith*, 297–98; Vance, *Hard Choices*, 194–95.

18.   Carter, *Keeping Faith*, 299–300; Vance, *Hard Choices*, 198–200; Quandt,

Peace Process, 271–72; Don Peretz, "Israeli Policies toward the Arab States and the Palestinians since 1967," 17–18.

19. Carter, *Keeping Faith*, 298–300; Temko, *To Win or to Die*, 214–15.

20. Mohamed Ibrahim Kamel, *The Camp David Accords: A Testimony* (London: KPI, 1986), 21–27; Silver, *Begin*, 178–80; Temko, *To Win or to Die*, 214–17; Vance, *Hard Choices*, 200; Quandt, *Camp David*, 159–60; Parker, *The Road to Camp David*, 120–21.

21. Carter, *Keeping Faith*, 300–305; Vance, *Hard Choices*, 201; Parker, *The Road to Camp David*, 123–25.

22. *Newsweek*, 91 (16 January 1978): 40–47.

23. Brzezinski, *Power and Principle*, 235–36.

24. Carter, *Keeping Faith*, 306–8; Vance, *Hard Choices*, 203–5; Kamel, *The Camp David Accords*, 78–95.

25. Brzezinski, *Power and Principle*, 246. See also Dayan, *Breakthrough*, 117–18.

26. Brzezinski, *Power and Principle*, 235–36.

27. Temko, *To Win or to Die*, 219–20; Silver, *Begin*, 187–88; Vance, *Hard Choices*, 207–11; Carter, *Keeping Faith*, 310–13; Dayan, *Breakthrough*, 121–29.

28. Ibid.

29. Dayan, *Breakthrough*, 129–37; Silver, *Begin*, 188–89; Vance, *Hard Choices*, 212–13.

30. Carter, *Keeping Faith*, 315–16; Vance, *Hard Choices*, 213–16; Dayan, *Breakthrough*, 138–48; Kamel, *The Camp David Accords*, 208–19; Matti Golan, *The Road to Peace: A Biography of Shimon Peres* (New York: Warner Books, 1989), 183–86; Quandt, *Camp David*, 196–201.

31. Vance, *Hard Choices*, 216.

32. The full text of this letter is in Kamel, *The Camp David Accords*, 225–28.

33. Vance, *Hard Choices*, 216–18; Carter, *Keeping Faith*, 315–17; Quandt, *Camp David*, 201–5.

34. Carter, *Keeping Faith*, 322–23; Quandt, *Camp David*, 207–8.

35. The Camp David negotiations are described in great detail in Carter, *Keeping Faith*, 327–401; Vance, *Hard Choices*, 219–26; Kamel, *The Camp David Accords*, 302–69; Quandt, *Camp David*, 206–58; Dayan, *Breakthrough*, 149–80; Parker, *The Road to Camp David*, 125–30. Unless otherwise noted, the discussion of the negotiations that follow is based on these sources.

36. Temko, *To Win or to Die*, 226–27; Kamel, *The Camp David Accords*, 289–92.

37. James Lunt, *Hussein of Jordan: Searching for a Just and Lasting Peace* (New York: William Morrow & Co., 1989), 177–78.

38. *Washington Post*, 18 September 1978, 1; *New York Times*, 18 September 1978; Vance, *Hard Choices*, 229; Quandt, *Camp David*, 259.

39. Kamel, *The Camp David Accords*, 361–71.

40. Dayan, *Breakthrough*, 249–58; Vance, *Hard Choices*, 229–42; Carter, *Keeping Faith*, 409–12; Silver, *Begin*, 204–5.

41. Memorandum to President Carter from Hamilton Jordan, 30 November 1978, Box 49, Hamilton Jordan Papers, Jimmy Carter Library, Atlanta, Georgia.

42. Carter, *Keeping Faith*, 413; Vance, *Hard Choices*, 242–43; Dayan, *Breakthrough*, 59–66.

43. *Time*, 113 (12 March 1979): 13–16; *Newsweek*, 93 (12 March 1979), 24–27; Carter, *Keeping Faith*, 414–15; Temko, *To Win or to Die*, 238–39.

44. Vance, *Hard Choices*, 244–45; Temko, *To Win or to Die*, 239–40.

45. Vance, *Hard Choices*, 245–62; Carter, *Keeping Faith*, 416–26; Dayan, *Breakthrough*, 270–78; Silver, *Begin*, 208–10.

46. Lunt, *Hussein of Jordan*, 180–81; Israeli, *Man of Defiance*, 248–53.

47. For an early but still excellent account of the revolution, see Barry Rubin, *Paved With Good Intentions: The American Experience in Iran* (New York: Oxford University Press, 1980), 190–336. For the revolution's impact on oil prices, see also Yergin, *The Prize*, 681–714, 748–50.

48. James A. Bill, *The Eagle and the Lion: The Tragedy of American-Iranian Relations* (New Haven: Yale University Press, 1988), 216–68; Gary Sick, *All Fall Down: America's Tragic Encounter with Iran* (New York: Random House, 1985), 80–142.

49. Vance, *Hard Choices*, 244–45. See also Brzezinski, *Power and Principle*, 354; Carter, *Keeping Faith*, 435.

50. An excellent analysis of the hostage crisis is Warren Christopher et al., *American Hostages in Iran: The Conduct of a Crisis* (New Haven: Yale University Press). See also Bill, *The Eagle and the Lion*, 295–303.

51. Two good surveys of the Soviet invasion of Afghanistan are Henry S. Bradsher, *Afghanistan and the Soviet Union* (Durham, N.C.: Duke University Press, 1985) and Thomas T. Hammond, *Red Flag over Afghanistan: The Communist Coup, the Soviet Invasion, and the Consequences* (Boulder: Westview Press, 1984). See also Robert O. Freedman, *Moscow and the Middle East: Soviet Policy since the Invasion of Afghanistan* (Cambridge: Cambridge University Press, 1991), 71–74.

52. Carter, *Keeping Faith*, 465.

53. Ibid., 471–72.

54. In addition to issuing the Carter Doctrine, the president took a series of other measures, including imposing a grain embargo on the Soviet Union, barring Soviet access to high technology and other strategic items, and asking the Senate to indefinitely postpone consideration of the Strategic Arms Limitation Agreement (SALT II), which had been signed in June. He also raised the possibility that the United States might boycott the 1980 Summer Olympics scheduled for Moscow. Garthoff, *Detente and Confrontation*, 943–52; Carter, *Keeping Faith*, 472–83.

55. Yergin, *The Prize*, 64. On Carter's energy policy, see also Burton I. Kaufman, *The Presidency of James Earl Carter, Jr.* (Lawrence: University Press of Kansas, 1993), 32–34, 57–58, 66–68, 107–9, 140–53, 169–77.

56. Brzezinski, *Power and Principle*, 83.

57. Yergin, *The Prize*, 633–42.

58. Freedman, *Moscow and the Middle East*, 53–54.

59. Garthoff, *Detente and Confrontation*, 952–55.

60. Gershon R. Kieval, *Party Politics in Israel and the Occupied Territories* (Westport: Greenwood Press, 1983), 161–67; Temko, *To Win or to Die*, 245–46; Israeli, *Man of Defiance*, 249–53; Dayan, *Breakthrough*, 303–13.

61. Carter, *Keeping Faith*, 490–95; Temko, *To Win or to Die*, 246–47; Israeli, *Man of Defiance*, 249–53.

62. Carter, *Keeping Faith*, 495–96; Temko, *To Win or to Die*, 248–49.

63. Carter, *Keeping Faith*, 495.

64. *Time*, 116 (25 August 1980), 34–35.

CHAPTER 8

1. Ronald Reagan, *An American Life* (New York: Simon & Schuster, 1990), 409. See also Lou Cannon, *President Reagan: The Role of a Lifetime* (New York: Simon & Schuster, 1991), 391.

2. Reagan, *An American Life*, 409.

3. Rabinovich, *The War for Lebanon*, 60–91; Schiff and Ya'ari, *Israel's Lebanon War*, 24–29; Carter, *Keeping Faith*, 304–5, 310–11, 352.

4. Rabinovich, *The War for Lebanon*, 60–91; Carter, *Keeping Faith*, 369; Helena Cobban, *The Palestinian Liberation Organization: People, Power and Politics* (Cambridge: Cambridge University Press, 1984), 82–84; David Kimche, *The Last Option: After Nasser, Arafat and Saddam Hussein* (New York: Charles Scribner's Sons, 1991), 130–38.

5. Rabinovich, *The War for Lebanon*, 91–92; Raymond Tanter, *Who's at the Helm?: Lessons of Lebanon* (Boulder: Westview Press, 1990), 11.

6. Rabinovich, *The War for Lebanon*, 94–97, 99–102, 106–15; Cobban, *The Palestinian Liberation Organization*, 94–95.

7. There was considerable debate within the administration over whether right-wing Phalangists purposely provoked the Syrians into placing missiles in Lebanon in order to compel Israel into war with Syria or whether Syria acted on its own accord. On this debate, see Tanter, *Who's at the Helm?*, 14–15. But most scholars hold the former view. See, for example, Schiff and Ya'ari, *Israel's Lebanon War*, 33; and Rabinovich, *The War for Lebanon*, 167–81.

8. Rabinovich, *The War for Lebanon*, 117–19; Schiff and Ya'ari, *Israel's Lebanon War*, 32–35; Helena Cobban, *The Superpowers and the Syrian-Israeli Conflict* (New York: Praeger; the Center for Strategic and International Studies, 1991), 35–36; Alexander M. Haig, Jr., *Caveat: Realism, Reagan, and Foreign Policy* (New York: Macmillan, 1984), 180; Reagan, *An American Life*, 412.

9. Tanter, *Who's at the Helm?*, 48–50; Reagan, *An American Life*, 412–13.

10. Two Israeli journalists, Ze'ev Schiff and Ehud Ya'ari, have argued that Israel's invasion of Lebanon in 1982 was a result of a conspiracy between Bashir Gemayel and Sharon to eradicate the PLO, drive the Syrians out of Lebanon, and install Gemayel as Lebanon's new president. According to Schiff and Ya'ari, Gemayel, in collusion with Sharon, had "step by step, piece by piece . . . jockeyed the prime minister of Israel into defending Christian interests [in Lebanon]" so that by his second term, Sharon was able "to woo Begin into taking steps that he probably would not have contemplated in his first term." Schiff and Ya'ari, *Israel's Lebanon War*, 30, 39. But one does not have to weave a story of conspiracy, which in its own way lifts much of the burden from Israel for its invasion of Lebanon in 1982, to explain why Begin decided to send Israeli forces into that country. Certainly the Israelis had their own reasons for wanting to destroy the PLO and force the Syrians to leave Lebanon. Also, as Schiff and Ya'ari acknowledge, the Israelis had been providing arms to the Christians since 1976, and the notion of a Jewish-Maronite (Christian) partnership was a long-standing one in Israel. Most historians writing about the Lebanese war, therefore, do not support this conspiracy theory even though they agree with major elements of it. See, for example, Rabinovich, *The War for Lebanon*, 105–34. See also Quandt, *Peace Process*, 340–41; Kimche, *The Last Option*, 145; Cobban, *The Superpowers and the Syrian-Israeli Conflict*, 37–39.

11. Anthony McDermott, *Egypt from Nasser to Mubarak: A Flawed Revolution* (London: Croom Helm, 1988), 59–67; Haig, *Caveat*, 171–72, 322–27, 330; Silver, *Begin*, 223–26.

12. Reagan, *An American Life*, 421; Haig, *Caveat*, 332–37. See also Rabinovich, *The War for Lebanon*, 125.

13. Haig, *Caveat*, 170. See also Tanter, *Who's at the Helm?* 35–36, 40; Howard Teicher and Gayle Radley Teicher, *Twin Pillars to Desert Storm: America's Flawed Vision in the Middle East from Nixon to Bush* (New York: William Morrow & Co., 1993), 194; Cobban, *The Superpowers and the Syrian-Israeli Conflict*, 81–82; Bob Schieffer and Gary Paul Gates, *The Acting President* (New York: E. P. Dutton, 1989), 156.

14. Caspar P. Weinberger, *Fighting for Peace: Seven Critical Years in the Pentagon* (New York: Warner Books, 1990), 136–40; Rabinovich, *The War for Lebanon*, 126; Teicher and Teicher, *Twin Pillars*, 194; Schieffer and Gates, *The Acting President*, 136.

15. Reagan, *An American Life*, 411; Cobban, *The Superpowers and the Syrian-Israeli Conflict*, 82–83.

16. Haig, *Caveat*, 174–90; Cannon, *The Role of a Lifetime*, 392–93. On Begin's visit to the United States, see also Reagan, *An American Life*, 424.

17. Ironically, Israel's attack on the Iraqi plant may have contributed to the president's victory on the AWACS. In order to reach Iraq, Israeli planes had to fly over Saudi Arabia without Saudi permission. The Saudis were able to use the Israeli overflight of their country as evidence of the threat Israel posed to the Arab states and as proof of their need for AWACS aircraft. Reagan, *An American Life*, 413; Haig, *Caveat*, 182–84.

18. Schiff and Ya'ari, *Israel's Lebanon War*, 47, 62; Kimche, *The Last Option*, 145–46.

19. For an analysis of the administration's position, which is also highly critical of Israel, see George W. Ball, *Error and Betrayal in Lebanon: An Analysis of Israel's Invasion of Lebanon and the Implications for U.S.–Israeli Relations* (Washington, D.C.: Foundation for Middle East Peace, 1984).

20. Reagan, *An American Life*, 422; Haig, *Caveat*, 339, 342–43. See also Cannon, *The Role of a Lifetime*, 397; Tanter, *Who's at the Helm?*, 5–6.

21. Tanter, *Who's at the Helm?*, 6–7; Cannon, *The Role of a Lifetime*, 395–96.

22. Reagan, *An American Life*, 420; Haig, *Caveat*, 338–39, 343.

23. Schiff and Ya'ari, *Israel's Lebanon War*, 61; Haig, *Caveat*, 336.

24. Rabinovich, *The War for Lebanon*, 135–39.

25. Haig, *Caveat*, 341; Reagan, *An American Life*, 423; Rabinovich, *The War for Lebanon*, 139–40.

26. Haig, *Caveat*, 342.

27. Ibid., 310–12.

28. Cannon, *The Role of a Lifetime*, 397; George P. Shultz, *Turmoil and Triumph: My Years as Secretary of State* (New York: Charles Scribner's Sons, 1993), 3–4.

29. Haig, *Caveat*, 345.

30. Ibid., 344–45.

31. Rabinovich, *The War for Lebanon*, 142; Kimche, *The Last Option*, 149.

32. Shultz, *Turmoil and Triumph*, 14–15; Haig, *Caveat*, 350–51; Cannon, *The Role of a Lifetime*, 399.

33. Haig, *Caveat*, 343, 346.

34. Hart, *Arafat*, 455–59; Wallach and Wallach, *Arafat*, 374–77.

35. Shultz, *Turmoil and Triumph*, 47–48; Rabinovich, *The War for Lebanon*, 151–52.

36. Shultz, *Turmoil and Triumph*, 19, 21, 40.

37. Ibid., 21, 40, 85; Teicher and Teicher, *Twin Pillars to Desert Storm*, 211–12.

38. Shultz, *Turmoil and Triumph*, 50–53; Kimche, *The Last Option*, 151–53.

39. Shultz, *Turmoil and Triumph*, 53–57.

40. Ibid., 54, 60; Reagan, *An American Life*, 425–26.

41. Reagan, *An American Life*, 425–28; Shultz, *Turmoil and Triumph*, 62–71; Reagan, *An American Life*, 428; Cannon, *The Role of a Lifetime*, 401; Silver, *Begin*, 233.

42. Shultz, *Turmoil and Triumph*, 71–72; Reagan, *An American Life*, 430; Cannon, *The Role of a Lifetime*, 406; Wallach and Wallach, *Arafat*, 378.

43. South Yemen (more accurately the People's Democratic Republic of South Yemen) was a Marxist-oriented state bordering on the Gulf of Aden that was established in 1967 following the British withdrawal from the Federation of South Arabia (the former Western Aden Protectorate). Occasional efforts to unite the two Yemens failed because of their very different economic and political systems and their mutual mistrust of each other. For a harsh indictment of Britain's decision to abandon its Aden protectorate and the subsequent establishment of South Yemen, see Kelly, *Arabia, the Gulf and the West*, esp. 1–101, 131–32, 469–73.

44. Shultz, *Triumph and Turmoil*, 72–83; Wallach and Wallach, *Arafat*, 377–78.

45. Shultz, *Turmoil and Triumph*, 85–96; Reagan, *An American Life*, 430.

46. Reagan, *An American Life*, 432–33; Shultz, *Triumph and Turmoil*, 96–98; Cannon, *The Role of a Lifetime*, 406–7.

47. Lunt, *Hussein of Jordan*, 186–87; Shultz, *Triumph and Turmoil*, 98–100.

48. Weinberger, *Fighting for Peace*, 147–48. See also Kimche, *The Last Option*, 157.

49. Lunt, *Hussein of Jordan*, 186–87; Shultz, *Turmoil and Triumph*, 100; Wallach and Wallach, *Arafat*, 363; Cobban, *The Palestinian Liberation Organization*, 113–14; Hart, *Arafat*, 447.

50. Shultz, *Turmoil and Triumph*, 100, 430–31. On the Habib mission, see also Wallach and Wallach, *Arafat*, 371–72; Hart, *Arafat*, 444, 456–57.

51. Rabinovich, *The War for Lebanon*, 176–78.

52. Thomas L. Friedman, *From Beirut to Jerusalem* (New York: Farrar, Straus, & Giroux, 1989), 159; Reagan, *An American Life*, 437–38.

53. Silver, *Begin*, 234–39; Shultz, *Turmoil and Triumph*, 103–7.

54. Shultz, *Turmoil and Triumph*, 107–11; Cannon, *The Role of a Lifetime*, 409; Kimche, *The Last Option*, 159–61.

55. Shultz, *Turmoil and Triumph*, 111–12; Reagan, *An American Life*, 438–39.

56. Rabinovich, *The War for Lebanon*, 154–55.

57. Shultz, *Turmoil and Triumph*, 433–36.

58. Cannon, *The Role of a Lifetime*, 410–11; Weinberger, *Fighting for Peace*, 154–55.

59. Weinberger, *Fighting for Peace*, 151–54; Schieffer and Gates, *The Acting President*, 214–15; Cannon, *The Role of a Lifetime*, 410–11.

60. Weinberger, *Fighting for Peace*, 155–56; Reagan, *An American Life*, 444.

61. Seale, *Asad of Syria*, 298–315.

62. Teicher and Teicher, *Twin Pillars to Desert Storm*, 203–4; Rabinovich, *The War for Lebanon*, 116–17, 128, 155, 177.

63. Seale, *Asad of Syria*, 316–34; Moshe Ma'oz, "The Emergence of Modern Syria," in *Syria under Assad: Domestic Constraints and Regional Risks*, eds. Moshe Ma'oz and Avner Yaniv (London: Croom Helm, 1986), 30–34; Amatzia Baram, "Ideology and Power Politics in Syrian-Iraqi Relations," in ibid., 133–38; Becker, *The PLO*, 224; Rabinovich, *The War for Lebanon*, 155; Teicher and Teicher, *Twin Pillars to Desert Storm*, 116–17.

64. *Moscow and the Middle East*, 92–93, 151–56; Dennis B. Ross, "Soviet Behavior toward the Lebanon War, 1982–84," in *Soviet Strategy in the Middle East*, ed. George W. Breslauer (Boston: Unwin Hyman, 1990), 99–111; Cobban, *The Superpowers and the Syrian-Israeli Conflict*, 53–56. On al-Asad's policy with respect to Lebanon, see also Seale, *Asad of Syria*, 334–50; Raymond A. Hinnebusch, "Egypt, Syria, and the Arab State System," in *The Arab-Israeli Conflict: Two Decades of Change*, eds. Yehuda Lukacs and Abdalla M. Battah (Boulder: Westview Press, 1988), 186–93; and Hinnebusch, "Syrian Policy in Lebanon and the Palestinians," *Arab Studies Quarterly* 8 (Winter, 1986): 1–20.

65. Rabinovich, *The War for Lebanon*, 177–78.

66. Temko, *To Win or to Die*, 282–90; Silver, *Begin*, 248–52; Kimche, *The Last Option*, 172–73.

67. Kimche, *The Last Option*, 174–78.

68. Reagan, *An American Life*, 447; Cannon, *The Role of a Lifetime*, 412, 414, 421–22; Weinberger, *Fighting for Peace*, 157–60.

69. Cannon, *The Role of a Lifetime*, 440–41; Schieffer and Gates, *The Acting President*, 215–16.

70. Cannon, *The Role of a Lifetime*, 443–44; Reagan, *An American Life*, 452–62.

71. Cannon, *The Role of a Lifetime*, 451.

72. Cannon, *The Role of a Lifetime*, 453–57; Reagan, *An American Life*, 464; Weinberger, *Fighting for Peace*, 162–69.

73. Shultz, *Turmoil and Triumph*, 233.

74. On this point, see also Reagan, *An American Life*, 463–64.

CHAPTER 9

1. Shultz, *Turmoil and Triumph*, 439.

2. Tanter, *Who's at the Helm?*, 89–91; Lunt, *Hussein of Jordan*, 187–88; Shultz, *Turmoil and Triumph*, 433–39.

3. Quandt, *Peace Process*, 347.

4. Teicher and Teicher, *Twin Pillars to Desert Storm*, 137–40.

5. Israel did return the Sinai to Egypt in 1982 but only after extended negotiations involving State Department officials over the removal of Israeli settlers from Yamit in the Sinai and over whether the coastal resort town of Taba was part of Egypt or Israel. Mubarak thought the Israelis were purposely trying to delay their withdrawal from the Sinai. The Israelis were convinced that after Egypt recovered the Sinai, it would not honor its treaty commitments to Israel, instead making its

reentry into the Arab world its top priority—at Israel's expense. For an account of the negotiations leading to the return of the Sinai by a member of the National Security Council involved in the negotiations, see Teicher and Teicher, *Twin Pillars to Desert Storm*, 172–77.

6. Lorenz, *Egypt and the Arabs*, 109; Lunt, *Hussein of Jordan*, 189; Teicher and Teicher, *Twin Pillars to Desert Storm*, 177–78.

7. Lunt, *Hussein of Jordan*, 190–91; Shultz, *Turmoil and Triumph*, 438.

8. Shultz, *Turmoil and Triumph*, 444–46; Lunt, *Hussein of Jordan*, 192–94; Teicher and Teicher, *Twin Pillars to Desert Storm*, 224–25.

9. Lunt, *Hussein of Jordan*, 194–98; Shultz, *Turmoil and Triumph*, 450–62.

10. Friedman, *From Beirut to Jerusalem*, 73, 107–25, 145–46, 152–55, 167–74; Hart, *Arafat*, 466; Lunt, *Hussein of Jordan*, 197–98; Shultz, *Turmoil and Triumph*, 462.

11. Wallach and Wallach, *Arafat*, 237–41; Hart, *Arafat*, 467–73.

12. Friedman, *From Beirut to Jerusalem*, 175. See also Wallach and Wallach, *Arafat*, 317–30.

13. Shultz, *Turmoil and Triumph*, 453.

14. Even Secretary of State Shultz recognized the dilemma Hussein faced as a result of Jordan's large Palestinian population and the opposition of other Arab leaders to negotiations with Israel without PLO representation. Shultz, *Turmoil and Triumph*, 454. See also Lunt, *Hussein of Jordan*, 204–6; Seale, *Asad of Syria*, 464–66.

15. Shultz, *Turmoil and Triumph*, 449–54, 457–60.

16. Cannon, *The Role of a Lifetime*, 605; Reagan, *An American Life*, 493–94; Shultz, *Turmoil and Triumph*, 653–55.

17. Teicher and Teicher, *Twin Pillars to Desert Storm*, 223.

18. Shultz, *Turmoil and Triumph*, 665–68.

19. Seale, *Asad of Syria*, 468–69; Cannon, *The Role of a Lifetime*, 606–7; Shultz, *Turmoil and Triumph*, 654–68; Reagan, *An American Life*, 494–98.

20. For the administration's immediate reaction to these incidents, see Shultz, *Turmoil and Triumph*, 669–75. See also Reagan, *An American Life*, 508–9.

21. Reagan, *An American Life*, 511; Shultz, *Turmoil and Triumph*, 677.

22. Teicher and Teicher, *Twin Pillars to Desert Storm*, 22–23; Yergin, *The Prize*, 577–80.

23. Teicher and Teicher, *Twin Pillars to Desert Storm*, 134–37.

24. Weinberger, *Fighting for Peace*, 176–77; Shultz, *Turmoil and Triumph*, 680–82; Reagan, *An American Life*, 517.

25. Shultz, *Turmoil and Triumph*, 649–51, 670–71.

26. Weinberger, *Fighting for Peace*, 183–201; Shultz, *Turmoil and Triumph*, 683–87; Reagan, *An American Life*, 517–20.

27. Weinberger, *Fighting for Peace*, 360, 362–63; Reagan, *An American Life*, 504–7.

28. The quote is from Cannon, *The Role of a Lifetime*, 604. See also Shultz, *Turmoil and Triumph*, 784–86; Weinberger, *Fighting for Peace*, 362–64; Teicher and Teicher, *Twin Pillars to Desert Storm*, 287.

29. Lunt, *Hussein of Jordan*, 207–8, 215; Wallach and Wallach, *Arafat*, 330; Kienle, *Ba'th v. Ba'th*, 152–69; Seale, *Asad of Syria*, 466.

30. The surreptitious selling of arms to Iran in return for the release of American hostages in Lebanon and the subsequent use of the proceeds from these

sales to support contra rebels in Nicaragua fighting the Sandinista government. See *Report of the Congressional Committees Investigating the Iran-Contra Affair*, abridged edition, (New York: Random House, 1988), esp. 11–34.

31. Shultz, *Turmoil and Triumph*, 839–40, 936–37; Quandt, *Peace Process*, 378–79.

32. Golan, *The Road to Peace*, 307–9, 323–29; Shultz, *Turmoil and Triumph*, 936–38.

33. Shultz, *Turmoil and Triumph*, 940–44; Golan, *The Road to Peace*, 330–31.

34. See below, p. 146–47.

35. Efraim Karsh, *Soviet Policy towards Syria since 1970* (New York: St. Martin's Press, 1991), 58–59, 163–77; Freedman, *Moscow and the Middle East*, 205–316; Galia Golan, "Gorbachev's Middle East Strategy," in *Soviet Strategy in the Middle East*, ed. George W. Breslauer (Boston: Unwin Hyman, 1990), 151–58. For the Soviet Union's early relations with the PLO, see also Galia Golan, *The Soviet Union and the Palestine Liberation Organization: An Uneasy Alliance* (New York: Praeger, 1980).

36. Shultz, *Turmoil and Triumph*, 944–48; Lunt, *Hussein of Jordan*, 206.

37. Weinberger, *Fighting for Peace*, 387–88; Shultz, *Turmoil and Triumph*, 925–26; John K. Cooley, *Payback: America's Long War in the Middle East* (Washington, D.C.: Brassey's), 1991, 109–10, 144–45.

38. Weinberger, *Fighting for Peace*, 388; Shultz, *Turmoil and Triumph*, 926; Cooley, *Payback*, 144.

39. Weinberger, *Fighting for Peace*, 390; Cooley, *Payback*, 145–46.

40. Weinberger, *Fighting for Peace*, 393–94; Teicher and Teicher, *Twin Pillars to Desert Storm*, 294.

41. Cooley, *Payback*, 146; Weinberger, *Fighting for Peace*, 391.

42. Shultz, *Turmoil and Triumph*, 926–35.

43. Ibid., 927; Weinberger, *Fighting for Peace*, 399–404.

44. Shultz, *Turmoil and Triumph*, 930–35; Weinberger, *Fighting for Peace*, 404–26; Cooley, *Payback*, 147–52.

45. Quandt, *Peace Process*, 360.

46. Ze'ev Schiff and Ehud Ya'ari, *Intifada: The Palestinian Uprising—Israel's Third Front* (New York: Simon & Schuster, 1990), esp. 17–50; Friedman, *From Beirut to Lebanon*, 370–78; Shultz, *Turmoil and Triumph*, 1016.

47. Schiff and Ya'ari, *Intifada*, 46–48, 93–94, 119–23; Friedman, *From Beirut to Jerusalem*, 366–70; Shultz, *Turmoil and Triumph*, 1017; Lunt, *Hussein of Jordan*, 209; Aaron David Miller, "The PLO in Retrospect: The Arab and Israeli Dimensions," in *The Arab-Israeli Conflict: Two Decades of Change*, eds. Yehuda Lukacs and Abdalla M. Battah (Boulder: Westview Press, 1988), 120–30; Golan, *The Road to Peace*, 333–34.

48. Shultz, *Turmoil and Triumph*, 1017; Lunt, *Hussein of Jordan*, 209–10.

49. Shultz, *Turmoil and Triumph*, 1018–23.

50. Naseer H. Aruri, "Palestinian Nationalism Since 1967: An Overview," in *The Arab-Israeli Conflict: Two Decades of Change*, Yehuda Lukacs and Abdalla M. Battah (Boulder: Westview Press, 1988), 78–81; Shultz, *Turmoil and Triumph*, 1023–26; Golan, *The Road to Peace*, 336.

51. Shultz, *Turmoil and Triumph*, 1026–34; Wallach and Wallach, *Arafat*, 332–33; Schiff and Ya'ari, *Intifada*, 296–302.

52. Shultz, *Turmoil and Triumph*, 1035–37.

53. Schiff and Ya'ari, *Intifada*, 302; Shultz, *Turmoil and Triumph*, 1037–40.

54. Shultz, *Turmoil and Triumph*, 1040–44; Schiff and Ya'ari, *Intifada*, 304–5.

55. Shultz, *Turmoil and Triumph*, 1045.

CHAPTER 10

1. Tanter, *Who's at the Helm?*, 150–57; Cobban, *The Superpowers and the Syrian-Israeli Conflict*, 110–11; Quandt, *Peace Process*, 384–85; Wallach and Wallach, *Arafat*, 386.

2. Bob Woodward, *The Commanders* (New York: Simon & Schuster, 1991), 225.

3. Ibid., 46, 300; Schiff and Ya'ari, *Intifada*, 309; Wallach and Wallach, *Arafat*, 392.

4. Both Baker's and Friedman's remarks are from Jonathan Marcus, "Discordant Voices: The U.S. Jewish Community and Israel during the 1980s," *International Affairs* 66 (1990): 556. See also Schiff and Ya'ari, *Intifada*, 309–10; Quandt, *Peace Process*, 389; Slater, *Rabin of Israel*, 345, 348; Lawrence Freedman and Efraim Karsh, *The Gulf Conflict 1990–1991: Diplomacy and War in the New World Order* (Princeton: Princeton University Press, 1993), 16–17.

5. According to former NSC staff member William Quandt, however, Bush's comment "was not a slip of the tongue." Quandt, *Peace Process*, 391–92. Remarks by other administration officials also raised questions about Israel's claim to East Jerusalem. On this point, see Marcus, "Discordant Voices," 556. See also Slater, *Rabin of Israel*, 349–52.

6. *U.S. News & World Report*, 108 (26 March 1990): 32–33; *New Republic*, 202 (26 March 1990): 10–11; ibid., (2 April 1990): 7–8.

7. Quandt, *Peace Process*, 392.

8. Slater, *Rabin of Israel*, 352–59.

9. *Congressional Quarterly Weekly Report*, 48 (21 April 1990): 1204–5.

10. Ibid., 48 (9 June 1990): 1802; ibid., (23 June 1990): 1978, 1986–87; Quandt, *Peace Process*, 393–94; Wallach and Wallach, *Arafat*, 409–10.

11. Elaine Sciolino, *The Outlaw State: Saddam Hussein's Quest for Power and the Gulf Crisis* (New York: John Wiley and Sons, 1991), 192–94; Adel Darwish and Gregory Alexander, *Unholy Babylon: The Secret History of Saddam's War* (New York: St. Martin's Press, 1991), 9–11; Amatzia Baram, "The Iraqi Invasion of Kuwait: Decision-Making in Baghdad," in *Iraq's Road to War*, eds. Amatzia Baram and Barry Rubin (New York: St. Martin's Press, 1993), 6–10, 15–16.

12. Although the Kennedy administration had been deeply concerned about Iraq's aggressive behavior and welcomed Kuwait's independence, it abstained from involving itself in the Kuwaiti-Iraqi dispute. Sciolino, *The Outlaw State*, 192; Freedman and Karsh, *The Gulf Conflict 1990–1991*, 42–44; Darwish and Alexander, *Unholy Babylon*, 4, 11–12, 195–96; Baram, "The Iraqi Invasion of Kuwait," 5–6.

13. Baram, "The Iraqi Invasion of Kuwait," 6–10, 16–18; Freedman and Karsh, *The Gulf Conflict 1990–1991*, 44–49; Sciolino, *The Outlaw State*, 196–200; Darwish and Alexander, *Unholy Babylon*, 256–65.

14. Joseph Kostiner, "Kuwait: Confusing Friend and Foe" in *Iraq's Road to War*, eds. Amatzia Baram and Barry Rubin (New York: St. Martin's Press, 1993), 111–14;

Freedman and Karsh, *The Gulf Conflict 1990–1991*, 48–50, 56–57; Darwish and Alexander, *Unholy Babylon*, 265–72; Woodward, *The Commanders*, 212–16.

15. Sciolino, *The Outlaw State*, 205–11.

16. For this and the following two paragraphs, see Freedman and Karsh, *The Gulf Conflict 1990–1991*, 69–72, 95–99, 143–44, 161–62; Baram, "The Iraqi Invasion of Iran," 11; Sciolino, *The Outlaw State*, 205–11, 213–15; Darwish and Alexander, *Unholy Babylon*, 265–72, 283–84; Wallach and Wallach, *Arafat*, 421–28; Jacob Goldberg, "Saudi Arabia: The Bank Vault Next Door," in *Iraq's Road to War*, Amatzia Baram and Barry Rubin (New York: St. Martin's Press, 1993), 126–31; Joseph Nevo, "Jordan's Relations with Iraq: Ally or Victim?" in ibid., 141–46; Barry Rubin, "Iraq and the PLO: Brother's Keepers, Losers Weepers," in ibid., 154–61; Michael Eppel, "Syria: Iraq's Radical Nemesis," in ibid., 180–87; Yoram Meital, "Egypt in the Gulf Crisis," in ibid., 193–98.

17. But as Maha Azzam has argued, support for Iraq was not limited to the Palestinian community in Jordan. Because of strong anti-Israeli and anti-American feeling and a "dormant hankering for an Arab awakening," support for Iraq "extended across the political spectrum in Jordan." Maha Azzam, "The Gulf Crisis: Perceptions in the Muslim World," *International Affairs* 67 (1991): esp. 475–76.

18. *Newsweek*, 116 (13 August 1990): 18. See also Barry Rubin, "The United States and Iraq: From Appeasement to War," in *Iraq's Road to War*, eds. Amatzia Baram and Barry Rubin (New York: St. Martin's Press, 1993), 260–65; Baram, "The Iraqi Invasion of Kuwait," 19–22; Freedman and Karsh, *The Gulf Conflict 1990–1991*, 47, 51–55, 57–61, 73–74.

19. The resolutions authorizing the embargo can be found conveniently in M. Weller, ed., *Iraq and Kuwait: The Hostilities and Their Aftermath* (Cambridge: Grotius, 1993), 2–5.

20. Margaret Thatcher, *The Downing Street Years* (New York: HarperCollins, 1993), 816–22; Freedman and Karsh, *The Gulf Conflict 1990–1991*, 74–84, 110–17, 145–53, 189–98; Darwish and Alexander, *Unholy Babylon*, 282–83.

21. Michael R. Beschloss and Strobe Talbott, *At the Highest Levels: The Inside Story of the End of the Cold War* (Boston: Little, Brown & Co., 1993), 246–47; Graham E. Fuller, "The Middle East in U.S.-Soviet Relations," *Middle East Journal* 44 (Summer 1990): 419–30; Galia Golan, *Moscow and the Middle East: New Thinking on Regional Conflict* (New York: Council on Foreign Relations Press, 1992), 54–59.

22. On this latter point, see especially Thatcher, *The Downing Street Years*, 826–27.

23. Mikhail Gorbachev, *Perestroika: New Thinking for Our Country and the World* (New York: Harper and Row, 1987), esp. 173–75; Beschloss and Talbott, *At the Highest Levels*, 247–67.

24. Darwish and Alexander, *Unholy Babylon*, 275–76.

25. Ibid., 293–94; H. Norman Schwarzkopf, *It Doesn't Take a Hero* (New York: Bantam Books, 1992), 296–328; Woodward, *The Commanders*, 243, 248–53.

26. Schwarzkopf, *It Doesn't Take a Hero*, 346–50; Rick Atkinson, *Crusade: The Untold Story of the Persian Gulf War* (Boston: Houghton Mifflin Co., 1993), 53–54; *Newsweek* 117 (28 January 1991): 60–61.

27. Freedman and Karsh, *The Gulf Conflict 1990–1991*, 134–42, 155–57, 172–75; Darwish and Alexander, *Unholy Babylon*, 292–93.

28. *The Economist* 316 (25 August 1990): 13–14; Woodward, *The Commanders,* 277.

29. Woodward, *The Commanders,* 261; Schwarzkopf, *It Doesn't Take a Hero,* 366–69.

30. *Congressional Quarterly Weekly Report* 48 (2 September 1990): 2838–39; *Time* 136 (10 September 1990): 27–28; Golan, *Moscow and the Middle East,* 54–60; Cooley, *Payback,* 206–7.

31. Sciolino, *The Outlaw State,* 232–35; Efraim Karsh and Inari Rautsi, *Saddam Hussein: A Political Biography* (New York: Free Press, 1991), 227–31.

32. Darwish and Alexander, *Unholy Babylon,* 295–97.

33. *Time* 136 (10 September 1990): 36–37.

34. *Newsweek* 116 (17 September 1990): 22.

35. Darwish and Alexander, *Unholy Babylon,* 297–98; Freedman and Karsh, *The Gulf Conflict 1990–1991,* 223–25.

36. Woodward, *The Commanders,* 297–303.

37. *Time* 136 (26 November 1990): 30–32; *U.S. News & World Report* 109 (26 November 1990): 26–28; Cooley, *Payback,* 206–7.

38. *Time* 136 (10 December 1990): 40–43; ibid., (17 December 1990): 28–29, 32. See also Freedman and Karsh, *The Gulf Conflict 1990–1991,* 211–15.

39. *Time* 136 (26 November 1990): 30–32.

40. *Time* 136 (3 December 1990): 67–68, 70; Freedman and Karsh, *The Gulf Conflict 1990–1991,* 228–33, 353.

41. Weller, *Iraq and Kuwait,* 6; *Time* 136 (10 December 1990), 26–27; ibid., (17 December 1990), 28–30; Sciolino, *The Outlaw State,* 237–39; Woodward, *The Commanders,* 333–35; Freedman and Karsh, *The Gulf Conflict 1990–1991,* 233–34, 238–40.

42. *Time* 136 (17 December 1990): 28, 32; *U.S. News & World Report* 109 (17 December 1990): 44–48.

43. The quote can be found in Jean Edward Smith, *George Bush's War* (New York: Henry Holt and Company, 1992), 4.

44. Woodward, *The Commanders,* 355–62; Freedman and Karsh, *The Gulf Conflict 1990–1991,* 290–92.

45. *U.S. News & World Report* 109 (31 December 1990/7 January 1991): 20.

46. Karsh and Rautsi, *Saddam Hussein,* 242–43.

47. Freedman and Karsh, *The Gulf Conflict 1990–1991,* 292–94.

48. Ibid., 292–94.

49. Ibid., 204–8, 286–88, 301; Schwarzkopf, *It Doesn't Take a Hero,* 320; Woodward, *The Commanders,* 347–50.

50. Woodward, *The Commanders,* 327–30, 345–50.

51. The most comprehensive military history of the war is Atkinson, *Crusade,* 31–487. But see also, Schwarzkopf, *It Doesn't Take a Hero,* 414–72; Freedman and Karsh, *The Gulf Conflict 1990–1991,* 286–409; Karsh and Rautsi, *Saddam Hussein,* 244–66. Except when noted, the account of the Persian Gulf War that follows in the next six paragraphs is based on these sources.

52. Slater, *Rabin of Israel,* 364–65; *Newsweek* 117 (28 January 1991): 25–26.

53. *Newsweek* 117 (11 March 1991): 27–29; Atkinson, *Crusade,* 451–54; Freedman and Karsh, *The Gulf Conflict 1990–1991,* 404–9.

54. Weller, *Iraq and Kuwait*, 7.

55. *Newsweek* 117 (11 March 1991), 26–28.

56. Smith, *George Bush's War*, esp. 1–12, 252–57.

CHAPTER 11

1. Quoted in *U.S. News & World Report* 110 (21 January 1991): 18. See also ibid. (25 February 1991): 30.

2. Maha Azzam, "The Gulf Crisis," 473–85.

3. *Time* 137 (28 January 1991): 38.

4. Ibid., 38–40; Martin Indyk, "Watershed in the Middle East," *Foreign Affairs* 71 (Winter 1992): 75; *Maclean's* 104 (18 March 1991): 28.

5. Indyk, "Watershed in the Middle East," 75–81.

6. Ibid., 81–85, 88; Alvin Z. Rubinstein, "New World Order or Hollow Victory?" *Foreign Affairs* 70 (Fall 1991): 59–62; *U.S. News & World Report* 110 (25 February 1991): 30–34.

7. Indyk, "Watershed in the Middle East," 88–89; Martin Indyk, "Peace Without the PLO," *Foreign Policy* 83 (Summer 1991): 30–37; Ken Matthews, *The Gulf Conflict and International Relations* (New York: Routledge, 1993), 77–79, 288, 291, 293. See also *U.S. News & World Report* 117 (25 February 1991): 34.

8. Kanan Makiya, *Cruelty and Silence: War, Tyranny, Uprising, and the Arab World* (New York: W. W. Norton & Co., 1993), 152–74.

9. Freedman and Karsh, *The Gulf Conflict 1990–1991*, 410–11.

10. Elizabeth Drew, "Letter from Washington," *New Yorker* 67 (11 April 1991): 93–94; Freedman and Karsh, *The Gulf Conflict 1990–1991*, 412–15, 417–18. See also *National Review* 43 (13 May 1991): 15–17.

11. Makiya, *Cruelty and Silence*, 202–8; Freedman and Karsh, *The Gulf Conflict 1990–1991*, 419–21.

12. *U.S. News & World Report* 110 (1 April 1991): 18–19; *New Republic* 204 (22 April 1991): 13–14; Freedman and Karsh, *The Gulf Conflict 1990–1991*, 421; *Time* 137 (6 May 1991): 76; David Gergen, "America's Missed Opportunities," *Foreign Affairs* 71 (Winter 1992): 10–11.

13. *Newsweek* 117 (22 April 1991): 21–23; *U.S. News & World Report* 110 (29 April 1991): 24–26. See also Elizabeth Drew, "Letter from Washington," *New Yorker* 67 (6 May 1991): 97–103; Freedman and Karsh, *The Gulf Conflict 1990–1991*, 421–25.

14. *U.S. News & World Report* 110 (10 June 1991): 44–45; ibid., 111 (8 July 1991): 21; Indyk, "Watershed in the Middle East," 89–90.

15. See, for example, Terry L. Deibel, "Bush's Foreign Policy: Mastery and Inaction," *Foreign Policy* 84 (Fall 1991): 3–23.

16. *U.S. News & World Report* 110 (18 March 1991): 55–59.

17. For an early analysis of Bush's Middle East policy, see M. Graeme Bannerman, "Arabs and Israelis: Slow Walk toward Peace," *Foreign Affairs* 72 (Winter 1993): 142–57. See also *Maclean's* 104 (25 March 1991): 28–30.

18. *Newsweek* 118 (5 August 1991): 20–21; Bannerman, "Arabs and Israelis," 149–50; Quandt, *Peace Process*, 339–401.

19. After Shamir's government fell in 1992, the former prime minister revealed

his disdain for the whole peace process when he remarked that had he stayed in office, he "would have conducted the autonomy negotiations for ten years, and in the meantime we would have reached half a million souls in Judea and Samaria." Quoted in Bannerman, "Arabs and Israelis," 150. See also, *New Statesman and Society* 4 (20 September 1991): 12–13; *Newsweek* 118 (5 August 1991): 19; Quandt, *Peace Process*, 402.

20. Slater, *Rabin of Israel*, 366–67.

21. *Congressional Quarterly Weekly Report* 50 (18 January 1992): 120; *New Statesman and Society* 4 (27 September 1991): 27; *Newsweek* 119 (9 March 1992): 42–43; *U.S. News & World Report* 112 (16 March 1992): 9; ibid., 111 (30 September 1991): 30–31. See also Norman Podhoretz, "America and Israel: An Ominous Change," *Commentary* 93 (January 1992): 21–25.

22. Quandt, *Peace Process*, 400–401, 403.

23. Indyk, "Watershed in the Middle East," 91.

24. Milton Viorst, "Report from Madrid," *New Yorker* 67 (9 December 1991): 60; Beschloss and Talbott, *At the Highest Levels*, 446–47; Golan, *Moscow and the Middle East*, 72–73; Quandt, *Peace Process*, 104.

25. *Vital Speeches of the Day* 58 (1 December 1991): 98–100.

26. Viorst, "Report from Madrid," 57, 62–78; Quandt, *Peace Process*, 405; Slater, *Rabin of Israel*, 370–71.

27. Viorst, "Report from Madrid," 73; Quandt, *Peace Process*, 404.

28. Viorst, "Report from Madrid," 76–78; Bannerman, "Arabs and Israelis," 151–52; Quandt, *Peace Process*, 404; Slater, *Rabin of Israel*, 370.

29. Viorst, "Report from Madrid," 80.

30. Bannerman, "Arabs and Israelis," 151–52.

31. *Newsweek* 119 (1 June 1992), 51.

32. Between 1984 and 1986, the leader of the Labor Party, Shimon Peres, served as prime minister as part of an arrangement with the Likud Party following elections that had resulted in a virtual standoff between the Labor and Likud Parties.

33. *Newsweek* 119 (6 July 1992): 44–47; ibid., (3 August 1992): 32–33; Quandt, *Peace Process*, 405–8; Slater, *Rabin of Israel*, 382–84, 387–89, 398, 401, 404, 408–9, 416–20, 422–26. See also Avishai Margalit, "The General's Main Chance," *New York Review of Books* 39 (11 June 1992): 17–22.

34. See, for example, Rabin's remarks while meeting with Bush at his vacation home in Kennebunkport, Maine, *Weekly Compilation of Presidential Documents* 28 (10 August 1992): 1411–12, and the President's News Conference, 11 August 1992, ibid., 1413–19. See also *Economist* 324 (15 August 1992): 33–34; *Facts on File* 52 (10 September 1992): 658–59.

35. Slater, *Rabin of Israel*, 430–31, 433–37, 442–43.

36. Ibid., 437, 443–49; Quandt, *Peace Process*, 410; *U.S. News & World Report* 114 (22 February 1993): 34–35; *Newsweek* 121 (11 January 1993): 44; *New York Times*, 14 February 1993.

37. *Economist* 327 (22 May 1993): 51–52.

38. *New York Times*, 1 August 1993.

39. Ibid., 5 August 1993; *Newsweek* 120 (7 September 1992): 42.

40. The three delegates were given a new status as officials of the PLO. Even so, Foreign Minister Shimon Peres announced that Israel would continue to negotiate with them. This was a highly significant development since it brought an official end

to Israel's prohibition in negotiating directly with members of the PLO. *New York Times*, 17 August 1993.

41. Ibid., 9, 13, and 23 August 1993.

42. Ibid., 3 and 5 September 1993.

43. Ibid., 27 August 1993.

44. Ibid., 28–31 August 1993 and 1 September 1993.

45. Ibid., 31 August 1993 and 4, 7, and 9 September 1993; *U.S. News & World Report* 115 (20 September 1993): 60–64.

46. Richard Falk, "Can U.S. Policy toward the Middle East Change Course?" *Middle East Journal* 47 (Winter 1993): 18–19; *New York Times*, 31 July 1993, 4, 5, and 31 August 1993, and 9 September 1993; *U.S. Department of State Dispatch* 4 (3 May 1993): 309–10.

47. *New York Times*, 14 September 1993.

48. Ibid., 14 and 15 September 1993.

49. For a summary of the official report on the massacre by a commission appointed by the Israeli government, see ibid., 27 June 1994.

50. Ibid., 14 September 1993; *Time* 141 (10 January 1994): 31.

51. *Time* 141 (31 January 1994): 91; *Newsweek* 123 (17 January 1994): 26.

52. Ibid.

53. *Newsweek* 123 (17 January 1994): 26; ibid., (21 February 1994): 31, 34; *New York Times*, 10 and 11 February 1994.

54. *Washington Post*, 6 March 1994, sec. C.

55. Robert I. Friedman, "Report from the West Bank: An Unholy Rage," *New Yorker* 70 (7 March 1994): 54–56; *Time* 143 (7 March 1994): 49–55.

56. *Time* 143 (7 March 1994): 53–55; ibid., (14 March 1994): 39–41; ibid., (18 April 1994): 42–43; *New York Times*, 26 February 1994.

57. *New York Times*, 24, 25, and 31 March 1994 and 9 May 1994.

58. Ibid., 16 May 1994.

59. Ibid., 16, 17, 18, and 24 May 1994, and 5 June 1994.

60. *Newsweek* 125 (8 August 1994): 24–25.

61. *New York Times*, 19 and 20 May 1994, 10, 17, and 20 June 1994, and 2 and 3 July 1994.

62. Ibid., 18 May 1994.

63. Ibid., 5 and 22 June 1994; *Newsweek* 125 (8 August 1994), 25.

64. *Wall Street Journal*, 6 March 1995.

65. *Wall Street Journal*, 11 January 1995; Fawaz A. Gerges, "Egyptian-Israeli Relations Turn Sour," *Foreign Affairs* 74 (May/June 1995): 69–78.

66. *New York Times*, 4, 5, and 15 June 1994.

67. *New York Times*, 15, 19, 22, 26 September 1994, 14, 15, 16, 21, 24 October 1994; *Wall Street Journal*, 25 April 1995; *U.S. News & World Report* 118 (6 February 1995): 45–46; Amos Perlmutter, "The Israel-PLO Accord Is Dead," *Foreign Affairs* 74 (May/June 1995): 59–61.

68. *New York Times*, 4 July and 21 October 1994; *Wall Street Journal*, 2 February 1995; Perlmutter, "The Israel-PLO Accord Is Dead," 6–66.

69. Quandt, "The Urge for Democracy," *Foreign Affairs* 73 (August 1994): 2–7; Perlmutter, "Arafat's Police State," ibid., 8–10; Perlmutter, "The Israel-PLO Accord Is Dead," 59.

70. *New York Times*, 28 May 1994 and 4 July 1994.

71. Both quotes are from ibid., 10 September 1993.

72. However, most analysts believed that Saddam hoped in some bizarre fashion to get the United Nations to lift the economic embargo it had imposed on Iraq after the Persian Gulf War, which was throttling the Iraqi economy. *Newsweek*, 124 (17 October 1994): 24–27.

73. *New York Times*, 11 October 1994.

74. *New York Times*, 11, 12, 13, 14, 15 October 1994; *Time* 144 (17 October 1994): 54; *Newsweek* 124 (17 October 1994): 24–30.

BIBLIOGRAPHIC ESSAY

An excellent overview of the literature on the United States and the Arab Middle East since 1945 and the place to begin any study of the subject is Douglas Little, "Gideon's Band: America and the Middle East Since 1945," *Diplomatic History* 18 (Fall 1994): 513–40. This should be supplemented with Thomas A. Bryson, *United States/Middle East Diplomatic Relations, 1784–1978: An Annotated Bibliography* (Metuchen, N.J.: Scarecrow Press, 1979).

Readers wanting to know more about the history of the Middle East should consult Sydney Nettleton Fisher and William Ochsenwald, *The Middle East: A History*, 4th ed. (New York: McGraw-Hill, 1990), which is comprehensive in coverage and the standard work on the subject; William L. Cleveland, *A History of the Modern Middle East* (Boulder: Westview Press, 1994), a highly readable and informed text; Eugene Fisher and M. Cherif Bassiouni, *Storm over the Arab World: A People in Revolution* (Chicago: Follett Publishing Co., 1972), a survey of the Arab world since World War I that is sympathetic to the spread of Arab nationalism; George Antonius, *The Arab Awakening: The Story of the Arab National Movement*, 2nd ed. (New York: Capricorn Books, 1965), a survey, first published in 1946, of the origin and growth of the Arab national movement from about 1850 through the establishment of the mandates (Iraq, Syria, and Palestine) after World War I; Albert Hourani, *A History of the Arab Peoples* (Cambridge: Harvard University Press, 1991), a brilliant and beautifully written book by one of the world's most eminent scholars of the Arab world; Bernard Lewis, *The Arabs in History*, 6th ed. (New York: Oxford University Press, 1993), a standard work, now in its sixth edition, which is really an interpretative essay on the Arab contribution to history; Peter Mansfield, *The Arabs*, 3rd ed. (London:

Harmondsworth, 1985), a lengthy and well-written account of the Arab people which, while conceding the vast impact of the Western invasion and colonization of the Arab world, notes its continued resistance to westernization; Malcolm H. Kerr, *The Arab Cold War: Gamal Abd al-Nasir and His Rivals, 1958–1970* (London: Oxford University Press, 1971), a short but highly important study that chronicles the inter-Arab rivalry that has been so prevalent, not only in the 12 years covered by Kerr, but throughout much of the twentieth century; Bruce Maddy-Weitzman, *The Crystallization of the Arab State System, 1945–1954* (Syracuse, N.Y.: Syracuse University Press, 1993), which discusses inter-Arab politics and the competing tensions between Arab nationalism and subregional Arab blocs; L. Carl Brown, *International Politics and the Middle East: Old Rules, Dangerous Game* (Princeton, N.J.: Princeton University Press, 1984), which points to Islam as the major unifying factor in the otherwise fractious Arab world; Hisham Sharabi, *Nationalism and Revolution in the Arab World* (Princeton, N.J.: Van Nostrand, 1966) which notes three systems of power in the Arab world: 1) the monarchical; 2) the republican; and 3) the revolutionary; A. I. Dawisha, *The Arab Radicals* (New York: Council on Foreign Relations, 1986), which surveys Arab radical states and movements and stresses their different goals rather than their commonalities; and David Pryce-Jones, *The Closed Circle: An Interpretation of the Arabs* (New York: Harper and Row, 1991), which argues the deep roots of Arab society and the inability of the West to understand the Arab character.

Useful for insight into America's Middle East policy are John Badeau, *The American Approach to the Arab World* (New York: Harper and Row, 1968), which deals with the framework in which policy is formulated and argues against the United States making commitments to either side in the Arab-Israeli dispute; Leon T. Hardar, *Quagmire: America in the Middle East* (Washington, D.C.: Cato Institute, 1992), which also advocates a policy of benign neglect; William Stivers, *Supremacy and Oil: Iran, Turkey, and the Anglo-American World Order, 1918–1930* (Ithaca, N.Y.: Cornell University Press, 1982); and Stivers, *American Confrontation with Revolutionary Change in the Middle East, 1948–83* (New York: St. Martin's Press, 1986), both of which are critical of America's resistance to change in the Middle East; Wilbur Crane Eveland, *Ropes of Sand: America's Failure in the Middle East* (New York: W. W. Norton & Co., 1980), a study of CIA activities in the Middle East by a former CIA agent which is critical of American presidents for ignoring CIA intelligence estimates; Michael A. Palmer, *Guardians of the Gulf: A History of America's Expanding Role in the Persian Gulf, 1833–1992* (New York: Free Press, 1992), which traces America's involvement in the Persian Gulf, which grew slowly during the nineteenth and early twentieth centuries, more quickly after World War II, and with astounding speed after the late 1970s; Willard A. Beling, ed., *The Middle East: Quest for an American Policy* (Albany: State University of New York Press, 1973), which contains chapters by prominent scholars on such matters as the "political ecology" of the Middle East and the domestic forces shaping American policy for the region; Charles A. Kupchan, "American Globalism in the Middle East: The Roots of Regional Security Policy," *Political Science Quarterly* 103 (Winter 1988–89): 585–611, which takes America's Middle East policy to task for its misunderstanding of regional political change and its exaggeration of the Soviet threat in the region; and Robert D. Kaplan, *The Arabists* (New York: The Free Press, 1993), a highly critical study of Arabists in the foreign service who for three decades, Kaplan maintains, dominated American policy on the Arab-Israeli dispute. For a rejoinder by one of these former diplomats, see Richard B. Parker, "'The Arabists': A Review Essay," *Journal of Palestine Studies* 24 (Autumn 1994): 67–77.

The two most comprehensive books on U.S. relations with the Middle East prior to 1940 are John A. DeNovo, *American Interests and Policies in the Middle East, 1900–1939* (Minneapolis: University of Minnesota Press, 1963), which focuses on cultural and religious as well as political and economic matters, and Robert W. Stookey, *America and the Arab States: An Uneasy Encounter* (New York: John Wiley and Sons, 1975), which places U.S.-Arab relations within the context of developments in the Arab world and is highly critical of America's Middle East policy. Two important essays on the interwar years are John A. DeNovo, "On the Sidelines: The United States and the Middle East between the Wars, 1919–1939" in *The Great Powers in the Middle East, 1919–1939*, ed. Uriel Dann (New York: Holmes and Meier, 1988); 225–37; and Barry Rubin, "America as Junior Partner: Anglo-American Relations in the Middle East, 1919–1939," in ibid., 238–51. Both DeNovo and Rubin agree that American policymakers between the wars regarded the Middle East with indifference. Rubin argues, however, that the interwar years were a time of American apprenticeship under British guidance which would be important after the war. For a highly partisan account of the interwar years, which argues that American policy toward Palestine was largely predicated on Zionist plans and that President Franklin Roosevelt explicitly identified himself with Zionism, see Hisham Ahmed, "From the Balfour Declaration to World War II: The U.S. Stand on Palestinian Self-Determination," *Arab Studies Quarterly* 12 (Winter/Spring 1990): 9–41.

For the World War II period, readers should consult Philip J. Baram, *The Department of State in the Middle East, 1919–1945* (Philadelphia: University of Pennsylvania Press, 1978); and Baram, "Undermining the British: Department of State Policies in Egypt and the Suez Canal before and during World War II," *Historian* 40 (August 1978): 631–48, which stress the continuity in America's Middle East policy, the homogenous and elitist nature of the upper and middle echelons of the State Department, and the growing competitiveness of the United States with Britain beginning around 1937; Thomas A. Bryson, *Seeds of Mideast Crisis: The United States Diplomatic Role in the Middle East during World War II* (Jefferson, N.C.: McFarland Press, 1981), which emphasizes the role of interest groups in determining America's policy but also maintains that their goals were generally consonant with the national interest and that when they were not, the latter prevailed; Nathan Godfried, *Bridging the Gap between Rich and Poor: American Economic Development Policy toward the Arab East, 1942–1949* (Westport, Conn.: Greenwood Press, 1987), and Godfried, "Economic Development and Regionalism: United States Foreign Relations in the Middle East, 1942–45," *Journal of Contemporary History* 22 (July 1987): 481–500, which point out that policymakers hoped after World War II that economic development in the Middle East would lessen the chances of regional conflict but believed that development had to be undertaken by the poor countries themselves; William R. Polk, *The United States and the Arab World*, 3rd ed. (Cambridge: Harvard University Press, 1975), which makes the point that, more than any other factor, Islam acted as the great unifier of the Arab world; and Barry Rubin, *The Great Powers in the Middle East, 1941–1947: The Road to the Cold War* (Totowa, N.J.: Frank Cass, 1980), which argues that as early as 1945 the State Department regarded Britain as a fading power in the Middle East and that America's Mideast policy at the end of World War II was predicated on preventing new or expanded spheres of influence in the region.

Other useful essays include John A. DeNovo, "The Culbertson Economic Mission and Anglo-American Tensions in the Middle East, 1944–1945," *Journal of American History* 63 (March 1977): 913–36, a study of a special economic mission headed by Culbertson to North Africa in 1944 to survey postwar prospects for American business, which documents Anglo-American differences in the Middle East during the war; James L. Gormly, "Keeping the Door Open in Saudi Arabia: The United States and the Dharan Airfield, 1945–46," *Diplomatic History* 4 (Spring 1980): 189–205, which makes the point that in promoting the construction of an airfield in Saudi Arabia during the war, the United States was as much concerned with increasing its influence in that oil-rich kingdom as with meeting military exigencies; and Douglas Little, "Pipeline Politics: America's *TAPLINE*, and the Arabs," *Business History Review* 64 (Summer 1990): 255–85, which examines Washington's successful effort to build a pipeline from Dharan to the Mediterranean in order to make Saudi oil available to Europe.

There are a number of surveys on U.S. relations with the Middle East since 1945. Among the most recent and best are: H. W. Brands, *Into the Labyrinth: The United States and the Middle East, 1945–1993* (New York: McGraw-Hill, 1994); T. G. Fraser, *The USA and the Middle East since World War 2* (New York: St. Martin's Press, 1991); George Lenczowski, *American Presidents and the Middle East* (Durham, N.C.: Duke University Press, 1990); Seth Tillman, *The United States in the Middle East: Interests and Obstacles* (Bloomington: Indiana University Press, 1982); and especially Steven L. Spiegel, *The Other Arab-Israeli Conflict: Making America's Middle East Policy, from Truman to Reagan* (Chicago: University of Chicago Press, 1985), which shows how global and regional considerations have affected U.S. policy since the Eisenhower administration. Stookey's *America and the Arab States* (cited earlier) also remains highly useful for the period through the Yom Kippur War of 1973.

The literature on the United States' role in the establishment of the state of Israel is massive and beyond the scope of this book. Among the most important works, however, are Michael J. Cohen, *Palestine and the Great Powers: 1945–1948* (Princeton, N.J.: Princeton University Press, 1982), a well-documented study that emphasizes the geopolitical interests of the United States in explaining President Truman's decision in 1948 to recognize Israel; Zvi Ganon, *Truman, American Jewry, and Israel, 1945–1948* (New York: Holmes and Meier, 1979), and John Snetsinger, *Truman, the Jewish Vote, and the Creation of Israel* (Stanford, Calif.: Hoover Institution Press, 1974), both of which emphasize the domestic political considerations behind Truman's decision; Evan M. Wilson, *Decision on Palestine: How the U.S. Came to Recognize Israel* (Stanford, Calif.: Hoover Institution Press, 1979), an analysis by the Palestine desk officer at the State Department during most of the period 1942–1968, which contends that Truman supported the partition of Palestine and the establishment of Israel more for political than humanitarian reasons; Bruce R. Kuniholm, "U.S. Policy in the Near East: The Triumphs and Tribulations of the Truman Administration" in Michael J. Lacy, ed., *The Truman Presidency* (New York: Cambridge University Press, 1989), 299–338, which agrees with Wilson that the State Department failed to sufficiently take into account the domestic political imperatives relevant to the Palestine question and that policymakers believed a compromise solution on Palestine was possible when it may have been impossible; and Kenneth Ray Bain, *The March to Zion: United States Policy and the Founding of Israel* (College Station, Tex.: Texas A&M University Press, 1979), which maintains that earlier works have exaggerated the differences between the White House and the State Department regarding Palestinian partition and Israeli recognition.

In addition to these works, the reader should consult the pertinent sections in Melvyn P. Leffler, *A Preponderance of Power: National Security, the Truman Administration, and the Cold War* (Stanford, Calif.: Stanford University Press, 1992); David McCullough, *Truman* (New York: Simon & Schuster, 1992); and Robert Donovan, *Conflict and Crisis: The Presidency of Harry S. Truman, 1945–1948* (New York: Norton, 1977). Leffler emphasizes political and national security reasons for Truman's decision to recognize Israel (to preempt Soviet influence in Israel), while McCullough stresses humanitarian concerns, and Donovan political and humanitarian concerns.

Useful memoirs bearing mainly on Truman's decision to recognize Israel, but which also shed light on other aspects of his administration's Middle East policy, include Harry S. Truman, *Memoirs* (Garden City, N.Y.: Doubleday &

Co., 1955–56); Dean Acheson, *Present at the Creation: My Years in the State Department* (New York: W. W. Norton & Co., 1969); Clark Clifford, *Counsel to the President: A Memoir* (New York: Random House, 1991); Abba Eban, *An Autobiography* (New York: Random House, 1977); and Chaim Weitzmann, *Trial and Error: An Autobiography* (New York: Harper, 1949). For Truman's diary and other private papers, see also Robert H. Ferrell, ed., *Off the Record: The Private Papers of Harry S. Truman* (New York: Harper and Row, 1980).

For the military history of the first Arab-Israeli war, see Jon Kimche, *Seven Fallen Pillars* (New York: Praeger, 1953), which also discusses the events leading up to and resulting from the war; Larry Collins and Dominique Lapierre, *O Jerusalem!* (New York: Simon & Schuster, 1972), a lengthy but well-written and informative account; and Edgar O'Ballance, *The Arab-Israeli War, 1948* (New York: Praeger, 1957), a book by the leading military historian of the Arab-Israeli conflicts. In addition, the reader should consult Barry Rubin, *The Arab States and the Palestine Conflict* (Syracuse, N.Y.: Syracuse University Press, 1981), which discusses Arab conflict as well as cooperation during the war; the pertinent chapters in Nadav Safran, *From War to War: The Arab-Israeli Confrontation, 1948–1967* (New York: Pegasus, 1969), which covers the Arab-Israeli conflict through 1967 and has good chapters on the arms buildup of each of the countries involved in that conflict; and Trevor N. Dupuy, *Elusive Victory: The Arab-Israeli Wars, 1947–1974* (New York: Harper and Row, 1978), which covers all the Arab-Israeli conflicts through the Yom Kippur War of 1973.

On Israel's decision in 1949 to make Jerusalem its capital, see the appropriate section in Michael Brecher, *Decisions in Israel's Foreign Policy* (New Haven: Yale University Press, 1975), and the pertinent chapters in Evan M. Wilson, *Jerusalem: Key to Peace* (Washington, D.C.: Middle East Institute, 1970). For a lengthy but balanced study of the Arab-Israeli dispute through the October 1973 war, consult Fred J. Khouri, *The Arab-Israeli Dilemma* (Syracuse, N.Y.: Syracuse University Press, 1976). A massive—and splendid—documentary history of the Arab-Israeli conflict from 1949 to 1973, sponsored by the American Society of International Law, is John Norton Moore, ed., *The Arab-Israeli Conflict: Readings and Documents*, 3 vols. (Princeton, N.J.: Princeton University Press, 1974). An abridged version of this work, (Princeton, N.J.: Princeton University Press, 1977) contains documents and readings through April 1976. Two other useful sourcebooks are Walter Laqueur and Barry Rubin, eds., *The Israel-Arab Reader: A Documentary History of the Middle East Conflict* (New York: Penguin Books, 1991), and Ralph H. Magnus, ed., *Documents on the Middle East* (Washington, D.C.: American Enterprise Institute, 1969).

On the Palestinian refugee problem after the establishment of Israel, see Edward H. Buehrig, *The U.N. and the Palestinian Refugees: A Study in Nonterritorial Administration* (Bloomington: University of Indiana Press,

1971), a study of the United Nations Relief and Works Agency for Palestinian refugees; Mohammed K. Shadid, *The United States and the Palestinians* (New York: St. Martin's Press, 1981), which notes three distinct phases in American policy with respect to the Palestinians: 1) 1948–1967 a policy of pacification; 2) 1967–1976 a policy of confrontation; and 3) 1976–1980 a policy of accommodation; and Ibrahim Abu-Lughod, "America's Palestine Policy," *Arab Studies Quarterly* 12 (Winter/Spring 1990): 191–201, which is highly critical of the United States for failing to recognize the indivisibility of the Arab people. See also the pertinent chapters in Howard M. Sachar, *Europe Leaves the Middle East, 1936–1954* (New York: Knopf, 1972), a lengthy and comprehensive study that provides good coverage of the Palestinian mandate issue; and David Schoenbaum, *The United States and the State of Israel* (New York: Oxford University Press, 1993), which points out Washington's growing displeasure with Israel's treatment of the Palestinians. A useful essay on the same subject is Fred H. Lawson, "The Truman Administration and the Palestinians," *Arab Studies Quarterly* 12 (Winter/Spring 1990): 43–65, which argues that concern for Western security in the Middle East led President Truman to pressure the Israelis to adopt a more conciliatory policy regarding the Arab population of Palestine.

The literature on the oil industry (including Middle East oil interests) is almost as overwhelming as that on the Arab-Israeli dispute. I deal with some of the historiography on this subject prior to 1976 in Burton I. Kaufman, *The Oil Cartel Case: A Documentary Study of the Antitrust Activity in the Cold War Era* (Westport, Conn.: Greenwood Press, 1978). But unquestionably the most comprehensive and finest study of the oil industry is Daniel Yergin's Pulitzer Prize winning *The Prize: The Epic Quest for Oil, Money and Power* (New York: Simon & Schuster, 1991). The reader should also consult Stephen J. Randall, *United States Foreign Oil Policy, 1919–1948: For Profits and Security* (Montreal: McGill-Queens University Press, 1985); Irving H. Anderson, *Aramco, the United States and Saudi Arabia: A Study of the Dynamics of Foreign Oil Policy, 1933–1950* (Princeton, N.J.: Princeton University Press, 1981); Aaron David Miller, *Search for Security: Saudi Arabian Oil and American Foreign Policy* (Chapel Hill, N.C.: University of North Carolina Press, 1980); Gerald D. Nash, *United States Oil Policy, 1890–1964* (Pittsburgh: University of Pittsburgh Press, 1968); David S. Painter, *Oil and the American Century: The Political Economy of U.S. Foreign Oil Policy, 1941–1954* (Baltimore: Johns Hopkins University Press, 1986); Michael B. Stoff, *Oil, War and American Security: The Search for a National Policy on Foreign Oil, 1941–1947* (New Haven: Yale University Press, 1980); Leonard Mosley, *Power Play: Oil in the Middle East* (New York: Random House, 1973); Anthony Sampson, *The Seven Sisters: The Great Oil Companies and the World They Shaped* (New York: Viking Press, 1975); and Christopher Rand, *Making Democracy Safe for Oil: Oilmen and the Islamic East* (Boston: Little, Brown & Co., 1975). All these authors emphasize, in one way or another, the public-private relationship that contributed to the expansion of American oil interests overseas. But Randall is particularly critical of Washington for giving the major oil companies virtual carte blanche in promoting their interests abroad without regard to the national interest. Three other good studies of the oil crisis of the 1970s and 1980s that was brought on by the rapid increase in oil prices by the Organization of Petroleum Exporting Countries (OPEC), are: Benjamin Shwadran, *Middle Eastern Oil Crises since 1973* (Boulder, Colo.: Westview Press, 1986); Dunkwart A. Rustow, *Oil and Turmoil: America Faces OPEC and the Middle East* (New York: Norton, 1982); and the essays in Raymond Vernon, ed., *The Oil Crisis* (New York: W. W. Norton & Co., 1975).

There are a number of excellent books and articles on Britain's reluctant withdrawal from the Middle East after World War II and the friction this sometimes caused between London and Washington. Two of the most important are William Roger Louis, *The British Empire in the Middle East, 1945–1951: Arab Nationalism, the United States, and Postwar Imperialism* (Oxford: Clarendon Press, 1984), a masterpiece of scholarship and analysis dealing primarily with Britain's unsuccessful effort to replace a system of formal rule and alliances with an informal system based on an equal partnership with each of the important Arab states, and Peter L. Hahn, *The United States, Great Britain, and Egypt, 1945–1956: Strategy and Diplomacy in the Early Cold War* (Chapel Hill: University of North Carolina Press, 1991), which notes President Truman's willingness to challenge British hegemony in the Middle East after the war and points to the quest for stability in the region as the guiding principle behind America's Mideast policy. Britain's differences with the United States in the early 1950s is also the theme of William Roger Louis's "American Anti-Colonialism and the Dissolution of the British Empire," *International Affairs* 61 (Summer 1985): 395–420; Shlomo Slonim, "Origins of the Tripartite Declaration on the Middle East," *Middle Eastern Studies* 23 (April 1987): 135–49; and Tore Tingvold Petersen "Anglo-American Rivalry in the Middle East: The Struggle for the Buaraimi Oasis, 1952–1957," *International History Review* 14 (February 1992): 71–91. For Britain's final withdrawal from Aden, Muscat, and Oman in southwest Arabia, see Glen Balfour-Paul, *The End of Empire in the Middle East: Britain's Relinquishment of Power in Her Last Three Arab Dependencies* (Cambridge: Cambridge University Press, 1991). For a highly critical account of Britain's relinquishment of power in the gulf states, consult J. B. Kelly, *Arabia, the Gulf, and the West* (London: Weidenfeld and Nicolson, 1980).

London's unsuccessful effort in the early 1950s to establish a Middle East Defense Organization (MEDO) before reluctantly withdrawing from Egypt in 1954, under pressure from Washington, can be followed in Peter Hahn, "Containment and Egyptian Nationalism: The Unsuccessful Effort to Establish the Middle East Command, 1950–1953," *Diplomatic History* 11 (Winter 1987): 23–40, and William Roger Louis, "The Tragedy of the

Anglo-Egyptian Settlement of 1954," in *Suez 1956: The Crisis and its Consequences*, eds. William Roger Louis and Roger Owen (Oxford: Clarendon Press, 1989), 43–71. Two articles that deal with the 1955 formation of the Baghdad Pact as an alternative to MEDO are Nigel John Ashton, "The Hijacking of a Pact: The Formation of the Baghdad Pact and Anglo-American Tensions in the Middle East, 1955–1958," *Review of International Studies* 19 (Spring 1993): 123–37; and Ayesha Jalal, "Towards the Baghdad Pact: South Asia and the Middle East Defence in the Cold War, 1947–1955," *International History Review* 11 (August 1989): 409–33. In "The Baghdad Pact: Cold War or Colonialism?" *Middle Eastern Studies* 27 (January 1991): 140–56, Richard L. Jasse challenges the view that the Baghdad Pact was part of a containment strategy, arguing instead that it was intended to maintain Britain's strategic position in a region considered vital for the defense of its empire.

There are a score of books and articles on the Suez crisis of 1956, which marked Britain's denouement as a major power in the Middle East. Among the most recent and best books are: Donald Neff, *Warriors at Suez: Eisenhower Takes America into the Middle East* (New York: Simon & Schuster, 1981), which argues that until the Suez crisis, the Eisenhower administration considered the Middle East little more than a sideshow in terms of its foreign policy but that afterward it assumed, almost by default, superpower status in the region; Diane B. Kunz, *The Economic Diplomacy of the Suez Crisis* (Chapel Hill: University of North Carolina Press, 1991), which examines how Eisenhower applied economic pressure against Britain, France, and Israel to end the Suez War; Steven Z. Freiberger, *Dawn over Suez: The Rise of American Power in the Middle East* (Chicago: Ivan Dee, 1992), which places the Suez crisis within the context of Eisenhower's concern about the expansion of Soviet influence in the Middle East and the transfer of influence and power in the region from Britain to the United States; Keith Kyle, *Suez* (New York: St. Martin's Press, 1991), a lengthy and detailed study which notes that after the Suez War Britain explicitly acknowledged that it was no longer a world power; W. Scott Lucas, *Divided We Stand: Britain, the U.S. and the Suez Crisis* (London: Holder and Stoughton, 1991), which is critical of British prime minister Anthony Eden for his obsession with secrecy in planning Britain's military intervention in Egypt; and William Roger Louis and Robert Owen, eds., *Suez 1956* (previously cited), a compilation of fine essays by such authors as Diane Kunz, Roger Bowie, and William Roger Louis, which looks at the long-term consequences of the Suez crisis. Other useful essays on the crisis include William Roger Louis, "Dulles, Suez, and the British," in *John Foster Dulles and the Diplomacy of the Cold War*, ed. Richard Immerman, (Princeton, N.J.: Princeton University Press), 133–58, and Louis, "American Anti-Colonialism and the Dissolution of the British Empire," *International Affairs* 61 (Summer 1985): 395–420, both of which argue that the British made the mistake of believing that Dulles rather than

Eisenhower controlled American foreign policy and that both would cooperate in overthrowing Nasser; and Howard J. Dooley, "Great Britain's 'Last
Battle' in the Middle East: Notes on Cabinet Planning during the Suez Crisis
of 1956," *International History Review* 11 (August 1989): 486–517, which discusses the activities of the British cabinet's Egypt Committee before and during the Suez crisis and argues that Prime Minister Anthony Eden intended
the Suez attack as a way of reestablishing British authority in the Middle
East.

In addition to these books, the replacement of Britain by the United
States during the Eisenhower administration as the major nonregional power
in the Middle East can be followed in William Stivers, "Eisenhower and the
Middle East," in *Reevaluating Eisenhower and American Foreign Policy in the
1950s*, eds. Richard A. Melanson and David Mayers, (Urbana: University of
Illinois Press, 1987), 192–219, which argues that while Eisenhower was theoretically committed to supporting Arab nationalism, in reality he regarded it
as a threat to regional stability; Harry N. Howard, "The Regional Pacts and
the Eisenhower Doctrine," *Annals of the American Academy of Political and
Social Science* 401 (May 1972): 85–94, which notes that although the
Eisenhower Doctrine was modeled after the Truman Doctrine, it was not
nearly as successful; Robert McMahon, "Eisenhower and the Third World: A
Critique of the Revisionists," *Political Science Quarterly* 101 (Fall 1986):
453–66, which points out Eisenhower's confusion of Arab nationalism with
communism; and Shimon Sharir, "The Collapse of Project Alpha," in *Suez
1956*, eds. William Roger Louis and Robert Owen (previously cited),
73–100, which traces the demise of the Anglo-American effort known as
Project Alpha to resolve the Arab-Israeli dispute.

For Eisenhower's intervention in Lebanon in 1958, see Fahim I. Qubain,
Crisis in Lebanon (Washington, D.C.: Middle East Institute, 1961), a balanced account that stresses the dependence of Lebanon on the confidence of
its fellow Arab states for its survival; Agnes G. Korbani, *U.S. Intervention in
Lebanon, 1958 and 1982: Presidential Decisionmaking* (New York: Praeger,
1991), which argues that both Eisenhower in 1958 and Ronald Reagan in
1982 failed to bring order and peace to Lebanon; Irene L. Gendzier, "The
Declassified Lebanon, 1948–1958: Elements of Continuity and Contrast in
U.S. Policy toward Lebanon," in *Toward a Viable Lebanon*, ed. Halim
Barakat, (London: Croom Helm, 1988), 187–207, which comments on how
the United States since 1948 favored Maronite Christians in their struggle
with Lebanese Muslims, notwithstanding Eisenhower's claims to the contrary; Michael B. Bishku, "The 1958 American Intervention in Lebanon: A
Historical Assessment," *American-Arab Affairs* 31 (Winter 1989/1990):
106–19, which argues that Eisenhower intervened in Lebanon because he
feared that failure to do so would endanger pro-Western regimes in the Arab
world and cause allies such as Turkey, Iran, and Pakistan to lose faith in the
United States; and Irene L. Gendzier, "The U.S. Perception of the Lebanese

Civil War According to Declassified Documents: A Preliminary Assessment" in *The Middle East and North Africa: Essays in Honor of J. C. Hurewitz*, ed. Reeva S. Simon (New York: Columbia University Press, 1990), 332–338, which maintains that the president sent troops to Lebanon to protect those whom, he believed, were unable to stop Nasser's advances. Useful histories of Lebanon include Helena Cobban, *The Making of Modern Lebanon* (Boulder, Colo.: Westview Press, 1985), a good short survey that emphasizes the continuity in Lebanese history notwithstanding the collapse of the Lebanese political edifice; and David Gilmour, *Lebanon: The Fractured Country* (New York: St. Martin's Press, 1983), which, in contrast to Cobban, views Lebanon as a country with no unity or sense of nationhood.

For the United States' policy with respect to Nasser and Egypt prior to and after the Suez crisis, see Gail E. Meyer, *Egypt and the United States: The Formative Years* (Cranbury, N.J.: Associated University Presses, 1980), which maintains that Washington's aversion to Arab nationalism prevented a constructive relationship with Nasser's Egypt; Barry Rubin, "America and the Egyptian Revolution, 1950–1957," *Political Science Quarterly* 97 (Spring 1982): 73–90, which traces the evolution in American policy from regarding Nasser as a political ally to viewing him as the force behind anti-Americanism in the Arab world; Henry William Brands, Jr., "What Eisenhower and Dulles Saw in Nasser: Personalities and Interests in U.S.-Egyptian Relations," *American-Arab Affairs* 17 (Summer 1986): 44–54, which argues that Eisenhower and Secretary of State Dulles believed that Nasser was the chief obstacle to peace in the Middle East and suspected him of having a "Hitlerite" personality; H. W. Brands, "The Cairo-Tehran Connection in Anglo-American Rivalry in the Middle East, 1951–1953," *International History Review* 11 (August 1989): 434–56, which notes how U.S. intervention in Iran in 1951 justified for Britain its intervention in Egypt and argues that the Eisenhower administration might have supported Nasser's overthrow had Nasser not prevented the establishment of MEDO, thereby turning America's interests away from Suez; H. W. Brands, *The Specter of Neutralism: The United States and the Emergence of the Third World, 1947–1960* (New York: Columbia University Press, 1989), which maintains that the United States opposed Nasser's neutralism because it represented a net loss of Western influence; William J. Burns, *Economic Aid and American Policy toward Egypt, 1955–1981* (Albany, N.Y.: State University of New York Press, 1985), which shows how the United States attempted to use economic aid to Egypt as a political lever; and Geoffrey Aronson, *From Sideshow to Center Stage: U.S. Policy Toward Egypt, 1946–1956* (Boulder, Colo.: Westview Press, 1986), which maintains that the United States' failed effort to apply economic pressure on Nasser helped drive him closer to the Soviet Union. A useful study on Egyptian policy toward other Arab powers is Joseph P. Lorenz, *Egypt and the Arabs: Foreign Policy and the Search for National Identity* (Boulder, Colo.: Westview Press, 1990), which maintains that the first Arab-Israeli war was critical in determining Egypt's Arab relationships for the next 25 years.

There are a number of biographies of Nasser that also have much to say about the relationship between the Egyptian leader, the Arab world, and the West. Among the most useful are Robert Stephens, *Nasser: A Political Biography* (New York: Simon & Schuster, 1971) and Anthony Nutting, *Nasser* (New York: E. P. Dutton & Co., 1972), both of which argue that even more than an Egyptian, a Muslim, and a self-proclaimed Arab, Nasser was a revolutionary of the Third World. In *The Struggle for the Arab World: Egypt's Nasser and the Arab League* (London: KPI, 1985), Tawfig Y. Hasou also describes Nasser as a political revolutionist who used the Arab League to tighten his hold on the Arab masses.

For the United States' response to the 1958 Iraqi revolution, see Nicholas G. Thatcher, "Reflections on U.S. Foreign Policy toward Iraq in the 1950s," in *The Iraqi Revolution of 1958: The Old Social Classes Revisited*, eds. Robert A. Fernea and William Roger Louis (London: I. B. Tauris, 1991): 62–76, which makes the point that prior to the revolution, the United States was willing to play a secondary role to Britain in Iraq; Frederick W. Axelgard, "U.S. Support for the British Position in Pre-Revolutionary Iraq," in ibid., 72–94, which makes the same point; and Alan Dowty, *Middle East Crisis: U.S. Decision-Making in 1958, 1970, and 1973* (Berkeley: University of California Press, 1984), which notes that the Iraqi revolution caught the United States by surprise and attributes it to poor intelligence and poor use of intelligence reports.

Useful histories of Iraq include Edith and E. F. Penrose, *Iraq: International Relations and National Development* (Boulder, Colo.: Westview Press, 1978), a general survey; Marion Farouk-Sluglett and Peter Sluglett, *Iraq since 1958: From Revolution to Dictatorship* (London: KPI Limited, 1987), which stresses fundamental political and socioeconomic changes since 1958, including new social classes; Amatzia Baram, *Culture, History and Ideology in the Formation of Ba'thist Iraq, 1968–89* (London: Macmillan, 1991), which maintains that the Ba'th leadership of Iraq has placed increasing emphasis on Iraqi localism rather than on an integrationist pan-Arab ideology; and Christine Moss Helms, *Iraq: Eastern Flank of the Arab World* (Washington, D.C.: Brookings Institution, 1984), which notes the continued tension between the state and nation in Iraq—between the central authority and a number of small, autonomous social groups. A solid history of the Ba'th Party in Iraq to 1966 is John F. Devlin, *The Ba'th Party: A History from Its Origins to 1966* (Stanford: Hoover Institution, 1976).

For the Eisenhower administration's clandestine scheme in 1957 to overthrow what it believed to be a communist-controlled government in Syria, see David W. Lesch, *Syria and the United States: Eisenhower's Cold War in the Middle East* (Boulder, Colo.: Westview Press, 1992) and Douglas Little, "Cold War and Covert Action: The United States and Syria, 1945–1958,"

Middle East Journal 44 (Winter 1990): 51–75. They should be supplemented with David W. Lesch, "The Saudi Role in the American-Syrian Crisis," *Middle East Policy* 1, no. 3 (1992): 33–48, which discusses how Saudi Arabia tried to assert itself politically in Syria at the expense of Nasser by playing a mediating role between Syria and the United States. On the Soviet Union's growing influence in Syria beginning in the mid-1950s, see Walter Z. Laqueur, "Syria: Nationalism and Communism," in *The Middle East in Transition: Studies in Contemporary History*, ed. Walter Z. Laqueur (Freeport, N.Y.: Books for Libraries Press, 1971), 325–36.

A general account of Syrian history through the Six-Day War of 1967 is Tabitha Patran, *Syria* (New York: Praeger, 1972). A standard work on Syrian politics is Patrick Seale, *The Struggle for Syria: A Study of Post-War Arab Politics* (London: Tauris & Co., 1986), which argues the central importance of Syria to Middle East politics. A provocative study that argues that scholars, fascinated by radical pan-Arabism, have neglected the importance of pan-Syrianism is Daniel Pipes, *Greater Syria: A History of Ambition* (New York: Oxford University Press, 1990).

The increased Soviet presence in the Middle East starting in the 1950s and the rivalry in the region between Moscow and Washington has received considerable attention by scholars. Among the more important works are Walter Laqueur, *The Struggle for the Middle East: The Soviet Union and the Mediterranean, 1958–1968* (New York: Macmillan, 1969), which details the estrangement and then reconciliation between the Soviet Union and Egypt in the late 1950s and 1960s; John C. Campbell, "The Soviet Union and the United States in the Middle East," *The Annals of the American Academy of Political and Social Science* 401 (August 1970): 51–59, which notes Soviet success in becoming a Middle East power as a result of opportunistic diplomacy, the deployment of military and naval power, and economic assistance; Aaron S. Klieman, *Soviet Russia and the Middle East* (Baltimore: Johns Hopkins University, 1970), which argues that the Soviet Union was determined to be a major player in the Middle East even in defiance of the Arab world; George Lenczowski, *Soviet Advances in the Middle East* (Washington, D.C.: American Enterprise Institute for Public Policy Research, 1971), which emphasizes the growing Soviet influence in the region and points to three strands in Soviet Mideast policy: 1) close political alignments with radical Arab states; 2) rearming those regimes; and 3) providing them with economic assistance; Galia Golan, *Soviet Policies in the Middle East from World War II to Gorbachev* (New York: Cambridge University Press, 1990), which argues that Moscow's primary interests in the Middle East have been defense of Soviet borders and the cold war struggle between communism and capitalism; Graham E. Fuller, "The Middle East in U.S.-Soviet Relations," *Middle East Journal* 44 (Summer 1990): 419–30, which points out how, for decades, American policy in the Middle East was predicated on Soviet actions in the area; Galia Golan, *Moscow and the Middle East: New Thinking on Regional*

Conflict (New York: Council on Foreign Relations Press, 1992), which points to new thinking on Soviet policy in the Middle East predicated on the idea of global interdependence and a renunciation of ideology; J. C. Hurewitz, ed., *Soviet-American Rivalry in the Middle East* (New York: Praeger, 1969), a collection of papers by prominent scholars on such topics as military and economic competition in the Middle East; Michael Confino and Shimon Shamir, eds., *The U.S.S.R. and the Middle East* (Jerusalem: Israel Universities Press, 1973), another series of papers by prominent scholars the central theme of which is the limits of Soviet policy in the Middle East because of the constraints of global bipolarity; George W. Breslauer, ed., *Soviet Strategy in the Middle East* (Boston: Unwin Hyman, 1989), a third collection of papers, which looks at the sources of Soviet strategy in terms of consensus and conflict; Ilana Kass, *Soviet Involvement in the Middle East: Policy Formulation, 1966–1973* (Boulder, Colo.: Westview Press, 1978), which emphasizes the role of different Soviet policy groups in formulating foreign policy and maintains that Soviet policy for the Middle East was not monolithic; Alvin Rubinstein, *Red Star on the Nile: The Soviet Egyptian Influence since the June War* (Princeton, N.J.: Princeton University Press, 1977), which stresses the limited effort by Moscow to influence Egypt; Efraim Karsh, *The Soviet Union and Syria: The Asad Years* (London: Routledge, 1988), which traces the development of close Soviet-Syrian relations despite the countries' mutual distrust; and Robert O. Freedman, *Soviet Policy toward the Middle East since 1970* (New York: Praeger, 1978); and Freedman, *Moscow and the Middle East: Soviet Policy since the Invasion of Afghanistan* (Cambridge: Cambridge University Press, 1991), both of which also point to the limits of Soviet influence in the region. For an excellent analysis of Soviet arms sales to the Middle East, which argues Soviet reluctance to give the Arab states more arms than were needed to protect themselves from an Israeli attack, see Jon D. Glassman, *Arms for the Arabs: The Soviet Union and War in the Middle East* (Baltimore: Johns Hopkins University Press, 1975).

Useful memoirs bearing on Eisenhower's Middle East policy, especially the 1956 Suez War, include Dwight D. Eisenhower, *The White House Years* (Garden City, N.Y.: Doubleday & Co., 1963 & 1965); Robert Murphy, *Diplomat among Warriors: The Unique World of a Foreign Service Expert* (Garden City, N.Y.: Doubleday & Co., 1964); Anthony Eden, *Full Circle: The Memoirs of Anthony Eden* (Boston: Houghton Mifflin, 1960); and Selwyn Lloyd, *Suez, 1956: A Personal Account* (London: Jonathan Cape, 1978). Murphy was undersecretary of state at the time of the Suez crisis and Lloyd was British foreign minister. Lloyd is particularly bitter at the United States for not cooperating with Britain against what he considered to be Nasser's defiance of international law.

A highly laudatory assessment of the Kennedy administration's Middle East policy is Mordechai Gazit, *President Kennedy's Policy toward the Arab States and Israel: Analysis and Documents* (Tel Aviv: Shiloah Center for

Middle Eastern and African Studies, 1983), which notes the concern Kennedy's cultivation of Nasser caused moderate Arab regimes. But this should be counterbalanced with two essays by Douglas Little, "The New Frontier on the Nile: JFK, Nasser, and Arab Nationalism," *Journal of American History* 75 (September 1988): 501–27; and "From Even-Handed to Empty-Handed: Seeking Order in the Middle East," in *Kennedy's Quest for Victory: American Foreign Policy, 1961–1963*, ed. Thomas Paterson (New York: Oxford University Press, 1989), 156–77. In these essays, Little points out Kennedy's success in keeping quiescent the potentially explosive Palestinian question and preventing expanded Soviet influence in the region. He also remarks that Kennedy came closer than any other American president to resolving the riddle of the Arab-Israeli dispute. Nevertheless, he acknowledges that Kennedy's evenhanded policy ended in failure. In "The United States, the Arabs, and Israel: Peace Efforts of Kennedy, Johnson and Nixon," *Annals of the American Academy of Political and Social Science* 401 (May 1972): 115–25, Don Peretz also argues that the efforts by Kennedy and his two successors to be honest brokers in the Arab-Israeli dispute failed because of the role of superpower competition, domestic politics, and the mutual distrust of Arabs and Israelis. Excerpts from the correspondence between Kennedy and Nasser and insight into the relationship between the two leaders can be found in Mohamed Hassanein Heikal, *The Cairo Documents: The Inside Story of Nasser and His Relationship with World Leaders, Rebels, and Statesmen* (Garden City, N.Y.: Doubleday & Co., 1973).

The wave of Arab discord and radical Arab nationalism that confronted the Kennedy administration is carefully—indeed, brilliantly—delineated in Malcolm H. Kerr, *The Arab Cold War* (previously cited). On the same subject, see Itamar Rabinovich, *Syria under the Ba'th 1963–66: The Army-Party Symbiosis* (Jerusalem: Israel University Press, 1972). For the threat that Arab radicalism posed for Jordan's King Hussein and how Hussein employed both mediation and repression to keep his monarchy intact, see Uriel Dann, *King Hussein and the Challenge of Arab Radicalism: Jordan, 1955–1967* (New York: Oxford University Press, 1989). For the importance that American financial aid has played in keeping Hussein in power, see Stephen S. Kaplan, "United States Aid and Regime Maintenance in Jordan, 1957–1973," *Public Policy* 23 (Spring 1975): 189–217. For the Yemeni civil war, consult Dana Adams Schmidt, *Yemen: The Unknown War* (New York: Holt, Rinehart and Winston, 1968), which points out that the 1962 coup d'état in Yemen began just as the new Kennedy administration was trying to break from a seeming American pattern of supporting reactionary regimes, thereby making support of the new republican regime almost certain. But see also Edward Weintal and Charles Bartlett, *Facing the Break: An Intimate Study of Crisis Diplomacy* (New York: Charles Scribner's Sons, 1967), which is critical of the administration's support of the rebel regime, maintaining that it encouraged Nasser in his campaign for leadership of the Arab world, and Michael B. Bishku,

"The Kennedy Administration, the U.N., and the Yemen Civil War," *Middle East Policy* 1, no. 4 (1992): 116–28, which argues that in the case of the Yemeni civil war, Kennedy misjudged Nasser's commitment to Arab nationalism because of his belief that Third World nationalists were essentially pragmatic leaders more interested in economic development than in spreading ideology. For a good, balanced history of Yemen, see Robin Bidwell, *The Two Yemens* (Boulder, Colo.: Westview Press, 1963).

On Lyndon Johnson's Middle East policy, see Douglas Little, "Choosing Sides: Lyndon Johnson and the Middle East," in *The Johnson Years: LBJ at Home and Abroad*, ed. Robert A. Divine, (Lawrence: University Press of Kansas, 1994), 150–97; and Little, "A Fool's Errand: America and the Middle East, 1961–69," in *The Diplomacy of the Crucial Decade: American Foreign Relations in the 1960s*, ed. Diane Kunz, (New York: Columbia University Press, 1994), 283–319, both of which maintain that the Johnson administration based its policy on closer relations with three Middle East "pillars" (Israel, Iran, and Saudi Arabia) at the very time that its ability to control their actions was declining; and Don Peretz, "The United States, the Arabs, and Israel: Peace Efforts of Kennedy, Johnson and Nixon" (previously cited).

There is a large literature on the June 1967 war. Useful books and articles include Walter Laqueur, *The Road to War: The Origins and Aftermath of the Arab-Israeli Conflict, 1967–8* (Baltimore: Penguin Books, 1968), an early but thoughtful analysis, which maintains that on the eve of the war there was no master Arab plan for a concerted military campaign against Israel; Michael Bar-Zohav, *Embassies in Crisis: Diplomats and Demagogues behind the Six Days War* (Englewood Cliffs, N.J.: Prentice Hall, 1970), a daily account of the two weeks preceding the outbreak of hostilities, which argues that the world came perilously close to World War III during that time; Donald Neff, *Warriors for Jerusalem: The Six Days that Changed the Middle East* (New York: Simon & Schuster, 1984), which is highly critical of Johnson, maintaining that his overwhelming support for Israel during the conflict has led to the impasse in the Middle East since the end of the war; Hal Kosut, ed., *Israel and the Arabs: The June 1967 War* (New York: Facts on File, 1968), a short factual account; Richard Parker, "The June 1967 War: Some Mysteries Explored," *Middle East Journal* 46 (Spring 1992): 177–97, which contends that the war was avoidable but happened as a result of a series of unfortunate policy decisions, mainly by Nasser, the potential consequences of which were not fully considered; William B. Quandt, "Lyndon Johnson and the June 1967 War: What Color Was the Light?" ibid.: 214–22, which argues that instead of giving Israel a green light to start the war or a red light against launching a preemptive attack, as historians have maintained, Johnson gave the Israelis a yellow light, not acting in collusion with them, but making it clear that he would not force them to withdraw from Egypt, as Eisenhower had done in 1956, if they launched a preemptive strike; Edgar O'Ballance,

The Third Arab-Israeli War (Hamden: Archon Books, 1972), the best military account of the war; Samir A. Mutawi, *Jordan in the 1967 War* (Cambridge: Cambridge University Press, 1987), which emphasizes how disastrous the war was militarily and diplomatically for Jordan; and Gershon R. Kieval, *Party Politics in Israel and the Occupied Territories* (Westport, Conn.: Greenwood Press, 1983), which makes the point that Israel was not prepared to deal with the territories after the conflict.

For an Arab view on the war by nine Arab scholars that portrays Israel as an aggressor state, see Ibrahim Abu-Lughod, ed., *The Arab-Israeli Confrontation of June 1967: An Arab Perspective* (Evanston, Ill.: Northwestern University Press, 1970). For the Israeli attack on the *Liberty* during the conflict, see James M. Ennes, Jr., *Assault on the Liberty: The True Story of the Israeli Attack on an American Intelligence Ship* (New York: Random House, 1979), which maintains that Israel attacked the vessel because it knew it was a spy ship and that the United States conspired with Israel to cover this up, and Clark Clifford, *Counsel to the President* (previously cited), which expresses Clifford's own skepticism about why the attack occurred. On the long-term consequences of the Six-Day War, see Aaron David Miller, "The Arab-Israeli Conflict, 1967–1987: A Retrospective," *Middle East Journal* 41 (1987): 349–60. See also, Yehuda Lukacs, ed., *The Israeli-Palestinian Conflict: A Documentary Study* (New York: Cambridge University Press, 1992), an excellent collection of documents that covers the period from 1967 to 1990 and has separate sections of U.S., Israeli, and Palestinian documents.

On the three-year war of attrition that followed the end of the conflict, when Israel was faced with substantial guerrilla activity across its borders and both Israel and Egypt used highly sophisticated military technology, see Edgar O'Ballance, *Arab Guerrilla Power: 1967–1972* (Hamden, Conn.: Shoe String Press, 1973); and O'Ballance, *Electronic War in the Middle East, 1968–1970* (New York: Faber and Faber, 1974).

On the split that developed between Syria and Iraq, beginning with the short-lived Ba'th coup in Iraq in 1963 and clearly evident after the Ba'ths returned to power in Iraq in 1968, see Eberhard Kienle, *Ba'th v. Ba'th: The Conflict Between Syria and Iraq* (London: I. B. Tauris & Co., 1990); and Amatzia Baram, "Ideology and Power Politics in Syrian-Iraq Relations," in *Syria Under Assad: Domestic Constraints and Regional Rivalries*, eds. Moshe Ma'oz and Avner Yaniv (London: Croom Helm, 1986), 125–39, which contends that the ideology of the two Ba'thist regimes not only failed to produce rapprochement between them but actually exacerbated other differences.

On the establishment of the PLO, see Jillian Becker, *The PLO: The Rise and Fall of the Palestine Liberation Organization* (London: Weidenfeld and Nicolson, 1984), a highly critical study which argues that the PLO was essentially a product of Nasser's ambitions to be leader of the Arab world and that its major result has been to strengthen its enemies, and Helena Cobban, *The Palestine Liberation Organization: People, Power and Politics* (Cambridge:

Cambridge University Press, 1984), which argues that the PLO helped define a political space for a people who had hitherto been largely ignored even by pan-Arabists. See also Zaha Bustami, "The Kennedy/Johnson Administrations and the Palestinians," *Arab Studies Quarterly* 12 (Winter/Spring 1990): 101–20, which comments upon the indifference of Kennedy and especially Johnson to the Palestinian people. A useful, albeit highly slanted, biography of PLO leader Yasir Arafat is Alan Hart, *Arafat: Terrorist or Peacemaker?* (London: Sidgwick and Jackson, 1984), which claims that there could have been a settlement of the Arab-Israeli dispute by 1980 had Israel had more courageous leaders. Also sympathetic to Arafat but more balanced is Janet Wallach and John Wallach, *Arafat: In the Eyes of the Beholder* (New York: Carol Publishing Group, 1990).

The memoir literature on the Johnson administration—and, for that matter, on the Kennedy administration—is generally disappointing insofar as the Middle East is concerned. But see Lyndon Johnson, *The Vantage Point: Perspectives of the Presidency, 1963–1969* (New York: Holt, Rinehart and Winston, 1971) in which Johnson remarks that his greatest concern with respect to the Middle East was that the Arab-Israeli dispute might lead to conflict between the United States and the Soviet Union; and Dean Rusk, *As I Saw It* (New York: W. W. Norton & Co., 1990), in which the former secretary of state remarks that, until the Six-Day War, the Middle East created few major problems for him. For Johnson's friendship with Israel see also Merle Miller, *Lyndon: An Oral Biography* (New York: G. P. Putnam's Sons, 1980).

A good introduction to President Richard Nixon's Middle East policy is Donald Neff, "Nixon's Middle East Policy: From Balance to Bias," *Arab Studies Quarterly* 12 (Winter/Spring 1991): 121–52, which argues that Nixon came to office politically unencumbered with respect to Israel and committed to a balanced policy for the region, yet became the most pro-Israeli president up to that time. On the October 1973 Arab-Israeli war, see Walter Laqueur, *Confrontation: The Middle East and World Politics* (New York: Quadrangle/New York Times Book Co., 1974), a thoughtful diplomatic and military analysis of the conflict which underscores how badly Israel misread the military potential and intentions of its adversaries; Edgar O'Ballance, *No Victor, No Vanquished: The Yom Kippur War* (San Rafael, Calif.: Presidio Press, 1978), still the best military account of the conflict; and Chaim Herzog, *The War of Atonement: October 1973* (Boston: Little, Brown & Co., 1975), which maintains that Israel failed to differentiate between the Bar-Lev Line as a warning system and as a defensive system. On the events leading to the war from the point of view of a prominent Egyptian journalist, see Mohamed Heikal, *The Road to Ramadan* (New York: New York Times Book Co., 1975). A highly critical, contemporary account of Soviet diplomacy during the war is Foy D. Kohler, Leon Goure, and Mose L. Harvey, *The Soviet Union and the October 1973 Middle East War: The Implications for*

Detente (Miami: University of Miami, Center for Advanced International Studies, 1974), which argues the Soviet Union's continued commitment to an "anti-imperialist" struggle.

On efforts to end the Arab-Israeli conflict following the war, including Secretary of State Henry Kissinger's step-by-step diplomacy, see William Quandt, *Peace Process: American Diplomacy and the Arab-Israeli Conflict Since 1967* (Washington, D.C.: Brookings Institution, 1993), which is both balanced and scholarly; Edward R. F. Sheehan, *The Arabs, Israelis, and Kissinger: A Secret History of American Diplomacy in the Middle East* (New York: Thomas Y. Crowell, 1976), which maintains that Kissinger was the first secretary of state to develop a coherent Arab policy for the United States; Ishaq I. Ghanayem and Alden H. Voth, *The Kissinger Legacy: American Middle East Policy* (New York: Praeger, 1984), which stresses Kissinger's political approach to diplomacy and his concern with concrete results; and Matti Golan, *The Secret Conversations of Henry Kissinger: Step-by-Step diplomacy in the Middle East* (New York: Bantam Books, 1976), a highly critical account of Kissinger's diplomatic efforts. A solid but also critical biography of Kissinger is Walter Isaacson, *Kissinger: A Biography* (New York: Simon & Schuster, 1992). Also useful is Harold H. Saunders, *The Other Wall: The Politics of the Arab-Israeli Peace Process* (Washington, D.C.: American Enterprise Institute for Public Policy Research, 1985), in which a high-level career diplomat and participant in the Middle East peace process throughout the 1970s discusses the efforts to end the Arab-Israeli conflict and maintains that his hardest task was just getting the parties to come to the bargaining table.

On the Lebanese civil war beginning in 1970, see Itamar Rabinovich, *The War for Lebanon, 1970–1983* (Ithaca, NY: Cornell University Press, 1984), which describes how a series of developments, including Palestinian migration into Beirut and the political mobilization and radicalization of Shi'ite Muslims, led to the internal unraveling of the nation. On Syrian intervention in Lebanon, see Naomi Joy Weinberger, *Syrian Intervention in Lebanon: The 1975–76 Civil War* (New York: Oxford University Press, 1986), which argues that despite Syria's paramount influence in Lebanon, Syria overestimated its leverage and miscalculated the political costs of its involvement in Lebanon's civil strife; A. I. Dawisha, *Syria and the Lebanese Crisis* (New York: St. Martin's Press, 1980), which notes Syria's special relationship with Lebanon as part of Greater Syria; and Raymond A. Hinnebusch, "Syrian Policy in Lebanon and the Palestinians," *Arab Studies Quarterly* 8 (Winter 1986): 1–20, which argues that Syria's zigzag policy toward Lebanon and the Palestinians was part of its largely unsuccessful bid for leadership of the Arab world.

For Syrian president Hafiz al-Asad's efforts to change Syria from a weak and vulnerable state to a strong, stable nation and regional power, see Moshe Ma'oz, "The Emergence of Modern Syria," in *Syria under Asad: Domestic*

Constraints and Regional Risks, eds. Moshe Ma'oz and Avner Yaniv (London: Croom Helm, 1986), 9–35. On al-Asad's relations with the Soviet Union, see Efraim Karsh, *Soviet Policy towards Syria since 1970* (previously cited).

For an excellent biography of al-Asad, see Patrick Seale, *Asad of Syria: The Struggle for the Middle East* (Berkeley: University of California Press, 1989), which points to Syria's relations with Egypt as one of al-Asad's principal preoccupations. A useful biography of al-Asad's Egyptian rival, Anwar Sadat, which, while laudatory in tone, nevertheless accuses him of hypocrisy for talking about peace even as he prepared for the October War is Raphael Israeli, *Man of Defiance: A Political Biography of Anwar Sadat* (London: Weidenfeld and Nicolson, 1985). On Jordan's King Hussein, see James D. Lunt, *Hussein of Jordan: Searching for a Just and Lasting Peace* (New York: William Morrow & Co., 1989).

In contrast to material about the Kennedy and Johnson administrations, there is a bountiful memoir literature dealing with American Middle East policy during the Nixon and Ford administrations. Most important are the two massive volumes by former national security adviser and secretary of state Henry Kissinger, *White House Years* (Boston: Little, Brown & Co., 1979) and *Years of Upheaval* (Boston: Little, Brown & Co., 1982), which are rich in character description, including personal observations on Nixon and Arab and Israeli leaders, as well as the details of step-by-step diplomacy. Also extremely useful is Richard Nixon, *The Memoirs of Richard Nixon* (New York: Gross and Dunlap, 1978), which reveals the former president's odyssey from one Middle East policy—broadening relations with the Arab states—to another—making Israel a pillar of American interests in the region. The great latitude that Gerald Ford gave Kissinger in most foreign policy matters, including those involving the Middle East, is clearly evident in Gerald Ford, *A Time to Heal: The Autobiography of Gerald R. Ford* (New York: Harper and Row, 1979). Other useful memoirs by Arab and Israeli leaders include Anwar el-Sadat, *In Search of Identity: An Autobiography* (New York: Harper and Row, 1978); Abba Eban, *Personal Witness: Israel through My Eyes* (New York: G. P. Putnam's Sons, 1992); and Moshe Dayan, *Story of My Life* (New York: William Morrow, 1976). Eban and Dayan disagree over whether the United States purposely delayed an airlift of supplies to Israel following the start of the October 1973 conflict. Eban maintains it did not; Dayan suggests it did.

For President Jimmy Carter's Middle East policy, see William B. Quandt, *Camp David: Peacemaking and Politics* (Washington, D.C.: Brookings Institution, 1986), which notes the disappointment that Carter felt as president in not being able to go beyond the Camp David Accords, especially with respect to the highly charged Palestinian issue; Thomas Parker, *The Road to Camp David: U.S. Negotiating Strategy towards the Arab-Israeli Conflict* (New York: Peter Lang, 1989), which describes the negotiations beginning at the end of the Six-Day War and culminating in the Camp David Accords as the greatest triumph of American diplomacy since the end of World War

II; and Steven L. Spiegel, "The Carter Approach to the Arab-Israeli Dispute," in *The Middle East and the United States: Perspectives and Policies,* eds. Haim Shaked and Itamar Rabinovich (New Brunswick, N.J.: Transaction Books, 1980), 93–117, which argues that Carter approached the Middle East with a false sense of moral rectitude and an inadequate knowledge of the region's history or social and political concerns; and the pertinent sections of Gaddis Smith, *Morality, Reason, and Power: American Diplomacy in the Carter Years* (New York: Hill and Wang, 1986), the title of which indicates what Smith believes were the three themes of Carter's foreign policy. On Carter's policy with respect to the Palestinians, see Janice J. Terry, "The Carter Administration and the Palestinians," *Arab Studies Quarterly* 12 (Winter/Spring 1990): 153–65, which takes Carter to task for abandoning a comprehensive resolution of the Arab-Israeli dispute, which would have involved some form of Palestinian self-determination, to an approach more along the lines of step-by-step diplomacy.

Two useful biographies of Israeli prime minister Menachem Begin are: Eric Silver, *Begin: A Biography* (London: Weidenfeld and Nicolson, 1984), which refers to Begin as a complex but not mysterious person, whose assertive Jewish nationalism and insistence on incorporating the West Bank of the Jordan into Israel were rooted in the Hasidic mysticism of his European childhood; and Ned Temko, *To Win or to Die: A Personal Portrait of Menachem Begin* (New York: William Morrow & Co., 1987), a study more sympathetic to Begin which stresses his humanity and flexibility.

The memoir literature on the Carter presidency is also extremely valuable. But see especially Jimmy Carter, *Keeping Faith: Memoirs of a President* (New York: Bantam Books, 1982), which is highly selective in content but provides a full account of the Camp David negotiations; Zbigniew Brzezinski, *Power and Principle: Memoirs of the National Security Adviser* (New York: Farrar, Straus & Giroux, 1983), which is rich in detail and frank about Brzezinski's differences with Secretary of State Cyrus Vance; and Cyrus Vance, *Hard Choices: Critical Years in America's Foreign Policy* (New York: Simon & Schuster, 1983), which notes the administration's conviction upon taking office that Kissinger's step-by-step diplomacy had run its course and new initiatives were needed. Also important for the negotiations between Israel and Egypt following Anwar Sadat's visit to Israel in 1977 is Moshe Dayan, *Breakthrough: A Personal Account of the Egypt-Israel Peace Negotiations* (New York: Knopf, 1981), which makes clear the strained relations that existed between the United States and Israel throughout much of Carter's administration. So does Yitzhak Rabin, *The Rabin Memoirs* (London: Weidenfeld and Nicolson, 1979), which also points out Carter's determination to bring the PLO to the negotiating table. For Egyptian foreign minister Mohamed Ibrahim Kamel's break with Sadat over the Camp David Accords, see Kamel, *The Camp David Accords: A Testimony* (London: KPI, 1986).

Not surprisingly, there is very little secondary work yet on Ronald Reagan's Middle East policy. But two useful, albeit highly critical, biographies of the former president are Bob Schieffer and Gary Paul Gates, *The Acting President* (New York: E. P. Dutton, 1989), and especially Lou Cannon, *The Role of a Lifetime* (New York: Simon & Schuster, 1991), which argues that, as president, Reagan acted out parts he played as a movie star. Cannon also provides considerable detail about Reagan's response to Arab terrorism and America's involvement in Lebanon. Also useful is Juliana S. Peck, *The Reagan Administration and the Palestinian Question: The First Thousand Days* (Washington, D.C.: Institute for Palestine Studies, 1984), which argues that Reagan's policies on the Palestinian question showed little consistency or continuity, and Ann M. Lesch, "U.S. Policy Toward the Palestinians in the 1980s," *Arab Studies Quarterly* 12 (Winter/Spring 1990): 167–89, which notes Reagan's increased sympathy for the Palestinians as a result of the war in Lebanon.

Making up for some of the dearth of secondary studies on Reagan's Middle East policy is the memoir literature, which is again extremely rich, especially with regard to America's involvement in Lebanon. In Ronald Reagan, *An American Life* (New York: Simon & Schuster, 1990), the former president emphasizes how strongly committed he was to Israel when he took office. But he also makes clear his growing disenchantment with the Israelis because of their intervention in Lebanon. More consistent in his strong support of Israel, including its incursion into Lebanon which he tacitly supported, was Reagan's first secretary of state, Alexander Haig, as he makes clear in Alexander M. Haig, Jr., *Caveat: Realism, Reagan, and Foreign Policy* (New York: Macmillan, 1984). On the sharp division within the administration over America's involvement in Lebanon, see also George P. Shultz, *Turmoil and Triumph: My Years as Secretary of State* (New York: Charles Scribner's Sons, 1993), a long and frank memoir in which Haig's successor defends American involvement; and Caspar P. Weinberger, *Fighting for Peace: Seven Critical Years in the Pentagon* (New York: Warner Books, 1990), in which the former secretary of defense makes clear his opposition to it and discusses the friction that developed between him and Shultz over the issue. See also Raymond Tanter, *Who's at the Helm? Lessons of Lebanon* (Boulder, Colo.: Westview Press, 1990), a critical analysis of Reagan's Lebanon policy by a staff member of the National Security Council from 1981 to 1982, which accuses Reagan of a lack of leadership; and Howard Teicher and Gayle Radley Teicher, *From Pillars to Desert Storm: America's Flawed Vision in the Middle East from Nixon to Bush* (New York: William Morrow & Co., 1993), another critical account of Reagan's Middle East policy by a former State Department and NSC official whose career was eventually short-circuited as a result of his involvement in Irangate, which, he argues, was extremely limited.

For Israel's involvement in Lebanon beginning in 1976 when it started to supply Lebanese Christians with arms and other military equipment, see

Ze'ev Schiff and Ehud Ya'ari, *Israel's Lebanon War* (New York: Simon & Schuster, 1984), which argues that Israel allowed itself in 1982 to be dragged into a war in Lebanon that its military leaders did not want. For a similar argument that also blames the war on Israel's excessively large military establishment, see Helena Cobban, *The Superpowers and the Syrian-Israel Conflict* (New York: Praeger; Center for Strategic and International Studies, 1991). For the Soviet Union's vacillating policy with respect to Lebanon and its determination to avoid undue risks, see Dennis B. Ross, "Soviet Behavior toward the Lebanon War, 1982–84" in *Soviet Strategy in the Middle East*, ed. George W. Breslauer (previously cited), 99–121. For a defense of Israel's Lebanon War by the director general of its foreign ministry from 1981 to 1987, see David Kimche, *The Last Option: After Nasser, Arafat and Saddam Hussein* (New York: Charles Scribner's Sons, 1991). For a favorable assessment by a Palestinian of Israel's military performance in Lebanon in June 1982, see Yazid Sayigh, "Israel's Military Performance in Lebanon, June 1982," *Journal of Palestine Studies* 13, no. 1 (1983): 24–65. For penetrating insight into the mentality of Arabs and Jews during the conflict by a Pulitzer Prize–winning journalist, see Thomas L. Friedman, *From Beirut to Jerusalem* (New York: Farrar, Straus, Giroux, 1989).

The war's impact on the PLO is discussed in Rashid Khalidi, "The Palestinian Dilemma: PLO Policy After Lebanon," *Journal of Palestine Studies* 15 (Autumn 1985): 88–103, which contends that almost all Palestinians by 1982 were willing to accept the existence of Israel alongside a Palestinian state. For the divisions within Israel over negotiating with the Palestinians, see Matti Golan, *The Road to Peace: A Biography of Shimon Peres* (New York: Warner Books, 1989). For the impact of the intifada on both Arab and Israeli leaders, see Ze'ev Schiff and Ehud Ya'ari, *Intifada: The Palestinian Uprising—Israel's Third Front* (New York: Simon & Schuster, 1990).

Although the monographic and memoir literature on the George Bush administration is still skimpy, there is already a large literature on the Persian Gulf War following Iraq's invasion of Kuwait in August 1990. The place to begin is Lawrence Freedman and Efraim Karsh, *The Gulf Conflict 1990–1991—Diplomacy and War in the New World Order* (Princeton, N.J.: Princeton University Press, 1993), a superb book which is comprehensive in scope and argues that President Bush regarded the gulf conflict as a defining moment in world history and as an opportunity to make fundamental changes in global politics. Freedman and Karsh also blame the war on Saddam Hussein's political insecurity, which in 1990 was compounded by his fear of the democratic fallout from the collapse of communism, Iraq's economic problems, and tension with Israel. See also Jean Edward Smith, *George Bush's War* (New York: Henry Holt & Co., 1992), which is highly critical of Bush, maintaining that he permitted his loathing of Saddam to cloud his judgment and pointing out that at the war's end Saddam was still in power; Adel Darwish and Gregory Alexander, *Unholy Babylon: The Secret*

History of Saddam's War (New York: St. Martin's Press, 1991), which criticizes the Reagan and Bush administrations for the military equipment Iraq received from the United States during the 1980s and for ignoring intelligence reports about Iraq's military buildup prior to its invasion of Kuwait; Alex Roberto Hybel, *Power over Rationality: The Bush Administration and the Gulf Crisis* (Albany: State University of New York Press, 1993), which also criticizes Bush for ignoring the intelligence community's warnings of an imminent Iraqi invasion of Kuwait; Bob Woodward, *The Commanders* (New York: Simon & Schuster, 1991), which, based on extensive interview with high-ranking Bush officials, describes the decision making process within the administration and the military planning that took place between the White House and the Pentagon; Barry Rubin, "The United States and Iraq: From Appeasement to War," in *Iraq's Road to War*, eds. Amatzia Baram and Barry Rubin (New York: St. Martin's Press, 1993), 255–72, which traces the difficult relationship that existed between Washington and Baghdad, as Iraq went from being a virtual ally to being the first Arab state to fight the United States; Yoram Meital, "Egypt in the Gulf Crisis," in ibid., 191–202, which maintains that Egypt's Hosni Mubarak came to believe that Hussein posed a threat to Egypt's most vital interests; Joseph Koistiner, "Kuwait: Confusing Friend and Foe," in ibid., 105–16, which maintains that Iraq's decision to occupy Kuwait grew out of Saddam's belief that Kuwait would provide him with the financial and strategic assets needed to solve Iraq's economic and strategic problems; Jacob Goldberg, "Saudi Arabia: The Bank Vault Next Door," in ibid., 117–34, which details the historic rivalry between Iraq and Saudi Arabia; Joseph Nevo, "Jordan's Relations with Iraq: Ally or Victim?" in ibid., 135–48, which remarks that Jordan's backing of Iraq was the result of a special relationship between the two countries first developed in the 1970s that made Jordan economically, politically, and militarily dependent on Iraq; Ken Matthews, *The Gulf Conflict and International Relations* (New York: Routledge, 1993), which examines such issues as the legal and economic context of the Gulf War and the role of the United Nations in the crisis; Elaine Sciolino, *The Outlaw State: Saddam Hussein's Quest for Power in the Gulf Crisis* (New York: John Wiley and Sons, 1991), in which a journalist in Iraq at the time of the war criticizes Hussein for putting his own pride and ambitions above the interests of the Iraqi people; Alan Geyer and Barbara G. Green, *Lines in the Sand: Justice and the Gulf War* (Westminster, Ky.: John Knox Press, 1992), a pacifist view of the war, which challenges the "just war" theory of international relations and, without exonerating Hussein, places much of the responsibility for the conflict on the United States; Marcia Lynn Whicker, James P. Pfiffner, and Raymond A. Moore, eds., *The Presidency and the Persian Gulf War* (Westport, Conn.: Praeger, 1993), a collection of thoughtful papers on the impact of the Gulf War on the American presidency that is largely critical of the president's decisionmaking process; and Ted Galen Carpenter, ed., *America Entangled:*

The Persian Gulf Crisis and Its Consequences (Washington, D.C.: Cato Institute, 1991), another collection of papers sponsored by a conservative think tank, which is highly critical of the Bush administration for frequent gaps between its rhetoric and its actual conduct of diplomacy. On the military history of the war see Rick Atkinson, *Crusade: The Untold Story of the Persian Gulf War* (Boston: Houghton Mifflin Co., 1993), which notes that while the conflict represented a significant military victory for the United States, it did not lead to the new world order Bush had talked about, and Bruce W. Watson, *Military Lessons of the Gulf War* (Novato, Calif.: Presidio Books, 1991).

On the aftermath of the war within the Arab world, see Muhhamad Faour, *The Arab World after Desert Storm* (Washington, D.C.: United States Institute of Peace Press, 1993), which points to a decline in pan-Arabism and the rise of "Islamism" as consequences of the conflict; Maha Azzam, "The Gulf Crisis: Perceptions in the Muslim World," *International Affairs* 67 (1991): 473–85, which also notes the destabilizing impact of the war in the Middle East; Martin Indyk, "Watershed in the Middle East," *Foreign Affairs* 71 (Winter 1992): 75–90, which, in contrast, points to the opportunity for successful diplomacy in the region made possible by the war; Terry L. Beibel, "Bush's Foreign Policy: Mastery and Inaction," *Foreign Policy* 84 (Fall 1991): 3–23, which is critical of the Bush administration for lacking a well-defined policy for the Middle East; M. Graeme Bannerman, "Arabs and Israelis: Slow Walk toward Peace," *Foreign Affairs* 72 (Winter 1993): 142–57, a more sympathetic analysis; Galia Golan, *Moscow and the Middle East: New Thinking on Regional Conflict* (previously cited); and John McCain, ed., *The Gulf War Aftermath: An Environmental Tragedy* (Dordrecht, Holland: Kluwer Academic Publishers, 1993), which deals with the ecological damage caused by the war. For an interesting discussion of whether a future Palestinian state will be democratic or dictatorial, and economically dependent or independent, see William B. Quandt, "The Urge for Democracy," *Foreign Affairs* 73 (July/August 1994): 2–7; Amos Perlmutter, "Arafat's Police State," ibid.: 8–11; and Shlomo Avineri, "Sidestepping Dependency," ibid., 12–15.

Useful memoirs having to do with the gulf conflict include Margaret Thatcher, *The Downing Street Years* (New York: HarperCollins, 1993), which reveals the former British prime minister's role in persuading Bush to force Hussein out of Kuwait, and Norman H. Schwarzkopf, *It Doesn't Take a Hero* (New York: Bantam Books, 1992), a military account of the war by the commander of the coalition forces that defeated Iraq. A good biography of Saddam Hussein is Efraim Karsh and Inari Rautsi, *Saddam Hussein: A Political Biography* (New York: Free Press, 1991).

INDEX

Abbas, Abu, 151
Abdullah, King, of Transjordan, 7, 10
Acheson, Dean, 8
Achille Lauro, 141
Aden, 5, 36, 47, 49–50
Afghanistan, Soviet invasion of, 116, 121
Agnew, Spiro, 80
Ajami, Fouad, 183
Algeria, 59, 61, 74, 107, 129
Alliance for Progress, 45
American Jewish Committee, 6
American Jewish community, 15, 31, 34, 45, 72, 108, 149, 151
American Public Affairs Committee, 150
Anderson, Dillon, 24
Anderson, Robert, 56
Andropov, Yuri, 134
Anglo-American Committee of Inquiry, 5–6
Anglo-American Oil Agreement, 2
Anglo-Iranian Oil Company, 1, 11, 19, 29
Arab-Israeli War of 1948–49, 8–10, 12, 13
Arab League, 4–5, 152, 155; and division of Palestine, 5–6; and Tripartite Declaration, 12

Arab Legion, 22, 52
Arab nationalism, 6–7, 11, 15, 26, 38, 45, 46, 65, 153. *See also* inter-Arab rivalry
Arab oil boycott (1973), 83–84, 87; and impact on U.S. Arab policy, 91–92
Arab oil embargo (1967), 62
Arab states, and Soviet Union, 21–22, 25. *See also* Soviet Union *and individual states*
Arab summit meetings, 46, 47, 61, 94, 100–101, 130, 146–47, 155
Arabian-American Oil Company, 7, 14–15, 37, 51, 84
Arafat, Yasir, 46, 74, 126–27, 132, 138–40, 147; and Hebron massacre, 178–79; and meeting with Rabin, 166, 176, 180; opposition to leadership of, 139–40, 143, 175, 178–79, 182
ARAMCO. See Arabian-American Oil Company
arms sales, 19, 21, 39, 48. *See also* United States, arms sales *to individual countries*; Soviet Union, and arms sales to Arabs
Arnett, Peter, 162

THE AUTHOR

Burton I. Kaufman is professor of history and director of the Center for Interdisciplinary Studies at Virginia Polytechnic Institute and State University. Before coming to Virginia Tech in 1988, he taught at the University of New Orleans and Kansas State University. His earlier books include *Trade and Aid: Eisenhower's Economic Foreign Policy, 1953–1961* (Johns Hopkins University Press, 1982); *The Presidency of James Earl Carter, Jr.* (University Press of Kansas, 1993); and *The Korean War: Challenges in Crisis, Credibility, and Command* (2nd edition, McGraw-Hill, 1996). He is winner of the Newcomen Award for best article in *Business History Review* and the Binkley-Stephenson Award for best article in the *Journal of American History*.